RFID *in* LOGISTICS

A Practical Introduction

RFID *in* LOGISTICS
A Practical Introduction

Erick C. Jones
Christopher A. Chung

CRC Press
Taylor & Francis Group
Boca Raton   London   New York

CRC Press is an imprint of the
Taylor & Francis Group, an **informa** business

CRC Press
Taylor & Francis Group
6000 Broken Sound Parkway NW, Suite 300
Boca Raton, FL 33487-2742

Library of Congress Cataloging-in-Publication Data

Jones, Erick C.
    RFID in logistics : a practical introduction / Erick C. Jones and Christopher A. Chung.
       p. cm.
    Includes bibliographical references and index.
    ISBN 978-0-8493-8526-1 (alk. paper)
    1. Radio frequency identification systems. 2. Business logistics--Data processing. I. Chung, Christopher A. II. Title.

TK6553.J628 3007
658.5--dc22   2007025639

Visit the Taylor & Francis Web site at
http://www.taylorandfrancis.com

and the CRC Press Web site at
http://www.crcpress.com

Contents

PART 2   *Integrating RFID into Logistics*

PART 4   RFID Application Overviews

Contents   **xxv**

Preface

ORIGINS OF RFID IN LOGISTICS

In 2003 while working as a newly hired assistant professor, I opened the Radio Frequency Identification (RFID) Supply Chain Logistics (RfSCL) lab in Lincoln, Nebraska, due to my current understanding of the importance of the development of this advance in automatic data capture technology. Previous experience as an industrial engineer for UPS had exposed me to the technology in 1993. Further experiences as a consultant with Tompkins Associates in the late 1990s implementing warehouse management, transportation management, and enterprise resource planning systems (WMS, TMS, and ERP, respectively) utilizing automatic data capture devices exposed me to the rigors of implementing these technologies. My goal for the lab was to allow industry and academia to work together for solutions that lead to research. The Auto-ID Research lab at MIT, which established EPC Global, provided leadership for developing passive RFID tags as possible replacements for bar codes in distribution supply chains. The RfSCL goal was to utilize the accepted industry Six Sigma methodologies to define industry problems and, in the process of solving problems, identify and pursue relevant research opportunities. The industry–university focus has led to our lab becoming one of the National Science Foundation's Industry University Cooperatives (NSF I/URC) in the Centers for Engineering Logistics and Distribution (CELDi).

As mandates for Wal-Mart and the Department of Defense (DOD) were given for the respective organizations' suppliers, many of these suppliers sought answers for integrating RFID into their supply chain. Many professors were not motivated to approach RFID due to the fact that it crossed many different fields of research, such as electrical engineering, computer science engineering, and industrial engineering, to name a few. The need to cross into different research fields made RFID more of a practical research area. Many suppliers set up their research labs and tested their products. These tests appeared to be self-serving, touting the high read rates and read accuracies of their products. When these products were tested by companies who bought these tags and readers, they did not perform as promised. This lack of confidence by organizations and suppliers, the public lawsuits for patent rights for RFID technologies, and mandates created the need for education about RFID.

During this time, because we were named as one of the first academic RFID labs, organizations approached us to test RFID technologies. They needed an unbiased opinion. As we began presenting the results of these first-generation tags (or GEN 1, or Class 0, 1 tags), industry partners suggested that we provide education seminars on RFID. During the process of presenting these seminars, the most common feedback from participants included questions regarding how the technology works, how it can be used in operations, and what other applications for this technology are. Other researchers, such as Satish Bukaputnam at Oklahoma State University (OSU), described the need to introduce this knowledge into the engineering academic curriculum as a course. In fact, both OSU and the University of Nebraska — Lincoln (UNL) were, as I know it, the first to introduce RFID into the engineering curriculum. The knowledge of electrostatic theory, sensor technology, production planning and control, and logistics was best taught in engineering from our perspective. Currently, business case aspects are now being taught in some business schools.

We did our best to put together a structured description of the basics of RFID and how to use it in the supply chain. While doing this, we realized that certain fundamental relations exist — for example, the integration of testing the technology to the integration of the technology into operations. This became section 2 of our book. Though this material has been presented in short courses and in academic lectures, the process of converting this information into book form has proven challenging. Often the conversion of theoretical presentations into practical implementation practice remains difficult. Drawing from our implementations and other contributors we organize some of these principles in practice in section 3 of our book.

INTENDED AUDIENCE

RFID in logistics in intended for the three academic audiences:

1. BS and MS industrial engineering students in a production and planning course
2. MBA and MS students with a specialization in logistics as a core course on logistics
3. Logistics, manufacturing, and distribution engineering professionals

HOW TO USE THIS BOOK

After a brief introductory chapter, the book is organized into several sections: Section 1, Understanding RFID; section 2, The RFID Integrated Logistics Model; and section 3, Principles in Practice. In our own teaching we cover all three sections in order. We believe that section 2 should be covered completely, as it represents the core of RFID in logistics. Because we refer to extensive use of passive RFID tags in logistics, it is recommended that you cover chapter 3 (RFID Passive System Components) and chapter 6 (RFID Standards) completely before starting section 2. Beyond this, the individual instructor can select historical topics from section 1 and apply topics from 2 to meet his specific audience's need.

The instructor is also faced with the choice of how much technical depth to use. To assist readers who want general concepts with minimal technical focus, we suggest reviewing the sections prior to creating a syllabus. Some sections can be skipped completely without losing continuity.

In teaching this material to both logistics professionals and engineering students, we have found that logistics professionals are less interested in the technical rigors than the engineering students. However, we have found that logistics professionals have returned to investigate the technical information as it became relevant to their operational testing.

About the Authors

Erick C. Jones, Ph.D., is an assistant professor at the University of Nebraska-Lincoln in the Industrial and Management Systems Engineering Department. His areas of specialization and teaching include Supply Chain Management, Engineering Management, and Total Quality Management.

Dr. Jones boasts a broad background that spans both industry and academia. Dr. Jones worked as an Industrial Engineering Supervisor for UPS, an Engineering Director for Academy Sports and Outdoors, a Project Manager for Tompkins Associates, and Executive Manager for Arthur Anderson, LLP, prior to his current position at the University of Nebraska-Lincoln.

His working experiences included consulting and implementing WMS, TMS, ERP, Retail systems, AS/RS, Work Measurement systems, facility designs, location modeling analysis, and organizational strategies. He has also been trained in and utilized common industry implementation techniques such as Six Sigma, Lean Techniques, 5S, along with other Quality Process Improvement Techniques for results

Dr. Jones currently chairs the University of Nebraska Certified Six Sigma Black Belt committee. This board consists of both academic and industry experts in Six Sigma. The committee awards UNL-backed Black Belts to qualified candidates. Jones is currently researching the best practices across industries for implementing Six Sigma and other Quality initiatives (Malcolm Baldridge, Deming, ISO) successfully.

Dr. Jones' research appointments include Nebraska site director of a National Science Foundation Industry University Cooperative that consists of a group of universities and which focuses on Logistics and Distribution Engineering called CELDI. He also is the director of the Radio Frequency Supply Chain Center at the University of Nebraska, which opened in 2003, prior to serious interest by most universities in the subject of RFID.

Dr. Jones' degrees are BSIE Texas A&M University, MSIE University of Houston, Central, and Ph.D. University of Houston, Central. His positions have included president of the IIE-Houston Chapter for more than three years, President of the BFSN at Texas A&M University, Alpha Phi Alpha Fraternitiy, Inc, Alpha Phi Mu, Sloan Foundation Fellow and Nebraska site director of the Minority Ph.D. program.

Christopher Chung, Ph.D., is an associate professor in the Department of Industrial Engineering at the University of Houston. Dr. Chung's research areas include Engineering Management, Simulation, and Computer Applications.

Dr. Chung's research has been funded by the Department of Justice, the Department of Homeland Security, and a number of commercial corporations. His research has been published in *Simulation*, the *Journal of Transportation Engineering*, the *Journal of Air Transportation*, and *the International Journal of Industrial Engineering*. Dr. Chung is also the author of *Simulation Modeling Handbook: A Practical Approach*.

Dr. Chung has industrial experience as a manufacturing quality engineer for the Michelin Tire Corporation and military experience as a U.S. Army bomb disposal officer. Dr. Chung also holds a USCG 50 ton master's captains license.

Dr. Chung received his B.E.S. degree from the Johns Hopkins University and his M.S.I.E. and Ph.D. from the University of Pittsburgh.

Part 1

Understanding RFID

INTRODUCTION

In this section of the book, we discuss basic RFID issues. It is intended to be the foundation for all of the other chapters in the book. Readers who are knowledgeable in all of these subjects may elect to proceed to subsequent chapters.

SECTION CONTENTS

RFID History
Basic Introduction to Common RFID Components
Passive RFID System Components
Active RFID System Components
RFID System Design
Important RFID Mandates
Standards Organizations and RFID Standards

1 RFID History

History is more or less bunk. It's tradition. We don't want tradition. We want to live in the present and the only history that is worth a tinker's dam is the history we made today.

> —Henry Ford, U.S. automobile industrialist (1863–1947),
> Interview in *Chicago Tribune*, May 25, 1916

Those who cannot remember the past are condemned to repeat it.

> —George Santayana, U.S. (Spanish-born) philosopher (1863–1952),
> *The Life of Reason*, Vol. 1, 1905

INTRODUCTION

The quotes above describe how history is important to us so we can learn from it. Though many people believe that RFID is a new technology, it has an extensive history. A more accurate description of RFID is as an emerging technology, and its emergence is best understood by evaluating the history of RFID. It can be said that to manage something effectively one must first understand it. RFID systems are complex entities that can be utilized in many ways. Managers will have to use insight to make sound decisions on how and when to use these systems. Perspective is an organizing framework that supports effective decisions and can be gained by reviewing historical events.

A sense of history in RFID is important for the following reasons. Some RFID technologies have stood the test of time and have become more pervasive in the supply chain. Other RFID technologies have been utilized in other industries, such as animal tracking, and present unique advantages. The convergence of RFID systems has been theorized to create innovations in current industries and to lead to the creation of new industries. Given that the history of RFID is integrated with the history of other automatic data capture devices such as bar codes, we approach chronicling RFID history in the following ways.

First, we describe the evolution of the logistics and supply chain management in the United States. Second, we investigate the development of data acquisition device usage in the distribution and logistics. Third, we overlay the development history of RFID technologies for supply chain activities. Finally, we introduce future plans for RFID technologies in logistics operations.

THE EVOLUTION OF LOGISTICS AND SUPPLY CHAIN MANAGEMENT IN THE UNITED STATES

A supply chain is an overall process that includes a complex set of activities that result in product delivery to customers. Supply chains have become more visible in the modern corporation. The term *visibility* has been used in modern-day planning of supply chains at the operational, tactical, and strategic levels of the supply chain. We provide a more complete discussion of RFID in logistics and its application in the supply chain later in this text. But the main concept of passive RFID technologies in providing visibility in many firms' supply chains is important to remember.

THE USE OF DATA ACQUISITION DEVICES IN DISTRIBUTION AND LOGISTICS

Bar Codes

Early History of the Bar Code

The passive RFID technologies are often compared to the bar code. The bar code is the most common type of automatic data capture (ADC) technology in use today. A brief review of bar coding technologies is important to compare RFID as an alternative ADC technology. The history of the bar code described in the book is an adaptation from Global Standards 1 (GS1; Finkenzeller 1999; Tompkins et al. 2005). Other sources provide this information, but these sources are some of the most viable in the RFID logistics industry. It is apparent that retail applications would probably be the most likely industry driver for bar coding development. In 1932 Wallace Flint, whose family was in the grocery wholesale business, proposed a system using punch cards and flow racks that automatically dispensed products to customers. This automated checkout system required the need for some type of bar code system. This was the first documented instance of the advantages of an automated checkout and bar codes in the grocery industry. Flint emerged again, forty years later, as the vice president of the National Association of Food Chains and an active supporter of standards for a code system. Because of his early experiences, Flint was a main supporter of bar code standardization efforts that led to the uniform product code (UPC). Several code formats were developed in the 1940s, 1950s, and 1960s, including a bull's-eye code, numeral codes, and various formats of bar codes.

The modern-day bar code originated in 1949 when Norman Woodland and Bernard Silver, an instructor and a student, respectively, at Drexel Technical Institute, began investigating capturing product information automatically at checkout. The story mentions that Woodland, while at the beach, came up with the idea to use Morse code and its dots and dashes to capture information on grocery products that could be communicated electronically. Woodland started to draw dots and dashes in the sand to simulate Morse code and then extended them downward with his fingers, creating thin lines resulting from the dots and thick lines from the dashes, resulting in a two-dimensional Morse code. Three years later, Silver and Woodland received a patent on what began as lines in the sand, and the linear bar code was created. Bar codes were not initially successful because industry did not immediately accept this automated identification.

Industry Acceptance

Railroads

Initially bar codes were introduced as a means for tracking railcars and were placed on the sides of railroad freight cars. As the freight car rolled past a trackside scanner, the car, its destination, and cargo were identified. The system failed due to the fact that the freight cars were unstable and bounced as they passed the scanner. Consequently, the accuracy of the scanning was poor.

Grocery Industry

The complexity of the grocery business in the early twentieth century was due to the required stocking and inventorying of tens of thousands of items in various types and sizes, including perishable items, from many suppliers. Perishable items required additional information needs due to inventory rotation requirements. Due to the many errors and inefficiencies created from manual processes, the grocery industry sought to automate data capture.

THE UNIVERSAL PRODUCT CODE

The best-known and most widespread use of bar codes has been on consumer products used in most grocery industries. In the late 1960s, supermarkets sought to automate point-of-sale information and testing of bar code technologies became paramount. For instance, in 1972 a Kroger store in Cincinnati operated using a bull's-eye code. The need for standardization led to the forming of a committee within the grocery industry to select a standard code to be used within the industry.

Supporters such as Wallace Flint, believing that automating the grocery checkout process could reduce labor costs, improve inventory control, speed up the process, and improve customer service, pushed for bar code usage. Six industry associations, representing both product manufacturers and supermarkets, created an industry-wide committee of industry leaders for this initiative. Proposals were solicited from various interested parties, and on April 3, 1973, the committee selected the universal product code, or UPC symbol (based on the proposal from IBM), as the industry standard. The success of the system since then has spurred the development of other coding systems. The UPC made its first commercial appearance on a package of Wrigley's gum sold in Marsh's Supermarket in Troy, Ohio, in June 1974.

The Economics of the UPC Bar Code

Financial analysis provided by the grocery industry projected that there would be over $40 million in savings to the industry from scanning by the mid-1970s. These projects pushed the industry to adopt this technology. Unfortunately, in the 1970s these numbers were not achieved and some predicted the end of the bar coding technology initiative. The usefulness of the bar code required the purchase of expensive scanners by a critical mass of retailers while manufacturers simultaneously adopted standardized protocols for reader and bar code label communication. Given that many organizations did not want to be first to invest in this technology, the adoption of bar coding seemed bleak during the first couple of years, as documented by a *Business Week* article "The Supermarket Scanner That Failed" (1976).

As scanning spread, however, the $40 million cost saving projection was far exceeded. A 1999 analysis by Price Waterhouse Coopers estimated that the Universal Product Code (UPC) represents $17 billion in savings to the grocery industry annually. Even more astounding, the study concluded that the industry has not yet taken advantage of billions of dollars of potential savings that could be derived from maximizing the use of the UPC. Savings were passed on to customers and consumers were able to realize reduced costs for products because of this innovative technology. UPC scanning generated efficiencies and productivity improvements that led to lower costs and/or greater customer service. In addition to the labor savings, retailers using bar coding now had access to detailed product movement data, which they turned into a profit center by selling the data to their suppliers. Similar to RFID technologies of today, consumer advocates initially resisted the innovation and jeopardized its success by insisting that retailers forego substantial cost savings by continuing to mark prices on individual units. As with most businesses, the rise of technology—in this case bar coding—benefited both manufacturers and retailers, but it was the retailer who benefited the most. This is similar to what is happening with RFID today. Retailers such as Wal-Mart will probably receive a larger benefit than manufacturers such as ConAgra and Gillette when using RFID technologies.

Bar Code Physics

Linear bar codes utilize a binary code (1s and 0s) to create unique identifiers. The lines and spaces are of varying thicknesses and printed in different combinations. To be scanned, there must be accurate printing and adequate contrast between the bars and spaces. Scanners employ various technologies to read codes. The two most common are lasers and cameras. Scanners may be fixed position, like most supermarket checkout scanners, or handheld devices, often used for the taking of inventories. There is a distinction between the code and the machine-readable representation of the code. The code is text that can be translated into a multiplicity of languages and or symbols. One of the first successful bar codes, Code 39 developed by Dr. David Allais, is widely used in logistical and defense applications. Code 39 is still in use today, although it is less sophisticated than some of the newer bar codes. Code 128 and Interleaved 2 of 5 are other codes that attained some success in niche markets.

Because the universal product code was the first bar code symbology widely adopted, foreign interest in UPC led to the adoption of the European Article Number (EAN) code format, similar to UPC, in December 1976. The 2005 Sunrise and the Global Trade Item Number initiatives from the Uniform Code Council (UCC) began on January 1, 2005. This is known as the fourteen-digit UPC. For a manufacturer of a product that has an existing eight- or ten-digit UPC bar code, there was no effect; however, retailers or wholesalers with scanners had to ensure that scanners were able to decode 8-, 12-, 13-, and 14-digit bar codes and that database systems could handle the extra digits. This additional factor increased the cost for manufactuing expensive readers and drove the total cost of ownership of a system higher. This added expense limited the adoption of the technology. A good Web site reference of this coordinated effort (labeled Sunrise GTIN) further details this initiative.

The most common UPC formats are the five versions of UPC and two versions of European article number (EAN). The Japanese article numbering (JAN) code has a single version identical to one of the EAN versions with the flag characters set to 49.

UPC and EAN symbols are fixed in length, can only encode numbers, and are continuous symbologies using four element widths.

UPC version A symbols have ten digits plus two overhead digits, whereas EAN symbols have twelve digits and one overhead digit. The first overhead digit of a UPC version A symbol is a number related to the type of product, whereas an EAN symbol uses the first two characters to designate the country of the

FIGURE 1.1 Common bar codes. (From: Adams, 2007.)

EAN international organization issuing the number. UPC is in fact a subset of the more general EAN code. Scanners equipped to read EAN symbols can read UPC symbols as well. However, UPC scanners will not necessarily read EAN symbols.

The UPC symbology was designed to make it ideal for coding products. UPC can be printed on packages using a variety of printing processes. The format allows the symbol to be scanned with any package orientation. Omnidirectional scanning allows any package orientation provided that the symbol faces the scanner. The UPC format can be scanned by handheld wands and can be printed by equipment in the store. Version A of the symbology has a first-pass read rate of 99 percent using a fixed laser scanner and has a substitution error rate of less than one error in 10,000 scanned symbols.

Nominal X dimension is 13 millimeters. A magnification factor of 0.8 to 2.0 is allowed and, as a result, makes a printable range of X dimension values of 10.4 to 24 mils. In other words, the nominal size of a UPC symbol is 1.469" wide by 1.02" high. The minimum recommended size is 80 percent of the nominal size, or 1.175" wide by .816" high. The maximum recommended size is 200 percent of the nominal size, or 2.938" wide by 2.04" high. Larger UPCs scan better. Smaller UPCs do not scan as well and sometimes not at all.

The UPC format can be printed using a variety of printing techniques because it allows for different ink spreading. The amount of ink spreading depends on printing press conditions, amount and viscosity of ink, and other factors that are difficult to precisely control. The UPC symbol is decoded by measuring the distance from leading edges to leading edge of bars, trailing edge to trailing edge of bars, and leading edge to leading edge of characters. Since relative distances are measured for decoding, uniform ink spread will not affect the symbol's readability. However, excessive ink spread will make the spaces very small, to the point that the reader will be unable to resolve them. Since UPC is a continuous code with exacting tolerances, it is more difficult to print on any equipment except printing presses.

Current Level of Use

Because computing technologies have become more efficient over the last several decades, the development of applications that can utilize bar codes has increased, leading to bar codes becoming more prevalent in our society. Bar codes are currently utilized in many retail stores such as supermarkets and hardware stores, as well as many industrial and military applications such as manufacturing, warehousing, and transportation operations. With ever increasing use, many companies have developed software to generate and manipulate bar codes. Some pundits believe that as newer technologies such as RFID are developed, we may eventually see a disappearance of bar codes as we know them today.

The developers of the UPC believed that there would be fewer than 10,000 companies, most in the U.S. grocery industry, who would use the UPC. To the contrary, currently there are over one million companies, in more than one hundred countries, in over twenty different industry sectors enjoying the benefits of scanning because of the UPC. UPC symbols are everywhere in the retail environment. They can also be found in industries as diverse as construction, utilities, and cosmetics. The UPC is extensively used in the supply chain by the suppliers of raw materials, manufacturers, and distributors. At the dawn of the twenty-first century, the Uniform Code Council, Inc., the administrator of the UPC, estimates that the UPC symbol was scanned over five billion times a day.

The linear bar code continues to evolve. Today, there are two-dimensional bar codes such as PDF 417 and MaxiCode, capable of incorporating the Gettysburg Address in a symbol one quarter of an inch square. RSS and composite symbologies will enable the bar code identification of very small items such as individual pills or a single strawberry. Rental car companies keep track of their fleet by means of bar codes on the car bumper. Airlines track passenger luggage, reducing the chance of loss. Researchers have placed tiny bar codes on individual bees to track the insects' mating habits. NASA relies on bar codes to monitor the thousands of heat tiles that need to be replaced after every space shuttle trip, and the movement of nuclear waste is tracked with a bar code inventory system. In the fashion world, designers stamp bar codes on their models to help coordinate fashion shows. The codes store information about what outfits each model should be wearing and when they are due on the runway.

Future Uses

The future of automatic identification, however, is probably in radio frequency (RFID). Tiny transmitters embedded in items do not require a line of sight to the scanner nor are they subject to degradation by exposure. Already in use in retail stores to help prevent shoplifting and on toll roads to speed traffic, the primary deterrent to wider use of RFID has been the cost of the silicon chips required. Today, the five-cent chip is close at hand. If the cost can be reduced to less than one cent per chip, in the future your breakfast cereal box will be a radio transmitter.

OVERLAYING THE HISTORY OF RFID DEVELOPMENT INTO THE SUPPLY CHAIN

One of the most comprehensive discussions of RFID history is provided through AIM technologies, "Shrouds of Time," authored by Landt and Catlin (2001). Other references are described by GS1, EPC Global, and other referenced Web sites. We include a summary from one of the premiere journals on RFID, the *RFID Journal*. We summarize the references to provide an overview of the history as it applies to RFID in logistics. The beginnings of radio frequency identification technology have been traced back to prior to World War II. Radar, which had been discovered in 1935 by Scottish physicist Sir Robert Alexander Watson-Watt, was utilized by both enemy and Allied air force traffic controllers and pilots in the war to identify aircraft. Unfortunately, the air traffic personnel could not uniquely identify friendly or enemy aircraft by using the radar. The main problem with radar was that there was no way to identify which planes belonged to the enemy and which were a country's own planes returning from a mission.

The Germans discovered that if pilots rolled their planes as they returned to base, it would change the radio signal reflected back. This crude method alerted the radar crew on the ground that these were German planes and not Allied aircraft. This plane roll created a uniquely identifiable signal that acted in essence as a unique reflected signal. This principle is what the base passive RFID systems are based upon.

Later, Watson-Watt headed a secret project by the British to develop an identification system. This identify friend or foe (IFF) system was the first active RFID system. A transmitter was placed on each British plane. When the transmitter received signals from radar stations on the ground, it began broadcasting a signal back that identified the aircraft as friendly. RFID works on this same basic concept. A signal is sent to a transponder, which wakes up and either reflects back a signal from the transponder's power and/or broadcasts a signal from its own power such as a batter inside the responding antenna or tag.

Advances in radar and RF communications systems continued through the 1950s and 1960s. Scientists and academics in the United States, Europe, and Japan did research and presented papers explaining how RF energy could be used to identify objects remotely.

Companies began commercializing antitheft systems that used radio waves to determine whether an item had been paid for or not. Electronic article surveillance tags are still used in retail packaging today at retailers such as JC Penney and Sears. They use a one-bit tag where the bit is either on or off. When someone pays for an item, a cashier deactivates the tag and the bit is turned off, and the person can leave the store. In contrast, if the person does not pay and tries to walk out of the store, readers at the door detect the tag and sound an alarm.

PRIOR TO IFF

Though the IFF development is one of the most commonly known stories of RFID origins, more detailed knowledge and history of RFID is described by Landt and Catlin (2001). The history described here is an adaptation of parts of that work. Though many focus on World War II as the beginning of RFID development, we will explore other events that contribute to theoretical understanding of RFID technologies. Given that RFID technologies include passive, active, and semi-active technologies, we provide other historical events that will allow the student to investigate and create investigative thought on all RFID technologies.

Many scientists believe that, at the beginning of time, electromagnetic energy created the universe, a concept often referred to as the Big Bang theory. Due to the fact that most RFID technologies use electromagnetic energy as the source of energy, this Big Bang may be considered the beginning of RFID technologies. Benjamin Franklin explored electromagnetism with his experiments in electricity in the 1700s. In the 1800s, Michael Faraday and James Maxwell contributed theories on electricity: the relationship of light and magnetic fields on electromagnetic energy, respectively. Michael Faraday, an English scientist, explored the relationship of light, radio waves, and electromagnetic energy. In 1864, James Maxwell, a Scottish physicist, published theory on electromagnetic fields that concluded that electric and magnetic energy travel in transverse waves moving at the speed of light.

In 1887, Heinrich Rudolf Hertz, a German physicist, confirmed Maxwell's theories and added theories about electromagnetic waves (radio waves), which showed as long transverse waves that travel at the speed of light and can be reflected, refracted, and polarized like light. Hertz was the first credited for transmitting and receiving radio waves, and his demonstrations were later duplicated by Aleksander Popov of Russia. Another key breakthrough for radio transmission was when Gugliemo Marconi successfully transmitted a radiotelegraphy across the Atlantic Ocean.

At the start of the twentieth century, in 1906, Ernst F. W. Alexanderson discovered the first continuous wave radio generation and transmission of radio signals, which signaled the beginning of modern radio communications where all aspects of radio waves were controlled.

The Manhattan project at Los Alamos Scientific Laboratory in 1922 was attributed to the birth of radar detection. The project described how radar sends radio waves for detecting and locating an object by the reflection of the radio waves. The refection can determine the position and speed of an object. Given that RFID is a combination of radio broadcast technology and radar, the convergence of these disciplines allowed for future RFID development. Sir Robert Alexander Watson-Watt was considered to be the inventor of the modern radar system in 1935.

In 1945, historians theorize, the first known device may have been invented by Theremin as an espionage reporting tool for the Russian government; the device was the first "bug," or covert listening device. This device was the first to use inducted energy from radio waves of one frequency to transmit an audio signal to another. This made the device difficult to detect, as it did not radiate any signal unless it was being remotely powered and listened to, and endowed it with (potentially) unlimited operational life.

This bug was embedded in a two-foot wooden replica of the Great Seal of the United States and presented to the American ambassador in Moscow, Averell Harriman, by Russian schoolchildren in 1946. This is currently on display at the National Security Agency (NSA) National Cryptologic Museum. The bug hung prominently for years, at least part of the time in the ambassador's study, before a tiny microphone was found in the eagle by a professional bug sweeper using a Marta kit, which happened to catch a signal from it while it was being used. During George F. Kennan's ambassadorship in 1952, a routine security check discovered that the seal contained a microphone and a resonant cavity, which could be stimulated from an outside radio signal. George Kennan's memoirs describe the event. In a theme now familiar, Kennan relates that Spaso House had been redecorated under Soviet supervision, without the presence of any American supervisors, giving them the opportunity "to perfect their wiring of the house. The ordinary, standard devices for the detection of electronic eavesdropping revealed nothing at all, but technicians decided to check again, in case our detection methods were out of date." The irony of the Great Seal bug was that it hung over the desk of the Ambassador to Moscow in plain sight. It was a simple resonate chamber, with a front wall that acted changed dimensions of the chamber when sound waves struck it. It had no power pack, wires, and no batteries. An ultra-high-frequency signal beamed to it from a van parked near the building was reflected from the bug after being modulated by sound waves from conversations striking the bug's diaphragm (Landt and Catlin, 2001).

How the Great Bug Seal Worked

The Ultimate Spy Book (1952) by H. Keith Melton further details how the Great Seal bug worked. It features a bald eagle, beneath whose beak the Soviets had drilled holes to allow sound to reach the device. Western experts were perplexed on how the device, also know as the *Thing*, worked, because it had neither batteries nor electrical circuits. Peter Wright of British intelligence discovered how it operated and later produced a copy of the device for use by both British and American intelligence. The Thing was initiated when a radio beam aimed at the antenna from a source outside of the building was sent, and then the sound wave struck the diaphragm, causing variations in the amount of space (and the capacitance) between it and the tuning post plate. These variations altered the charge on the antenna, creating modulations in the reflected radio beam. These were picked up and interpreted by the receiver.

RESEARCH ON RFID

One of the first works exploring RFID was the paper by Harry Stockman entitled "Communication by Means of Reflected Power" (1948). This transcript discussed the basic problems of researching reflected-power communication but discussed the usage of the technology. It also predicted that "considerable research and development work has to be done before the remaining basic problems in reflected-power communication are solved, and before the field of useful applications is explored." For this prediction to become valid, advances in transistor technologies, integrated circuits, microprocessors, development of communication networks, and computing power which happened over the next 30 years would spur cost economics of RFID type technologies.

Also, in the 1950s, other technical developments in radio and radar along with the IFF exploration of long-range transponder systems for identification include F. L. Vernon's "Application of the Microwave Homdyne" (1952) and D. B. Harris's "Radio Transmission Systems with Modulatable Passive Transponder" (1960). These developments also led to future patents for RFID technology.

IN THE TWENTIETH CENTURY

R. F. Harrington studied the electromagnetic theory related to RFID and published papers in the 1960s: "Field Measurements Using Active Scatterers" and "Theory of Loaded Scatterers" in 1963–1964, Robert Richardson's *Remotely activated radio frequency powered devices* in 1969, Otto Rittenback's *Communication by radar beams* in 1969, J. H. Vogelman's *Passive data transmission techniques utilizing radar echos* in 1968, and J. P. Vinding's *Interrogator–responder identification system* in 1967.

Commercial activities were beginning in the 1960s. Sensormatic and Checkpoint were founded in the late 1960s. Knogo developed electronic article surveillance (EAS) equipment to counter theft using one-bit tags. Fundamentally, the presence or absence of a tag was detected and the tags were made inexpensively and could provide effective antitheft measures. Most of these systems used microwave or inductive technology. This EAS technology was the first widespread use of RFID technology.

RFID PATENTS

The first U.S. patents for RFID tags were from Mario W. Cardullo and Charles Watson in 1973. Mario W. Cardullo received the first U.S. patent for an active RFID tag with rewritable memory on January 23, 1973. That same year, Charles Watson, a California entrepreneur, received a patent for a passive transponder used to unlock a door without a key. The electronic door lock operated with a card that communicated with an embedded transponder that communicated a signal to a reader near the door. When the reader detected a valid identity number stored within the RFID tag, the reader unlocked the door. Watson licensed the technology to lock makers and other similar companies.

The testing of these technologies was still relevant when one of the authors worked for United Parcel Services (UPS) in the early 1990s in the Strategic Systems Group. Unfortunately, the reliability and the cost-effectiveness were not viable even twenty years later at a company as successful at UPS.

TOLL ROAD AND ANIMAL TRACKING

Also in the 1970s, Los Alamos National Laboratory, at the request of the United States Department of Energy, developed a system for tracking nuclear materials. Scientists developed the idea of putting a transponder in a truck and readers at the gates of secure facilities. The gate's antenna would wake up the transponder in the truck, which would respond with an ID and potentially other data, such as the driver's ID, and then the gate would automatically open.

There was a realization of how RFID technologies—specifically, electronic vehicle identification—could change transportation. This was evidenced in the transportation efforts are included work at Los Alamos and by the International Bridge and Turnpike and Tunnel Association (IBTTA) and the United States Federal Highway Administration. Unfortunately, the IBTTA and U.S. Federal Highway Administration held a conference in 1973 and concluded that there was no national interest in developing a standard for electronic vehicle identification. In the late 1970s, companies realized the potential commercial aspects of RFID. Companies such as Identronix, a spin-off from Los Alamos Scientific Lab; Amtech, which later became part of Intermec; and Transcore were developed.

In the mid-1980s, this type of system was commercialized when former Los Alamos scientists left and formed companies that developed automated toll payment systems. These systems have become widely used on roads, bridges, and tunnels around the world. Organizations such as the Port Authority of New York and New Jersey tested electronic toll collection systems built by General Electric, Westinghouse, Philips, and Glenayre.

In the 1970s, animal tracking efforts were initially investigated using microwave systems at Los Alamos and using inductive technologies in Europe. Animal ID was pursued in Europe by Alfa Laval, Nedeap, and others.

Other forward-moving occurrences in the 1970s included the use of modulated backscatter. In 1975, Alfred Koelle, Steven Depp, and Robert Freyman introduced a research paper "Short-Range Radio-Telemetry for Electronic Identification Using Modulated Backscatter," which is the foundation for current RFID passive tags. Other events include the development of the Raytheon's "Raytag" along with other events from RCA and Fairchild in RFID development. Richard Klensch of RCA developed the electronic identification system in 1975, and Sterzer of RCA developed an electronic license plate for motor vehicles in 1977. Thomas Meyers and Ashley Leigh of the Fairchild organization developed a passive encoding microwave transponder in 1978.

In the 1980s, RFID history documents many commercial implementations. The most common implementations in the United States were for transportation, personnel, and animals. In Europe, interests were in short-range systems for animals, industrial, and business applications. Toll roads in Italy, France, Spain, Portugal, and Norway were equipped with RFID. The U.S. Association of American Railroads and the Container Handling Cooperative Program were active with RFID initiatives. Though testing of RFID for collecting tolls had been going on for many years, the first commercial application began in Europe in 1987 in Norway. This was followed quickly in the United States by the Dallas North Turnpike in 1989. Port Authority of New York and New Jersey began commercial operation of RFID for buses going through the Lincoln Tunnel. RFID was finding a home with electronic toll collection.

Also, Los Alamos was requested by the U.S. Department of Agriculture to develop passive RFID tags to track cows. The goal was to facilitate the tracking of the amount of hormones and medicines that were administered to cows when

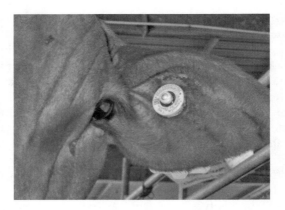

FIGURE 1.2   Cattle tagging.

they were ill. The challenge of ensuring that each cow received the correct dosage affected multiple economic factors. Los Alamos came up with a passive RFID system that used 125-kHz radio waves. A transponder encapsulated in glass is injected under the cow's skin and draws energy from the reader and reflects back a modulated signal to the reader using a technique known as backscatter. This system is still used in cows around the world today. These low-frequency transponders were also put in cards and used to control the access to buildings.

Over time, companies commercialized 125-kHz systems. Later, other companies developed systems that operate on higher radio spectrum to high frequency (13.56 MHz). This frequency was chosen because it was unregulated and unused in most parts of the world. This frequency offered greater range and faster data transfer rates. Companies in Europe began using it to track reusable containers and other assets. The 13.56-MHz frequency RFID systems are used for access control, payment systems (Mobile Speed Pass), contact less smart cards, and as an antitheft device in cars. The cars have a reader in the steering column that reads the passive RFID tag in the plastic housing around the key. The car is rendered disabled if the ID number it is programmed to look for is not found.

In the early 1990s, IBM engineers developed and patented an ultra-high-frequency (UHF) RFID system that offers longer read ranges—20 feet under good conditions—and faster data transfer. IBM did some early pilots with Wal-Mart but never commercialized this technology, and when IBM ran into financial trouble in the mid-1990s it sold its patents to Intermec, a material handling systems provider. Intermec has installed it in numerous different applications, from warehouse tracking to farming. Intermec invested in the future of this technology because it was inexpensive due to the low volume of sales and lack of international standards.

In the 1990s, electronic toll collection using RFID technologies expanded to wide-scale deployment of electronic toll collection in the United States. An open highway electronic tolling system opened in Oklahoma in 1991 in which cars pass scanning points at highway speeds (no need for cameras or barriers). The world's first combined toll collection and traffic management system was installed in the

FIGURE 1.3   Harris County Toll Road Authority tag.

Houston area by the Harris County Toll Road Authority in 1992. Both of the authors personally were able to witness the construction of the toll road in Houston.

Later, the Kansas Turnpike used a system based on the Title 21 Standard, which allows usage by other states, such as Georgia, which also used the same standard. The Title 21 Standard was designed to have a multi-protocol capability in electronic toll collection applications. Also, in the northeastern United States, seven regional toll agencies formed the E-Z Pass Interagency Group (IAG) in 1990 to develop a regionally compatible electronic toll collection system. Also, toll tags were integrated for multi-use like parking garages, toll booths, gated communities, and business campuses; for example, the Dallas TollTag. Texas instruments began developing the Texas Instruments Registration and Identification System (TIRIS) used for starting cars.

The development of computer engineering technology that allowed microwave Schottky diodes fabricated on a regular CMOS integrated circuit permitted the construction of microwave RFID tags. These tags contained a single circuit, which previously had been limited to inductively coupled RFID transponders, thus allowing for cheaper active tags and readers.

The Federal Communications Commission (FCC) allocated a spectrum in the 5.9-GHz band for expansion of intelligent transportation systems, which will spur wider RFID development and applications. RFID systems have been installed in numerous different applications, from warehouse tracking to farming. But the technology was expensive at the time due to the low volume of sales and the lack of open, international standards.

DEVELOPMENT OF COST-EFFECTIVE PROTOCOL

In early 1999, the Uniform Code Council, EAN International, Proctor & Gamble, and Gillette established the Auto-ID Center at the Massachusetts Institute of Technology (MIT). Two research professors, David Brock and Sanjay Sarma, initiated the idea of integrating low-cost RFID tags in products in order to track them through the supply chain. Their idea of transmitting a unique number from the RFID tag in order to promote the cost-effectiveness of the technology was novel. The idea of using a simple microchip that stored very little information as opposed to using a more complex chip that may require batteries and require more memory allowed for cost-effective implementation. Data associated with the serial number on the tag would be stored in a database that would be accessible over the Internet.

Sarma and Brock changed the way people used RFID in the supply chain. Previously, RFID tags were considered mobile databases that contained information about the product, case, pallet, or container on which they were attached. Sarma and Brock promoted the idea of RFID as an associating networking technology that linked objects to databases through the Internet through the tag. This was an important change to businesses because this enabled the idea of visibility. For example, a manufacturer could automatically let a business partner know when a shipment was leaving the dock at a manufacturing facility or warehouse, and a retailer could automatically let the manufacturer know when the goods arrived.

Between 1999 and 2003, the Auto-ID Center gained industry acceptance of the passive RFID tagging system with the support of more than one hundred large end-user companies, the U.S. Department of Defense, and RFID vendors. Auto-ID research labs were opened in Australia, the United Kingdom, Switzerland, Japan, and China. The Auto-ID center is credited with developing two air interface protocols (Class 1 and Class 0), the EPC numbering scheme, and a network architecture for associating data on an RFID tag. The technology was licensed to the Uniform Code Council (UCC) in 2003. The UCC created EPC Global as a joint venture between the Auto-ID Center and EAN International in order to commercialize EPC technology. The Auto-ID Center closed its doors in October 2003, and its research responsibilities were passed on to Auto-ID labs. GS1 EPC Global is now the organization that is responsible for providing standards for RFID technologies. EAN has become Global Standards 1 or (GS1) and UCC has become GS1 US, and they currently seek to manage bar codes, RFID, EDI, and ecommerce standards.

The industry support is evidenced in the fact that some of the biggest retailers in the world—Albertsons, Metro, Target, Tesco, Wal-Mart—and the U.S. Department of Defense have initiated plans to use EPC technology to track goods in their supply chain. The pharmaceutical, tire, defense, and other industries are also moving to adopt the technology. EPC Global ratified a second-generation standard in December 2004 in order to compensate for some of the shortcomings of the first-generation technologies, improving challenges such as read distance and better integration between vendor products.

REFERENCES

Cardullo and Watson. History of RFID Technology, *RFID Journal*. Accessed August 30, 2007 from http://www.rfidjournal.com/article/articleview/1338/1/129/

Finkenzeller, K. (1999). *RFID handbook*. John Wiley & Sons.

Harrington, R. F. Theory of loaded scatterers. Proceedings of Institution of Electrical Engineers (IEE), VIII, n4, April 1964, n4444E, pp. 617–623.

Harris, D. B. (1960). *Radio transmission systems with modulatable passive responder*. U.S. Patent No. 2,927,321, 1 March.

Klensch, R. J. (1975). *Electronic identification system*. U.S. Patent No. 3,914,762, 21 October.

Koelle, Alfred R., Depp, Steven W., Freyman, Robert W., Short-Range Radio-Telemetry for Electronic Identification, Using Modulated RF Backscatter, Proceedings of the IEEE, V63, n8, August 1976, pp. 1260–1261.

Landt, J., and B. Catlin. (2001). *Shrouds of time*. Pittsburgh, PA: The Association of Automatic Identification and Data Capture Technologies.

Leary, W. (2004). With food low, space crew must cut back. *New York Times*, 10 December.

Melton, H. Keith, with forewords by William Colby and Oleg Kalugin. *The Ultimate SPY Book*. London & New York: Dorling Kindersley, Ltd., 1996. *Ultimate Spy*. New York: DK Publishing, 2002.

Meyers, T. D., and A. P. Leigh. (1978). *Passive encoding microwave transponder*. US Patent 4,068,232, 10 January.

Rittenback, O. (1969). *Communication by radar beams*. U.S. Patent No. 3,460,139, 5 August.

Stockman, Harry. Communication by means of Reflected Power, *Proceedings of the IRE*, pp. 1196–1204, October, 1948.

Vernon, F. L. (1952). Application of the microwave homodyne. *IRE Trans*. AP-4:110–116.

Vogelman, J. H. (1968). *Passive data transmission techniques using radar echos*. U.S. Patent No. 3,391,404.

ADDITIONAL REFERENCES

Baldwin, H., S. Depp, A. Koelle, and R. Freyman. (1978). *Interrogation and detection system*. U.S. Patent No. 4,075,632, 21 February.

Carreau, M. (2004). Space station crew endures food shortage. *Houston Chronicle*, 10 December.

Cetinkaya, S., F. Mutlu, and C. Y. Lee. (2006). A comparison of outbound dispatch policies for integrated inventory and transportation decisions, *European Journal of Operations Research* 171(3):1094–1112.

Chappell, G., D. Durdan, G. Gilbert, L. Ginsberg, J. Smith, and J. Tobolski. (2002). *Auto-ID on delivery: The value of auto-ID technology in retail stores*. MIT Auto-ID Center White Paper, Accenture.

Clampitt, H. G. (2006). *RFID certification textbook*. Edited by Erick C. Jones. PWD Group.

Clampitt, H. G., D. Galarde, M. Hendricks, M. Johnson, A. De La Serna, and S. Smith. (2006). *The RFID certification textbook*. 2d ed. Edited by Erick C. Jones. Houston, Tex.: PWD Group.

Dinade, (1967). A new interrogation, navigation and detection system. *Microwave Journal* 70–78.

Foote, R. S. (1981). Prospects for non-stop toll collection using automatic vehicle identification. *Traffic Quarterly* 35(3):445–460.

Foote, R. S. Automatic bus identification. NTIS DOT-FH-11-7778 TS-7930-ABI.

Gibbs, P. *Physics chronology* [Online]. Available at http://webplaza.pt.lu/public/fklaess/html/historia.html [Accessed]

Hauslen, R. A. (1977). The promise of automatic vehicle identification. *IEEE Transactions on Vehicular Technology* VT-26(1):30–38.

Henoch, B., and E. Berglind. (1982). *Apparatus for synchronized reception in connection with system for recording objects*. U.S. Patent No. 4,333,078, 1 June.

Henoch, B., and E. Berglind. (1982). *Apparatus for producing a single side band*. U.S. Patent No. 4,358,765, 9 November.

Hoover, D. R. (1982). *Passive sensing and encoding transponder*. U.S. Patent No. 4,343,252, 17 August.

Kamata, S., Y. Kimura, and J. Sakuragi. (1978). *Foreground subject-identifying apparatus*. U.S. Patent No. 4,069,472, 17 January.

Klensch, R. J., J. Rosen, and H. Staras. (1973), A microwave automatic vehicle identification system. *RCA Review* 34(4):566–579.

Lacy, S. (2005). RFID: Plenty of mixed signals. *BusinessWeek Online*, 31 January [Online]. Available at http://www.businessweek.com/technology/content/jan2005/tc20050131_5897_tc024.htm [Accessed]

Sterzer, F. (1974). An electronic license plate for motor vehicles. *RCA Review* 35(2):167–175.

The supermarket scanner that failed. (1976). *Business Week*, 22 March.

Tompkins, J. A., J. A. White, Y. A. Bozer, and J. M. A. Tanchoco. (2003). *Facilities planning.* 3d ed. Hoboken, N.J.: John Wiley & Sons.

Works, G. A., J. C. Murray, E. D. Ostroff, and N. Freedman. (1973). *Remotely powered tran-sponders.* U.S. Patent No. 3,745,569, July.

Zaleski, J. F. (1974). *Passive microwave receiver-transmitter.* U.S. Patent No. 3,836,961, September.

OTHER WORKS CITED

Adams, Russ. Describes the basics of barcodes. Adams Communications.

AIM. Available at http://www.aimglobal.org/technologies/rfid/ [Accessed]

Barcode 1 [Online]. Available at http://www.adams1.com/pub/russadam/upccode.html [Accessed]

Biggus, J. *Sketches of the history of electromagnetics* [Online]. http://history.hyperjeff.net/electromagnetism.html [Accessed]

Emerson, D. T. (1998). *The work of Jagadis Chandra Bose: 100 Years of mm-wave research* [Online]. Available at http://www.tuc.nrao.edu/~demerson/bose/bose.html [Accessed]

EPC Global North America homepage [Online]. Available at http://www.epcglobalna.org/default.aspx [Accessed]

GS1US. *The origins of a code* [Online]. Available at http://www.gs1us.org/About/History/UPCBackground/BarCodeOrigin/tabid/74/Default.aspx [Accessed]

GS1US. *History* [Online]. Available at http://www.gs1us.org/About/History/tabid/64/Default.aspx [Accessed]

History of RFID technology. *RFID Journal* [Online]. Available at http://www.rfidjournal.com/article/articleview/1338/2/129/ [Accessed]

Marsh, M., ed. *Transponder News* [Online]. Available at http://rapidttp.com/transponder/ [Accessed]

Nystrom, J. *A scientific history behind our electromagnetic understanding* [Online]. Available at http://www.ee.uidaho.edu/ee/em/ee330/ee330_his/ee330_his.html [Accessed]

Spencer, R. *History—A ridiculously brief history of electricity and magnetism* [Online]. Available at http://maxwell.byu.edu/~spencerr/phys442/node4.html [Accessed]

Sunrise GTIN [Online]. Available at http://www.adams1.com/pub/russadam/2005-sunrise-gtin.pdf [Accessed]

Taylor, L. S. *Gallery of electromagnetic personalities* [Online]. Available at http://www.ee.umd.edu/~taylor/frame1.html [Accessed]

2 Basic Introduction to Common RFID Components

The design and implementation of a successful RFID system is a complex process. One of the most important sets of decisions that the RFID engineer must make involves the selection of individual system components. Making informed decisions with respect to this process will increase the probability of producing a fully functional, reliable system. Conversely, less than informed decisions can easily result in a poorly performing system or, even worse, having to redesign the system from scratch. A poor implementation of any new technology such as RFID can increase the resistance to other attempts at using technology to increase productivity.

With these thoughts in mind, the objective of this chapter is to introduce the basic components that are required for a functioning RFID system. For now, we will begin by describing the general nature of each component and then follow up with more detailed information. Each of these specific individual components, as well as their implementation, is discussed in greater depth throughout the remainder of this book.

GENERAL COMPONENT OVERVIEW

We will begin with a generic discussion of general RFID system components. At this high-level viewpoint in our discussion, the exact nature of the system process we are attempting to apply RFID is not of paramount importance. As long as it is a system that requires inventory to be tracked, the following discussion is applicable.

As with many other types of automatic identification systems, an RFID system requires a number of interrelated components. From a very high-level perspective, an RFID system must contain a set of tags, one or more antennas, and a reader. Figure 2.1 illustrates how these components work in conjunction with each other.

TAGS

Tags are the devices attached to the items or material that the RFID system is intended to track. The tags may be placed directly on individual items such as in the case of consumer goods or on shipping containers or pallets that hold multiple items. Tags come in all sorts of shapes and sizes.

The primary function of the tag is to transmit data to the rest of the RFID system. Tags generally contain three basic parts. These include:

- The electronic integrated circuit
- A miniature antenna
- A substrate to hold the integrated circuit and the antenna together and to the inventory item

FIGURE 2.1   Basic RFID system components.

Tags are also classified depending on how they are powered. These classifications include:

- Passive
- Active
- Semi-passive

The following figure illustrates just one of many types of common RFID tags. In Figure 2.2, the PayPass passive RFID tag is illustrated. This tag is used in retail systems across the country. In the subsequent tag section of this chapter, we will describe and illustrate a number of different types of tags.

FIGURE 2.2   Common RFID tag.

FIGURE 2.3   Common type of RFID reader.

SCANNERS AND READERS

The RFID reader is a device that creates an electromagnetic signal, which is transmitted to the RFID tags through one or more antennas. Under normal operation, the reader is continuously transmitting the electromagnetic signal in search of one or more RFID tags. The RFID reader also performs a second function of monitoring for electromagnetic signals from the RFID tags via the same antenna. Figure 2.3 illustrates a common type of RFID reader. This particular reader is manufactured by the Symbol Corporation.

ANTENNAS

The function of the antenna is to both transmit and receive electromagnetic signals between the tags and the reader. The effective electromagnetic field that the antenna transmits is in RFID terms known as the interrogation zone. That is, the antenna creates a three-dimensional space that is used to communicate with the RFID tags. In order to obtain successful communication, the tags must be within range of the antenna or in the interrogation zone. Figure 2.4 illustrates a common type of RFID antenna. This antenna is manufactured by the Symbol Corporation.

HOST

The host is a computer system that communicates with the RFID reader. It is the host that actually makes sense of the input from the reader. The host will typically have a number of software applications to support the RFID system. One application is commonly known as RFID middleware. This software is used by the user to set up and control the reader. Another needed software application involves data management. This includes functions that perform database and inventory tracking functions.

Now that you are familiar with the basic purpose of each of the major RFID system components, we will examine each individual component in greater detail. In addition, we will identify some of the major manufacturers of each type of component.

FIGURE 2.4   Common RFID antenna.

TAGS

RFID tags come in an incredible array of shapes, sizes, and capabilities. While we cannot describe every possible type of tag, we will describe RFID tags in more detail. This will include describing the differences and advantages and disadvantages of the different types of tags that are commercially available. These differences between tags will be examined with respect to:

- Power sources
- Frequencies
- Writing capabilities
- Tag components
- Tag generations
- Tag costs

POWER SOURCES

All RFID tags must receive power in some form or another. Power is required by the tag in order to communicate information to the reader via the antenna. There are at least three different means currently available to power RFID tags. These include passive tags, active tags, and semi-passive tags. Each type of tag has its own advantages and disadvantages that must be carefully considered when designing and RFID system. The type of tag required can have the tendency to drive the selection of the rest of the components of the system.

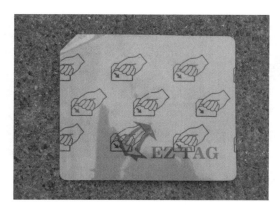

FIGURE 2.5   Common passive tag.

PASSIVE TAGS

Passive tags do not contain a power source. To power the tag circuitry, the tag relies on electromagnetic power obtained from the RFID systems antenna. Since passive tags do not contain their own power sources, the designs can be simpler and less expensive. They can also have an unlimited shelf life in comparison to active tags. This has made the passive tag the focus of most government and commercial RFID mandates.

The downside of all passive tags is their extremely limited range. Since passive tags depend on power from the reader and antenna, with the current technology, passive tags must be in close proximity to the reader and antenna in order to obtain sufficient power to transmit a signal.

Many RFID experts believe that passive tags are the future of RFID. In the last few years, the unit price of passive RFID tags has steadily gone down in cost. This is a result of, at least, increased scales of production. Some industry analysts believe that when the cost of individual tags reaches five cents, significant acceptance will be achieved. At that point, RFID tags may be placed on many consumables. Should this happen, the vision of consumers bypassing the checkout counter may soon follow.

ACTIVE TAGS

In contrast to passive tags, active tags contain an onboard power source. This is usually in the form of a small battery. The battery powers both the tag's internal circuitry and the onboard antenna. The additional circuitry required by the battery as well as the battery itself requires that active tags be larger and more expensive than passive tags. Many active tags, for example, have plastic housings. These cannot simply be adhered to high-volume inventory in the same manner as a film or Mylar-based passive tag. Because of this, specific consideration must be made to affixing the active tag to the inventory or pallet being tracked.

As a result of the additional power offered by the battery, the range of active tags is generally far superior to that of passive tags. Active tags can have transmission ranges measured in hundreds or even thousands of feet instead of just a few feet, as is normal in the case of passive tags.

FIGURE 2.6   Common active tag.

Active tags conserve battery power by normally existing in a sleep mode. The tag is woken up or activated by entrance into an RFID system interrogation zone. The powered tag then provides data to the RFID system as requested. The ability to normally exist in a sleep mode greatly lengthens the operational life of an active tag. The minimal power consumption in the normal sleep mode enables many tags to remain operational for several years. The actual length of the battery life will be dependent on the number of times that the tag is activated. Thus, the RFID engineer will have to design or set up an active RFID system so that in the event that tagged material is stored within an interrogation zone the tags will not be continuously activated until their batteries are exhausted.

RFID active tag batteries come in many shapes and sizes. Many RFID-specific batteries superficially resemble normal commercial equivalents. However, the RFID batteries are likely to function at a higher voltage of 3.6 versus 1.5 for smaller cells, as in the case with many defense-related RFID tags. To avoid potential damage to both RFID and other conventional battery equipment, it is imperative that control be maintained over both the storage and replacement of RFID-specific batteries.

The high power demands of RFID active tag batteries may also require different battery chemistry than conventional equipment. Whereas most electronics utilize alkaline, nickel-cadmium, or nickel metal hydride batteries, RFID batteries are more likely to be based on substantially more costly advanced battery technology such as lithium chemistry. The higher cost associated with lithium batteries may also lead the RFID tag manufacturer to produce rechargeable systems.

Active tags can also be more sophisticated than passive tags. In some cases, active tags can be interfaced with other technologies such as the global positioning system (GPS) and/or satellite communication systems. The global positioning system is a set of U.S. government satellites orbiting around the earth. A GPS receiver communicates with the GPS satellites. Nowadays, receivers can be found in cell phones, radios, and wristwatches. If the minimum required number of satellite signals can be acquired by the GPS receiver, the system can determine its location within as little as ten meters. This means that GPS interfaced tags can be placed on large shipping containers or tractor trailer rigs to determine both the identification and location of product.

The larger size and greater expense of active tags does prevent their use on smaller, cheaper types of products, particularly those with high volume. That means

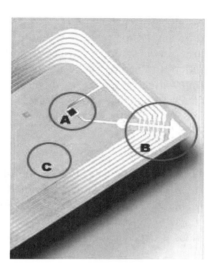

FIGURE 2.7   Active tag battery.

that it is unlikely that active tags will ever be used at the individual consumer product level. As you would expect, expensive active tags are obviously not considered disposable and may be intended to be recycled according to operating policy.

Semi-Active Tags

Tags can also be designed with features found in both passive and active tags. These are attempts to retain the advantages while eliminating the disadvantages of each type. Semi-active tags typically use an internal battery to power circuitry that is internal to the tag itself. Typically, circuitry on semi-active tags includes sensors for monitoring environmental conditions such as temperature and humidity. Sensors can also be powered to detect vibration or movement. These are typically used to monitor the possibility of damage or unauthorized movement during transport or storage.

However, in contrast to active tags, the semi-active tag does not use its internal power source to communicate with the antenna. For communications functions, the semi-passive tag relies on electromagnetic field power received from the system's antenna. By conserving its internal power in this manner, the internal battery life can be greatly extended.

SAW RFID Tags

SAW (surface acoustic wave) tags are passive RFID tags that operate in a fundamentally different way from typical RFID tags. Typical RFID tags are based on semiconductor physics to provide power for transmission of their ID number. SAW tags convert an incoming wave from the interrogator into nanoscale surface acoustic waves on the surface of the chip. The wave travels past a set of acoustic wave reflectors that encode the wave into a unique pulse train. This pulse train is converted to a radio wave to be sent back to the reader.

These tags operate at a globally legal 2.45-GHz frequency. Due to the nature of the tags, there is no need for any DC power to operate the tag, allowing for greater read range. They have sufficient data storage capacity to comply with EPC or other global standards. In addition, the nature of the tag allows the distance between reader and tag to be calculated and provides for direct measurement of tag temperature. The tags have an operating range of −100 degrees to 200°C. They can also survive high-energy X-rays and gamma-ray sterilization.

TAG FREQUENCIES

Tags primarily operate at either high frequency (HF) or ultra-high frequency (UHF). HF is most often 13.56 MHz, while UHF can range from 902 to 928 in the United States. The 2400–2500 MHz range may also used. Some active tags for specialized applications may utilize microwave frequencies. The use of either HF or UHF tags for more normal applications is dependent on the range required and the materials present in the system.

HF tags are generally limited in ranges measured in inches. This lends HF tags to inventory applications where the items are in close proximity to each other and in close proximity to a reader. UHF tags operating between 902 and 928 MHz, on the other hand, can be utilized out to several feet or even yards. The greater range of UHF tags makes them more applicable to shipping dock type applications; 2400- to 2500-MHz tags may have a range between one and four feet.

Both the packaging material and the material itself is a significant RFID system issue as some materials are known as radio frequency absorbing while others are radio frequency reflecting. Examples of radio frequency reflecting materials are metallic items or containers. The RF reflecting characteristic of metals can prevent the tag antenna from absorbing sufficient RF energy to be powered by deflecting the RF wave.

Examples of RF absorbing materials are liquids. Liquids reduce the effectiveness of the RF wave by absorbing the energy. The reduced strength RF signal then does not have sufficient power to activate the tag.

WRITING CAPABILITIES

When the tag enters the interrogation zone, the data stored in the tag is transmitted to the RFID reader antenna. The data can be ASCII, hex characters, or decimal characters. The data that is stored in the tag is dependent on the tag's writing capability. The three general types of writing capabilities are:

- Read only
- Write once, read many
- Read/write

Read Only

Read-only tags are tags where the identification data is entered by the tag's manufacturer. Thus, these types of tags must be either specified by the manufacturer and accepted by the purchaser or specified by the purchaser. In many cases, the identification data is used by a number of different organizations. Therefore, it is actually easier to control if the identification data is assigned by the manufacturer. A typical example is the E-ZPass tollway system. A vehicle is assigned a tag with a specific number regardless of which tollway system the tag is purchased through. Since the tag number is controlled, it may be used on other tollway systems in the tag consortium.

Write Once, Read Many

Write once, read many (WORM) tags are not programmed by the manufacturer. The purchaser is given the opportunity to write the identification data to the tag. However, with the WORM type of tag, this identification data cannot be erased. This means that once the data is written it cannot be changed. However, in some cases, if additional memory space is available, additional identification data can be added. Generally, in the event that incorrect data is written to the tag, the tag must be discarded.

Read/Write

As with WORM tags, read/write tags are not programmed by the manufacturer. It is the purchaser who programs the tags. The advantage of the read/write tag is that the purchaser can reprogram the identification data held by the tag. Thus, any identification data writing errors can be corrected. Read/write tags are generally the most sophisticated type of the three types of tags. Often additional information may be stored. It is also possible to lock certain areas of the tag's memory so that it cannot be erased.

TAG COMPONENTS

Passive, active, and semi-passive tags all contain a minimum of:

- Integrated circuitry or chip
- An antenna
- A substrate or tag housing

The components are illustrated in Figure 2.8.

Of course, more sophisticated active tags will also contain the battery and specialized integrated components such as GPS circuitry or monitors for humidity, temperature, vibration, or movement.

Tag Integrated Circuitry

The tag integrated circuit or chip is that part of the tag that contains the data that is transmitted. It also contains the logic to decode the RF signal from the reader and code the data recorded on the chip for subsequent transmission by the tag's antenna. Passive tags commonly have the capability to transmit ninety-six bits of data. Active tags, on the other hand, are limited only by the other system components integrated with the RFID tag.

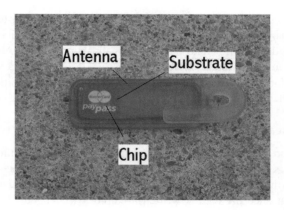

FIGURE 2.8   Tag components.

Tag Antennas

Not to be confused with the system reader antenna, the tag antenna is an integral component on the actual RFID tag. The tag antenna is used to both receive and send radio frequency waves. In the case of passive tags, the tag antenna receives the radio frequency energy and passes the energy on to the tag's integrated circuitry. The integrated circuitry's response to the radio frequency energy is then transmitted back out through the tag's antenna.

The configuration of the tag's antenna is dependent on what type of frequency is used by the tag. HF tag antennas will most likely be shaped as coils, UHF antennas will be more linear in shape. Figure 2.9 illustrates these designs.

Another tag antenna issue is the size of the antenna itself. This is a critical issue because the size of the antenna is related to its ability to both absorb RF energy and transmit RF energy. Since greater range is generally desired regardless of the type of tag that is used, most tag antenna designs attempt to maximize the size of the antenna. Thus, a larger part of any tag is going to consist of antenna.

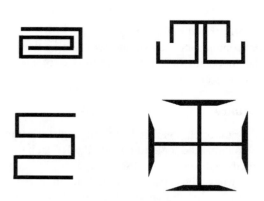

FIGURE 2.9   Tag antenna designs.

A significant antenna issue revolves around the potential placement of the tag on the intended object. The effectiveness of the antenna may depend on how it is oriented with respect to the product, which in turn is dependent on how it is positioned with respect to the reader's antenna. To address this issue, some RFID tags contain multiple antennas or antennas that have different branches. All of these attempts are aimed at increasing the RFID system's ability to obtain more reliable communication. The successful placement of tags on objects requires that the RFID engineer conduct some experimentation in order to determine the optimum position. The subject of tag placement testing will be covered in greater depth in a later section of this book.

Tag Substrate or Tag Housing

The tag substrate performs two primary functions. First, on the front surface, it provides a surface or housing for the other tag components. Second, on the back surface, it can provide means for attaching the adhesive or tape for positioning the tag to the item. A variety of materials can be used for the tag substrate. Common materials are thin plastics, including Mylar.

Table 2.1 summarizes the major differences between the three major types of RFID tags. SAW tags are not included in this table.

TAG GENERATIONS

One of the vastly superior characteristics inherent in RFID tags over bar codes is the ability to change data that is transmitted to the antenna and reader. Bar codes, once printed, can only provide a fixed set of data. The most current RFID tags can be reprogrammed. However, to reach this point, RFID tags have undergone evolution.

An earlier generation of RFID tags, referred to as Generation 1 Class 0, are programmed by the tag manufacturer. With this class of tags, there is no way for the local end-user to modify the data. This limitation means that a lot of coordination is needed between the manufacturer and the end-user. The end-user also has to be extremely careful not to make any tag placement errors. An incorrectly affixed tag could result in a wasted tag. This lack of flexibility somewhat reduces the benefits of the entire RFID system.

TABLE 2.1
RFID Technology Comparison

	Passive	Active	Semi-Passive
Power source	External Electromagnetic antenna field	On-board battery	On-board battery for internal circuitry External electromagnetic field for transmission
Range	Measured in feet	Up to thousands of feet	Measured in feet
Size	Smaller	Larger	Larger
Data storage	Less	More	More
Cost	Less	More	More

Newer Gen 1 Class 1 tags are known as write once, read many (WORM). With the proper equipment, the end-user can program blank tags. This reduces waste, as the tags are programmed as the need arises.

The latest tag protocol is known as Generation 2 Class 1. These are also WORM-type tags. The major difference between Generation 1 Class 1 and Generation 2 Class 1 tags is that the Generation 2 protocol is intended to have increased global acceptance.

SCANNERS AND READERS

As previously discussed, RFID tags receive an electromagnetic signal that is transmitted through the system's antennas. The RFID tags then subsequently return a signal to the system. For these functions, either a simple scanner or complex readers may be utilized.

SCANNERS

In simple systems, the electromagnetic signal may be transmitted from a simple scanner. Simple scanners may be handheld or mounted to mobile equipment such as a forklift. This means that scanners are primarily used for situations where you go to the material rather than the material coming to you. Scanners are also commonly used for situations where RFID data must be verified. Both of these requirements imply that a relatively low rate of reads is required. An application that is well suited to scanner use is order fulfillment. Here the individual processing the order may travel throughout a warehouse picking individual items from stock. As each item is picked, it is scanned and removed from the on-hand inventory database.

Typically, the data gathered by scanners is downloaded or linked to other information systems components. Figure 2.10 illustrates a typical handheld RFID scanner.

FIGURE 2.10 Typical handheld RFID scanner.

READERS

In more complex or rapidly moving systems, the electromagnetic signal is transmitted by a smart reader. Smart readers may be commonly seen in conveyor or loading

FIGURE 2.11   Common types of RFID reader.

dock portal applications. With smart readers, the characteristics of the radio frequency field generated by the reader is controlled by the RFID middleware installed on the host computer. These include the size of the interrogation zone field and the radio frequency that the interrogation zone field uses. The reader also monitors the interrogation zone for tag transmissions. Figure 2.11 illustrates a common type of RFID reader.

Reader Frequencies

Readers may use one of two common types of radio frequencies. These include HF and UHF. As previously described in the tag section of this chapter, HF is most often 13.56 MHz, whereas UHF can range from 902 to 928 in the United States. It goes without saying that the reader and the tags must operate on the same frequency in order to properly function.

Reader Interrogation Modes

Most readers will have a setup protocol, including the mode in which the reader is to interrogate tags within the interrogation zone. With passive tags this is not an issue. However, with active tags, the RFID engineer must decide whether to set up the system with continuous or intermittent interrogation. If any tagged material is present in the interrogation zone and the RFID system is set up for continuous interrogation, the active tag's batteries may be quickly depleted.

One method of sidestepping this problem is to reduce the interrogation zones size. This, however, will prevent the RFID system from being able to maintain any kind of vigilance over potentially expensive tagged material. On the other hand, a large interrogation zone can be maintained and the reader can only activate the interrogation zone on an intermittent basis. The downside to this approach is that all of the material can be monitored but only at specific intervals. Between interrogation intervals, the presence or location of the tagged material is unknown.

FIGURE 2.12   Large common RFID antenna.

ANTENNAS

As previously discussed, an RFID antenna as illustrated in Figure 2.12 is used to transmit the radio frequency signal from the reader to the tags. An RFID antenna is also used to receive the radio frequency signal from the tag for subsequent processing by the RFID reader.

In situations where the orientation of the tag with respect to the reader will not change, it is possible to have a single antenna. This can work in manufacturing applications where a product is undergoing a process. However, in more complex situations where the orientation of the tag is not guaranteed, it is normal for RFID systems to utilize more than one antenna. Generally speaking, for a given sized interrogation zone for an antenna, the greater the number of antennas, the greater the probability of a successful read by the system.

RFID antennas are commonly contained within an outer rectangular-shaped plastic housing. The housing protects the antenna and associated electronic components from damage. The housing also protects the antenna from minor environmental hazards such as dust. Thus, many RFID antennas have little resemblance to the type of antenna that you may be used to seeing. The plastic housing also provides a means of attaching the antenna in position.

The positioning of the antennas is also an important issue. As previously discussed, both the packaging material and the item to be tracked can affect the ability of the RFID system to conduct a successful read. In the classical loading dock application, it would be standard to include an antenna on each side of the portal. In a forklift-type application, the antennas may be positioned above the driver's safety cage. Lastly, in a shrink-wrap application, the antennas would be positioned in locations around the turntable, which would still allow access to the table.

Another antenna placement issue is the height of the antenna. In some applications, the material will not necessarily be passing through a specific portal. In many cases, the range of the antenna and the size of the interrogation zone can be increased by raising the antenna above ground level. Some experimentation will be necessary in order to determine the optimal sized zone. The subject of effectively testing and positioning antennas is covered in depth later in this text.

Yet another possible antenna issue is a situation where the antenna cannot be allowed to interfere with the surface movement of the material. In situations like this, it is possible to mount the antenna suspended from the ceiling with the field oriented downwards. This method works particularly well when the tags can be placed on the topmost horizontal surface. In this case, the system has an unobstructed view of the tags and the successful read rate is likely to be very high.

HOSTS

As previously described, the host is a computer system with application specific software. The software can include RFID middleware to set up and control the reader and some type of database software to control the information received from the reader.

COMMUNICATION PROTOCOLS

The reader may have the capability of communicating to the host via more than one type of communication protocol. The choice of communications protocol can depend on the distance between the reader and the host, the required data transfer rate, and the system budget. Common types of protocols include RS-232, RS-485, and Ethernet-based systems.

RS-232

RS-232 is the simplest of the protocols likely to be available with an RFID system. RS stands for recommended standard by the Electronics Industry Association (EIA). This serial protocol is commonly utilized in industry to communicate directly between a host computer and one or more devices via individual dedicated cables. RS-232 ports have either nine or twenty-five pins. A nine pin port is illustrated in Figure 2.13. While reliable, RS-232 suffers from slow data transfer rates of 20K and limited transmission cable lengths of fifty feet. While some transmission distance issues may be overcome, other issues may make another protocol more attractive. For example, RS-232 cable is more expensive than other alternatives such as Ethernet. Despite many industry announcements of the death of RS-232, the protocol continues to be utilized in the industrial environment.

FIGURE 2.13 RS-232 port.

RS-485

RS-485 is a more capable serial communication protocol than RS-232. Advancements include increased data transfer rates and increased transmission distances. The RS–85 specifications include up to a 100K data transfer rate and a 4000-foot transmission distance. It also permits the communication to more than one device via a bus cable architecture. Up to ten receiving devices can be utilized. RS-485 also has the improved capability over RS-232 of being differential. Among other things, this means that the system is less susceptible to problems associated with voltage shifts and electrical noise. Like RS-232 cable, RS-485 cable is more expensive than Ethernet cable.

Ethernet

Another possibility for communication between the RFID reader and the host computer is Ethernet. The attraction of an Ethernet-based system is that most facilities probably already have an Ethernet network in place. Ethernet also has a much higher data transfer rate than either RS-232 or RS–85. Newer Ethernet systems have the capability to transfer data at 100 M. If one does not already exist, Ethernet cable can be more inexpensively obtained and installed than either RS-232 or RS-485 cable.

FIGURE 2.14 Ethernet port.

SUMMARY

The objective of this chapter was to provide a high-level, easy-to-understand introduction to the various components required to implement an RFID system. These
components include tags, antennas, readers, scanners, and hosts. Tags are classified
as either passive or active depending on the source of power. Antennas come in
many shapes and sizes depending on the application. Readers send power through
the antenna to active the tags. Scanners are less sophisticated handheld versions of
readers. Hosts are the computer systems that control the entire RFID system.

   With a basic understanding of these various components, it will now be possible
to discuss specific commercially available RFID components, RFID system configurations, and RFID applications.

CHAPTER QUESTIONS

1. What are the four basic components of any RFID system?
2. What are the three main components present in a passive RFID tag?
3. What are the fundamental differences between passive and active tags and
    systems?
4. Under what conditions would you want to use HF versus UHF for an
    RFID system?
5. What techniques are used in tag design to reduce the tag positioning
    sensitivity?
6. What technique can be used to conserve the battery life of active tagged
    material while still maintaining some level of control?
7. What type of communications protocol would you normally want to use for
    an RFID system?

3 Passive RFID System Components

INTRODUCTION

In this chapter, we provide a more in-depth examination of passive RFID system components than in the common RFID systems components chapter. As with the active RFID system components chapter, for details on how these components are actually used in a system, readers are directed to the applications section of the book.

As discussed in the common RFID systems components chapter, passive RFID systems are distinguished from active RFID systems primarily by the absence of an internal power source in the tag. The lack of an internal power source yields both advantages and disadvantages to the RFID system designer.

MAJOR ADVANTAGES TO PASSIVE RFID SYSTEMS

The major advantages of passive RFID systems include:

- Lower expense
- Smaller sizes
- Greater operational life
- Environmental robustness

LOWER EXPENSE

Passive tags are well known for their lower expense in comparison to active tags. The lower expense is a result of having lower capabilities and no internal battery requirement. The lower expense of passive RFID tags is a great advantage in applications that do not require the greater capabilities of active RFID tags. For example, the use of passive RFID tags on consumer products is rapidly approaching. In this application, the RFID tag will obviously be disposable in nature, as the consumer product will permanently leave the logistical system. With extremely low-cost tags, the small increased expense of the tag becomes negligible. The same cannot be said of the much more expensive active RFID tags.

SMALLER SIZES

Currently, very small-sized passive tags are in use. The completely operational Trovan passive tag, for example, is approximately the size of a grain of rice. This small size allows great flexibility in applications and mounting positions. Tags of this type are used currently for:

- Companion animal tracking
- Individual sports competitions

The small size allows passive RFID tags to be implanted between the shoulder blades of companion animals or pets. Neither the animal nor the owner can physically detect the presence of the tag under normal conditions. It is only when the animal's identity needs to be determined that the tag has any impact.

The small size of passive tags also means that they are very light. This is important in cases where individual sports competition times need to be recorded. The champion tag, for example, is a passive RFID tag positioned in a housing that can be attached to a runner's shoe. The runner's time is recorded as he runs across an RFID antenna mat at the finish line. Runners cannot object to the presence of the tag. The tag is so small and light as to not interfere with the competitor's performance.

GREATER OPERATIONAL LIFE

Greater operational life is achieved through the lack of an internal power source. Since no internal power source is necessary, the tag cannot be nonoperational as a result of battery depletion. Active tags, in contrast, must have their batteries replaced every three to five years, depending, of course, on the exact nature of the usage. The operational life, can in fact, be almost infinite as long as the tag is not damaged. A more likely source of obsolescence would be an upgrade in the RFID infrastructure. This would most likely come about in the form of a change in protocol standards.

ENVIRONMENTAL ROBUSTNESS

Since passive RFID tags do not need to have a provision for replacing an internal power source, they may be hermetically sealed during the manufacturing process. This makes passive RFID tags inherently environmentally robust. This robustness allows passive RFID tags to be subject to environments where the operation of any nonhermetically sealed tag could be compromised. In the case of the Champion tag, the tag is subject to rain and perspiration. Since the tag is sealed, these sources of moisture cannot enter the tag.

MAJOR DISADVANTAGES TO PASSIVE RFID SYSTEMS

The major disadvantages to passive RFID systems include:

- Less range
- Less identification capability

LESS RANGE

Passive RFID tags generally have much less range than active tags. Part of this is a result of the fact that passive tags must acquire power from the electromagnetic transmissions from the RFID reader antenna. The other part is due to the limited size of the antenna in the passive RFID tag. The end result is that the range of passive RFID tags is measured in a few inches or feet, whereas active RFID tags may transmit one hundred meters or more.

The lesser range capabilities of passive tags are both a blessing and a curse. From a blessing standpoint, the reduced range is advantageous for privacy reasons. For example, few consumers would be interested in carrying a credit card that could be activated by any reader hundreds of feet away. Imagine being charged for goods as you passed by any number of readers in a department store. Similarly, E-passports incorporate a passive RFID chip to transmit personal data to the port of entry RFID reader. For both privacy and security purposes, the government would not want this data accessible to unauthorized individuals. Even with the short-range passive RFID tags, manufacturers are beginning to bring out transmission-proof passport cases and wallets. Supposedly, these will help prevent illicit activation of passive tags.

The downside to lesser range is that a passive RFID system is much more sensitive to bad reads. The system must insure that the tag is in closer proximity to the RFID reader antenna. In many applications, this is not a problem. The tag user deliberately places the passive tag near the scanner. This is the case with credit cards, passports, and companion pets. However, with other applications such as individual sports competitions, the placement of the tag is not as certain. For example, it is recommended that two separate antenna mats be utilized at the finish line in races. If the primary mat does not pick up the runner's tag, hopefully the backup mat will acquire the signal.

LESS IDENTIFICATION CAPABILITY

A second major disadvantage to passive tags is their lesser identification capability. In many cases, passive tags can only hold and transmit a single ten-space unique alphanumeric string. In systems of this type, the identification code must be linked to an external database in order for the identification code to become meaningful.

The E-passport perhaps represents one of the most advanced applications of passive tag identification capability. The passive tag embedded in the back cover of the E-passport holds the individual's name, date of birth, place of birth, passport number, and even a digital photograph. The data is also encrypted. It is necessary to possess the key in order to translate the encoded data. However, in contrast to the capabilities of active tags, even this amount of data is limited.

CHAPTER ORGANIZATION

The remainder of this chapter focuses on a sample of specific passive RFID chips that are readily available for use by RFID system designers and engineers. New tags are being developed every day. Similarly, older tags are being constantly phased out. The inclusion of specific chips does not imply any endorsement, nor does the absence of any specific chips mean that they are not suitable for particular applications. The passive tags presented here are merely representative of the capabilities of passive chips in general.

TROVAN ELECTRONIC IDENTIFICATION SYSTEMS

Trovan Electronic Identification Systems is a privately held United Kingdom company that has been in business since 1988. It produces a variety of passive RFID tags. Trovan is the market leader in animal tagging applications. Its products are currently used by commercial organizations including Volkswagon, Daimler-Benz, Coca Cola, Nissan, Merck, and many others. Trovan products are also used by over sixty government agencies in thirteen countries around the world.

TROVAN PASSIVE TAGS

The Trovan tags have thirty-nine bits of data available for use. The tags are written with unique identification numbers during manufacture. With this number of bits, there are 550 billion unique code numbers. The Trovan Web site is www.trovan.com.

The intended uses, capabilities, and dimensions of the following Trovan passive RFID Tags will be summarized:

- ID 100 series
- ID 200 and 300 series
- ID 400 series
- ID 600 series
- ID 700 series
- ID 800 series
- ID 1000 series

ID 100 Series

FIGURE 3.1   Trovan 100 series tag.

The 100 series tags are used in animal as well as industrial applications. This includes implantation in both animals and humans. The tags are stated as currently being utilized in over three hundred zoos worldwide. The tags are encapsulated in glass. They are approximately the size of a grain of rice at 0.45 inches long and 0.08 inches in diameter. The read range depending on the reader is approximately 9 to 14 inches. The basic 100 series tag is illustrated in Figure 3.1.

A ruggedized version of the tag is also available for industrial applications and garment identification. This tag has a capsule that is approximately twice as thick as the normal 100 series tag. As a result, the tag is slightly larger, at 0.51 inches long and 0.18 inches in diameter. The tag is also listed as being able to withstand temperatures as high as 180° centrigade. This tag is illustrated in Figure 3.2.

As many of the major applications involve animal implantation, the ID-100US tags feature pre-sterilized transponders and a dedicated lancet delivery device. This tool is illustrated in Figure 3.3. The RFID tag can be seen near the tip. The lancet has a special gauge to insure that the tag has been properly inserted.

FIGURE 3.2   Trovan hardened 100 series tag.

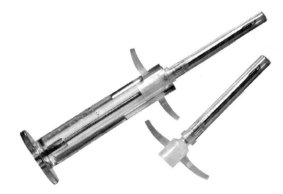

FIGURE 3.3   Trovan implantation tool.

ID 200 and 300 Series

The 200 series circular transponder is a passive tag in the form of a donut. The pre-drilled, countersunk hole allows the tag to be screwed or riveted to a host product. The 200 series tag is 1.02 inches in diameter and 0.18 inches thick. The range of the 200 series is between 13 and 24 inches depending on the reader. The 300 series pellet transponder is similar to the 200 series minus

FIGURE 3.4   Trovan 200 and 300 series tags.

the mounting hole. This also allows the tag to be more compact. It has a diameter of 0.50 inches and a thickness of 0.19 inches. The range of the series 300 is between 9 and 18 inches. Figure 3.4 illustrates the 200 and 300 series tags.

ID 400 Series

The 400 series tag utilizes a card form factor. It is primarily utilized as an identification card. It is suitable for use in security, time, and attendance, and entertainment applications where the identification number can be linked to an external database. The read range of the card is 20 to 33 inches. It is 3.4 by 2.12 inches. The 400 series card is illustrated in Figure 3.5.

FIGURE 3.5   Trovan 400 series card.

ID 600 Series

The 600 series tag is designed for use with vehicles. It possesses the characteristic of having a very wide operating temperature range of −20°C to 200°C. Its range is between 18 and 27 inches. Its dimensions are 2.4 inches long, 1.34 inches wide, and 0.55 inches thick. The ID 600 is illustrated in Figure 3.6.

FIGURE 3.6   Trovan 600 series tag.   **FIGURE 3.7**   Trovan 700 series tag.

ID 700 Series

The 700 series metal mount transponder is designed to be mounted on kegs, vehicles, or other metal boxes. It may be mounted by welding or epoxying. It is specifically designed to handle conditions requiring durability and physical ruggedness. It has a read range of approximately 10 inches. It is 1.69 inches in diameter and 0.24 inches thick. Figure 3.7 illustrates the ID 700 series tag.

ID 800 Series

The 800 series rod transponder is designed for extremely rugged applications, including those requiring extended immersion in water. The read range is approximately 29 inches. The 800 is 5 inches long and 1 inch in diameter. The 800 series is illustrated in Figure 3.8.

ID 1000 Series

The 1000 series tags are similar to the 200 series tags. However, their intended use is for pallet tracking and animal ear tags. They are donut-shaped with a variety of diameters from 0.5 to 2.0 inches. The smaller sizes have 9-inch ranges while the larger sizes have 20-inch ranges. Figure 3.9 illustrates a few of the 1000 series tags.

FIGURE 3.8   Trovan 800 series tag.

FIGURE 3.9   Trovan 1000 series tags.   **FIGURE 3.10**   Trovan Workabout Pro Reader.

TROVAN PORTABLE READERS

Trovan offers a number of portable readers for use with their passive RFID tags. The readers that Trovan offers include:

- LID WAPR Workabout Pro Reader
- GR-250 High-Performance Reader
- LID Pocket Series Readers

LID WAPR Workabout Pro Reader

The LID WAPR Workabout Pro Reader is the most sophisticated portable reader offered by Trovan. This reader combines RFID and barcode scanning with keyboard entry in a single device. It features the Windows CE NET operating system. The screen is color and is also touch sensitive. The reader has USB and docking port connectors. Bluetooth connectivity is standard. The read range depends on the tag being scanned. The maximum range is approximately 5 inches. The reader is 8.7 inches long and 3 inches wide. Figure 3.10 illustrates the Workabout Pro Reader.

GR-250 High-Performance Reader

The GR-250 High-Performance Reader is designed to maximize the read range and read area. It sacrifices some of the capability of the Walkabout Pro Reader in order to improve performance. The GR-250 does not have a color touch screen or a keyboard. The screen is a two-line, sixteen-character LCD display. The reader can store up to 3072 identification codes. As with the Walkabout Pro Reader, ranges vary with tag type. The maximum range is 29 inches with the Trovan ID 500 tag. The reader is 11.7 inches long, 6.9 inches wide, and 4.5 inches tall. The reader is also sealed for better withstanding of environmental conditions. The GR-250 is illustrated in Figure 3.11.

FIGURE 3.11   GR-250 High-Performance Reader.

LID-5xx Pocket Series Readers

Trovan offers a series of pocket readers with different capabilities. The readers are all 12.5 cm long, 7 cm wide, and 2.4 cm thick. All of the readers possess a two-line sixteen-character LCD display. The maximum read range of all of the readers is 5 inches. The LID 560 basic pocket reader will read and display tags only. It has no onboard memory or comms ports. It is the most economical solution. The LID 571 reader can store up to 1600 codes and has an RS-232 interface and an IRDA interface. The LID 571 can also provide a date and time

FIGURE 3.12 Trovan LID 560 Pocket Reader.

stamp. The LID 572 is similar to the LID 571 with the exception of a USB port. A Bluetooth option is available. The basic pocket reader is illustrated in Figure 3.12.

LD-650 Stationary Readers

Trovan also offers a range of stationary readers that are modular in design. Decoder and antenna types can be mixed and matched according to application requirements and are available in a number of packaging options. These feature high performance and resistance to EMI, and they can be used to read transponders on metal. LID-650 series readers are suitable for use in industrial environments and can be equipped with ruggedized housings as needed.

SMARTCODE

SmartCode was founded in 1998. It has headquarters in New York, London, and Hong Kong. SmartCode is a world leader in providing low-cost, high-performance RFID solutions. The company manufactures RFID inlays and passive tags. Smart-Code also offers active tags, which will be discussed separately in the active tag chapter. The SmartCode Web site is www.smartcodecorp.com.

SMARTCODE INLAYS

SmartCode inlays are passive RFID tags constructed on a polymer substrate. The tags are typically distributed on reels. Customers can use the inlays between layers of paper or foil to create passive tags for a variety of inexpensive operations. These include product labels, tickets, and tracking tags. The inlays are available in a wide variety of antenna forms for use in particular applications. The tags can be as small as 30 mm by 30 mm. The largest tags are 100 mm by 100 mm. The weight varies between 80 and 200 mg. They are write once, read many types of tags. They operate on frequencies of 869 MHz/902–928 MHz and have a range up to twenty-five feet. Up to 256 bits of memory can be programmed on the tags. The tags can operate between −25°C and 80°C. A variety of SmartCode RFID inlays are illustrated in Figure 3.13.

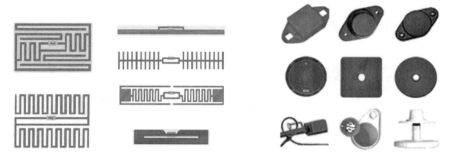

FIGURE 3.13   SmartCode RFID inlays.   **FIGURE 3.14**   SmartCode passive tags.

SMARTCODE PASSIVE TAGS

SmartCode also manufactures complete passive RFID tags. Passive tags are available in read-only and read/write format. The tags operate on frequencies of 125 KHz/13.56 MHz/915 MHz/2.45 GHz for read/write. Up to 16K of memory is available. The tags can be as small as 0.8 mm and weigh between 6 and 54 g. The tags have a range up to six meters. The operating temperature range is −40°C to 70°C. Figure 3.14 illustrates a variety of SmartCode passive tags.

SYMBOL TECHNOLOGIES

The New York–based Symbol Technologies Corporation has long been associated with automatic identification systems beginning with bar code technology. Symbol has continued in automatic identification with RFID technology. The company manufactures both passive RFID Gen 1 and Gen 2 inlays and tags. The Symbol Technologies Web site is www.symbol.com.

RFX 3000 SERIES INLAYS

The RFX 3000 series of passive RFID tag inlays come in a variety of shapes and sizes. These tags are Gen 1 Class 0 with read rates up to four hundred per second. The tags are general purpose in nature, suitable for boxes, cartons, plastic bottles, and totes. The antennas are either single-dipole designs or dual-dipole designs with omnidirectional polarization. The dual-dipole design antennas incorporate two antennas to improve read/write capability at any angle in any direction. The following figures illustrate some common Symbol Technologies inlays.

RFX 3000 1 × 1 Read/Write Tag

The RFX 3000 1 × 1 tag can be read at up to five feet and written to at up to three feet. It is 1.00 inches by 1.383 inches. It utilizes a single-dipole antenna design. In addition to general use, it is designed for plastic parts, bottles, totes, and containers. The RFX 3000 1 × 1 tag is illustrated in Figure 3.15.

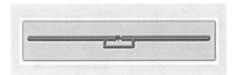

FIGURE 3.15   RFX 3000 1 × 1 read/
write tag.

FIGURE 3.16   RFX 3000 1 × 6 read/write tag.

RFX 3000 1 × 6 Read/Write Tag

This tag can be read up to twenty-five feet away and written to up to eight feet away. It utilizes a single-dipole antenna design. It is a large tag with dimensions of 6.342 inches by 0.670 inches. Its intended uses are cartons and corrugated cardboard containers. This tag is illustrated in Figure 3.16.

RFX 3000 2 × 2 Read/Write Tag

This tag is also designed for plastic parts, bottles, containers, and totes. It differs from the RFX 3000 1 × 1 tag by having a dual-dipole antenna design. It can read up to twenty feet away and be written to up to eight feet away. It is 2.234 inches by 2.234 inches. The RFX 3000 is illustrated in Figure 3.17.

RFX 3000 4 × 4 Read/Write Tag

The RFX 3000 4 × 4 tag is the largest, most capable of the 3000 series tags. This tag is designed for use with cartons and corrugated cardboard containers. It has a dual-dipole antenna design with a read range of thirty feet and a write range of eight feet. It is 3.692 inches by 3.692 inches. The tag is illustrated in Figure 3.18.

FIGURE 3.17   RFX 3000 2 × 2
read/write tag.

FIGURE 3.18   RFX 3000 4 × 4 read/
write tag.

GEN 2 RFX 6000 SERIES READ/WRITE INLAY

The Gen 2 RFX 6000 series tags are UHF EPC compliant tags. They have 96-bit memory for a unique ID with 32-bit access password and 32-bit kill password. They have a read rate of up to four hundred times per second. The tags have an expected life of up to ten years with 1000 write cycles. The temperature operating range is −40°C to 65°C. The 6000 series also incorporates both single- and dual-dipole antenna designs.

RFX 6000 1 × 1 Series Read/Write Inlay

This tag is intended primarily for use on plastic bottles, parts, containers, and trays. It utilizes a single-dipole design antenna. It has a read range of up to five feet and a write range of up to three feet. The tag measures 1.00 inches by 1.383 inches. The RFX 6000 1 × 1 is illustrated in Figure 3.19.

FIGURE 3.19 RFX 6000 1 × 1 series read/write inlay.

RFX 6000 2 × 4 Series Read/Write Inlay

The RFX 6000 2 × 4 tag is intended for use with cartons, boxes, and corrugated cardboard containers. It has a dual-dipole antenna design with a read range of up to fifteen feet and a write range of up to six feet. It measures 1.700 inches by 3.875 inches. The RFX 6000 2 × 4 is illustrated in Figure 3.20.

CARGO TAG

The Symbol Technologies EPC Global Gen 2 Class 1 cargo tag is intended for all-weather applications. It is designed to be robust enough to withstand vibration, shock, rain, and temperature extremes. The tag has mounting holes, so it can be mounted with screws or rivets or it can be glued. A small area is also available for a conventional bar code. The tag has an aluminum backplate to enhance the tags signal. The tag can be read at up to forty feet. It contains 96-bit memory with 16-bit control for lock and kill features. It operates in UHF at 860–960 MHz. It is 6 inches by 6 inches with a 4 inch by 4 inch antenna. It weighs 9.8 ounces. It can operate between −20°C and 85°C. The cargo tag is illustrated in Figure 3.21.

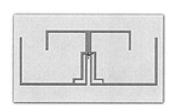

FIGURE 3.20 RFX 6000 2 × 4 series read/write inlay.

FIGURE 3.21 Symbol cargo tag.

SYMBOL ANTENNAS

Symbol manufactures a wide variety of antennas. In this section, we will summarize the features of following antennas:

- AN200 general-purpose antenna
- AN400 high-performance area antenna

FIGURE 3.22   Symbol AN200 general-purpose antenna.

AN200 General-Purpose Antenna

The AN200 is designed as a general-purpose antenna for use in both indoor and outdoor applications. These antennas are intended for use in pairs with left- and right-hand polarization. The antenna is relatively small, at 11.1 inches wide by 11.1 inches long and 1.9 inches thick. It weighs approximately three pounds. The operating temperature range is −40°C to 65°C. It has been tested specifically for rain, humidity, and salt spray. The AN200 is illustrated in Figure 3.22.

AN400 High-Performance Area Antenna

The AN400 is designed for long-range and wide area applications. It can be mounted on both ceilings and walls. The antenna and housing is constructed of aluminum with a polycarbonate cover. The AN400 is 28.3 inches long, 12.5 inches wide, and 1.5 inches thick. The antenna can operate between 0°C and 50°C. It is approximately eight pounds in weight. The AN400 high-performance area antenna is illustrated in Figure 3.23.

FIGURE 3.23   AN400 high-performance area antenna.

SYMBOL READERS

Symbol manufactures both mobile and fixed readers. The mobile reader is the RD5000. The fixed readers are designated as the XR400, XR440, and XR480. These readers use the same form factor. The difference between the models includes increased sophistication and a greater number of read points. The XR400 has one read point, whereas the other two have four and eight read points, respectively.

RD5000

The RD5000 is designed as a mobile reader for mounting on forklifts, mobile carts, and other material handling equipment. It operates in conjunction with a mobile computer such as the Symbol VC5090. It is 7 inches long, 9 inches wide, and 2 inches tall. It weighs 3 pounds 10 ounces. It is powered by a removeable, rechargeable 7.2-volt lithium-ion battery. The reader has a special feature that only powers the reader when the platform is in motion. This helps preserve the battery life. The operating temperature is −20°C to 50°C. The RD5000 is illustrated in Figure 3.24.

FIGURE 3.24 Symbol RD5000 mobile reader.

XR400 Series

The XR400 is a multiprotocol fixed reader that operates between 902 and 928 MHz. It has Ethernet capability and USB and RS-232 ports. Feedback is provided with green, yellow, and red LEDs to indicate power, activity, and errors. The XR400 is 11.75 inches long, 8.75 inches wide, and 2.00 inches thick. It weighs 4.85 pounds. The reader can operate in temperatures between −20°C and 50°C. Figure 3.25 illustrates the XR400 reader.

FIGURE 3.25   Symbol XR400 reader.

INTERMEC

Intermec's line of passive read/write RFID tags is marketed under the Intellitag name. The tags operate at 915 MHz. Their tags come in a variety of form factors. Applications include container tags, identification cards, and windshield tags.

INTELLITAG WINDSHIELD TAG

This tag is intended to be affixed to vehicle windshields for highway toll and security access applications. The substrate is flexible and has an adhesive backing for mounting. The tag measures 3.1 inches by 1.81 inches by 0.051 inches. It can operate between −40°C and 85°C. It has a read range of approximately thirteen feet. This enables the tag to be read by overhead antenna readers. The Intellitag windshield tag is illustrated in Figure 3.26.

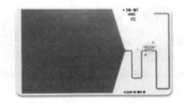

FIGURE 3.26   Intermec Intellitag windshield tag.

INTELLITAG CONTAINER TAG

FIGURE 3.27   Intermec Intellitag container tag.

The Intellitag container tag is a general-purpose tag designed to be used with pallets, cartons, and containers. It measures 4.13 inches by 1.28 inches by 0.125 inches. It has a read range of approximately thirteen feet. The container tag is also available in other formats specifically suited for reusable plastic containers. The basic Intellitag container tag is illustrated in Figure 3.27.

INTELLITAG ID CARD

The Intellitag ID card is listed as being the first credit card format 915-MHz RFID card to have both long-range read and write capabilities. The card is specified as having a read range of eight feet. It has a total of 110 bytes of memory for use. It can operate between 0°C and 50°C. Applications include border security, customer loyalty, and luggage tags. The card is also available with a magnetic stripe. The Intellitag ID card is illustrated in Figure 3.28.

FIGURE 3.28   Intermec Intellitag ID card.

INTERMEC READERS

Intermec offers fixed readers, handheld readers, and vehicle mount readers. The designations for these readers are:

- IF series of fixed readers
- IP4 handheld reader handle with Intermec 700 series computer
- IV7 vehicle mount reader

IF Series of Fixed Readers

The IF series of fixed readers includes the IF 30, IF 4, and IF 5. The series is intended for dock doors, portals, and conveyors. The IF is set up for 865-MHz, 869-MHz, and 915-MHz frequencies.

The IF 30 can read tags from up to fifteen feet. It also has the capability to filter out tag information prior to transmission to the host. This prevents

FIGURE 3.29   Intermec IF 30 fixed reader.

redundant information being sent to the host computer. The IF 30 has both Ethernet and RS-232 ports. The dimensions are 12.27 inches long, 8.90 inches wide, and 3.25 inches tall. It weighs 6.75 pounds. The IF 30 is illustrated in Figure 3.29.

IP4 Handheld Reader Handle with Intermec 700 Series Computer

The IP4 reader is actually a reader designed to be an accessory handle for the Intermec 700 series of portable computers. This combination allows users to perform exception reading when it would be difficult to perform scans or writes with fixed readers. The system can be interfaced with existing networks for data transmission. Figure 3.30 illustrates the IP4 reader and Intermec 700 series computer.

IV7 Vehicle Mount Reader

The IV7 is designed to be mounted directly to a vehicle such as a forklift. It combines the power of a fixed reader with the mobility of a portable reader. The IV7 is particularly useful when the number of dock doors exceeds the number of forklifts. It allows hands-free scans for operators. The IV7 is intended to be interfaced with Intermec's CV60 vehicle mount computer. The IV7 vehicle mount reader is illustrated in Figure 3.31.

FIGURE 3.30   Intermec IP4.   **FIGURE 3.31**   Intermec IV7 vehicle mount reader.

SUMMARY

In this chapter, we presented some representative passive RFID system components. As with active RFID components, there are many more manufacturers than those presented here. Users are encouraged to identify as many different manufacturers as needed to insure that the equipment best suits their needs.

REFERENCES

Intermec. Intermec Supply Chain Solutions & Inventory Tracking. www.intermec.com (accessed August 29, 2007).
SmartCode. SmartCode Corp. www.smartcodecorp.com (accessed August 29, 2007).
Symbol Technologies. Enterprise Mobility Products and Services. www.symbol.com (accessed August 24, 2007).
Trovan. Trovan Electronic Identification Systems. www.trovan.com (accessed August 29, 2007).

4 Active RFID System Components

INTRODUCTION

In this chapter, we provide a more in-depth examination of active RFID system components than in the common RFID systems components chapter. For details on how these components are actually used in a system, readers are directed to the applications section of the book.

As discussed in the common RFID systems components chapter, active RFID systems are distinguished from passive RFID systems primarily by the presence of an internal power source in the tag. The existence of an internal power source yields both advantages and disadvantages to the RFID system designer.

MAJOR ADVANTAGES TO ACTIVE RFID SYSTEMS

The major advantages include:

- Greater range
- Greater identification capability

GREATER RANGE

The presence of an internal power source enables active tags to possess greater read ranges than passive tags. Active tag ranges are measured in meters rather than inches or feet as in the case with passive tags. This increased range enables an active RFID system to employ fewer reader antennas and read a larger number of tags from a given position than a passive system. The greater range enables active tags to be used for:

- Expensive large asset tracking
- Container control

In the case of expensive large asset tracking, the greater range of active tags allows a number of expensive and/or large assets to be inventoried simultaneously with a small number of antennas. A typical example of this would be a vehicle yard. Some active tag systems have a read range as great as one hundred meters. A large number of vehicles could be near instantaneously inventoried within the one hundred–meter radius of an active RFID system.

Similarly, storage units such as intermodal shipping containers can be inventoried and tracked with the greater range of active RFID tags. The common storage method of stacking multiple shipping containers makes normal inventory techniques difficult to execute. With the same one hundred–meter range previously discussed, mobile inventory vehicles can easily read the active tags while driving between rows of containers.

GREATER IDENTIFICATION CAPABILITY

The internal power source allows active RFID tags to be far more flexible and capable than passive tags. The internal power also allows greater memory to be utilized. In contrast to 16 or 64 Kbits of memory in passive tags, there may be significantly more memory in active tags. The Savi active RFID tags, for example, contain 128 Kbits of user available memory. Active tags may also be interfaced with environmental sensors for humidity and vibration. Even GPS capabilities can be built into active tags. This allows tags to transmit not only identification information but also the tags' physical location.

MAJOR DISADVANTAGES TO ACTIVE RFID SYSTEMS

The major disadvantages of active RFID systems include:

- More expensive
- Less operational life
- Larger physical size

MORE EXPENSIVE

Active RFID tags are generally far more expensive than passive tags. This is generally a result of the additional circuitry and components required for the increased capabilities of active tags. For this reason, active tags are currently only being utilized in applications where the active tags' enhanced capabilities can be taken advantage of and where the tags can be recycled. Unfortunately, recent history indicates that many shipping container type tags never actually end up being returned for reuse. As the use of active tags becomes more widespread, this disadvantage may become less of an issue.

LESS OPERATIONAL LIFE

Since active RFID tags possess an internal battery, their operational time is limited by the battery life. This is a serious issue because most active tags are far more expensive than passive tags. Many active tags actually have batteries that cannot be replaced by the user in the field. Unless the manufacturer is willing to replace the batteries, these types of tags must be discarded. Fortunately, many sealed active tags of this type can operate for up to ten years if the tag is not subjected to frequent identification collection operations.

Some active tags have the capability to have batteries replaced in the field by the users. However, the battery life is generally shorter than that of the nonreplaceable active tags. Still, the battery life can be as long as three to five years. However, this is only possible when tag information is collected on a very limited schedule. For example, in some Savi active tags, the five-year battery life is only achievable with two collections per day.

Several approaches can be taken to minimize this weakness. One approach is to utilize very power-dense battery chemistry. Rather than utilizing conventional alkaline batteries, manufacturers may specify far more expensive lithium-based batteries. Another approach is to design the tag so that the battery can be easily replaced in the field rather than having to return the tag to the manufacturer. Even replacing the battery in the field can be burdensome. If the tag is mounted in an inaccessible position or is protected from theft, battery replacement can become a serious issue when a large number of tags is involved. If frequent tag battery replacement is anticipated, users should insure that the battery can be replaced while the tag is still mounted.

LARGER PHYSICAL SIZE

The increased range and data transmission capabilities of active tags naturally require that their physical size and weight is larger in comparison to passive tags. This automatically precludes the use of active RFID tags in any application where these characteristics would be detrimental. Typical examples of this would involve the use with either human beings or animals. The presence of the tag might prevent the host from functioning in a normal manner.

The remainder of this chapter focuses on specific active RFID tags that are available for use by RFID system designers and engineers. As with the passive tag chapter, the active tags presented in this chapter do not constitute any sort of endorsement. The absence of any particular active tags should not be interpreted as being unsuitable for any particular application.

SAVI CORPORATION

The California-based Savi Corporation was founded in 1989. It is predominately involved in active RFID systems and is probably the market leader in this area. Savi is heavily involved in defense applications for both the United States and NATO countries. Specific applications include the tracking of expensive assets and containers through logistical systems. Savi was acquired by Lockheed Martin in 2006. The Savi Web site is www.savi.com.

SAVI ACTIVE TAGS

Most Savi tags are based on similar highly developed active RFID technology. The tags generally operate on 433 MHz at 28K bps. Their range is approximately two hundred feet with mobile RFID readers and three hundred feet with fixed readers. The difference in tags lies mainly in their intended end application. Their tags are categorized as either asset or data-rich tags. The following Savi Tags are reviewed:

- ST-602
- ST-604
- ST-654
- ST-656

SaviTag ST-602

The small ST-602 is classified as an asset tag. It is designed to be attached to relatively small inventory items. It is 2.4 inches by 1.7 inches by 0.48 inches. The tag weighs approximately one ounce. The tag is powered by a 3-volt, 540-mA nonreplaceable, nonrechargeable lithium ion battery. The battery life is listed as four years with ten reads per day. The tag has sixteen bytes of memory for identification and sixteen bytes of user memory. The tag returns the tag identification, the tag status, and the reader identification. The ST-602 is illustrated in Figure 4.1.

FIGURE 4.1   Savi ST-602.

SaviTag ST-604

The ST-604 tag is designed for users needing more battery life than the ST-602. The ST-604 is 6.25 inches by 1.7 inches by 1.3 inches. It has the same sixteen-byte identification and user memory as the ST-602. The tag also returns the tag ID, the tag status, and the reader ID. The battery life is much longer than the ST-602, ten years with ten reads per day. As with the ST-602, the battery is nonreplaceable and nonrechargeable. The ST-604 is illustrated in Figure 4.2.

FIGURE 4.2   Savi ST-604.

SaviTag ST-654

The Savi ST-654 is intended for use on shipping containers. It is classified by Savi as a data-rich tag. The ST-654 has 128 Kbytes of memory in comparison to the ST-602's and ST-604's sixteen bytes. This allows the user a great deal of flexibility. Aside from the tag ID, the user can also program the contents of the container that the tag is attached to. The tag is similar in size to the ST-604 at 6.25 inches by 2.12 inches by 1.125 inches. The tag is also more sophisticated than the ST-604 in that the 3.6-volt lithium battery may be replaced in the field without special tools. However, the expected battery life is less, at five years with two collections per day. The tag also has a buzzer for assistance in location. Figure 4.3 illustrates the ST-654.

SaviTag ST-656

The ST-656 is designed to be used on large International Standards Organization (ISO) shipping containers. It can be attached to the left door of an ISO-compliant container. It is weatherproofed in order to operate under adverse conditions. The housing has the appearance of a clamp with a front and back case. In position, the tag is inside of the container. The front case is 4.75 inches by 4.5 inches by 1.5 inches.

FIGURE 4.3   Savi ST-654.

The back case is 4.6 inches by 3.2 inches by 2 inches. Like the ST-654, the ST-656 utilizes a replaceable 3.6-volt lithium battery. The battery life is also the same, five years with two collections per day. The battery is replaceable without special tools. The tag also has a beeper for location and other alarms. The ST-656 is illustrated in Figure 4.4.

SAVI FIXED READERS

FIGURE 4.4   Savi ST-656.

Savi offers both fixed and mobile readers. In this section, we will review fixed readers. The Savi fixed readers are intended to be positioned permanently in storage yards, terminals, and warehouses. The readers can be interfaced together through an Ethernet network.

The following Savi fixed readers will be reviewed:

- SR-650
- Savi Signposts

SR-650 Fixed Reader

The SR-650 fixed reader is a long-range omnidirectional antenna/reader. Its intended use is for asset inventory. The reader operates on a frequency of 433 MHz. It is compatible with all Savi active tags. The range of the antenna is one hundred meters. The antenna/reader is designed to be weatherproof, with a polypropylene housing with UV inhibitors. It can operate between −32°C and 60°C. It is circular in shape with a diameter of 12 inches and a height of 5 inches. Figure 4.5 illustrates the SR-650 fixed reader.

FIGURE 4.5   Savi SR-650 fixed reader.

Savi Signpost

The other fixed reader that Savi offers is the Signpost. The Signposts are designed for use in dock portals and vehicle gates through which tagged material
passes. This prevents unintentional cross-reads from
occurring that might be possible with the omnidirectional SR-650. By utilizing a number of Signposts, the RFID system can positively determine
the location of the tags. The Signposts can read
tags traveling as fast as sixty miles per hour. The

FIGURE 4.6   Savi Signpost.

Signposts are available in short, medium, and long range. The model designations are
SP-65X-111, SP-65X-211, and SP-65X-311. The long-range model has a range of up to
twelve feet. Figure 4.6 illustrates a Savi Signpost.

SAVI MOBILE READERS

When the permanent nature of fixed readers is less appropriate, Savi offers a mobile
solution based on the SMR-650 antenna reader. Readers of this type are particularly useful for commissioning tags. This reader has a range of two hundred feet.
This unit interfaces with a PC through a DB-9 pin RS-232 port. The dimensions are
6.25 inches by 1.5 inches by 1 inch. The weight is 6.4 ounces. The unit uses a 3.7-volt,
420-mAh lithium-ion battery. The battery life is listed as three to four days of continuous operation. Figure 4.7 illustrates the SMR-650 antenna/reader.

The unit can be attached to either the Intermec 751 G/A computer or a conventional notebook computer. An SMR-650 attached to the Intermec 751 G/A is illustrated in Figure 4.8.

MARK IV INDUSTRIES

Mark IV Industries manufactures active RFID tags primarily for the electronic toll
industry. Their RoadCheck Flat Pack Transponders (FPT) line of RFID tags come in a

FIGURE 4.7   Savi SMR-650 antenna/
reader.

FIGURE 4.8   Savi SMR-650 attached
to the Intermec.

variety of form factors for internal, external, and license plate mount styles. The tags transmit on a frequency of 915 MHz at 500 Kbits per second. They have 256 bits of memory. The internal lithium battery can operate the tags for up to ten years. However, most organizations specify replacement between three and five years. The operating temperature range is −40°C to 70°C. The Mark IV Industries Web site is www.ivhs.com.

MARK IV TRANSPONDERS

Mark IV offers a total of five transponders for different vehicle applications. These include:

- Internal flat pack transponder
- License plate transponder
- Roof mount transponder
- Fusion transponder
- Ubiquity transponder

Mark IV Internal Flat Pack Transponder

The internal version typically mounts behind the rearview mirror so that it does not interfere with the driver's vision. The basic form factor is 3.5 inches wide, 3.0 inches high, and 0.6 inches thick. It weighs 2.5 ounces. Figure 4.9 illustrates basic internal form factor.

License Plate Transponder

Some vehicles possess antennas internally laminated into the windshield. Vehicles with this type of windshield often experience transmission problems with the normal internal RFID tags. To address this problem, Mark IV offers the license plate transponder form factor with similar performance specifications as the internal flat pack form factor. The license plate tag is illustrated in Figure 4.10.

Figure 4.9   Mark IV internal flat pack transponder.

Figure 4.10   Mark IV license plate transponder.

Roof-Mounted Transponder

Mark IV has also developed an RFID tag for situations in which both a line of sight problem may exist and the tag needs to be mounted so that it is out of reach. This may occur with heavy trucks and buses. The roof-mounted transponder fulfills these needs. This tag is illustrated in Figure 4.11.

FIGURE 4.11 Mark IV roof-mounted transponder.

Fusion Transponder

Mark IV also offers a more sophisticated active RFID tag for commercial use. This tag is known as the fusion transponder. This 915-MHz tag is 3.1 inches wide, 4.3 inches high, and 0.9 inches thick. Its additional capabilities include audiovisual driver capabilities and enhanced read/write abilities. The audiovisual capabilities include LEDs to provide the driver with feedback as to the success of toll transactions. The write capability of the tags means that toll systems can program special data to calculate toll payments. These tags have a lithium battery that is listed as having a life of five years. The fusion transponder is illustrated in Figure 4.12.

Ubiquity Transponder

The final RFID transponder that Mark IV offers is both active and passive. This tag enables commercial operators to utilize virtually all toll systems in the United States, including the Inter Agency Group EZ-Pass system and the Tier 21 California and Colorado system. In addition, it has the capability of utilizing a variety of weigh station systems. The Ubiquity transponder is illustrated in Figure 4.13.

FIGURE 4.12 Mark IV fusion transponder.

FIGURE 4.13 Mark IV Ubiquity transponder.

FIGURE 4.14   Mark IV Badger reader.   **FIGURE 4.15**   Mark IV MGate reader.

MARK IV READERS

Mark IV offers a number of readers for use in electronic toll collection systems. These include:

- Badger Reader
- MGate Reader

Badger Reader

The Badger reader is Mark IV's product for general applications. It is capable of interfacing with eight regular lane antennas or four high-speed lane antennas. For larger applications, several Badger readers may be interfaced together. Vehicles traveling as fast as one hundred miles per hour can be detected with the Badger. The Badger operates on a frequency of 915 MHz. Both RS-232 and RS 422 interfaces are available to communicate with the host computer. The Badger's dimensions are 20.95 inches by 19.00 inches by 12.85 inches. The Badger can operate in temperatures between −40°C and 158°C. The Badger reader is illustrated in Figure 4.14.

MGate Reader

The low-cost MGate reader is designed for less demanding applications than the Badger reader. The MGate has also been used as a temporary mobile replacement for permanent facilities under construction or repair. The MGate is 12 inches by 3.4 inches by 4.1 inches. With these dimensions, the MGate is one of the smallest ETC capable readers. The MGate can operate between −40°C and 70°C. The MGate is illustrated in Figure 4.15.

MARK IV ANTENNAS

Due to the nature of electronic toll collection systems, Mark IV offers its antennas separate from its readers. In most applications, a number of antennas will be attached to a single reader. Each of these antennas will be mounted either above or alongside the traffic lane. The lane antenna is 37 inches by 30 inches by 4 inches. The outer

housing is fiberglass. It is hermetically sealed
to withstand exposure to the elements. The
antenna can operate in temperatures between
−40°C and 158°C. Figure 4.16 illustrates one
of Mark IV's lane antennas.

SUMMARY

In this chapter, we have reviewed actual product offerings from two manufacturers in the
active RFID system market. For logistics
chain type applications, we examined tags
and antenna/reader systems from one of the

FIGURE 4.16   Mark IV lane antenna.

market leaders, Savi Technology. For electronic tollway collection operations, we
examined the tags, readers, and antennas from the EZ-Pass manufacturer Mark IV
Industries. These are obviously not the only manufacturers that supply active RFID
system components to those markets. Likewise, many other markets exist that utilize
active RFID systems. Readers are encouraged to explore the offerings from as many
manufacturers as necessary to meet their needs.

REFERENCES

Mark IV Industries. MARKIV Industries Corp. www.ivhs.com (accessed August 29, 2007).
Savi Technologies. Savi Technology Homepage: RFID Visibility for Supply Chain Networks.
    www.savi.com (accessed August 29, 2007).

5 RFID System Design

SYSTEM DESIGN APPROACH

In order to be effective in conducting this type of analysis, the investigative team or engineer should seek to collect information effectively. An approach suggested by Foster (2003), a six-step design life cycle for products and processes, is shown in Figure 5.1. The steps are listed below:

- Idea generation
- Preliminary design
- Prototype development
- Final definition
- Product design and evaluation
- Implementation

As we tailor this process for RFID system design cycle we suggest the following steps:

- Gain ideas through understanding
- Preliminary design
- Prototype development
- Choose an alternative
- Test and retest the chosen alternative
- Implement the solution

STEP 1: GAIN IDEAS THROUGH UNDERSTANDING

In this step we seek to document the environment that is being investigated. Techniques such as flow charting and values stream mapping should be utilized to understand the operations. Validation of these types of tools by operations is critical to allow for operational understanding. Dialogue with operators, managers, and technicians is recommended for keen understanding of common problems that RFID may improve and or create. The collection of operational data in specific areas such as parts or product selected per hour will provide estimates on how much equipment may be needed for operations. Understanding of the source of the data may provide an evaluation of the credibility of the information. Oftentimes this type of analysis is accomplished by evaluating the real operation by using an on-site analysis. RFID on-site analysis can be demonstrated in three parts: equipment evaluation, environment evaluation, and human factor evaluation.

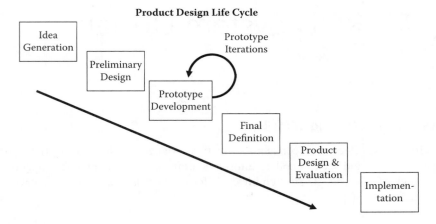

FIGURE 5.1   Design life cycle.

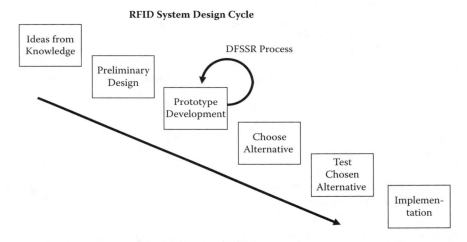

FIGURE 5.2   RFID system design cycle.

ON-SITE ANALYSIS

An on-site analysis is an excellent tool for identifying problem areas prior to deploying an RFID instiutive. Consider the three parts of an on-site analysis: equipment evaluation, environmental evaluation, and human factor evaluation.

Equipment Evaluation

The first part of the analysis should be the equipment evaluation, which would include estimating needs, reviewing costs, and training that will be required when using RFID equipment. This would include some of the following tasks:

- Identifying the number of readers required for optimal read response. The number of readers must be determined along with how many antennas will be necessary for boosting the signal in the given environment
- Identifying the number of tags required for tagging new items, retagging of bad labels, and tagging of miscellaneous items such as returns.

What type of products that will be tagged will have physical problems with the RFID technologies? For example, products encased with metal tubing may have problems with Gen 1 passive RFID tags.

In Appendix 5.1 (Clampitt, 2006), a sample RFID dock door survey shows typical areas that need to be assessed.

Environmental Evaluation

Environmental evaluation allows for identification and creation of physical and logical read zones such as portals that will not hinder operation. If readers and/or physical enhancements to facilities will be necessary for integrating RFID into the environment, what violation of leases, rental agreement, or building codes may originate? Also, process flows for material handling traffic, replenishment of max–min volume, and other environmental interference must be evaluated. Most pundits recommend that you walk the process and observe operations. Often some operational understanding can only be achieved by a substantial amount of keen observation. Appendix 5.2 provides an RFID environmental evaluation.

Radio Frequency Interference Testing

Another form of environmental testing includes the identification of sources of electromagnetic interference (EMI) in the environment. Often after production operations are clearly understood it is becomes important to understand the radio frequency environment. First, checking for documented wireless protocol is important to make sure you understand which frequencies are being used and the potential conflicts with RFID frequencies. Next, we suggest utilizing equipment to evaluate frequencies. A spectrum analyzer can be utilized to evaluate potential frequency problems in an environment. A sample exercise on using a spectrum analyzer to do an EMI survey is shown in Appendix 5.3.

Human Factor Evaluation

Often the human element of the process and operations is overlooked when performing an assessment. It is important to consider not only what is being done but also who is doing the work. Consider not only the people who will be doing the job tasks; we suggest that you also evaluate who will be performing the implementation. Oftentimes job satisfaction is overlooked and a technical initiative such as system implementation is sabotaged by disgruntled workers. We suggest that both a work measurement and time study analysis be performed, along with a job satisfaction analysis for technical personnel. We provide an overview of work measurement in Appendix 5.4 and a cognitive turnover job satisfaction survey and case study in Appendix 5.5.

STEP 2: CREATE PRELIMINARY DESIGNS

After collecting relevant information, RFID technologies can be evaluated and selected based on the solution that will best fit the operation. After the understanding of the environment has been made clear, the knowledge of RFID technologies will allow for a better analysis of relevant technologies for the operation.

STEP 3: PROTOTYPE DEVELOPMENT

Best practices suggest that you create an initial scenario or prototyped environment to evaluate the chosen solution. We suggest using the Design for Six Sigma Research (DFSSR) methodology when designing operational prototypes. This is covered in detail in the RFID implementation chapter.

STEP 4: CHOOSE AN ALTERNATIVE

After testing the solutions for performance cost justification, a return on investment analysis should be evaluated. Choosing the best valued RFID solution is important to satisfy both short-term needs such as mandate compliance and long-term needs such as operational efficiencies. A five-year cost analysis technique should be implored for this type of evaluation. We suggest using the RFID ROI chapter as a guide for cost evaluation details. Make sure there is corporate and workplace buy-in in the chosen solutions. Some suggest involving both decision-makers and personnel who utilize the solution most in the process as a means for attaining buy-in.

STEP 5: TEST AND RETEST THE CHOSEN ALTERNATIVE

Testing protocols and minimum specification should be set for operational acceptance. Testing should be categorized into subsystem testing and full system testing procedures. It is critical that end-users of the system are involved in the testing to identify problem prior to rollout.

STEP 6: IMPLEMENT THE SOLUTION

Effective project management is key to implementing an RFID solution. Coordinating efforts and identifying key milestone using techniques such as Program Evaluation and Review Technique (PERT) and Central Path Method (CPM) are critical. More details are provided in the project management chapter.

APPENDIX 5.1

SAMPLE RFID DOCK DOOR SURVEY

A dock door survey may allow users to evaluate performance expectations/specifications to identify and/or model potential RF, EMI (electromagnetic interference), and other interference sources. These elements hinder an RFID system's performance, reliability and introduce uncertainty regarding the overall system throughput and integrity.

This sample may allow understanding of how to measure RF signal strength, stray signal, multipath, bounce, RF signal absorption/reflection characteristics, harmonic effects, shading, emitted and conducted RF signal strength, loss profiles, and full spectral analyses for the intended operational RFID. Recommended practices prior to a survey include:

- Gather business requirements
- Interview managers and users
- Define information for security requirements
- Gather site-specific documentation
- Document existing network characteristics
- Gather permits, license (electrical), and zoning (fire marshal) requirements
- Note indoor- or outdoor-specific information

Other operational considerations include:

- Bill of material items comprising materials, components, subassembly, assembly, or product nature
- Packaged items—individual or mixed fundamental items in a single package
- Transport units comprising packages or other discernible items
- Unit load or palletized unit—to carry transport units or other discernible items
- Container units—for accommodating pallets or other discernible items
- Transportation vehicles—to carry container units or other discernible items
- Throughput speeds of pallets, cartons, or items on forklifts, pallet jacks, or conveyors

The site survey may identify the variables that would most affect your client's RFID project. Understanding the conflicts of these variables helps to ensure that the RFID technology will be optimized. Some of the variables that can affect positive RFID outcomes are:

- RF-absorbing water/liquid content in food stuffs and manufactured goods
- RF-absorbing water content in corrugated cardboard packaging, with added variability due to changing relative humidity of indoor/outdoor climates
- RF-reflecting and/or RF-shielding metal content in both goods and packaging, even foils and metallic inks

DOCK DOORS CHECKLIST

Dock Door Characterization

- Dimensions (height × width × depth)
- Note reflective surfaces
- Leveling ramp
- Door
- Side posts
- Are there protective posts/fences for the antennas?

- Does the door go straight up, parallel to the floor, or roll?
- What is the distance between the dock doors?
- Are all docks the exact same configuration?
- Do they use a screen?
- Can the dock door or screen be partially open?
- Are there fire extinguishers present whose view cannot be blocked?
- Study customers' work flow process and note exactly what each employee does
- Note the kind of traffic, busy periods, quiet periods, volume
- Do they use forklifts? What speed?
- Do they use pallet jacks? What speed?
- Do they manually load with totes? What speed?
- Are wireless handhelds or forklifts used at dock? Note any communication devices including cellular phones
- Are adjacent docks typically used simultaneously?
- Do they stage pallets between docks? Do they park or store other items temporarily?
- How do they load pallets in the trailer?
- Do they pivot pallets? For example, one loaded from the narrow side, one from the wide side of the pallet?
- What kind of product is loaded?
- Do they double stack (or more) pallets?
- Do they dual stack pallets; for example, two adjacent?
- Do they quadruple load pallets; for example, two adjacent, double stacked?

Mounting

- Best location for reader mounting
- Center of dock is not very serviceable
- Are antenna cables sufficiently long?
- What kind of brackets will be required?
- How can you protect the antennas from forklifts?

Input Sensors

- Where can photoelectric sensors be mounted if required?
- Do you need a narrow detection beam or is a less expensive wide beam sensor okay?
- Can the sensors be inadvertently activated? Is that an issue?
- Where can magnetic door or screen switches be mounted if required?
- Is direction detection required (this may be complex—don't want to push for this)?

Output Sensors

- Are visual indicators required?
- Does the site have restrictions on visual indicator colors?

- Are audible outputs required?
- Equipment requirements
- How many readers per dock?
- How many antennas per dock?
- What types of antennas per dock?
- Mounting brackets required for readers and antennas?
- How do you keep the antennas from getting misaligned?
- Are spare readers and antennas required?
- Will you need to attenuate power?
- Network design and connectivity to each reader
- LAN test panel
- Electrical power for readers
- Security issues for location
- Grounding availability

APPENDIX 5.2 (Adapted from Clampitt, 2005)

RFID ENVIRONMENTAL EVALUATION

Many operations contain metal, carbon, and absorptive instruments in their physical environment. Operations such as maintenance warehouses, electronics manufacturers, and some distribution operations operate in these conditions. System design should be well thought out for RFID technologies to be successful. A dirty environment is defined in the text as an operation in which radio frequency transmissions may be difficult and provide an unreliable environment for RFID technologies to operate. Tagged materials that present difficulties for RF include lucent materials and opaque materials.

Lucent materials or materials that allow RF energy to penetrate such as paper, plastics, cloth, and cardboard have the highest confirmed successful read in an RFID system. These items can be tagged arbitrarily and can be scanned successfully.

OPAQUE MATERIALS

Opaque materials present the most problems. First, conductive materials that block or reflect RF energy such as metals, pastes, carbon-impregnated plastic (black), conductive plastics, and foil-lined packaging scatter or block RF signals. Second, absorptive materials, which weaken RF energy, such as most liquids and moist fibers, green wood, moist wipes, and damp paper, absorb RF energy, preventing the tag from reaching full capacitance.

The best practice is to containerize the opaque materials into some type of RF lucent material and scan those products.

Common Problems

- Liquid items such as water do not scan
- Metal items such as metal cans and toothpaste do not scan

- Items located in the middle of pallets do not scan
- Fast-moving pallets do not scan all tagged items

Best Practices

- Recontainerize into scannable containers
- Use alternate scanning method
- Move tags to outside of items
- Speed through the portal is insignificant
- In a dense reader environment, change the reader from Talk first, then listen to Listen first, then talk. This solution will affect your read rate, causing a longer time to attain reads, but you may still attain the scan
- Limit speeds for mobile reader to allow time for the waves to manipulate the environment
- Tag pallets with difficult items such that the tags are facing outward toward the reader
- Tag materials such as water where there is conductive material such as the bottle cap
- Antennas may have to be adjusted in order to capture the effective read area for your specific application
- The reader may need to be configured and adjusted similar to a portal configuration to account for dead areas within the scanning area. Antennas may also have to be adjusted such that the wrong product is not scanned at the wrong area
- Mount RFID tags to allow for the greatest possible surface area presentation to the reader
- Configure pallet to minimize shadowing, which is when tags are oriented on top of each other with a container in between. This shadowing causes the signal of one tag to mask the signal of all the tags situated behind it
- Consider the liquid line and air space within cases and pallets to enable better reads on absorptive materials
- Utilize alternative tag types for better results on absorptive products
- For opaque items, seek to add a scannable layer to the tag or change the tag substrate to be reflective so the tags will scan
- Tag products on the outer side of the carton facing the antennas
- Test the pallet portal limits and dead zones
- Alter the multiplexing sequence of multiple antennas to give preferential read by the antenna better suited for capturing difficult tag geometry
- Ensure that the reader wake and sleep settings are optimized to capture scans
- Evaluate the link margin if the reader field appears limited. Evaluate settings by:
  - Increased gain in antenna
  - Increased output power
- Evaluate VSWR for reader power airborne
- Evaluate connectors and coaxial cables

- Evaluate tag to reader polarization
- Enhance tag with packaging on hard to scan packages, add one inch of air space with packaging or spacers such as foam, paper, or other more conducive materials
- Include movements such as rotation to improve scanning. Utilize stretch wrap locations that rotate 360 degrees multiple times for hard-to-scan products on mixed pallets

APPENDIX 5.3

USING A SPECTRUM ANALYZER TO TEST EMI

Oftentimes electronic devices operate by radiating excessive amounts of electromagnetic energy and are susceptible to such energy from internal or external sources. Thus, determining electromagnetic compatibility or electromagnetic compatibility (EMC) is necessary. Electromagnetic interference (EMI) occurs when radiated or conducted energy adversely affects circuit performance and disrupts a device's EMC. Many types of electronic circuits radiate or are susceptible to EMI and may need to be shielded to ensure proper performance. Establishing basic electromagnetic compatibility in any electronic device generally requires detailed engineering. The first goal is to identify and reduce EMI generated from internal sources. Many manufacturers accomplish the reduction through engineering designs in which an electronic circuit is shielded in such a manner to generate less EMI. Residual EMI may then be suppressed or contained within the enclosure by appropriate filtering and shielding methods. Filtering cables at the point where they enter or leave the enclosure will reduce conducted emissions. A tool that is commonly utilized to identify the EMI levels in a facility is known as a spectrum analyzer. A sample spectrum analyzer is shown in Figure 5.3. Below is a typical screen when viewing a spectrum analyzer.

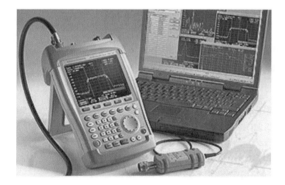

FIGURE 5.3 Handheld spectrum analyzer R&S FSH3/FSH6 (model 3.0) spectrum analyzer R&S FSH3/FSH6 (model 3.0).

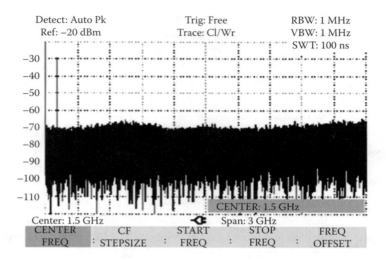

FIGURE 5.4   Spectrum analyzer start screen.

GENERAL DIRECTIONS FOR USING A SPECTRUM ANALYZER

The analyzer displays the frequency spectrum from 100 kHz to 3 GHz. See Figure 5.4 for the sample start screen.

- At 100 MHz, the generator signal is displayed as a vertical line. Generator harmonics can also be seen as lines at frequencies that are multiples of 100 MHz.
- To analyze the generator signal at 100 MHz in more detail, reduce the frequency span. Set the Rohde & Schwarz FSH Handheld Spectrum Analyser (R&S FSH) center frequency to 100 MHz and reduce the span to 10 MHz.

Centering the frequency to 915 MHz to capture RFID frequencies is necessary for identifying problems in the right frequencies.

The general procedures are as follows:

- Press Frequency button
- Enter 915 MHz
- Set span = 30 MHz
- Press Span button
- Enter 30 MHz
- Press the Marker button
- The marker automatically selects the trace maximum
- Use the soft keys to set marker
- Or rotate dial to move marker

See Figure 5.5 for more details.

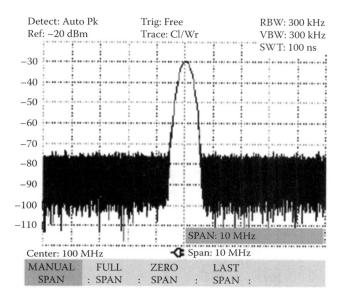

Detect: Auto Pk   Trig: Free   RBW: 300 kHz
Ref: −20 dBm   Trace: Cl/Wr   VBW: 300 kHz
                                 SWT: 100 ns

FIGURE 5.5 Centering the frequency to 915 MHz to capture RFID frequencies.

GENERAL GUIDELINES AND NOTES

- Setting the resolution and bandwidths
  - Resolution bandwidth controls the density of frequencies displayed. Lower resolution BWs will have a cleaner display but at the expense of accuracy
  - BW settings are displayed on the top right of the screen
  - A video BW setting rule of thumb is ResBW/10; see Figures 5.6 and 5.7 for sample captures of this step
- General method to set BW
  - Press the BW Function key
  - Press the manual Res BW soft key
  - Use the up/down arrows or alphanumeric keypad to enter 100 kHz
  - Press the Manual Video BW soft key
  - Use the up/down arrows or the alphanumeric keypad to enter 10 kHz
- To facilitate our measurement readings, we will activate Video Averaging
  - Press the Trace Function key
  - Press the Trace Mode soft key
  - Use the up/down arrow or the dial to select average
  - Save settings
- Other
  - Monitor the relative interference amplitude using the spectrum analyzer
  - Your measurements should correspond with the gridlines
- Throughout your measurements maintain consistency with:
  - Relative orientation with respect to the spectrum analyzer; for example, antenna orientation

- Your body position relative to the spectrum analyzer antenna
- Observers should maintain a good distance away so as not to interfere with the measurements

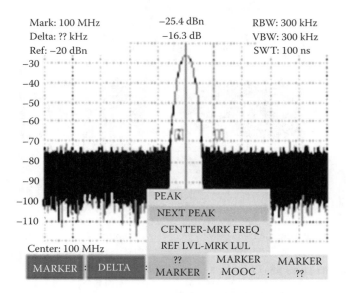

FIGURE 5.6   Identification of next peak.

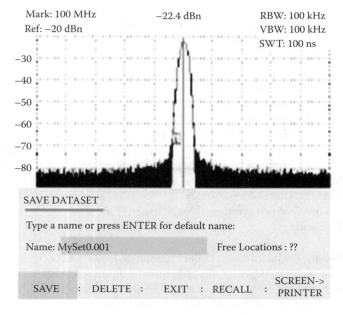

FIGURE 5.7   Saving a set of readings.

APPENDIX 5.4

Overview of Work Measurement and Time Studies

Brief History of Industrial Engineering

Work measurement and time studies is a common skill that is developed by industrial engineers. Though it is a foundational skill, most industrial engineers utilize this understanding to implement Enterprise Reserve Planning (ERP), Warehouse Management Systems (WMS), and other decision support systems in today's workforce. Operations research, statistical quality control, and logistics training provide future decisions support decision designers for complex computers systems, Six Sigma black belts and champions, and logistics engineers, respectively. Before our overview of work measurement we will provide an overview of today's industrial engineer.

The following formal definition of industrial engineering has been adopted by the Institute for Industrial Engineers:

> Industrial Engineering is concerned with the design, improvement, and installation of integrated systems of people, materials, information, equipment, and energy. It draws upon specialized knowledge and skill in the mathematical, physical, and social sciences together with the principles and methods of engineering analysis and design to specify, predict, and evaluate the results to be obtained from such systems.

Although the term *industrial* is often associated with manufacturing organizations, here it is intended to apply to any organization. The basic principles of industrial engineering are being applied widely in agriculture, hospitals, banks, government organizations, and others (Turner et al., 1987).

There is considerable commonality among the different branches of engineering, but each branch has distinguishing characteristics that are important to recognize. Industrial engineering emerged as a profession as a result of the industrial revolution and the accompanying need for technically trained people who could plan, organize, and direct the operations of large, complex systems. In the 1880s, industrial operations were conducted in more of specialty jobs shop manner and many first-line supervisors commonly abused workers. Most operations did not provide training or procedures and so supervisors managed from personal perspective, commonly abusing good workers whom they personally did not care for. Supervisors were expected to work men as hard as they could. Any improved efficiency in work methods usually came from the worker himself in his effort to find an easier way to get his work done. There was virtually no attention given to overall coordination of a factory or process (Turner et al., 1987).

Emergence of Work Measurement

Frederick W. Taylor, commonly referred to as the father of scientific management and industrial engineering, is credited with recognizing the potential improvements to be gained from analyzing the work content of a job and redesigning the job for greater efficiency. Taylor's methods brought about significant and rapid increases in productivity. Later developments stemming from Taylor's work led to improvements in the overall planning and scheduling of an entire production process.

Frank B. Gilbreth extended Taylor's work by his contribution to work management, which involved the identification, analysis, and measurement of fundamental motions involved in performing work. Work motions were classified as reach, grasp, transport, and so on, and by using motion pictures of workers performing their tasks, Gilbreth was able to measure the average time to perform each basic motion under varying conditions. This permitted, for the first time, jobs to be designed and the time required to perform the job to be known before the fact. This was a fundamental step in the development of industrial engineering as a profession based on science rather than art.

Time studies, as practiced today at companies such as United Parcel Service (UPS), consist of understanding operations, following best practices, and allowing for a normal work pace. Work measurement and standardizing operations are the precursors to performing a time study. Workers who are timed should be seasoned workers who have been trained in prescribed work methods and should be timed on a normal day. Consequently, time studies are mostly used to confirm a predetermined motion system.

Gilbreth's work derived into databases that have captured this information over many different environments and that can create predetermined work standards. These predetermined work measurement systems such as MODAPS, MTM, and others are computerized, and consulting firms implement standards using these systems. Most consultants boast a 20 percent increase in worker productivity when implementing these standards.

Another early pioneer in industrial engineering was Henry L. Gantt, who devised the so-called Gantt chart. The Gantt chart was a significant contribution in that it provided a systematic graphical procedure for preplanning and scheduling work activities, reviewing progress, and updating the schedule. Gantt charts are still in widespread use today.

W. A. Shewhart developed the fundamental principles of statistical quality control in 1924. This was another important development in providing a scientific base to industrial engineering practice. Many other industrial engineering pioneers contributed to the early development of the profession. During the 1920s and 1930s, much fundamental work was done on economic aspects of managerial decisions, inventory problems, incentive plans, factory layout problems, material handling problems, and principles of organization.

MORE ON INDUSTRIAL ENGINEERING

The period from 1900 through 1930 is generally referred to as scientific management. The next IE period began in the late 1920s and continues to the present time. This period is when operations research began to influence industrial engineering practices. The next period of IE includes computer systems and distribution and logistics and continues to grow. Though this is not an exhaustive list of all IE teachings such as total quality management, Six Sigma, Lean, JIT, manufacturing engineering, and others that are commonly taught in IE, the foundational periods provide foundations for the latter.

Industrial Engineering Organizations

Much can be learned about any profession by tracing the organizations that members of the profession form and/or join. The American Society of Mechanical Engineers provided the first forum for a discussion of the works of early pioneers, particularly Taylor and his associates. Then, in 1912 the Society to Promote the Science of Management was formed. The name was changed in 1915 to the Taylor Society.

The Society of Industrial Engineers was formed prior to 1920. The American Management Association was formed in 1922, and many industrial engineers were active in this organization. In 1934 the Taylor Society and the Society of Industrial Engineers were combined to form the Society for Advancement of Management.

The American Institute of Industrial Engineers (AIIE) was founded in 1948. The AIIE provided, for the first time, a professional organization devoted exclusively to the interests and development of the industrial engineering profession. Previously, IEs were associated with organizations whose main interests were in management or another branch of engineering.

The AIIE was an instant success in all respects. Within one year, student chapters were formed at eleven major universities. The official publication of the AIIE, the *Journal of Industrial Engineering*, also made its initial appearance the following year, the first issue being published in June 1949. In 1969, the journal was divided into two publications. *Industrial Engineering* is published monthly and is devoted primarily to industrial engineering practice. *UE Transactions* is published quarterly and is devoted primarily to research and new developments within the profession.

In 1981, through a vote of its membership, the institute changed its corporate name from AIIE to IIE. By dropping the word American, the institute officially recognized the international nature of its activities. The IIE has members in more than eighty countries around the world.

Many practicing industrial engineers belong to other organizations that are related to the IE field. Some of these are

- Operations Research Society of America
- The Institute for Management Sciences
- Association for Computing Machinery
- American Society for Quality Control
- Society for Decision Sciences
- American Production and Inventory Control Society
- Society of American Value Engineers
- American Association of Cost Engineers
- Society of Manufacturing Engineers
- Robot Society of America

The IIE is the technical society for all industrial engineers, beginning with university students who are majoring in industrial engineering. A very important part of the overall organization is the university chapters. Students participating in these chapters receive the IIE publications and are considered an integral part of the overall organization (Turner et al., 1987).

APPENDIX 5.5

COGNITIVE TURNOVER JOB SATISFACTION SURVEY

Background

Because of the difficulty of measuring knowledge worker production, dissatisfied knowledge workers may take advantage of the situation. This mindset of dissatisfaction may produce behavior in which personnel seek more financial satisfaction by giving themselves a stealth raise—cutting back the effective hours they perform knowledge work at the office. They may dedicate more mental effort to another activity that is not job related that brings them more satisfaction (Barber and Weinstein 1999). Businesses lose $150 billion annually in health insurance and disability claims, lost productivity, and other expenses attributable to burnout, stress-related problems, and mental illness (Bassman 1992). Further quantification of the bottom-line impact of indirect cost is demonstrated by the high cost of absenteeism, which is estimated at approximately $40 billion per year in the United States (Gaudine and Saks 2001).

Previous studies on turnover and burnout categorize costs into three groups: direct costs, indirect costs, and opportunity costs. Direct costs include disability claims, workers' compensation claims, increased medical costs, and litigation costs, including wrongful discharge, hiring new personnel, training cost, advertisement for new personnel, and time spent interviewing new personnel. Indirect costs include costs associated with poor quality, high turnover, absenteeism, poor customer relationships, or even sabotage. Opportunity costs include costs associated with lowered employee commitment, lack of discretionary effort, commitments outside of the job, time spent talking about problems instead of working, and loss of creativity.

Cognitive turnover (CT) is a term copyrighted in this research to describe a mindset that is created by a combination of turnover thoughts/cognitions brought about by burnout conditions. While everyone may manifest this mindset periodically, excessive CT (eCT) may be detrimental to the individual and the organization he works for. Subtle acts such as absenteeism, poor quality, and lack of discretionary effort have been related to worker burnout and are common predecessors to quitting and becoming another turnover statistic, Noncommitment type behavior may stem from employee stress and burnout created by management or organizational abuse; hence, an eCT will have lowered productivity due to the lack of commitment.

Engineering managers may be able to avoid the negative consequences to the organization and employee by identifying the nonproductive knowledge worker experiencing eCT. However, it is probably more productive to seek aggregate or group information that will facilitate improvements in attitude, innovation, and productivity of the organization and may prevent ineffective events such as reduced employee productivity and sabotage.

Cognitive turnover is a combination of a turnover thought process and the results of burnout. Similar to preturnover thought processes, high degrees of burnout among major proportions of a group suggest low productivity. High burnout implies little slack in a person's coping capacities and perhaps deficits in them. High measures of burnout are strong indicators of these phenomena, but the inverse, low burnout, does not necessarily indicate high productivity (Golembiewski and Muzenrider, 1986).

TABLE 5.1
SECtCS Method Phases

Phase 1: Develop test instrument	Develop a customized test instrument (questionnaire) for the knowledge worker population, administer the questionnaire, and collect and record scores. Conduct reliability testing on the questionnaire. This testing continued until the questionnaire was reliable (SECtCS questionnaire)
Phase 2: Develop mathematical model	Use the data collected in phase 1 and incorporate it into a mathematical model to give a valid CT index score (SECtCS model)
Phase 3: Statistical process control charts	Use data from the model developed in phase 2 for the statistical measurement of individuals with respect to all respondents and identify at-risk CT index scores. (SECtCS Evaluator-i) Establish a tracking mechanism for at-risk, and low-risk respondents. The respondents are required to retake the questionnaire every three months in order to complete the SPC charts
Phase 4: Intervention	Educate, implement, and monitor the solution (SECtCS intervention)
Phase 5: Intervention measurement	Remeasure the respondents after they have been subjected to the intervention and compare to the results of phase 3 (SECtCS Evaluator-r)
Phase 6: Evaluation of intervention	Document the results and conclusions and add to solutions database

Intervention note: Any intervention, like organizational mentorship, has to be coordinated for effectiveness. Intervention contributors must be provided with guidelines so that there will be data consistency. These guidelines will also allow for efficient collection of feedback.

This research focused on the high measures of burnout in conjunction with preturnover indicators.

The researchers have developed a methodology that is being explored as a means to consistently measure knowledge workers' CT. SECtCS, or Statistical Evaluation of Cognitive Turnover Control System, is a methodology that attempts to identify, measure, and document CT. This copyrighted methodology can only be used by the researchers in this study. The items produced from this study can be used by engineering managers and will be further described in the results and conclusions. The six phases of the SECtCS Research Methodology for Knowledge Workers (note that this chapter focuses on the first two) is shown in Table 5.1.

Phase 1: Develop Test Instrument

The test instrument that was developed to test CT is based on variables that organizations can actually do something about. Unlike other satisfaction questionnaires, the variables or constructs were chosen from organizational variables that organizations know what to do when there are problems. For instance, if pay is a problem, then organizations can raise pay, or if facilities are a problem, then organizations can choose to update facilities. The constructs are shown in Table 5.2. A questionnaire is given to measure these variables and then tested for reliability and reduced for the measured population or company.

TABLE 5.2
General Definitions of Constructs

Cognitive Turnover Determinant	Construct	Construct Definitions
Burnout (B)	Depersonalization	Distancing oneself from others
Burnout	Personal accomplishment	Performing well on things that matter
Burnout	Emotional exhaustion	Ability to cope in high-stress situations
Turnover (T)	Overall job satisfaction	Job satisfaction that determines turnover
Turnover	Goals	Feeling that goals are attainable and have meaning
Turnover	Comfort	The space and physical conditions of the job are adequate to perform at the job
Turnover	Challenge	Feeling that job is not boring and has reasonable challenges
Turnover	Financial rewards	Financial compensation is reasonable and fair
Turnover	Relationship with coworkers	Ability and willingness to work with others
Turnover	Resource adequacy	Organization provides adequate supplies and training to perform at job
Turnover	Promotions	Opportunity for fair chance at promotions

Subjects completed three questionnaires. The first was comprised of 109 questions concerning the job satisfaction constructs and the burnout constructs. A second questionnaire asked for the person's more direct appraisal of their level of CT. Respondents were assured that their answers would remain anonymous. Respondents were given both a verbal and written description of the CT and the levels of CT. A description of each range is given in Table 5.3. The respondents then self-scored their level of CT given the range from 1 to 10. Subjects were asked to rate, on a scale of 1 (strongly agree) to 5 (strongly disagree), statements that indicated how they felt about their employer. An example is "My employer is concerned about giving everyone a chance to get ahead." They were also asked to rate specific job satisfaction questions

TABLE 5.3
CT Scoring Matrix

Score	CT	Considering Leaving	Description
1–2	No	No	Not burned out
3–4	No	Occasionally	Light burnout
5–7	Yes	Open for other jobs	Medium to high
8–10	Yes	Strongly considering	High

Note: CT scores range from 1 to 10, with 1 representing low level of Cognitive Turnover and 10 representing high levels of the CT.

on a scale of 1 to 5: 1 (very dissatisfied) to 5 (very satisfied). An example is "On my present job, how do I feel about my pay and the amount of work I do?" The mean values were calculated for each construct and for an overall value.

As was mentioned before, the initial version of the questionnaire and rating scale was pilot tested and critiqued by other researchers. After feedback from other researchers, ambiguous or confusing items were identified and eliminated. This was an effort to achieve face validity.

Phase 2: Mathematical Model Results

For this research, a population of engineers across eight different companies was measured. The mean value for each construct of turnover and burnout was determined. The mean scores from the questionnaire constructs were calculated from the values attained from the responses to the questions. The mean value and standard deviations are listed in Table 5.4.

The result of the analysis of variance shows that only four variables had a significant effect on the Cognitive Turnover. The p values indicate that these variables have a significant effect on CT at an alpha level of 0.10.

The turnover variables "challenges" and "promotions" and the burnout variables "depersonalization" and "personal achievement" were significant for predicting engineers' CT in this study. Most of the job satisfaction constructs were not shown to be valid (goals, comfort, financial rewards, relationships with coworkers, and resource adequacy) and only one out of the three burnout constructs was not shown to be valid (emotional exhaustion). These constructs had a weak impact on CT for this group.

TABLE 5.4
Construct Means and Standard Deviations

Construct	Mean	Standard Deviation
Depersonalization (B)	2.55	0.68
Emotional exhaustion (B)	2.60	0.62
Personal achievement (B)	3.68	0.57
Goals (T)	3.62	0.67
Comfort (T)	3.34	0.83
Challenges (T)	3.46	0.84
Finances (T)	3.23	0.66
Relationships (T)	3.73	1.11
Resources (T)	3.69	0.82
Promotions (T)	2.94	0.83
Satisfaction (T)	3.60	0.72

Note: These scores are measured on 5-point Likert scales with 1 = not very satisfied and 5 = very satisfied and 1 = strongly disagree and 5 = strongly agree.

TABLE 5.5
Model Translation Description

Construct	What It Measures	Type of Effect
Challenges	Feeling that the job is not boring and has reasonable challenges	Direct impact on CT. If you feel the job is too challenging, then you will have a higher CT index score
Depersonalization	Distancing oneself from others	Has largest direct effect on CT. If you feel that you are involved as part of the team, you will have a higher CT index score
Personal achievement	Performing well on things that matter	Has largest opposite effect on CT. This means that if you believe you perform well, your CT index score will be lower
Promotion	Opportunity for fair chance of promotion	Has opposite effect on CT. If you believe that you can be promoted, you will have a lower CT index score

Based on the results, the mathematical model for predicting CT for engineers was given by the following equation:

$$F(x) = 1.199(\text{Challenges}) + 1.575(\text{Depersonalization}) -$$
$$1.712(\text{Personal achievement}) - 0.935(\text{Promotion}) + 5.122$$

(A5.1)

Table 5.5 summarizes the four variables in the model that showed significant prediction for CT and describes the impact of each on CT.

The function $F(x)$ will be a number between 1 and 10. Scores that are approximately 1–4 represent low cognitions to leave and generally low burnout indications. Scores 5–8 represent moderate burnout and leaving cognitions. Scores 9 and above represent eCT, which may lead to detrimental burnout and possible sabotage if departure is not imminent (refer back to Table 5.3 for chart).

It is important to note that because only four variables were necessary to determine the CT level, it might be possible for the engineering manager to reduce the fifty-nine–question questionnaire to nineteen questions. The danger in utilizing the nineteen-item questionnaire is that these results are based on a small sample size from exploratory research. The engineering manager should evaluate the limitations before using the nineteen-question questionnaire. The benefit of using the reduced question form is that it may be easier to implement. The researchers suggest using the current developed questionnaire and performing phase two for the engineering manager's specific knowledge worker group in order to attain the most effective questionnaire.

Study Limitations

Some limitations to this research were the sample size and questionnaire biases. This study used only fifty-one knowledge workers across organizations for the creation of the mathematical model. Currently, more populations are being targeted for further validation of the mathematical model. This should be taken into account when utilizing the model for possible sample bias when using the questionnaire and modeler. Also, questionnaire biases can occur when implementing the testing of the questionnaire. Respondents may not answer the questionnaire honestly if they feel threatened by what will happen if they score on the high end of the index. The researchers recommend utilizing tools such as a digital simulator or online questionnaire software to offset some of the fears of being identified and possible ramifications. Future research includes the development of a manager's checklist, which will allow managers to observe specific behaviors enabling the manager to score the employee for CT. If the nineteen-question questionnaire is utilized, it is important to note that this research is exploratory and caution should be used before the results are acted upon. Future research may focus on industry specific models.

Lessons Learned and Recommendations

Our findings yielded several lesson learned and many recommendations. First, knowledge worker management is difficult but crucial to companies' future growth and bottom line. Second, analyses of the empirical data on the CT indices presented here suggest that companies need to focus their current practice away from solely financial measures and toward providing challenging work and reduce isolated tasks that cause depersonalization and increase team activities, increase recognition of personal achievement, and provide realistic promotion opportunities. In this study, the high level of depersonalization may suggest that when knowledge workers perform isolated tasks they could have higher levels of CT. The engineering manager may be able to improve this component with team-based tasks. Further, the high negative coefficient for personal achievement on CT indices suggests that recognition of knowledge workers can have a strong positive effect on CT. The other two significant variables were promotion and challenges, which may not be under the direct control of the engineering manager.

Finally, one opportunity for improvement that companies miss is giving real feedback to employees. Companies should address the problems with performance by brainstorming and communicating with employees about possible solutions. By using the first two phases of the SECtCS methodology the engineering manager has a method for identifying some of the main components of the CT. The first two phases allow the organization to identify the most significant measures of eCT for the chosen group of knowledge workers. The complete methodology, which is not fully presented in this chapter, is designed to measure relevant components of eCT, remeasure implemented solutions effectiveness, document efforts, and provide feedback.

Feel free to contact the authors of this volume for a copy of the questionnaires.

REFERENCES

Barber, L., and M. Weinstein. (1999). *Work like your dog: Fifty ways to work less, play more, and earn more*. New York: Villard.
Bassman, E. S. (1992). *Abuse in the workplace, management remedies and bottom line impact*. Westport, Conn.: Quorum Books.
Foster, T. (2003). *Managing quality: An integrative approach*. 2d ed. New York: Prentice Hall.
Gaudine, A. P., and A. M. Saks. (2001). Effects of an absenteeism feedback intervention on employee absence behaviors. *Journal of Organizational Behavior* 22:15–29.
Golembiewski, R. T., and R. F. Munzenrider. (1986). The epidemiology of the progressive burnout: A primer. *Journal of Health and Human Resources Administration*, 9, 16–37.

ADDITIONAL REFERENCES

Bauch, G. T., and C. A. Chung. A statistical project control tool for engineering managers. *Project Management Journal* 32(2):37–44.
Bohlen, G. A., D. R. Lee, and P. A. Sweeney. (1998). Why and how project managers attempt to influence their team members. *Engineering Management Journal* 10(4):21–28.
Bureau of Labor. (1966). *Labor letter*. Washington, D.C.: U.S. Department of Labor.
Cherniss, C. (1980b). *Staff burnout: Job stress in human services*. Beverly Hills, Calif.: Sage.
Chung, C. A. (2003). *Simulation modeling handbook, a practical approach*. New York: CRC Press.
Clampitt, H. G. (2006). *RFID certificate handbook*. Edited by Erick C. Jones. Houston, Tex.: PWD Group.
Cook, J.D., S. J. Hepworth, T. D. Wall, and P. B. Warr. (1989). *The experience of work*. San Diego: Press Limited.
Cronbach, L. J. (1951). Coefficient alpha and the internal structure of tests. *Psychometrika* 16:297–334.
Evans J. R., and W. M. Lindsay. (1993). *The management and control of quality*. St. Paul, Minn.: West Publishing Company.
Fisher, K., and M. D. Fisher. (1987). *The distributed mind: Achieving high performance through the collective intelligence of knowledge work teams*. New York: Wiley.
Leach, F. J., and J. D. Westbrook. (2000). Motivation and job satisfaction in one government and development environment. *Engineering Management Journal* 12(4):3–10.
Locke, E. A. (1976). The nature and causes of job satisfaction. In *Handbook of industrial and organizational psychology*, edited by M. D. Dunnette. Chicago: Rand McNally.
Lofquist, L. H., and R. V. Dawis. (1967). *Adjustment to work: A psychological view of man's problems in a work-oriented society*. New York: Appleton-Century-Crofts.
Maslach, C. (1976). Burn-out. Human behavior. *Job stress and burnout: Research, theory, and intervention perspectives*. Beverly Hills, CA: Sage.
Mobley, W. H. (1982). *Employee turnover: Causes, consequences,and control*. Reading, Mass.: Addison-Wesley.
Mowday, R. T., L. W. Porter, and R. M. Steers. (1982). *Employee-organization linkages*. New York: Academic Press.
Nunnally, J. C. (1978). *Psychometric theory*. 2d ed. New York: McGraw-Hill.
Spector, P. E. *Summated rating scale construction: An introduction*. New York: Sage.
Turner, W. C., J. H. Mize, and K. E. Case. (1987). *Introduction to industrial and systems engineering*. Englewood Cliffs, N.J.: Prentice Hall.

6 Important RFID Mandates

INTRODUCTION

Mandates by large suppliers such as Wal-Mart and the Department of Defense (DOD) are driving development, use, and price of RFID passive technologies in the supply chain. Due to these mandates becoming a main driver for RFID technologies, we provide an overview of the most important organizations mandating that suppliers use RFID technologies. We will discuss DOD, Wal-Mart, and other companies that are considered leaders in supporting RFID.

DEPARTMENT OF DEFENSE (DOD) MANDATE

The DOD has developed a plan for passive RFID tagging with the war fighter as their customer. The mandate and dates are mainly laid out in the implementation plan. RFID technology will be implemented through a phased approach, applied both to supplier requirements and DOD sites. The implementation approach that DOD follows according to United States Department of Defense Suppliers' Passive RFID Information Guide Version 1.07 is as follows (DOD, 2004):

- Commencing January 1, 2005
  RFID tagging will be required for all DOD manufacturers and suppliers who have new contracts issued on or after October 1, 2004, according to the following implementation guidelines:
  The following classes of supply will require RFID tags to be placed on all individual cases, all cases packaged within palletized unit loads, and all palletized unit loads:
    - Class I Subclass—Packaged Operational Rations
    - Class II—Clothing, Individual Equipment, and Tools.
    - Class VI—Personal Demand Items
    - Class IX—Weapon Systems Repair Parts & Components
  when these commodities are being shipped to the following locations:
    - Defense Distribution Depot, Susquehanna, PA (DDSP)
    - Defense Distribution Depot, San Joaquin, CA (DDJC)
- Commencing January 1, 2006
  In addition to the requirements above, RFID tagging will be required for all DOD manufacturers and suppliers who have new contracts issued on or after October 1, 2004, according to the following implementation guidelines:

The following classes of supply will require RFID tags to be placed on all individual cases, all cases packaged within palletized unit loads, and all palletized unit loads (pending appropriate safety certification):
  - Class I—Subsistence and Comfort Items
  - Class III—Packaged Petroleum, Lubricants, Oils, Preservatives, Chemicals & Additives
  - Class IV—Construction & Barrier Equipment
  - Class V—Ammunition of all types
  - Class VII—Major End Items
  - Class VIII—Pharmaceuticals and Medical Materials
- Commencing January 1, 2007

RFID tagging will be required for all DOD manufacturers and suppliers who have new contracts issued after October 1, 2004, according to the following implementation guidelines:

All classes of supply will require RFID tags on all individual cases, all cases packaged within palletized unit loads, all pallets, and all unit packs for unique identification (UID) items.

RFID tagging will be required on commodities shipped to any DOD location.

GUIDELINES AND REQUIREMENTS

The cost of implementing and operating RFID technology is considered a normal cost of business. If DOD customers desire the inclusion of a passive RFID tag on shipments for these type purchases, this requirement must be specifically requested of the shipping supplier/vendor and the shipment must be accompanied by an appropriate advanced shipment notification (ASN) containing the shipment information associated to the appropriate RFID tag.

All solicitations awarded on or after October 1, 2004, for delivery of material on or after January 1, 2005, require that passive RFID tags be affixed at the case, pallet, and Unique Identifier (UID) item packaging level for material delivered to the Department of Defense, in accordance with the implementation plan, which is located above under the section entitled: "Implementation Approach." The plan can also be found at: http://www.dodrfid.org/supplierimplementationplan.htm.

WAL-MART MANDATE

In recent years, Wal-Mart has been working with the Auto-ID Center to develop and test RFID technology that will allow companies to track goods using a universal electronic product code (EPC). Their long-term goal is to use smart shelves at the retailer to monitor how many items are on each shelf. When inventory is low, software would signal management that products such as Gillette razors need to be brought from the storeroom. Readers in the storeroom would monitor inventory and alert the distribution center when more product is needed and automatically send a replenishment order, and this continues as a pull system throughout the supply chain (Roberti, 2003).

But Wal-Mart and other sponsors of the Auto-ID Center have always envisioned that it might take as long as ten years before RFID tags would become inexpensive enough to put on individual items in stores (Roberti, 2003). To date, at Wal-Mart RFID has been used successfully in closed-loop supply chains. Generally, the mandate requires that suppliers provide pallet-level RFID tag that can be scanned at ten feet wide of the dock door at all times. The RFID EPC tag, which is based on the pallet bar code that uses EAN.UCC Global Trade Identification Number (GTIN) or Serial Shipping Customer Code (SSCC), is the required tag. Wal-Mart suppliers have been communicated the requirement and all updates to the standards through Wal-Mart's Retail Link, which is their online communications link to suppliers. The Wal-Mart RFID mandate means its top one hundred suppliers not only have to put tags on pallets and cases, they must also install RFID readers in their manufacturing facilities, warehouses, and distribution centers. They, in turn, can require their suppliers to tag shipments, and so on through the supply chain (Roberti, 2003).

Wal-Mart is unlikely to back off its requirement because the retailer is convinced that the benefits are justifiable. Sanford C. Bernstein & Co., a New York investment research house, estimates that Wal-Mart could save nearly $8.4 billion per year when RFID is fully deployed throughout its supply chain and in stores. Wal-Mart has been studying the potential of RFID for more than a decade before rolling out the standard. Wal-Mart communicates to its suppliers what they need to do to fulfill the retailer's requirements, but after that, they are held accountable (Roberti, 2003).

OTHER ORGANIZATIONS

Other companies with mandates similar to Wal-Mart include Metro Corporation in Germany. Metro is the fifth-largest retailer in the world and Germany's largest retailer. Its mandate is very similar to the Wal-Mart standard, which is important to RFID pundits due to the fact that both Wal-Mart and Metro use many of the same suppliers. Tesco and Marks & Spencer, larger retailers in the United Kingdom, also have initiated RFID mandates, providing further influence for suppliers to use RFID technologies.

Many pundits expect RFID use at the pallet and case level to take off rapidly because of something economists call the *network effect*, which basically says that the more people use a physical network (say, the Internet) or shared service (Google), the more valuable it becomes (Roberti, 2003). That encourages even more people to use the network, creating exponential growth, a tipping point, or a group-think type of mentality (Roberti, 2003).

REFERENCES

Roberti, M. Analysis: RFID—Wal-Mart's Network Effect, September 15, 2003(a) http://www.cioinsight.com/print_article/0.3668.a=61672.00.asp.

Roberti, M. Case Study: Wal-Mart's Race for RFID, September 15, 2003(b) http://www.esp.eweek.com/article/Case+Study+WalMarts+Race+for+RFID/102963_4..aspx.

United States Department of Defense. United States Department of Defense Suppliers' Passive RFID Information Guide, November, 2004. http://www.acq.os.mil/log/rfid/implementation_plan.htm.

7 Standards Organizations and RFID Standards

INTRODUCTION

Standards describe data content, air interface protocol, conformance testing, and applications usage. Data content describes how content is stored and formatted. The air interface describes how the tags will talk to each other. The conformance standards describe how to test for acceptable performance. Application standards describe how various devices such as shipping labels are used.

INTERNATIONAL STANDARDS ORGANIZATION (ISO) STANDARDS

The International Standards Organization or ISO has been one of the key organizations in the world for standardizing equipment and operations for over twenty years. RFID standards at the item level are described for ISO under the ISO-IEC Automatic Identification and Data Capture (AIDC) Standard. The section labeled JTC-1 SC31/ WG4 is often referred to as the EPC Global Standard.

The International Standards Organization is an international association of national standards bodies of 148 countries with one member per country. It was founded in 1947 with the headquarters in Geneva, Switzerland. ISO produces guidelines, procedures, and policies on a wide range of issues and applications. Standards produced by ISO provide a template for member bodies to develop their own standards. Regulators may adopt these ISO standards unchanged or modify them to suit local conditions or requirements. The result is standards that are internationally compatible, consistent, and clear.

ISO STANDARDS AND RFID

Decisions about RFID ISO standards are made by two groups. The ISO and IEC (International Electro-Technical Commission) jointly sponsor Joint Technical Committee number one (JTC 1) to address subjects of interest to both organizations. JTC 1 has several subcommittees to address specific issues, including SC 31 (AIM, 2003). SC 31, Automatic Identification and Data Capture Techniques, oversees standardization of data formats, data syntax, data structures, data encoding, and technologies for the process of automatic identification and data capture. There are four work groups from this subcommittee: Data Carriers (WG1), Data Syntax (WG2), Conformance (WG3), and RFID (WG4) (AIM, 2003).

RFID standards at the item level are described for ISO under the ISO-IEC Automatic Identification and Data Capture (AIDC) Standard. See Figure 7.1. The section

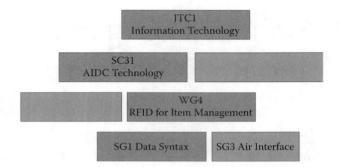

FIGURE 7.1   ISO/IEC standard structure (RFID Standards, 2006).

is labeled JTC-1 SC31/WG4. This is often referred to as the EPC Global Standard for
(1) Class 0 Gen 1, (2) Class 1 Gen 1, and (3) Gen 2.

The ISO/IEC standard structure is described in SG1, SG3, and WG3. The SG1 is
responsible for data content and includes the ISO/IEC 15961 data protocol-application
interface description and the ISO/IEC 15962 data protocol-data encoding rules.
SG3 is responsible for ISO/IEC 18000 series air interface standards at <135 KHz,
13.56 MHz, 433 MHz, 860–960 MHz, and 2.45 GHz. The ISO/IEC 18000,
Radio-Frequency Identification Standard for Item Management–Air Interface is
described in the following parts.

- Part 1: Air Interface Communication for Globally Accepted Frequencies
- Part 2: Air Interface Communication below 135 KHz
- Part 3: Air Interface Communication at 13.56 MHz
- Part 4: Air Interface Communication at 2.45 GHz
- Part 5: Air Interface Communication at 5.8 GHz
- Part 6: Air Interface at 860–930 MHz
- Part 7: Air Interface at 433.92 MHz

18000-1 Part 1: Generic Parameters for the Air Interface for Globally Accepted Frequencies (ISO/IEC 1800-RFID Air Interface Standards, 2006)

The scope of this standard is to describe the reference architecture for radio frequency identification for item management and to establish the parameters that will
be determined in any standardized air interface definition in the ISO 18000 series.
The subsequent parts of this standard providing specific values for air interface definition parameters will then, once approved, provide the frequency specific values
and value ranges from which compliance to (or noncompliance with) this standard
can be established.

This standard limits its scope to transactions and data exchanges across the
air interface at reference point delta. The means of generating and managing such
transactions, other than a requirement to achieve the transactional performance
determined within this standard, are outside the scope of this standard, as is the

definition or specification of any supporting hardware, firmware, software, or associated equipments.

This standard is an enabling standard that supports and promotes several RFID implementations without making conclusions about the relative technical merits of any available option for any possible application.

18000-2 PART 2: PARAMETERS FOR AIR INTERFACE COMMUNICATIONS BELOW 135 kHz

This document specifies the physical layer that shall be used for communication between the interrogator and the tag. The interrogator shall be capable of communicating with tags of both type A (FDX) and type B (HDX).

The Protocol and the Commands

The method to detect and communicate with one tag among several tags (anticollision).

Tag Types

This standard specifies two types of tags: type A (FDX) and type B (HDX).

These two types differ only in their physical layer. Both types support the same anticollision and protocol.

FDX tags are permanently powered by the interrogator, including during the tag-to-interrogator transmission. They operate at 125 kHz.

HDX tags are powered by the interrogator, except during the tag-to-interrogator transmission. They operate at 134.2 kHz.

An optional anticollision is described in the informative annex D.

Compliance Rules

Tag
To claim compliance with this standard, a tag shall be of either type A or B.

Interrogator
To claim compliance with this standard, an interrogator shall support both types A and B.

Depending on the application, it may be configured as type A only, type B only, or types A and B. When configured in types A and B, and when in the inventory phase, the interrogator will alternate between type A and type B interrogation.

18000-3 PART 3: PARAMETERS FOR AIR INTERFACE COMMUNICATIONS AT 13.56 MHz

This standard is to provide physical layer, collision management system and protocol values for RFID systems for item identification operating at 13.56 MHz in accordance with the requirements of ISO 18000-1. This standard provides parameter value for each MODE determined in the requirements clause below.

In this version of the standard, two noncontending MODES are defined:

- The modes are not interoperable
- The modes, while not interoperable, are noncontending

Intellectual Property

Both of the MODES require a license from the owner of the Intellectual Property, which shall be available on terms in accordance with ISO Policy. Details of Intellectual property are shown at the end of Clause 7. Neither of the MODES in this version of the Standard may be used without a license

18000-4 PART 4: PARAMETERS FOR AIR INTERFACE COMMUNICATIONS AT 2.45 GHz

Frequency

This standard is intended to address RFID devices operating in the 2450 MHz industrial, scientific, and medical (ISM) frequency band.

Interface Definitions

This standard supports a standard API (ISO/IEC 18000-1) and standard air interface implementations for wireless, noncontact information system equipment for item management applications. Typical applications operate at ranges greater than one meter.

There are two modes. Mode 1 is a passive tag, mode 2 is a battery assisted tag.

- Mode 1: Passive Backscatter RFID System
  The FHSS backscatter option or the narrow band operation RFID system shall include an interrogator that runs the FHSS backscatter option 1 RFID protocol or in narrow band operation, as well as one or more tags within the interrogation zone.
- Mode 2: Long-Range High Data Rate RFID System
  This clause describes a RFID system offering a gross data rate up to 384 kbps at the air interface in case of read/write (R/W) tag. In case of a read only (R/O) tag, the data rate is 76.8 kbps. The tag is battery assisted but backscattering. By using battery-powered tags, such a system is well designed for long-range RFID applications. This air interface description does not explicitly claim a need for battery assistance in the tag; real passive tags or tags for mixed operation are also conceivable.

18000-5 PART 5: PARAMETERS FOR AIR INTERFACE COMMUNICATIONS AT 5.8 GHz

This standard is to provide physical layer, anticollision system, and protocol values for RFID systems for item identification operating at 5.8–5.9 GHz in accordance with the requirements of ISO 18000-1. This standard provides parameter value for each mode determined in the requirements section below.

In this version of the standard, two noncontending modes are defined:

- None of the modes is interoperable
- All of the modes, while not interoperable, are noncontending

Intellectual Property

Some of the modes require a license from the owner of the intellectual property, which shall be available on terms in accordance with ISO policy. Details of intellectual property are shown at the end of each mode.

Mode 1 in this version of the standard may be used without a license.

This part has been withdrawn, due to lack of global acceptance. The physical, anticollision, and transmission protocols determined in this mode are consistent with the approach taken in ISO/IEC 15693. This section provides the normative part of mode 1 by reference.

The physical layer for the mode 1 air interface at 5.8 GHz shall be consistent and compliant to CEN 12253. The data link and MAC layers shall be compliant to CEN 12795.

The anticollision system and protocols for the mode 1 air interface at 5.8 GHz shall be consistent and compliant to CEN 12834.

18000-6 Part 6: Parameters for Air Interface Communications at 860–930 MHz

This standard describes:

- The physical interactions between the interrogator and the tag
- The protocols and the commands
- The collision arbitration schemes

For the forward link, type A uses pulse interval encoding and type B uses biphase modulation and Manchester encoding. For the collision arbitration, type A uses an Aloha-based mechanism and type B uses an adaptive binary tree mechanism. Both types use the same biphase space FM0 return link encoding.

18000-7 Part 7: Parameters for Air Interface Communications at 433 MHz

This standard is intended to address RFID devices operating in the 433 MHz frequency band.

Work Group on RFID for Item Management (WG 4) (AIM, 2003)

This work group's purpose is to provide standards for interoperability of wireless, noncontact omnidirectional radio frequency identification devices capable of receiving, storing, and transmitting data while operating at power levels that are in freely available international frequency bands in the area of item-level identification and management across the supply chain such as finished good asset management, raw material asset management, material traceability, inventory control, electronic article surveillance, warranty data, production control/robotics, and facilities management. The proposed RFID item management work would align without duplicating and coexist with the approved work of other international standards committees. It is their intent to utilize the prevailing standards, by normative reference, where appropriate:

- WG 4's subgroup (SG) 1 responsible for:
- ISO/IEC 15961 data protocol - application interface
- ISO/IEC 15962 data protocol - data encoding rules

WG 4's SG3 responsible for:

- ISO/IEC 18000 series air interface standards at <135 KHz, 13.56 MHz, 433 MHz, 860–960 MHz, and 2.45 GHz
- Application standards illustrate how products are to be used, such as where to place a label.
- Conformance standards provide instructions on how a specific device is to be evaluated to ensure it complies with a standard.

ISO Standards Summary

The ISO standards related to RFID include:

- ISO 11784, 11785, 14223: RFID standards for animal tracking; 14223 is the air interface standard.
- ISO 10536, 14443, 15693: RFID standards for smart cards
- ISO 10374: RFID for rail and ship freight containers
- ISO 15961, 15962, 15963: RFID for item management
- ISO 18000 Series: cover both active and passive RFID technologies (ISO/IEC 18000-RFID Air Interface Standards, 2006)
  - 18000-1 Part 1: Generic Parameters for the Air Interface for Globally Accepted Frequencies
  - 18000-2 Part 2: Parameters for Air Interface Communications below 135 kHz
  - 18000-3 Part 3: Parameters for Air Interface Communications at 13.56 MHz
  - 18000-4 Part 4: Parameters for Air Interface Communications at 2.45 GHz
  - 18000-5 Part 5: Parameters for Air Interface Communications at 5.8 GHz (Withdrawn)
  - 18000-6 Part 6: Parameters for Air Interface Communications at 860 to 930 MHz
  - 18000-7 Part 7: Parameters for Air Interface Communications at 433 MHz

- ISO 15418, 15434, 15459, 24721, 15961, 15962: Data Content
- ISO 18046, 18047 (RFID device conformance tests methods for active/passive)
- Application standards: ISO 10374, ISO 18185, 11785
- ISO/IEC TR 24710: Radio frequency identification for item management
- ISO/IEC TR 18047-7: Information technology—Radio frequency identification device conformance test methods, Part 7: Test methods for active air interface communications at 433 MHz
- ISO/IEC 15434: Information technology—Syntax for high-capacity automatic data capture (ADC) media (AIM, 2003)

EPC GLOBAL STANDARDS

The foundation for the RFID passive tag is the identifier, which is called the electronic product code (EPC). EPC is a joint venture of GS1 and GS1 US. It is an organization set up to achieve global adoption of the EPC RFID standard. We provide a brief history of the EPC Global, Auto-ID Center, GS1 and GS2 organizations.

- EPC Global was formed in October 2003 from the confines of the Auto-ID Center.
- The Auto-ID Center was founded by David Brock and Sanjay Sarma and supported financially by companies such as Procter & Gamble and Gillette. The Uniform Code Council was also a main supporter of the Auto-ID Center. The center created a global passive RFID-based item identification system that may eventually replace the barcodes. This code that was developed is called the electronic product code.

GS1 AND GS1 US

The global standards organization, which includes GS1 and GS1 US, seeks to provide member organizations a common data structure for information collected and manipulated using automatic data capture technologies. GS1, previously known as EAN International, managed the European article number product identification structure, which was commonly used as a supply chain identifier in Europe. GS1 US™, previously known as the Uniform Code Council, Inc. (UCC; GSI GSMP, 2007), managed the UCC identification structure mainly in the United States. The bar code was often referred to as the UCC-128 bar code. The protocols have been used for over a decade to enhance data identification throughout the supply chain.

Electronic Product Code Type 1

01-0000A89-00016F-000169DC0

Header	EPC Manager	Object Class	Serial Number
8 bits	28 bits	24 bits	36 bits

FIGURE 7.2   EPC tag data content.

The combining of these structures and management of the protocol allow more global coordination. GS1 groups these activities into the GS1 system. They support the following areas (GSI GSMP, 2007):

- Bar codes: Numbering and bar coding
- eCom: EDI (electronic data interchange)
- Global Data Synchronisation Network (GDSN): data synchronization
- EPC Global: RFID (radio frequency identification)

They continue to support this standardization effort through their global standards management process (GSMP). GS1 is governed by a management board composed of key leaders from multinational firms, retailers, manufacturers, and other GS1 member organizations. EPC Global, Inc. and GS1 GDSN, Inc. have separate management boards.

Using radio identification technology (RFID), a tag communicates its number to a reader. The reader then passes the number to a computer or local application system, known as the object name service (ONS). ONS tells the computer systems where to locate information on the network about the object carrying an EPC, such as when the item was produced. Commonly, the physical markup language (PML) is used as a common language in the EPC Global network to define data on physical objects. Initially, the Savant software technology was envisioned to act as the central nervous system of the EPC Global network. Savant was designed to manage and move information in a way that does not overload existing corporate and public networks (*RFID Gazette*, 2004). Currently this function can be handled by edgeware or middleware software commonly provided by hardware vendors and distributors.

The EPC air interface protocol is intended to describe the following elements, including (1) air interface (waveforms of different symbols), (2) command set, and (3) operating procedure (how to use command set to identify/modify tags).

The air interface protocol describes how the reader talks with the tag, start-up signals, tree traversal negotiation, and command communication. The start-up signal sends RF signals to the tag population. The tree traversal negotiation is the process in which the tag backscatters or reflects the data and how the reader acknowledges that data and maps the path through the population. The command communication

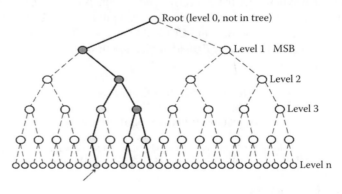

FIGURE 7.3   Air interface protocol.

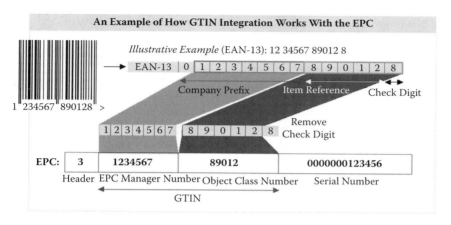

FIGURE 7.4 GTIN and EPC.

describes commands to retrieve data after confirmation that the tag has been identified.

EPC/GTIN INTEGRATION

Due to the fact that EPC Global was a joint venture between EAN International and the Uniform Code Council in order to provide the standard for passive RFID tag nomenclature, the nomenclature is based on a family of bar codes. The UPC/UCC/EAN families of bar codes are known as the global trade item number (GTIN), a worldwide system of supply chain identification. The basic UPC bar code extends to include country, classification, and product information.

EPC GENERATION 2

The EPC Generation 2 tag, which is now becoming the more commonly used tag, was developed and widely used by mid-2006. It focused on supply chain customer requirements. The standard had some unique development items. It was not based on a system from any one technology provider and it was developed by a broad consensus of chip, reader, and tag manufacturers. The main improvement of the Gen 2 tag was standardizing tags to a common standard, not multiple competing standards. Oher Gen 2 tag advantages over the first-generation passive RFID tags include

- Open standard—available from multiple sources
- Interoperable equipment
- System performance exceeds requirements
- High reliability—always detects items in the field
- Global operation
- Standard enables low-cost tags/readers
- Protocol detects late arriving tags or intermittently powered tags
- Tags can be permanently killed by a reader

EPC Class	Description	Functionality	Remarks
0	Read Only	Passive Tags	Data can be written only once during tag manufacturing and read many times
1	Write Once and Read Only	Passive Tags	Data can be written only once by tag manufacturer or user and read many times
2	Read/Write	Passive Tags	User can read/write data many times
3	Read/Write	Semi-passive Tags	Can be coupled with on board sensors for capturing parameters like temperatures, pressure etc.
4	Read/Write	Active Tags	Can be coupled with on board sensors and act as radio wave transmitter to communicate with reader

FIGURE 7.5   EPC tag classes.

OTHER STANDARDS

It is envisioned that the passive RFID standards will be integrated with other standards such as the U.S. Department of Defense's unique identifier (UID) standard. The UID is based on identification requirements for military products over $5,000. Other standards are targeted to be integrated with passive RFID standards, including other countries' EAN's, animal identification standards, and smart cards, to name a few.

THE ELECTRONIC PRODUCT CODE DETAILS

An electronic data signal provides the unique identification for a passive tag that is received by an RFID reader. This signal is formatted into a consistent code referred to as the electronic product code or EPC. This code is similar to the standardized framework provided in a universal product code or UPC used in most bar coding systems. The EPC structure consists of header, manager number, object class, and a serial number. The header identifies the length, type, and structure for the specific EPC standards version number. The manager number identifies the company or enterprise using the EPC number. The object class refers to the class or type of product similar to a stockkeeping unit, or SKU. The serial number is the specific instance of the object class being tagged. The 96-bit tag has additional fields that allow for more information and additional traceability.

The EPC identifier is a meta-coding scheme designed to support the needs of various industries by both accommodating existing coding schemes where possible and defining new schemes where necessary. The various coding schemes are referred to as *domain identifiers* to indicate that they provide object identification within certain domains such as a particular industry or group of industries. As such, the electronic product code represents a family of coding schemes (or name spaces) and a means to make them unique across all possible EPC-compliant tags.

To better understand the overall framework of the EPC tag data standards, it is helpful to distinguish between three levels of identification: pure identity layer, encoding layer, and physical realization layer. The pure identity layer is associated with a physical or logical item. The encoding layer is the EPC specification. The physical realization is the RFID tag.

Four types of EPCs have been defined as follows:

- 96 Bit
- 64 Bit, type I
- 64 Bit, type II
- 64 Bit, type III

A 64-bit EPC may uniquely identify sixteen thousand companies with a range of 9 to 1 million classes of products and 33 million serial numbers within a class.

The 96-bit EPC may uniquely identify 268 million companies with 16 million classes of products and 68 billion serial numbers in each class.

Organization by effectively using software can associate RFID tags with other identification schemas. The schemas include the following:

- EAN.UCC, serialized global trade item number (SGTIN)
- EAN.UCC, serial shipping container code (SSCC)
- EAN.UCC, global location number (GLAN)
- EAN.UCC, global returnable asset identifier (GRAI)
- EAN.UCC, global individual asset identifier (GIAI)
- A general identifier (GID)

SERIALIZED GLOBAL TRADE ITEM NUMBER (SGTIN)

The serialized global trade item number is a new identity type based on the EAN. UCC global trade item number (GTIN). A GTIN by itself does not represent a pure EPC identity because it does not uniquely identify a single physical object. Instead a GTIN identifies a particular class of object, such as a particular kind of product or SKU. The coding structure for the 96-bit tag is given in Table 7.1.

TABLE 7.1
96 Bit Tag Coding Structure

	Header	Filter Value	Partition	Company Prefix	Item Reference	Serial Number
SGTIN-96	8	3	3	20-40	24-4	38
	0011 0000 (Binary value)	(Refer to Table 5 for values)	(Refer to Table 7 for values)	999,999– 999,999,999,999 (Maximum decimal range[a])	9,999,999–9 (Maximum decimal range[a])	274,877,906,943 (Maximum decimal value)

[a] Maxium decimal value range of Company Prefix and Item Reference fields vary according to contents of the Partition field.

TABLE 7.2
Serial Shipping Container Code (SSCC)

	Header	Filter Value	Partition	Company Prefix	Location Reference	Serial Number
SSCC-96	8	3	3	20-40	38-18	24
	0011 0001 (Binary value)	(Refer to Table 9 for values)	(Refer to Table 11 for values)	999,999– 999,999,999,999 (Maximum decimal range[a])	99,999,999,999– 99,999 (Maximum decimal range[a])	[Not used]

[a] Maxium decimal value range of Company Prefix and Location Reference fields vary according to contents of the Partition field.

Unlike the GTIN, the SSCC is already intended for assignment to individual objects and therefore does not require any additional fields to serve as an EPC pure identity. Its specific coding structure for the 96-bit version is given in Table 7.2. A lower capacity 64-bit version is also defined.

SERIALIZED GLOBAL LOCATION NUMBER (SGLN)

A serialized GLN can represent either a discrete, unique physical location, such as a dock door or a warehouse slot, or an aggregate physical location, such as an entire warehouse. It may also represent a logical entity; for example, an organization that performs a business function, such as placing a purchase order. The coding structure for the 96-bit version is given in Table 7.3.

GLOBAL RETURNABLE ASSET IDENTIFIER (GRAI)

Unlike the GTIN, the GRAI is already intended for assignment to individual objects; therefore, it does not require any additional fields to serve as an EPC pure identity. The coding structure is given in Table 7.4.

TABLE 7.3
SGLN 96 Bit Code

	Header	Filter Value	Partition	Company Prefix	Location Reference	Serial Number
GIAI-96	8	3	3	20-40	21-1	41
	0011 0010 (Binary value)	(Refer to Table 13 for values)	(Refer to Table 15 for values)	999,999– 999,999,999,999 (Maximum decimal range[a])	999,999–0 (Maximum decimal range[a])	2,199,023,255,551 (Maximum decimal value) [Not used]

[a] Maxium decimal value range of Company Prefix and Location Reference fields vary according to contents of the Partition field.

TABLE 7.4
GRAI Code Structure

	Header	Filter Value	Company Prefix Index	Asset Type	Serial Number
GRAI-64	8	3	14	20	19
	0000 1010 (Binary value)	(Refer to Table 17 for values)	16,383 (Maximum decimal value)	999,999–0 (Maximum decimal range[a])	524,287 (Maximum decimal value)

[a] Maxium decimal value range of Asset Type fields varies with Company Prefix.

TABLE 7.5
GIAI Code Structure

	Header	Filter Value	Partition	Company Prefix	Individual Asset Reference
GIAI-96	8	3	3	20-40	62-42
	0011 0100 (Binary value)	(Refer to Table 21 for values)	(Refer to Table 23 for values)	999,999– 999,999,999,999 (Maximum decimal range[a])	4,611,686,018,427,387,903– 4,398,046,511,103 (Maximum decimal range[a])

[a] Maxium decimal value range of Company Prefix and Individual Asset Reference fields vary according to contents of the Partition field.

GLOBAL INDIVIDUAL ASSET IDENTIFIER (GIAI)

Like the GRAI, the GIAI is already intended for assignment to individual objects; therefore, it does not require any additional fields to serve as an EPC pure identity. The coding structure is shown in Table 7.5.

GLOBAL IDENTIFIER (GID-96)

GID is a 96-bit coding scheme that does not use a pre-existing standard. The GID is composed of three fields—the general manager number, object class, and serial number. Encoding of the GID includes a fourth field, the header, to guarantee uniqueness in the EPC name space.

Serialization, the ability to uniquely identify objects, is the key benefit to using the EPC standards. This serialization allows for item-level tracking and security against counterfeiting. Anticounterfeiting is one of the main advantages that RFID poses over bar coding. Another important component of the EPC standard includes the air interface and command set, often called the *specification protocol*. They are often listed as classes. Table 7.7 provides a summary of the EPC classes.

TABLE 7.6
GID 96 Code Structure

	Header	General Manager Number	Object Class	Serial Number
GID-96	8	28	24	36
	0011 0101 (Binary value)	268,435,455 (Maximum decimal value)	16,777,215 (Maximum decimal value)	68.719,476,735 (Maximum decimal value)

TABLE 7.7
Summary of EPC Classes

Class	Frequency	Description
0	900 MHz	Read only (0) Read/write (0+)
1	13.56MHz ISM band	Write once, read many (WORM) Read/write
1	860–930MHz (UHF)	WORMRead/write

THE DEPARTMENT OF DEFENSE (DOD) UID (DOD, 2004)

The DOD vision for RFID is to utilize RFID to facilitate accurate, hands-free data capture in support of business processes in an integrated DOD supply chain enterprise as an integral part of a comprehensive suite of automatic identification technology (AIT). The key to future functionality of the unique item data in the DOD supply chain will be the ability to temporarily associate conditional state information about an item.

DOD expects to fully embrace the use of EPC technology as well as approved EPC tag data constructs in a supporting DOD data environment. The efficiencies of RFID provide another valuable component of the suite of AITs. Active RFID has already improved the ability to track and trace material through the supply chain. Combining the passive RFID technology will create greater efficiencies and data accuracy. Leveraging RFID to the fullest extent possible will improve the ability to get the war fighter the right material, at the right place, at the right time, and in the right condition.

DOD definitions apply to passive RFID technology and tags in support of the DOD requirement to mark/tag material shipments to DOD activities in accordance with the DOD RFID policy:

- EPC technology: Passive RFID technology (readers, tags, etc.) that is built to the most current published EPC Global Class 0 and Class 1 specifications and that meets interoperability test requirements as prescribed by EPC Global. EPC technology will include ultra-high-frequency generation 2 (UHF Gen 2) when this specification is approved and published by EPC Global™.

- UID (unique identification): Unit Pack A MIL-STD-129 defined unit pack, specifically, the first tie, wrap, or container applied to a single item, or to a group of items, of a single stock number, preserved or unpreserved, that constitutes a complete or identifiable package.
- Bulk commodities: These items will not be tagged in accordance with passive RFID tagging requirements. Bulk commodities are products carried or shipped in rail tank cars; tanker trucks; other bulk, wheeled conveyances; or pipelines. In addition, munitions and explosives will not be tagged until the following certification requirements are met for the passive RFID tag: electromagnetic effects on the environment (E3), Hazards of Electromagnetic Radiation to Ordnance (HERO), Hazards of Electromagnetic Radiation to Fuel (HERF), and Hazards of Electromagnetic Radiation to Personnel (HERP).
- Case: Either an exterior container within a palletized unit load or an individual shipping container.
- Exterior container: A MIL-STD-129 defined container, bundle, or assembly that is sufficient by reason of material, design, and construction to protect unit packs and intermediate containers and their contents during shipment and storage. It can be a unit pack or a container with a combination of unit packs or intermediate containers. An exterior container may or may not be used as a shipping container.
- Shipping container: A MIL-STD-129 defined exterior container which meets carrier regulations and is of sufficient strength, by reason of material, design, and construction, to be shipped safely without further packing (e.g., wooden boxes or crates, fiber and metal drums, and corrugated and solid fiberboard boxes).
- Palletized unit load: A MIL-STD-129 defined quantity of items, packed or unpacked, arranged on a pallet in a specified manner and secured, strapped, or fastened on the pallet so that the whole palletized load is handled as a single unit. A palletized or skidded load is not considered to be a shipping container.

RFID technology will be implemented through a phased approach, applied both to supplier requirements and DOD sites. Shipments of goods and materials will be phased in by procurement methods, classes/commodities, location, and layers of packaging for passive RFID.

For DOD suppliers, RFID can be implemented using two options:

- EPC Global tag data construct
- DOD tag data construct

Suppliers that are EPC Global subscribers and possess a unique EPC manager number may choose to use an EPC tag data construct to encode tags per the rules that follow. Suppliers that choose to employ the DOD tag data construct will use the commercial and government entity (CAGE) code previously assigned to them and encode the tags per the rules that follow. Regardless of the selected encoding scheme, suppliers are responsible for ensuring that each tag contains a unique identifier.

TABLE 7.8

Acceptable RFID Tag Data Constructs for Supplier Originated Shipments

Class	User Memory Size (bits)	Tag Data Construct	Controlling Organization	Requires EPC Global Membership to Use Construct?
0	64	SGTIN-64 GRAI-64 GIAI-64 SSCC-64	EPC	Yes
	64	DOD-64	DOD	No
	64	SGTIN-64 GRAI-64 GIAI-64 SSCC-64	EPC	Yes
	64	DOD-64	DOD	No
0	96	SGTIN-64 GRAI-64 GIAI-64 SSCC-64	EPC	Yes
0	96	DOD-96	DOD	No
1	96	SGTIN-64 GRAI-64 GIAI-64 SSCC-64	EPC	Yes
1	96	DOD-96	DOD	No

Table 7.8 indicates the acceptable tag data constructs and the relationships between the various combinations of tag class, size, data construct, and the organization that controls the data construct.

Based on your membership in EPC Global, select either an EPC Global tag data construct option or a DOD tag data construct option and precede to the corresponding following section for details on how to encode RFID tags using the selected option.

EPC GLOBAL TAG DATA CONSTRUCT OPTION

This option should be selected by a DOD supplier that is

- Already a member of EPC Global and has an assigned company prefix
- Intends to join EPC Global and obtain a company prefix

This company prefix is required for encoding of all RFID tag classes and sizes. Table 7.9 summarizes the selection of an encoding scheme for either 64- or 96-bit tags based on the type of object being tagged and its usage. In general, the DOD is integrating the RFID passive technology with the UID standard that exists for item-level tracking.

TABLE 7.9
Selecting the Proper Tag Data Construct

Tag Requirement	EPC Data Construct	When Used
UID unit pack	SGTIN-64 SGTIN-96	On item packaging for items meeting the DOD criteria for assignment of UID where a serial number is used to augment a GTIN that is used for the unique identification of trade items worldwide within the EAN.UCC system
	GRAI-64 GRAI-96	On item packaging for items meeting the DOD criteria for assignment of UID (reusable package or transport equipment of specific or certain value)
Case, Transport package, Palletized unit load	GIAI-64 GIAI-96	On item packaging for items meeting the DOD criteria for assignment of UID (used to uniquely identify an entity that is part of the fixed inventory of a company; GIAI can be used to identify any fixed asset of an organization)
	SGTIN-64 SGTIN-96	Items shipped as either pure case or pallet (see above)
	SSCC-64 SSCC-96	Items shipped as either pure or mixed case, or pallet (SSCC can be used by all parties in the supply chain as a reference number to the relevant information held in computer database or file)

FCC PART 15 RADIATION REGULATION (*RFID GAZETTE*, 2005)

Though standards are important, the regulation of the RFID technologies has been more localized at the state level and focused on privacy issues; for example, the California anti-RFID legislation. A safety regulation that relates to RFID and human safety is given by the FCC as part 15. Part 15 of the FCC's rules for low-powered devices affects RFID technologies. RFID devices are referred to as *intentional radiators*. These low-powered devices do not raise a serious threat of interference with other devices and hence can be operated without a license. All the same, RFID devices have to meet the RF emissions limitations and power restrictions as laid down by the FCC.

Such intentional radiators as RFID need to obtain certification from the FCC. Obtaining the certification requires an application containing legal information about the device and the filing party; a technical report that includes RF test results; a block diagram of the instrument; and an explanation of the manner in which the instrument complies with FCC regulations. Intentional radiators operating at different frequencies are governed by different rules as per part 15. RFID products using the UHF 902–928 MHz band has to comply with rules in Section 15.247. The section stipulates that the systems should employ a frequency-hopping spread spectrum modulation technique so as to derive the maximum reader transmitted power allowances. UHF readers are allowed to operate at a maximum power of 1 watt and can go up to 4 watts if they have a directional antenna and hop across at least 50 channels. (*RFID Gazette*, 2005)

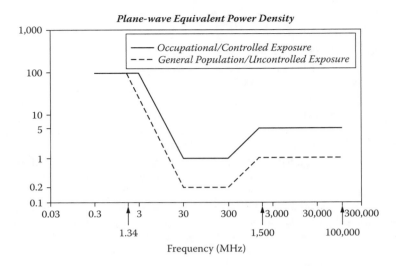

FIGURE 7.6   FCC limits for maximum permissible exposure.

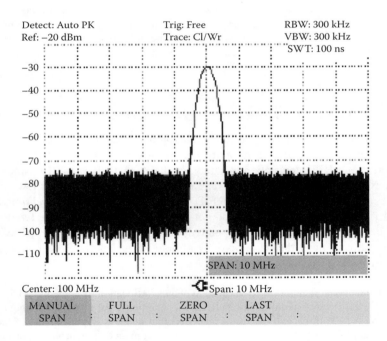

FIGURE 7.7   Sample analyzer reading for exposure.

The FCC has rules for human exposure to RF energy, as given forth in several of its bulletins. Bulletins 56 and 65 outline the amount of power a person can absorb in both a magnitude and a rate. It also provides limits for maximum electric and magnetic field exposure with limits on average exposure during any given time.

TABLE 7.10
FCC Limits for Maximum Permissible Exposure

(A) Limits for Occupational/Controlled Exposure

Frequency Range (MHz)	Electric Field Strength (E) (V/m)	Magnetic Field Strength (H) (A/m)	Power Density (S) (mW/cm²)	Averaging Time |E|², |H|² or S (minutes)
0.3–3.0	614	1.63	(100)[a]	6
3.0–30	1842/f	4.89/f	(900/f²)[b]	6
30–300	61.4	0.163	1.0	6
300–1500	—	—	F/300	6
1500–100,000	—	—	5	6

(B) Limits for General Population/Uncontrolled Exposure

Frequency Range (MHz)	Electric Field Strength (E) (V/m)	Magnetic Field Strength (H) (A/m)	Power Density (S) (mW/cm²)	Averaging Time |E|², |H|² or S (minutes)
0.3–1.34	614	1.63	(100)[a]	30
1.34–30	824/f	2.19/f	(180/f²)[b]	30
30–300	27.5	0.073	0.2	30
300–1500	—	—	f/1500	30
1500–100,000	—	—	1.0	30

[a] Plane-wave equivalent power density.
[b] f = frequency in MHz.

TABLE 7.11
FCC Limits for Localized (Partial Body) Exposure

Specific Absorption Rate (SAR)

Occupational/Controlled Exposure (100 kHz–6 GHz)	General Uncontrolled/Exposure (100 kHz–6 GHz)
< 0.4 W/kg whole-body	< 0.08 W/kg whole-body
≤ 8 W/kg partial-body	≤ 1.6 W/kg partial-body

Since RFID devices are low power, it is highly unlikely that any of these limits will be reached in a zone, except when a person may be standing in front of an antenna that is radiating at full power. The power output can be measured for each individual antenna to ensure that no excessive exposure will occur. The FCC limits are summarized in the following tables found at the FCC Web site.

REFERENCES

The AIM Global (2003), "Standards Groups related to Automatic Identification and Data Capture," http://www.aimglobal.org/standards/rfidstds/sc31.asp.

FCC OET Bulletin 56, Hazards of radio frequency and magnetic fields, and Bulletin 65, Human exposures to radio frequency and electromagnetic fields. http://www.fcc.gov/ Bueaus/Engineering_Technology/Documents/bulletins/oet56/oet56e4.pdf. Accessed August 28, 2007.

EPC Tag Data Standards Version 1.1 Rev. 1.24, Standard Specification, April 1, 2004. http:// www.barcodebook.com/EPC_Tag_Specs.pdf.

GSMP Glossary of Terms and Acronyms. http://www.gsl.org.services/gsmp/support/qa/docs/ general/GSMP_Glossary_&_Acronyms_List.pdf.

The High Tech Aid, ISO/IEC 18000—RFID Air Interface Standards, Mar 2, 2006. http:// www.hightechaid.com/standards/18000.htm.

The High Tech Aid, "RFID Standards—SC31," Mar 2, 2006. http://www.hightechaid.com/ standards/RFID_Standards_SC31.htm.

RFID Gazette, The Future Is Here: A Beginner's Guide to RFID, Jun 28, 2004. http://www. rfidgazette.org/2004/06/rfid_101.html.

RFID Regulations by FCC, December 7, 2005. http://www.rfidgazette.org/2005/12/rfid_ regulation.html.

United States Department of Defense Suppliers' Passive RFID Information Guide, Version 1.0 12 3.6.1

Part 2

Integrating RFID into Logistics

INTRODUCTION

In this section, we specifically discuss how RFID relates to logistical operations. We begin with an overview of logistics and discuss inventory concepts and planning levels.

SECTION CONTENTS

RFID in Logistics
Inventory Control Basics
RFID Supply Chain Planning Levels

8 RFID in Logistics

> If you knew how much work went into it, you wouldn't call it genius.
>
> **—Michelangelo**

INTRODUCTION

The quote above describes how much work and knowledge is required to truly integrate RFID into logistics. In order to ensure success it is important that automatic data capture integrators and managers understand logistics.

In this chapter we discuss how RFID supports

- Information use in the supply chain
- Open- and closed-loop systems as an intelligent agent
- Real-time item visibility that facilitates inventory control
- Supply chain planning and operational optimization
- Organizational improvement with best practices

RFID SUPPORTS INFORMATION USE IN THE SUPPLY CHAIN

In this text we discuss how RFID-captured information influences supply chain performance with data analysis, inventory management, transportation, and supply chain visibility.

Data analysis includes the evaluations concerning facilities, inventory, transportation, costs, prices, and customers throughout the supply chain.

Inventory management includes raw materials, work in process, and finished goods within a supply chain. Changing inventory policies can affect the supply chain's efficiency and responsiveness.

Transportation visibility provides information about inventory transported from point to point in the supply chain. Transportation includes many combinations of modes and routes, each with its own performance characteristics. Transportation modes have a large impact on supply chain responsiveness and cost.

Supply chain visibility provides information including status updates that allow for evaluation of the physical locations in the supply chain network where product is stored, assembled, or fabricated. The two major types of facilities are production sites and storage sites. The location, capacity, and flexibility of facilities have a significant impact on the supply chain's performance.

In this section we discuss the role that information plays in the supply chain, as well as key information-related decisions that supply chain managers must make.

The fundamental concepts of supply chain management are described in the next sections, but other academic texts provide more extensive discussion on the topic. We highlight an overview of the topic provided by one of the best known texts on the subject authored by Chopra and Miendl (2006). We suggest those who want a more extensive review of the topic should refer to this text and others referenced at the end of the chapter. We provide a description of the topic as it applies to RFID and automatic data capture technologies.

DATA ANALYSIS

RFID captures information or data but is relatively useless unless it can be used. Data analysis or information gathering is necessary for the use of RFID to be justified. Even without RFID, data analysis is important to organizational success in all areas of the supply chain. Data capturing, whether through automated means or manually, affects a supply chain in many different ways. Consider the following:

- Information provides critical working knowledge between all partners in a supply chain. This critical knowledge is necessary for coordinating organizational activities, minimizing costs such as labor, and maximizing profits for supply chain partners.
- Information is required for the operation of day-to-day business transactions in all levels of the supply chain. Without information, business would not exist; at the base level a business must have information on a customer order otherwise they are not in business. For example, a manufacturing company requires a production schedule or a system that coordinates different manufacturing processes required to produce a part. A production scheduling system uses information to create schedules that allow the factory to manufacture the correct lots, economic quantities, and optimized arrival times. The timing of products is important in order for the organizations to minimize costs, reduce excess inventories, and satisfy customer demand. Warehouse management systems, or WMS, use information to create inventory visibility within the walls of a warehouse or distribution center (DC) in order to promote efficient operational execution. Oftentimes a company may use the same information in an enterprise resource planning (ERP) system to manage and update information from the aforementioned systems to update accounting systems, ordering systems, and transportation systems to provide more efficient enterprise or organizational management.
- Information, some suggest, has become more important than the product to customer satisfaction because it makes the company more nimble by increasing the responsiveness and efficiency. In general, information capturing technology's increasing importance is due to the fact that it has effectively improved business. Though information can support efficiencies, many companies have found that if integrated incorrectly, it can result in company failure. For example, large-scale ERP systems that are expensive to implement have caused companies to fail when implemented incorrectly. Organizations such as Kmart and others have filed law suits when such

failures occur during implementation. Organizations should decide what information is necessary for reducing cost and improving their responsiveness within a supply chain.

OPERATIONAL STRATEGIES

Though many describe the benefits of RFID, it has to fit into a company's operational strategy. Operational strategies have to effectively utilize the previously mentioned information and information systems for operations to remain effective. Generally, forecast-based systems that use inventory to buffer variability are generally considered push systems, order driven systems are considered pull systems. Push systems are associated with material requirements planning (MRP), or modern enterprise resource planning (ERP) systems that use scheduling and forecasting to effectively schedule suppliers part types, quantities, and delivery dates. Again, pull systems are associated with order-driven Kanban systems, which fulfill only the actual requirements from customer demand. Kanban refers to the Japanese card-based system that only fills orders from internal or external customers when the customer requests a product. The requests are initiated by the cards, green for requesting product and red for stopping all requests. These Kanban systems are often referred to just-in-time (JIT) systems. In these JIT systems, when buffer or safety stock is required to meet larger demand volumes, it is tightly controlled and amounts are minimized. Modern execution systems such as warehouse management systems (WMS) and transportation management systems (TMS) and related execution modules in enterprise resource systems (ERP) use these strategies in their programmed logic. The effectiveness of these types of systems is predicated on timeliness of the collected information. RFID, bar codes, and other automatic identification systems allow these types of systems to effectively reduce operational costs.

COORDINATION

An advantage of automatic data capture technologies, it is suggested, is to offer supply chain management the ability to provide standardized information that can be easily coordinated. When supply chain information coordination occurs successfully, all partners of a supply chain work together and are able to maximize total supply chain profitability. Unfortunately, supply chain partners prefer to optimize their individual performance. Due to the competitive nature of business today, information provides a unique opportunity to provide shared information between partners and provide long-term viability for all involved. This suggests that the lack of coordination can result in a significant loss of supply chain profit. Coordination among different stages in a supply chain requires each partner to share information with other partners. This level of trust and deciding on what information to share is an important challenge for today's supply chain partners.

AGGREGATE PLANNING

One of the main goals for implementing RFID and other automatic data capture (ADC) technologies is to minimize labor. If these labor savings are realized and can be effectively captured, then tasks such as aggregate manpower planning can be automated. Aggregate planning is most effective with accurate forecasting. The more real-time information that is captured allows for forecasts to become more accurate and promotes better planning. If information is captured more often and accurately, it may promote more accurate forecasting about future demand and conditions. Obtaining forecasting information frequently means using sophisticated techniques for data capture in order to estimate future sales or market conditions. Managers must decide how they will make forecasts and to what extent they will rely on forecasts to make decisions. These decisions will dictate the type of data capture technique that is most beneficial. Organizations or firms traditionally use forecasts at a tactical level to schedule production or at a strategic level to determine whether to build new plants or when to strategically enter a new market.

Forecasts are useless unless a company uses them, so they must plan to act on the forecast. Aggregate planning transforms forecasts into useful plans that support scheduling of labor. A key decision is how to integrate an aggregate plan throughout the entire supply chain. The aggregate plan can become an important tool that provides information that can be shared across the supply chain. The usefulness is that this prior knowledge will allow other partners to effectively calculate demand on their firm's suppliers, vendors, and customer commitments.

RFID AND OTHER ENABLING TECHNOLOGIES

Information-sharing technologies along with RFID exist in logistics to share and analyze information in the supply chain. Common technologies such as EDI and Web-based application systems provide significant productivity increases due to their information-sharing capabilities. We describe these technologies in the next section.

EDI

Electronic data interchange (EDI) refers to the electronic transmission of standard business documents in a predetermined format from one company's business computer to its trading partner's computer (Cannon 1993). EDI relies on two standards, ANSI and EDIFACT, to ensure standardized business communication. EDI allows a firm to transmit information, such as point-of-sale demand for information, purchase orders, and inventory status information, to users within the firm and to customers and trading partners. Previously, EDI systems were implemented generally by larger firms because of the expense required for dedicated software and advanced hardware. Currently, more companies are using Web-based EDI due to the fact that the Internet version of EDI has reduced the cost of implementing EDI. Others choose to just send information over the Web that is not in EDI format.

The Internet provides several advantages for EDI with respect to information sharing. The Internet conveys much more information and therefore offers much more visibility than EDI. Better visibility improves decisions across the supply chain. Internet communication among stages in the supply chain is also easier because the Web provides a common information transmission and design platform. The Web has enabled modernized transmission for applications and the use of the Web to convey business information — e-commerce — and has become a major force in business operations.

WEB-BASED APPLICATION SYSTEMS

The use of the Web for both business-to-consumer (B2C) and business-to-business (B2B) is growing quickly. The Web will have significant implications for supply chain management in the coming years. Thomas Freidman, a leader on political thought, mentions that the Web is allowing small companies to compete with large companies in both B2C and B2B transactions. Unlike the failed dot-bomb companies in the early twentieth century, well-thought-out small businesses are able to use competitive leveraging Web-based transactions.

Many software firms offer Web-based systems. Some advantages that Web-based supply chain systems provide include:

- Unlimited access on the Web
- A common platform, unlike the complexity of EDI
- Cost-effective implementation

Because many firms are concerned with Internet security, some prefer the complex EDI protocols that provide more extensive security than Web-based systems. However, given the new Web-based EDI protocol standards and the cost implications, the Web-based systems will begin to replace EDI systems in the coming years.

BUSINESS SYSTEMS

For most ADC technologies to become effective, they must be integrated into business systems. The most common type of systems that RFID technologies are integrated into are ERP, WMS, and SCM systems. Enterprise resource planning (ERP) systems were created to provide the transactional tracking and enterprise visibility of information from within a company and with business partners in their supply chain. These systems provide real-time access to the latest information kept in the system database in order to support decisions that will enhance operational performance. Modern ERP systems keep track of the information in their databases and provide real-time access by utilizing application software that provides access through the Internet to view this information. Strategic planning systems such as supply chain management (SCM) software use the information in ERP systems to make analytical decisions that support operation and provide information visibility. SCM systems analyze where operations will move and change strategically in the future. An ERP system provides information to operations that show current operational conditions, whereas SCM systems help a company decide on their future direction.

INFORMATION EFFICIENCY

Though RFID provides information quickly, the key to successfully using information is how it is used to improve operations. Information can be used to improve organizational responsiveness and efficiency. Information can be used to improve the performance of operations if it allows the other operation to be more responsive. The benefits of responsiveness over efficiency are that responsiveness allows an organization to change to meet new business needs. Responsiveness may allow for the creation of new sales and markets, whereas efficiency may only reduce existing costs. Information can help an organization improve efficiency and productivity by decreasing inventory, labor, and transportation costs. Accurate information can further improve responsiveness by helping a supply chain better match changing markets and their changing customer demands.

Common literature suggests that we are living in the information age. Information in many sources such as academic publications, trade journals, magazines, newsletters, blogs, e-magazines, and so on is introduced every day. The explosion of information on the Web due to Web search companies such as Yahoo, Google, and Microsoft allow people to perform Web searches for information on almost anything.

Supply chain information provides the organization strategic advantage over competition and is key to running a business efficiently and effectively in an ever-changing and more complex environment. Information plays a key role in the management of the supply chain as evidenced in such uses as forecasts, aggregate manpower planning, and customer inquiries.

Concepts such as just-in-time (JIT) manufacturing and delivery, vendor-managed inventory (VMI), and cross-docking require timely information within the supply chain. JIT uses timely information to optimize the scheduling of deliveries or manufacturing in such a way as to minimize inventories. The VMI concept allows vendors to review information from a supplier and order only what is needed in a specific time period, which allows them reduce excess inventory. These concepts leverage the concept of information in the supply chain. In the next section we describe some of the concepts for leveraging information in the supply chain. They will introduce the bullwhip effect, which is a general term that describes the inefficiencies realized in supply chain operations with imperfect information. We will discuss the determinants and current ways that information can offset these inefficiencies, including electronic commerce, Web-based systems, and RFID.

E-COMMERCE

Electronic commerce, or e-commerce, refers to a technology that allows businesses to operate a common transaction that was traditionally performed in a paper-based system and is now performed electronically. It includes EDI, e-mail, electronic funds transfers, electronic publishing, image processing, electronic bulletin boards, blogs, Internet voice mail, Internet video meetings, mp3 sharing, shared databases, point-of-sale bar code systems in supermarkets, and all manner of Web-based business systems.

Some well-known companies such as General Electric Corporation, one of the world's largest diversified manufacturers of a wide variety of products, uses Web-based transactions systems and EDI as a regular part of its business practices in most divisions. Other companies use EDI, Internet-based systems, electronic fore-casting, and warehouse management systems to gain competitiveness.

During the last few years of the twentieth century, IPOs of the dot-com companies were occurring almost everyday and their share prices rose steadily, even though many of these companies had no customers. These pure play e-tailers, which represented Internet-based retailers without traditional brick-and-mortar operations, have all but disappeared. One that survived and thrived is Amazon.com. Amazon has significantly expanded its product line, and is one of the few successful "pure play" e-tailers that survived the dot-com bust. One of the authors, who was a consultant during the time of the e-tailer craze, recalls that the main failure of the movement was the lack of a real business plan; instead, the focus was on developing a "killer ap" or creative front-end software and Web sites as the major objective. Some of the primary portals (Yahoo and Google, for example) require big money to allow direct access to an e-commerce site. These failed e-tailers were also referred to as dot-bomb companies instead of "dot-com" companies.

A new phenomenon derived from these companies' failures, which was recently documented by Thomas Friedman in his landmark text *The World is Flat* (2005), is that smarter versions of these e-businesses initiatives are reappearing and competing against larger companies in local markets domestically and internationally. Most profits for Internet activities are business-to-business Web-based systems accounts. They represent a much greater share of the electronic commerce marketplace than Web-based retailers.

RFID AS PART OF THE INFORMATION SUPPLY CHAIN

Radio frequency identification (RFID) tags are emerging as the bar codes of the future. As we discussed in the earlier chapters, bar codes, which have become common in retailing, were only commonly accepted in 1985. The expectation is that though active RFID tags were commercially viable in 1973 and utilized in toll roads and animal tracking in the mid-1980s and passive tags were arguably commercially viable in 2005, mass acceptance in logistics is expected by 2010. This emerging technology may achieve the fastest acceptance in history.

Common applications include (1) E-ZPass for paying bridge or highway tolls, (2) tagging of library books in some libraries, and (3) tagging of cargo containers at most of the world's ports. Reconciling shipments against bills of lading or packing and customer orders can be performed succinctly and accurately eliminating the need to perform these functions manually. Beyond the supply chain, RFID technologies have broader applications such as emergency human identification for finding abducted children in Mexico or mountain climbers in Colorado who may become lost in an avalanche. Such applications of RFID technology benefits are touted yet fiercely debated as to how they may threaten individual rights and privacy. In the application chapters you will find details of these applications and their challenges. We now further detail how RFID technologies provide information strategically to allow organizations to improve operational effectiveness.

RFID AS AN INTELLIGENT AGENT SYSTEM

Because of the differing automatic identification technologies such as bar code, RFID passive, RFID active, SAW tags, and sensor tags, they must be integrated for use in the supply chain. We suggest using RFID technologies as an intelligent agent system (IAS) that supports real-time decision support systems as a solution for this integration challenge.

The idea of an intelligent agent is pervasive control system frameworks. Control frameworks can be classified as hierarchical, heterarchical, and hybrid (Shukla and Chen 1996; Heragu et al. 2002). We consider RFID tags that have a master–slave relationship that exists between higher and lower levels a hierarchical automatic identification framework. An operational example would be using bar codes affixed to cartons to write information to passive RFID pallet tags. The information is passed to the next highest unit load, case to pallet level with each technology acting as an independent system. This is similar to the control system concept, in which response to input data is passed up the chain of command and higher level controllers pass down command data for execution by the lower level controllers. In control systems this works well when there is little interference between the technologies; RFID integration does present this problem (Szelke and Kerr, 1994; Brussel et al. 1998). We will refer to this type of system as an open system. A heterarchical framework is present when there are interactions between the lower level controllers which are permitted to engage in one-on-one communication assuming there is no hierarchy or higher level controller. For RFID systems this represents the use of reading tags on a common protocol such as the EPC Global passive standard where multiple readers can read standardized tags. We refer to this type of system in our text as a closed system. Hybrid frameworks (Tawegoum, Castelain, and Gentina 1994; Brussell et al. 1998; Maturana, Shen, and Norrie 1999; Ottaway and Burns 2000; Heragu et al. 2002) discuss how these frameworks capture the benefits of hierarchical and heterarchical frameworks while avoiding their pitfalls. For RFID technologies to work with other auto-ID technologies in the short run, this type of approach will be necessary to realize organizational savings.

A practical example of how the integration of multiple RFID technologies that operate at different frequencies can be used is modeled in control frameworks so that real-time information can be used to determine an inventory policy is given as: a high-frequency (HF) 13.56 passive tag is used to track retail over-the-counter drugs at the item level, ultra-high-frequency (UHF) 915-MHz passive RFID tags can be used to track inventory at the case- and pallet-level inventory, and UHF 303-MHz active tags track the status of inventory on tractor trailers. Popular industrial literature assumes that linking information with relational databases provides real-time information on the status at the item level (i.e., the active tag can show the status of the drugs because the tags were relationally linked as they moved up in container level).

The flaws in this assumption may be that different technologies have different error rates in scanning validation; human error of integrating these relations, such as database programming; and they do not have common standards. The current mandate from Wal-Mart encompasses only one standard, the electronic product code (EPC) global standard for Generations 1 and 2 UHF 856–915 MHz passive tags.

Further, this EPC global standard is currently accepted in the United States but has been not completely adopted by other countries. Also, current FDA initiatives for over-the-counter drug tracking incorporate the 13.56-MHz RFID tags. The lack of understanding of how the mixed RFID technologies will have negative impacts, such as higher error rates and lower productivity, provides a gap that I seek to investigate during this research project. One of the authors identified this gap when testing technologies for NASA ISS. The most operationally valid solutions included multiple RFID technologies (Jones 2007).

SUMMARY OF RFID AND INFORMATION ENABLERS

This section provides understanding of key technologies and how all the technologies differ and how they can be integrated to work for operational effectiveness. This will allow warehouse management system algorithms such as "bucket brigade" calculations, picking route optimization, and other effective system updates that will improve operations. Further insights into safety stock minimization, customer order optimization, and pick/stock labor minimization will be affected and discussed later in the text.

RFID PROVIDES TIMELY VISIBILITY IN LOGISTICS

RFID supports information in the supply chain by enabling visibility. The concept of visibility describes the ability of anyone, including customers, to have access to inventory, orders, raw materials, and delivery points at any time. Visibility is currently provided by a mixture of automatic identification, or auto-ID, technologies such as bar codes, smart labels, ISBN, and UPC codes, along with others. The opportunity for RFID is that its non-line-of-sight scanning, the integration of the aforementioned auto-ID identifiers into RFID nomenclature, and the push for standardized technology protocols will provide large supply chain savings.

The real-time nature of RFID is considered a benefit and currently a challenge. The benefit is that you have the latest information to make the best decisions; the drawback is that the amount of data currently presents a data storage problem for operational systems.

Better visibility provides reduced inventory, labor and assets management using inventory policies, scheduling, and decision support system information. This is exemplified by the fact that:

- RFID supports reduced inventory costs with more effective labor policies
- RFID supports labor reduction with more effective scheduling
- RFID supports the reduction of expensive assets such as facilities, trucks, containers, and railroad time because of more accurate information in decision support systems

The ability for RFID to provide timely information and visibility into the supply chain are based on three components of RFID technologies. They are

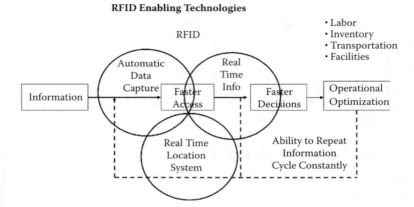

FIGURE 8.1   RFID-enabling technologies.

- Automatic data capture
- Real-time information
- Real-time location system

The RFID enabling technologies diagram shown in Figure 8.1 represents these components as interconnecting orbits.

The figure also shows how RFID supports timely information in the supply chain by enabling information to be accessed faster. This implies that faster decisions can be made, which produces operational optimization that can be effectively repeated. In the figure, one of the boxes represents the RFID information flow. The ability to allow resident information collected automatically in real-time leads to faster, more effective decisions is where RFID shows future promise. Business costs are reduced as operations become more productive by reducing labor, transportation, and facility cost of moving inventory in the supply chain.

Many organizations see that the benefit of using RFID is that they can effectively manipulate inventory. Inventory exists in the supply chain because of the variance between supply and demand. This variance is necessary for manufacturers where it is economical to manufacture in large lot quantities and then store for future sales. The variance is also present in retail stores where inventory is held for future customer demand. Oftentimes businesses suggest that inventory is a marketing vehicle creating demand by passing customers. The main role inventory plays is to satisfy customer demand by having product available when the customers want it. Another significant role that inventory plays is reducing cost by exploiting economies of scale that may exist during production and distribution. Given that economy of scale is believed to have such a large impact on inventory, we will present some relevant information regarding inventory in the supply chain.

INVENTORY IN THE SUPPLY CHAIN

Supply chain inventory is commonly described in the form of raw materials, work-in-process (WIP), and finished goods. Inventory in most operations is one of the most costly aspects. The effective manipulation of inventory will dictate the long-term success of most organizations. If the inventory is not managed well, it will create excessive costs and may negatively impact customer satisfaction.

Chopra and Meindl (2006) suggest that inventory also has a significant impact on the material flow time in a supply chain. Material flow time is the time that elapses between the points at which material enters the supply chain to the point at which it exits. In the next section we will consider a common example for demonstrating the effects of inventory mathematically. Again we will demonstrate the examples that were adapted from the Chopra and Meindl (2006) text. Consider that the throughput is the rate at which sales occur. If inventory is represented by I, flow time by F, and throughput by T, the three can be related using Little's law as follows:

$$I = FT$$

For example, if the flow time of an auto assembly process is ten hours and the throughput is fifty units per hour, Little's law tells us that the inventory is $50 \times 10 = 500$ units. If we were able to reduce inventory to 250 units while holding throughput constant, we would reduce our flow time to five hours (250/50). We note that in this relationship, inventory and throughput must have constant units. One can see that those inventory and flow times are related and that throughput is often determined by customer demand. The goal of many operations is to reduce the amount of inventory needed without increasing cost or reducing responsiveness.

RESPONSIVENESS

The responsiveness to customer needs and demand is crucial to business success. Inventory provides leverage that allows companies to be responsive and flexible. Managing inventory effectively requires decisions such as whether to locate inventory close to the customer by locating a main warehouse centrally or stocking distribution centers seasonally using a centralized stocking concept. Each inventory strategy will have trade-offs that need to be evaluated by each organization's strategic mission as well as short-term and long-term goals. Some of the strategies to effectively manage inventory include effective use of:

- Inventory turns
- Safety stock inventory
- Seasonal inventory
- Product availability
- Inventory measurement

Inventory Turns

Inventory turns refers to the rotation or cycling of inventory to minimize inventory and optimize space. Inventory turns or inventory cycling can be defined as the average amount of inventory used to satisfy demand between receipts of supplier shipments. The size of the inventory turns is a result of the production, transportation, or purchase of material in large lots. Companies produce or purchase in large lots to exploit economies of scale in the production, transportation, or purchase process. Commonly, the increase in lot size reduces the turn ration and traditionally increases carrying costs.

Safety Stock Inventory

Safety stock inventory is inventory held in case demand exceeds expectations; it is held to offset the uncertainty of demand forecasts. Because demand is uncertain and inventory may not meet actual customer demand, companies hold safety inventory to satisfy an unexpectedly high demand and meet customer needs. If a company does not have enough inventory, it may lose sales, profit, and customer confidence. Thus, choosing safety inventory involves making a trade-off between the costs of having too much inventory and the costs of losing sales, market share, and long-term customers due to not having enough inventory.

Seasonal Inventory

Seasonal inventory is inventory in addition to safety stock that is used to support predictable variability in demand due to a repeatable period or season. Common seasons include a company's peak selling season, such as Christmas or Thanksgiving holidays for retailers. Companies using seasonal inventory build up inventory in periods of low demand and store it for periods of high demand when they will not have the capacity to produce all that is demanded. The decision for most organizations is how much seasonal inventory to store. They must compare the costs of storing additional seasonal inventory against the cost of having the ability to satisfy fluctuations in customer demand.

Product Availability

Product availability is the amount of inventory that is available to be sold during a specified time period. Oftentimes products can be categorized into many statuses, such as damaged, committed, and reserved, as opposed to noncommitted inventory. The ability to support high levels of product availability provides greater customer demand responsiveness but increases cost because inventory has to be held with no prior commitment or order and oftentimes this excess inventory is held but rarely used. In contrast, a low level of product availability provides reduced inventory holding cost but may result in customer failure and loss of current and future sales. Companies must investigate whether having high product availability, which may be more expensive, is worth the risk of not meeting customer demand. Some companies have found that if customers are looking at only costs and are not loyal to any retailer, then reducing costs is more prudent.

Inventory Measurement

Given the importance of inventory, data is often collected and assessed in order to ensure proper management. Some common metrics are described below:

- Inventory amount measures the amount of inventory in dollars or units over a time period such as days, months, and years.
- Obsolete inventory products with more than a specified number of days of inventory identify the products for which the firm is carrying a high level of inventory.
- Safety inventory measures the amount of inventory on hand when a replenishment order arrives. Average safety inventory should be measured by SKU in both units and days of demand. It can be estimated by averaging over time the minimum inventory on hand in each replenishment cycle.
- Seasonal inventory measures the amount of both cycle and safety inventory that is purchased solely due to seasonal changes in demand.
- Fill rate measures the fraction of orders/demand that was met on time from inventory.
- Time out of stock measures the amount of time that a particular SKU had zero inventory.

There is an underlying trade-off that organizations make with regards to inventory decisions between customer needs, wants, and satisfaction against the cost of inventory. Excess inventory generally makes the supply chain more responsive and flexible to the customer wants. A higher level of inventory may also create a reduction in production and transportation costs because of improved economies of scale in both functions. All must consider the additional carrying cost of holding excess inventory. Moreover, these inventory costs in the supply chain can be greatly affected by a lack of supply chain coordination, commonly referred to as the bullwhip effect.

THE BULLWHIP EFFECT

The bullwhip effect has been evaluated by both practitioners and academics. Chopra and Meindl (2006) provide a brief history of the bullwhip effect. The problem was identified when Proctor & Gamble (P&G) were studying replenishment patterns for one of its best-selling products. They recognized that there was greater variability between (1) orders placed by distributors against retail store sales and (2) orders placed by distributors against requested materials from suppliers. Given that the product had consistent demand over the years, the large discrepancy was not expected. P&G coined the term *bullwhip effect* for this phenomenon. It also has been referred to as the whiplash or whipsaw effect. Other organization such as Hewlett-Packard experienced the bullwhip effect in patterns of sales for products such as printers.

An example of this bullwhip pattern of increasing variance as you move up the supply chain is shown in Figure 8.2.

Many researchers and practitioners have attempted to discover the origins of this effect due to the fact that it creates excess cost in the form of inventory in the supply chain. Some believe, when working with constant, highly predictable demand, that the effect is produced when companies order products in batch quantities at operational supply chain levels.

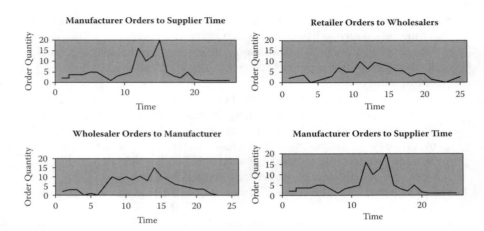

FIGURE 8.2   Increasing variability of orders up the supply chain. (From: Lee, Padmanabhan, and S. Whang (1997) and Chopra and Meindl (2006).)

The grocery industry, which exhibits this type of demand, sought to reduce the bullwhip effect with an efficient consumer response (ECR) initiative in which the food delivery supply chain would reduce a projected excess of one hundred days of inventory from the supply chain. The stated goal of the ECR initiative was to save $30 billion annually by reducing the bullwhip effect in food deliveries logistics (Crawford 2004).

In some cases, solutions that may reduce the effects of the bullwhip effect on demand forecasting, order batching, price fluctuations, and creative order gaming are suggested by researchers (Lee, Padmanabhan, and Whang 1997; Chopra and Meindl 2006). They include sharing of information, supplier alignment, stable price structure, and incentives to prevent gaming.

First, the sharing of information from all parties from common data such as a point-of-sale (POS) data can help create forecasts on these data. Other techniques include electronic data interchange, or EDI as it is commonly described. EDI and other Web-based exchange formats provide a means for integrating information between company software platforms.

Second, supplier alignment allows for the coordination of pricing, transportation, and inventory planning efforts operations in the supply chain. Fixed costs, which create order batching behavior, and economies of scale costs such as transportation can be limited with real-time information. Things such as smaller batch lot quantities and effective transportation scheduling are allowed by information that provides alignment. Another trend encouraging small batch ordering is the outsourcing of logistics to third parties. Logistics companies can consolidate loads from multiple suppliers. Logistics outsourcing to companies such as UPS Supply Chain Solutions is expanding rapidly.

Third, supplier pricing is designed to motivate customers to buy in large batches and store items for future use. This behavior is called price stabilization and is designed to reduce sales demand variation. This is evident in comparing a retailer that runs frequent promotions to warehouse stores that offer everyday low pricing. The warehouse stores have more stable demand than department stores in which promotional sales account for most of their business. Finally, exaggeration of orders to manipulate pricing, often referred to as *gaming*, can be affected dramatically by information. These order forecasts can be smoothed using past demand, not sales forecasting.

SUMMARY

In summary, the effective use of information to manage inventory can counteract the bullwhip effect created by partners in the supply chain acting in their own best interests. The need for timely information can be supported by RFID technologies.

RFID technologies provide an opportunity to reduce the uncertainty leading to the bullwhip effect through more real-time information. Given the costs of holding excess inventory in capital, obsolescence (or spoilage), handling costs, occupancy costs, pilferage, damage, taxes, and insurance, it may be worthwhile to use real-time information in evaluating inventory reduction.

REFERENCES

Brussel, H. V., J. Wyns, P. Valckernaers, and L. Bongaerts. (1998). Reference architecture for holonic manufacturing systems: PROSA. *Computers in Industry* 37:255–274.

Cannon, E. (1993). *EDI guide: A step by step approach.* New York: Van Nostrand Reinhold.

Chopra, S., and P. Meindl. (2006). *Supply chain management strategy, planning, and operation.* 2d ed. Upper Saddle River, N.J.: Prentice Hall.

Crawford, F. 1994. Efficient consumer responses. *Food Processing,* 55(2), 34–42.

Heragu, S. S., R. J. Graves, B. Kim, and A. St. Onge. (2002). Holonic/intelligent agent based framework for manufacturing systems control. *IEEE Trans. on Systems, Man and Cybernetics.*

Lee, H. L., V. Padmanabhan, and S. Whang. (1997). The bullwhip effect in supply chains. *Sloan Management Review* 38(3):93–102.

Maturana, F., Shen, W., and Norrie, D. H. (1999). MetaMorph: An adaptive agent-based architecture for intelligent manufacturing. *International Journal of Production Research* 37(10):2159–2173.

Ottaway, T. A., and J. R. Burns. (2000). An adaptive production control system utilizing agent technology. *International Journal of Production Research* 38(4):721–737.

Shukla, C. S., and Chen, F. F. (1996). The state of the art in intelligent real-time FMS control: A comprehensive survey. *Journal of Intelligent Manufacturing* 7:441–455.

Szelke, E., and Kerr, R. M. (1994). Knowledge-based reactive scheduling. *International Journal of Production, Planning, and Control,* 5(2), London: Taylor & Francis, 124–145.

Tawegoum, R., Castelain, E., and Gentina, J. C. (1994). Hierarchical and dynamic production control in flexible manufacturing systems. *Robotics and Computer-Integrated Manufacturing* 11(4):327–334.

ADDITIONAL REFERENCES

Amiri, A. (2006). Designing a distribution network in a supply chain system: Formulation and efficient solution procedure. *European Journal of Operational Research* 171(2):567–576.

AT Kearney. (2004). *RFID/EPC: Managing the transition (2004–2007).* White Paper, AT Kearney Consulting.

Atali, A., H. L. Lee, and Ö. Özer. (2004). *If the inventory manager knew: Value of RFID under imperfect inventory information.* Working Paper, Stanford University.

Buckner, M., R. Crutcher, M. R. Moore, and B. Whitus. (2002). Miclog RFID tag program enables total asset visibility. *MILCOM 2002 Proceedings* 2:1422–1426.

Chappell, G., D. Durdan, G. Gilbert, L. Ginsberg, J. Smith, and J. Tobolski. (2002). Auto-ID on delivery: The value of auto-ID technology in retail stores. MIT Auto-ID Center White Paper, Accenture.

Elhedhli, S., and J. L. Goffin. (2005). Efficient production-distribution system design. *Management Science* 51(7):1151–1164.

Eskigun, E., R. Uzsoy, P. V. Preckel, and G. Beaujon. (2005). Outbound supply chain network design with mode selection, lead times and capacitated vehicle distribution centers. *European Journal of Operational Research* 165(1):182–206.

Fleisch, E., and C. Tellkamp. (2005). Inventory inaccuracy and supply chain performance: A simulation study of a retail supply chain. *International Journal of Production Economics* 95(3):373–385.

Friedman, T. L. (2005). *The world is flat: A brief history of the twenty-first century.* New York: Farrar, Straus & Giroux.

Iglehart, D. L., and R. C. Morey. (1972). Inventory systems with imperfect asset information. *Management Science* 18(8):B388–B394.

Ingalls, R. G., and D. J. Morrice. (2004). PERT scheduling with resource constraints using qualitative simulation graphs. *Project Management Journal* 35(3):5–14.

Ingalls, R. G., D. J. Morrice, and A. B. Whinston. (2000). The implementation of temporal intervals in qualitative simulation graphs. *ACM Transactions on Modeling and Computer Simulation* 10(3):215–240.

Ingalls, R. G., D. J. Morrice, E. Yücesan, A. B. Whinston. (2003). Execution conditions: A formalization of event cancellation in simulation graphs. *INFORMS Journal on Computing* 15(3).

Johnson, J. C., D. F. Wood, D. L. Wardlow, and P. R. Murphy, Jr. (1999). *Contemporary logistics*, 7th ed. Upper Saddle River, N.J.: Prentice Hall.

Jones, E. C., and T. Farnham. (2007). *Using RFID to track inventory on NASA ISS.* Working Paper, University of Nebraska.

Kang, Y., and S. B. Gershwin. (2005). Information inaccuracy in inventory systems—Stock loss and stockout. *IIE Transactions* 37(9):843–859.

Kim, B.-I., R. J. Graves, S. S. Heragu, and A. St. Onge. (2002). Intelligent agent based model for a industrial order picking problem. *IIE Transactions* 34(7):601–612.

Klose, A., and A. Drexl. (2005). Lower bounds for the capacitated facility location problem based on column generation. *Management Science* 51(11):1689–1705.

Kök, A. G., and K. H. Shang. (2004). *Replenishment and inspection policies for systems with inventory record inaccuracy.* Working Paper, Duke University.

Lacy, S. (2005). RFID: Plenty of mixed signals. *BusinessWeek Online*, 31 January [Online]. Available at [Accessed]

Lee, H., B. Peleg, P. Rajwat, S. Sarma, and B. Subirana. (2005). *Assessing the value of RFID technology and the EPC standard for manufacturers.* White Paper, EPCGlobal.

Lee, H. L., and Ö. Özer. (2005). *Unlocking the value of RFID.* White Paper, Stanford University.

Lee, H. L., and S. Whang. (2005). Higher supply chain security at lower cost: Lessons from total quality management. *International Journal of Production Economics* 96(3):289–300.

Melo, M. T., S. Nickel, and F. Saldanha da Gama. (2006). Dynamic multi-commodity capacitated facility location: A mathematical modeling framework for strategic supply chain planning. *Computers and Operations Research* 33(1):181–208.

Pisello, T. (2004). *The three Rs of RFID: Rewards, risk and ROI* [Online]. Available at Technology-Evaluation.com [Accessed]

Sabri, E. H., and B. M. Beamon. (2000). A multi-objective approach to simultaneous strategic and operational planning in supply chain design. *OMEGA* 28(5):581–598.

Santoso, T., S. Ahmed, M. Goetschalckx, and A. Shapiro. (2005). A stochastic programming approach for supply chain network design under uncertainty. *European Journal of Operational Research* 167(1):96–115.

Shen, Z. J. M. (2005). Multi-commodity supply chain design problem. *IIE Transactions* 37(8):753–762.

Talluri, S., and R. C. Baker. (2002). A multi-phase mathematical programming approach for effective supply chain design. *European Journal of Operational Research* 141(3):544–558.

Teo, C. P., and J. Shu. (2004). Warehouse-retailer network design problem. *Operations Research* 52(3):396–408.

Turner, W. C., J. H. Mize, and K. E. Case. (1987). *Introduction to industrial and systems engineering*. Englewood Cliffs, N.J.: Prentice Hall.

9 Inventory Control Basics

If you have an important point to make, don't try to be subtle or clever. Use a pile driver. Hit the point once. Then come back and hit it again. Then hit it a third time — a tremendous whack.

—**Winston Churchill**

INTRODUCTION

The above quote describes the authors' view of inventory control. Inventory control is one of the most important topics in most operations. The basic industrial engineering curriculum provides many concepts on how to effectively manage inventory such that businesses maximize profits. Inventory decisions such as how much and what type as well as what type of material handling equipment is needed has driven operational costs. The important trade-offs of how much inventory is needed to meet customer service and minimize costs associated with inventory must be addressed continuously in many organizations. Managers of inventory, planners, and engineers seek to provide solutions that allow an organization to maintain inventory levels that both minimize the costs of holding inventory and the cost of losing a customer because of lack of inventory.

In this section we discuss closed-loop inventory control. The approaches discussed here are relatively unsophisticated. There is a large amount of information available in other academic texts along with consultative materials available in industry. A generally accepted text that summarizes inventory control in the logistics field is Johnson et al. (1999), and we utilize some their theories to further explore how RFID affects inventory control in logistics. We seek to explore certain aspects of inventory control principles so that the impact of RFID technologies can be recognized.

ADC AND INVENTORY CARRYING COSTS

The main advantages of automatic data capture (ADC) technologies such as RFID are reduction of labor and reduction in inventory. It is critical that the reduction of inventory is quantified in order to justify the investment in ADC technologies. Johnson et al. (1999) suggests that inventory carrying costs fall into several categories. They include the following:

- Storage costs are the costs associated with occupying space in a storeroom, warehouse or distribution center. Inventory costs such as insurance for fire, flood, and theft are included in the expense of storing goods.
- Theft or inventory shrinkage identifies when more items are recorded entering warehouses than leaving.
- Obsolescence describes when items in an inventory eventually become out of date.
- Depreciation or deterioration describes inventory as a function of time, not usage.
- Interest refers to the interest charges for the money invested in inventories. Oftentimes this represents the investment into company inventories as opposed to money that can be invested in other investments.
- Taxes refer to when inventories are taxed. Traditionally the tax is derived on the basis of the inventory on hand on a certain date. Most companies make a concentrated effort to have inventory present on that day be as low as possible.
- Carrying costs includes inventory tax and costs associated with avoiding or evading the inventory taxes.

Consider products such as fresh produce, which may deteriorate in only a few days. The depreciation portion of a produce company's carrying costs might be as high as 50 percent per day. Other products depreciate completely given their expiration dates, including products such as dairy products, drugs, bread, some soft drinks, and film. For these products the rate of depreciation can be calculated because expired products that are unsold must be removed from the shelf.

Specialized inventory costs are related to pets and livestock, which have costs related to being watered and fed. Security costs for high-value items such as computer chips may increase inventory carrying costs.

Inventory carrying charges are expressed as a percentage of the inventory's value and a widely cited estimate is that carrying costs approximate 25 percent per year of a product's value. See Table 9.1.

Opportunity costs are not traditionally included in most carrying costs calculations. Most companies must consider the trade-off of holding inventory against having inventory to meet the fluctuations of customer demand.

OUT-OF-STOCK COSTS

Out-of-stock costs refers to when an item is not available to a customer when the customer wants to purchase the product, item, or service

**TABLE 9.1
Component Breakdown
of the 25 Percent Figure**

Insurance	0.25%
Storage facilities	0.25
Taxes	0.50
Transportation	0.50
Handling costs	2.50
Depreciation	5.00
Interest	6.00
Obsolescence	10.00
Total	25.00%

Source: Adapted from Alford and Bangs, eds., 1955, pp. 396–397.

contract. Out-of-stock costs are difficult to predict or forecast and may result in creating loss of customer satisfaction. The difficulty of determining cost that is lost due to out-of-stock or the loss of a customer due to out-of-stock inventory is due to the fact that detailed knowledge of customer behavior is required. The determination of what type of buyer is necessary in addition to identifying whether you have customers or clients. Clients typically demonstrate some form of customer loyalty and will still purchase products in the future despite an out of stock event. If a client is continually disappointed by out-of-stock, then future sales from this client may represent lost sales. Customers may be more price and convenience driven and may not represent repeated lost sales due to out-of-stocks. The out of stock may represent a one-time loss for this type of buyer. Customers can have many varied reactions to stock-outs. The typical buyer responses can be categorized as:

- Future sale
- Lost sale
- Loss of client

Consider a set of five hundred buyers who experienced an out-of-stock event for a given product. The three types of buyer responses may suggest that of the 500 customers, 50 will return as a future sell (they are considered clients); 325 (customers) buyers may go to another store, which represents a lost sale; and 125 (clients) buyers may never return to the company. The percentages represented by future sale, lost sale, and loss of the customer are 10 percent, 65 percent, and 25 percent, respectively. These percentages can be considered probabilities of the events taking place and can be used to determine the average cost of an out-of-stock event.

Table 9.2 illustrates a procedure utilized by Johnson et al. (1999). Each cost is multiplied by the likelihood that it will occur and the results are added. A delayed sale has no cost because the customer is brand loyal and purchases the product when it is again available. The lost sale alternative results in loss of the profit that would have been made on the customer's purchase. The lost customer situation is the worst. The customer tries the competitor's product and prefers it to the product originally requested. The customer is lost, and the cost involved is that of developing a new brand-loyal customer. These costs are usually determined by a firm's marketing department, but we use the suggested numbers for demonstration purposes.

TABLE 9.2
Determination of the Average Cost of a Stock-Out

Alternative	Loss ($)	Probability	Average Cost ($)
Brand-loyal customer	0.00	0.10	0.00
Switches and comes back	37.00	0.65	24.05
Lost customer	1,200.00	0.25	300.00
Average cost of a stock-out	1.00	324.05	

Safety Stocks for Out-of-Stock Inventory

Safety stock is excess inventory that companies utilize to prevent loss sales due to out-of-stock inventory. It is envisioned that RFID technologies may prevent the need for this excess inventory. The RFID technologies will provide more effective analysis that will allow for eliminating or minimizing the amount of safety stock. Also, as we demonstrate later, expansion on economic order quantities can be explored using RFID technologies. A basic analysis for evaluating safety stock is described in Johnson et al. (1998) and is demonstrated in Table 9.3. A more detailed discussion of how RFID impacts safety stock is described later in this chapter.

Consider the example demonstrated by Johnson et al. (1999) to demonstrate safety stock analysis. In this example, goods are ordered from a wholesaler in multiples of ten. It is given that the carrying cost for an additional set of ten units is $1,200. The trade-off is shown that by stocking an additional ten units of safety stock and maintaining it throughout the year, the firm is able to prevent twenty stock-outs. The average cost of a stock-out has already been given in the examples as $324.05. We derive that saving twenty stock-outs saves the firm $6,481.00. The analysis demonstrates that the savings justifies the investment costs. Alternatively, the organization may consider maintaining safety stock throughout the year of twenty units. The analysis reveals that this adds $1,200 to the costs but prevents sixteen additional out-of-stock inventory losses, creating a savings of $5,184.80.

The optimum quantity of safety stock is sixty units. With this quantity, the carrying cost of ten additional units is $1,200, but $1,296.20 is saved. If the safety stocks are increased from sixty to seventy units, the additional carrying cost is again $1,200, while the savings are only $972.15. The analysis concludes that the firm would be more profitable by permitting three stock-outs to occur each year. This example provides a common method for evaluating impacts out-of-stock inventory on customer service.

The fact that companies choose to maintain safety stocks indicates that a company wants to meet customer demand for out-of-stock items but, as mentioned

---

TABLE 9.3
Safety

Number of Units of Safety Stock	Total Value of Safety Stock ($480 per Unit)	25% Annual Carrying Cost	Carrying Cost of Incremental Safety Stock	Number of Additional Orders Filled	Additional Stock-Out Costs Avoided
10	$4,800	$1,200	$1,200	20	$6,481.00
20	9,600	2,400	1,200	16	5,184.80
30	14,400	3,600	1,200	12	3,888.60
40	19,200	4,800	1,200	8	2,592.40
50	24,000	6,000	1,200	6	1,944.30
60	28,800	7,200	1,200	4	1,296.20
70	33,600	8,400	1,200	3	972.15

before, not all companies utilize this type of strategy. Many companies choose not to maintain safety stock due to the high carrying cost for inventory and because their customers' buying behaviors may not indicate that this would be profitable. Mass merchandisers such as Wal-Mart or Sam's Club typically do not replace many items that do not provide the appropriate profit margins because customers are not loyal to buying the manufacturer's brand at their retail stores. In these situations, customer behavior is to buy as much as they need because the items may not be available in the future. They understand that certain low margin items or special promotion items at the retailer are demand based and that the retailer may not have that product in the future. This is evidenced in popular close-out stores such as Big Lots and Hobby Lobby in which the firm buys large quantities of a product and sell it at a discount. When the product is sold out there is no expectation of that product appearing at the store in the future.

ECONOMIC ORDER QUANTITY

Our safety stock level discussion describes the minimum inventory a company tries to keep on hand. Commonly, determining the inventory level, how it should be reordered, and how much should be ordered each time is determined by the economic order quantity (EOQ). The EOQ and related models have been extensively studied in inventory control literature. There are researchers who have described how the fundamentals of this inventory theory will be expanded using RFID technologies in the form of adjusting advanced EOQ models. We describe this in upcoming sections in this chapter. We have included more detailed texts that explore the complete topic of production planning and control and inventory theory in manufacturing in our reference section. A brief overview of EOQ and samples are given. Most academic texts utilize the same equations provided in this adapted overview.

As described in Hopp and Spearman (2001), the EOQ model is an extension of using scientific management, industrial engineering, and advanced mathematics to solve inventory problems. The EOQ was originated by Ford W. Harris (1913) in order to determine economic manufacturing lot sizes. The EOQ model has been widely studied and the basics of the model are addressed in most introductory production planning, operations management, and industrial engineering textbooks. Though the EOQ may be considered common knowledge in the operations management and industrial engineering field, we will consider examples and a description of EOQ, fixed order systems, and just-in-time inventories from the widely accepted Johnson et al. (1999) text.

The EOQ relates to the problem of how much inventory to order in order to optimize manufacturing schedules. The typical inventory order size problem deals with calculating the proper order size based on minimizing the total of two costs: (1) the costs of carrying the inventory, which are in direct proportion to the size of the order that will arrive, and (2) the costs of ordering, which mainly involve the paperwork associated with handling each order, irrespective of its size. Consider if there were no inventory carrying costs, customers would hold inventory and avoid reordering. If there were no costs associated with ordering, one would place orders continually

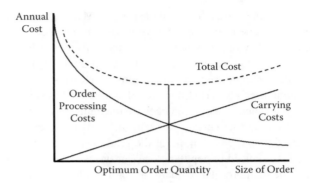

FIGURE 9.1 Determining EOQ by use of a graph.

and maintain no inventory at all, aside from safety stocks. Figure 9.1 shows the two costs on a graph and indicates the point at which they are minimized.

Mathematically, the economic order quantity is determined using this formula:

$$EOQ = \frac{2AB}{I}$$

Where:

    EOQ = the most economic order size, in dollars

      A = annual usage, in dollars

      B = company costs per order of placing the order

      I = carrying costs of the inventory (expressed as an annual percentage)

If $1,000 worth of an item is used each year, if the order costs are $25 per order submitted, and if carrying costs are 20 percent, what is the EOQ?

$$EOQ = \sqrt{\frac{2 \times 1000 \times 25}{0.20}} = \sqrt{250,000} = \$500 \text{ order size}$$

Because of the assumption of even outward flow of goods, inventory carrying costs are applied to one half the order size that would be the average inventory on hand, as illustrated in Table 9.4.

EOQs, once calculated, may not be the same as the lot sizes (units) that the product is bought and sold at by a company. EOQs can also be calculated in terms of the number of units that should be ordered. The formula is

$$EOQ = \sqrt{\frac{2 \left(\text{annual use of number of units} \right) \left(\text{cost of placing an order} \right)}{\text{annual carrying cost per item per year}}}$$

Assume that an item in the Table 9.4 example costs $5. Substituting numbers in the new formula yields

TABLE 9.4
EOQ Calculations

Number of Orders per Year	Order Size	Ordering Cost	Carrying Cost of Average Inventory in Stock	Total Cost
1	$1,000	$125	$100	$125
2	500	50	50	100
3	333	75	33	108
4	250	100	25	125
5	200	125	20	145

$$EOQ = \sqrt{\frac{2 \times 1000 \times 25}{0.20}} = \sqrt{\frac{10000}{1}} = 100 \text{ units}$$

The earlier EOQ formula and Table 9.4 shows that $500 was the best order size, and because the product is priced at $5.00 per unit, the answer is the same.

The simple EOQ formulation just given does not take into account large volume discounts. We can review Table 9.4 and visualize how discounts would have an impact on total costs. By imputing different values into the table horizontally, volume discounts can be evaluated and marketed to increase future business.

INVENTORY FLOWS

In the previous section we utilize the figures from the EOQ and the safety stock calculations as an analysis tool. We cannot utilize these same calculations to determine inventory policy. We must first take the given information and use it to develop an inventory flow diagram. Assume that the EOQ in this instance has been determined to be 120 units, that the safety stock level is sixty units, that average demand is thirty units per day, and that the replenishment or order cycle is two days. On day one (see Figure 9.2), an EOQ of 120 units arrives.

We will consider a common inventory flow diagram suggested in other texts. Consider the following: total inventory (point A) is 180 units (one EOQ plus sixty units of safety stock). Demand is steady at thirty units per day. On day three, total inventory has declined to 120 units (point B), which is the reorder point, because it takes two days to receive an order and during this time sixty units would be sold. If the inventory policy mandates that safety stock is not to be used under normal circumstances, reordering at 120 units means that sixty units (safety stock) will be on hand two days later when the EOQ arrives. The EOQ of 120 units arrives at point C, and then total inventory increases to 180 units at point D.

If the rate of sales doubles to sixty units per day, the reorder point is hit at 120 units (point E), and an additional EOQ is ordered. However, it will not arrive for two days. A day after the reordering, the regular inventory is exhausted, and at point F the safety stock is starting to be used. At point G, the EOQ arrives just as the safety stock is about to be exhausted. If the EOQ arrived later than day eight, a stock-out would have occurred. The new EOQ boosts the inventory to 120 units, which is also the reorder point. Therefore, at point H another EOQ is ordered. Starting on day eight, the demand settles back to the old average of thirty units per day.

If it appeared that the demand rate of sixty units per day were going to become the average demand rate, the EOQ would need to be recalculated. Recall that a basic input into the EOQ formula is annual sales of the product. If this number changes, then the EOQ must be determined again.

Starting at point H, demand is again thirty units per day. The next EOQ arrives on schedule at point I, and total inventory increases to 180 units at point J. The reorder point is at 120 units, and an EOQ is ordered on day twelve. Demand stays constant, but the transportation mode delivering the EOQ is delayed one day. Instead of arriving on day fourteen, it arrives on day fifteen. Safety stock is entered at point L on day fourteen. A stock-out is again prevented because the EOQ arrives at point M. Note that safety stock protects against two problem areas: increased rate of demand and an increased replenishment cycle.

When an EOQ is used, as illustrated in Figure 9.2, the time between orders varies. The normal time between orders was four days, but when sales doubled the time between orders was only two days. One requirement for the effective utilization of an EOQ is that the level of inventory in the system must be monitored constantly. The ability of RFID to allow for this type of monitoring holds great promise for using EOQ theories more effectively. Then, when the reorder point is hit, an EOQ is ordered. With the advent of computerization, many firms have the capability to constantly monitor their inventory and hence have the option of using an EOQ system. A reorder point for each item can be established in the computer's memory so it can indicate when the stock has been depleted to a point where a new order should be placed. The integration of RFID will allow for middle wear, decision support, and execution systems to transmit the purchase order to the vendor electronically.

A variation of the EOQ method is the fixed-order quantity method, used in repetitive purchases of the same commodity. This method can be initiated with RFID technologies triggering the reorder points. An example would be a materials

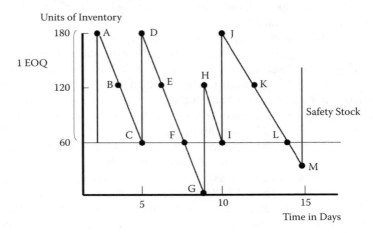

FIGURE 9.2   Inventory flow diagram.

retailer located in China that buys product by the barge load (approximately 1,000 tons per load). The retailer would wait until its product is out of stock before ordering another barge load. RFID would enable this type of activity by triggering the checkout counter POS checkout system to order the next lot of products from the China manufacturer directly. Tying the technical knowledge of the quantity to order with the automatic information capture of RFID will provide tremendous value in the future.

FIXED-ORDER-INTERVAL SYSTEM

An alternative inventory concept that is also commonly used is known as the fixed-order-interval system. In this system EOQs are not used; instead, orders are placed at fixed intervals, such as every three days or twice a month. In the EOQ system, the time interval fluctuates, with the order size remaining the same. In fixed-interval systems, the opposite holds, and order sizes may vary.

Fixed-interval systems are used in many situations. One situation is when the firm does not maintain automatically updated stock levels. Such firms are manually checked to verify the levels of all items and determine which stocks are running low. This task is assigned on a regular basis and may be laborious. Another situation is when vendors offer the firm significant discounts if it will place its orders at certain fixed time intervals. Because the discounts are greater than the advantages of using the EOQ system, the fixed-interval ordering system is utilized. Further, an additional condition is when the firm buys free onboard (FOB) origin and tries to utilize its private trucking fleet whenever possible. If one of the firm's trucks travels empty in one direction without freight, commonly called a deadhead, from a point near a supply source back to the firm's plant on a regular basis, the firm may decide to buy FOB origin and carry supplies in its own truck.

The fixed-order-interval system is commonly used with a safety stock inventory. It usually requires more safety stock than the EOQ system because the EOQ system requires constant monitoring of its inventory levels. In an EOQ system, if sales start to increase, the reorder point will be moved to an earlier time and a new order will be placed. Stock-outs can still take place but only during the restocking cycle after the new order has been placed. With the fixed-order-interval system, the inventory levels are not monitored and a stock-out can occur during both the order cycle and the time before order placement.

Most fixed-order-interval systems do borrow one element from EOQ system. Next to each bin or slot in the warehouse is a bar code, card, or indicator that will allow for determination of the minimum quantity for that product. When the order pickers note that the stocks have been reduced to this level, they notify their supervisor, who decides whether the reorder should occur immediately or on the next scheduled date.

Cyclical buying is a very specialized form of fixed-interval ordering. This practice occurs in the women's fashion industry, in which retailers place their orders directly with the manufacturer for each season's fashions, and there is almost no possibility to reorder. Another example is a grocery retailer's purchase of Halloween pumpkins or Christmas trees.

JUST-IN-TIME INVENTORY SYSTEMS

An inventory system that has received widespread attention is the just-in-time (JIT) system. The concept is related to the fixed-order-interval system, and customers place orders with their suppliers on set schedules that frequently involve daily or hourly deliveries. In comparison to the EOQ system, the concept is based on the assumption that ordering costs are negligible; hence, firms order frequently to minimize inventory holding costs. In JIT systems, inventory is kept at a minimum because the processes create perpetual motion and continuous movement.

In addition to the JIT inventory systems, there are several other, more traditional systems for replenishing inventory stocks. Nearly all inventory systems require some formal stock-level monitoring capability. In practice, today the JIT systems may be incorporated into execution systems that are stand-alone, often termed *best of breed*, within a larger enterprise-wide system. Software applications that create perpetual execution of larger tasks include warehouse management systems (WMS), transportation management systems (TMS), and order management systems (OMS).

RFID AND INVENTORY CONTROL

Some researchers suggest that operational labor can be reduced in distribution operations by as much as 30 percent. A.T. Kearney (2004), a notable supply chain consulting firm, suggests that labor savings of 7.5 percent is possible from reduction inventory cycle counting by using RFID. Distribution inbound receiving along with inventory cycle counting inventory reductions were recognized by Accenture consulting (Lacy 2005). Other researchers have reported savings in stocking and retail checkout operations (Chappel et al. 2002).

Opportunities in which RFID passive implementations can save money in operations in the future include:

- Automatic replenishment from reserve stocking area
- Safety stock reduction
- Automatic picking and stocking routing
- Automatic order generation from current inventory availability

AUTOMATIC REPLENISHMENT

Optimizing replenishments within warehouse or distribution centers (replenish primary picking locations, cross-docking, and kitting operations), within retail operations (replenish shelves from the back room to the retail floor), and within the supply chain (replenish or stock inventory between different nodes in the supply chain) are the practical applications for implementing RFID.

SAFETY STOCK REDUCTION

Researchers have investigated inventory control models and their impact on safety stock. Some research suggests that transactional errors lead to variability in planning and inflate the need for safety stock. Transaction errors create excess inventory due to miscounting of inventory and buffer stock becomes necessary to meet demand

for these error-effected items. The buffer stock for errors and the excess stock maintained due to the bullwhip effect created by inventory timing creates a large amount
of excess inventory (Kök and Shang 2004; Lee et al. 2005).

Commonly, the optimal amount of inventory ordered that was traditionally
derived by the economic order quantity (EOQ) or included a reorder component is
represented by a continuous review (Q, R) system. Oftentimes, to account for the
scheduling and lack of real-time information, an adjusted periodic review system is
used that includes safety stock inventory. Recently, researchers have addressed how
RFID can influence the amount of inventory in these situations (Lee and Özer 2005;
Gauker and Seifer 2006). Consider the following model from Lee et al. (2005):

Here, lead time is defined as placing an emergent order q ($q = \alpha Q$, $\alpha < 1$) ($q = \alpha Q$,
$\alpha < 1$) at any time point b based on RFID real-time information as l and cost to place
the emergent order is $k(l)$.

l is much less than the lead time of the regular order (Q). Additionally, the probability the emergent order will arrive before the regular order to be $p(l)$ if the regular
order is already on its way and an emergent order is released anyway.

Moreover, assume that expected total cost associated with inventory position
IP and RFID reading point b without releasing emergent order is $C_0(IP,b)$ and the
according total cost with emergent order release is $C_1(IP,b)$.

So we can compare the two different costs under periodic review without RFID
implementation and continuous review with given RFID real-time information in
order to decide whether an emergent order should be placed.

$$C_1\big(IP,b\big) = K\big(l\big) + P\big(l\big) * C_0\big(IP,b\big) + \big(1 - P\big(l\big)\big) * C_0\big(IP + q, b\big)$$

Other researchers such Gauker and Seifert (2006) utilize similar continuous
review application models to determine inventory levels in a real-time manner. In
summary, current research models suggest that inventory can be reduced using RFID
technologies due to the fact their real-time data capture abilities allow for common
periodic models to move closer to the theoretical optimal continuous review models.
The largest challenge is moving this theory to practice. In order for this model to
work in practice, a fixed infrastructure of antennas and readers at the operational
level is required, which would in reality cost operations more in process redesign
than the theoretical inventory reduction savings.

PICKING AND ROUTING

Using RFID technology, such as real-time locator systems, the promise of capital-
izing on employee location information and inventory status to optimize employees
order picking and stocking routes is attainable. This use of RFID builds on picking
routes and stocking strategies commonly used in WMS.

An RFID system's ability to provide real-time information will further help
optimize order picking schedules. The opportunities to reduce labor cost in these
activities may be realized and the significance in labor savings may be large. Labor
reduction of 20 percent for picking and stocking labor is commonly mentioned by
users of WMS systems that employ these types of algorithms.

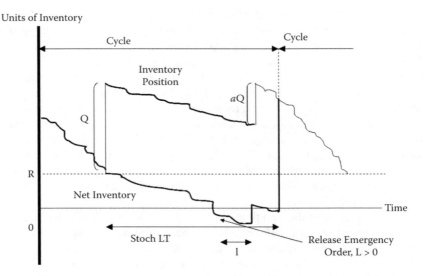

FIGURE 9.3 Lee and Özer's RFID continuous review application model. (From Lee and Özer 2006.)

ORDER BATCHING OF WAVES

Using RFID to group orders, commonly called *waves*, is automatically based on the latest inventory availability. The opportunity to use inventory as it is being received at the dock for immediate shipments can be utilized, dramatically reducing labor for stocking, replenishment, and picking. This theory, commonly called *cross-docking*, requires a considerable amount of receiving labor to be realized. The promise of RFID will truly enable this one of many opportunities to effectively organize, group, and fulfill orders automatically.

Next, the importance of order wave batching is critical in high-speed operations, but inventory inaccuracies can reduce the quality of this batching of orders and reduce their effectiveness. Specifically, in order management modules of WMS or ERP systems, the order bid process within the software schema, orders compete against one another for resources to meet their specific goals, described as the bid process in the negotiation schema. The real-time ability of RFID to provide inventory accuracy and identify secondary location of the inventory immediately can improve the accuracy of the wave batches.

SUMMARY

In summary, the contribution of RFID systems to closed-loop distribution logistics can produce significant contributions in the three areas mentioned above: (1) inventory reduction with respect to safety stock reduction, (2) optimization of order grouping and releases, and (3) labor reduction with respect to picking and stocking labor.

The real benefit of RFID will be based on its ability to provide the inventory accuracy benefits of current technologies such as bar codes and translate the non-line-of-sight benefits into inventory savings. The areas that will be investigated in the future from a closed-loop perspective in distribution operations include the aforementioned areas summarized below:

- Physical and cycle inventory counts
- Inventory replenishment
- Order picking
- Inventory stocking
- Order cross-docking
- Order kitting
- Many other common distribution operations

The realization of these savings will more than likely result as RFID is integration into common execution software such as WMS, LES, and TMS will quantify labor savings. That is RFID captures the data and their software enables the data to execute operational functions.

We previously discussed the benefits of RFID technology as a closed-loop systems framework. Traditional automatic identification systems are closed loop in the fact that they are static and traditionally are used within one tier of the supply chain. Consider a tote bar code or pallet tag that is used within a company's distribution center or between other distribution centers. Rarely is this bar code integrated between other unknown partners or even the customer to evaluate the history of that unit load — as opposed to a system in which information is passed from one intelligent automatic identification technology to another.

Consider each technology acting as an intelligent agent. So if a customer desires to know the history of a product, the UPC transfers information to a bar code, which transfers information to a passive RFID tag, which transfers information to an active RFID tag, which passes information to a global positioning system (GPS). This daisy chain–type of interlinking provides an open-loop concept that provides all potential players in the supply chain effective visibility. This nesting of auto-ID technologies may be an intermediate step to profitability for most intermediate RFID implementations. We next consider a framework that describes this type of technolgy.

REFERENCES

Alford, L. P., and Bangs, J. R. (eds.) (1955). *Producton Handbook*. New York: Ronald Press.

Gauker, G., and R. Seifert. (2006). Item-level RFID in the retail supply chain. *Production and Operations Management*.

Harris, F. W. (1913). How many parts to make at once. *Factory: The Magazine of Management* 10(2):135–136, 152. (1990). Reprinted in *Operation Research* 38(6):947–950.

Hopp, W. J., and M. L. Spearman. (2001). *Factory physics: Foundations of manufacturing management*. 2d ed. New York: Irwin McGraw Hill.

Johnson, J. C., D. F. Wood, D. L. Wardlow, and P. R. Murphy, Jr. (1999). *Contemporary logistics*, 7th ed. Upper Saddle River, N.J.: Prentice Hall.

Kök, A. G., and K. H. Shang. (2004). *Replenishment and inspection policies for systems with inventory record inaccuracy*. Working Paper, Duke University.

Lacy, S. (2005). RFID: Plenty of mixed signals. *BusinessWeek Online*, 31 January [Online]. Available at [Accessed]

Lee, H. L., and Ö. Özer. (2005). *Unlocking the value of RFID. Production and Operations Management*, 16(1), 40–64.

Lee, H. L., and S. Whang. (2005). Higher supply chain security at lower cost: Lessons from total quality management. *International Journal of Production Economics* 96(3):289–300.

ADDITIONAL REFERENCES

Amiri, A. (2006). Designing a distribution network in a supply chain system: Formulation and efficient solution procedure. *European Journal of Operational Research* 171(2):567–576.

AT Kearney. (2004). *RFID/EPC: Managing the transition (2004–2007)*. White Paper, AT Kearney Consulting.

Atali, A., H. L. Lee, and Ö. Özer. (2004). *If the inventory manager knew: Value of RFID under imperfect inventory information*. Working Paper, Stanford University.

Bongaerts, L. (1998). Integration of scheduling and control in holonic manufacturing systems. Ph.D. thesis, Katholieke Universiteit Leuven, Belgium.

Brussel, H. V., J. Wyns, P. Valckernaers, and L. Bongaerts. (1998). Reference architecture for holonic manufacturing systems: PROSA. *Computers in Industry* 37:255–274.

Buckner, M., R. Crutcher, M. R. Moore, and B. Whitus, (2002). Miclog RFID tag program enables total asset visibility. *MILCOM 2002 Proceedings* 2:1422–1426.

Carreau, M. (2004). Space station crew endures food shortage. *Houston Chronicle*, 10 December.

Cavalierei, S., V. Cesarotti, and V. Introna. (2003). A multiagent model for coordinated distribution chain planning. *Journal of Organizational Computing and Electronic Commerce* 13(3–4):267–287.

Cetinkaya, S., F. Mutlu, and C. Y. Lee. (2006). A comparison of outbound dispatch policies for integrated inventory and transportation decisions. *European Journal of Operations Research* 171(3):1094–1112.

Chan, Y. P., and S. F. Baker. (2005). The multiple depot, multiple traveling salesmen facility-location problem: Vehicle range, service frequency, and heuristic implementations. *Mathematical and Computer Modelling* 41(8–9):1035–1053.

Chappell, G., D. G. G. Durdan, L. Ginsberg, J. Smith, and J. Tobolski. (2002). *Auto-ID on delivery: The value of auto-ID technology in retail stores*. MIT Auto-ID Center White Paper, Accenture.

Chopra, S., and P. Meindl. *Supply chain management strategy, planning, and operation*. 2d ed. Upper Saddle River, N.J.: Prentice Hall.

Chu, C. W. (2005). A heuristic algorithm for the truckload and less-than-truckload problem. *European Journal of Operational Research* 165(3):657–667.

Clampitt, H. G., and E. C. Jones. (2006). *RFID certification textbook*. PWD Group.

Elhedhli, S., and J. L. Goffin. (2005). Efficient production-distribution system design. *Management Science* 51(7):1151–1164.

Eskigun, E., R. Uzsoy, P. V. Preckel, and G. Beaujon. (2005). Outbound supply chain network design with mode selection, lead times and capacitated vehicle distribution centers. *European Journal of Operational Research* 165(1):182–206.

Fisher, M. J., M. L. Outwater, D. N. Ahantou, and R. Calix. (2005). Innovative framework for modeling freight transportation in Los Angeles County, California. Freight analysis, evaluation, and modeling. *2005 Thomas B. Deen Distinguished Lecture Transportation Research Record* 1906:105–112.

Fleisch, E., and C. Tellkamp. (2005). Inventory inaccuracy and supply chain performance: A simulation study of a retail supply chain. *International Journal of Production Economics* 95(3):373–385.

Friedman, T. L. (2005). *The world is flat: A brief history of the twenty-first century.* New York: Farrar, Straus & Giroux.

Hau, L. L., and Ö. Özer. (2005). *Unlocking the value of RFID.* White Paper, Stanford University.

Heragu, S. S. (1997). *Facilities design.* Boston: PWS Publishing Company.

Heragu, S. S., R. J. Graves, B. Kim, and A. St. Onge. (2002). Holonic/intelligent agent based framework for manufacturing systems control. *IEEE Trans. on Systems, Man and Cybernetics.*

Iglehart, D. L., and R. C. Morey. (1972). Inventory systems with imperfect asset information. *Management Science* 18(8):B388–B394.

Ingalls, R. G., and D. J. Morrice. (2004). PERT scheduling with resource constraints using qualitative simulation graphs. *Project Management Journal* 35(3):5–14.

Ingalls, R. G., D. J. Morrice, and A. B. Whinston. (2000). The implementation of temporal intervals in qualitative simulation graphs. *ACM Transactions on Modeling and Computer Simulation* 10(3):215–240.

Ingalls, R. G., D. J. Morrice, E. Yücesan, and A. B. Whinston. (2003). Execution conditions: A formalization of event cancellation in simulation graphs. *INFORMS Journal on Computing* 15(3).

Jones, E. (in press). The engineering economics of RFID in specialized manufacturing. *The Engineering Economist.*

Jones, E. C., and G. Anantakrishnan. (2004). A training simulator for radio frequency identification education. *Journal of Engineering Systems Simulators* 1(4):44–51.

Jones, E. C., and S. Bukkaptnam. (2005). RFID: Fundamentals and applications. Paper read at the Centers for Engineering Logistics and Distribution (CELDi) Research Conference, 11 April.

Jones, E. C., and M. Eren. (2006). *Observation the effect of reader polarization on RF tags.* Working Paper.

Kang, Y., and S. B. Gershwin. (2005). Information inaccuracy in inventory systems—Stock loss and stockout. *IIE Transactions* 37(9):843–859.

Kim, B.-I., R. J. Graves, S. S. Heragu, and A. St. Onge. (2002). Intelligent agent based model for a industrial order picking problem. *IIE Transactions* 34(7):601–612.

Klose, A., and A. Drexl. (2005). Lower bounds for the capacitated facility location problem based on column generation. *Management Science* 51(11):1689–1705.

Koo, P. H., W. S. Lee, and D. W. Jang. (2004). Fleet sizing and vehicle routing for container transportation in a static environment. *OR Spectrum* 26(2):193–209.

Kumara, S. R. T., P. Ranjan, A. Surana, and V. Narayanan. (2003). Decision making in logistics: A chaos theory based analysis. *CIRP Annals-Manufacturing Technology* 52(1):381–384.

Landt, J., and B. Catlin. (2001). *Shrouds of time.* Pittsburgh, PA: The Association of Automatic Identification and Data Capture Technologies.

Lapierre, S. D., A. B. Ruiz, and D. W. Jang. (2004). Designing distribution networks: Formulations and solution heuristic. *Transportation Science* 38(2):174–187.

Leary, W. (2004). With food low, space crew must cut back. *New York Times,* 10 December.

Lee, H., B. Peleg, P. Rajwat, S. Sarma, and B. Subirana. (2005). *Assessing the value of RFID technology and the EPC standard for manufacturers.* White Paper, EPCGlobal.

Maturana, F., Shen, W., and Norrie, D. H. (1999). MetaMorph: An adaptive agent-based architecture for intelligent manufacturing. *International Journal of Production Research* 37(10):2159–2173.

Melo, M. T., S. Nickel, and F. Saldanha da Gama. (2006). Dynamic multi-commodity capacitated facility location: A mathematical modeling framework for strategic supply chain planning. *Computers and Operations Research* 33(1):181–208.

Min, H., V. Jayaraman, and R. Srivastava. (1998). Combined location-routing problems: A synthesis and future research directions. *European Journal of Operational Research* 108(1):1–15.

Ottaway, T. A., and J. R. Burns. (2000). An adaptive production control system utilizing agent technology. *International Journal of Production Research* 38(4):721–737.

Parunak, H. V. D. (1991).Characterizing the manufacturing scheduling problem. *Journal of Manufacturing Systems* 10(3):241–259.

Pisello, T. (2004). *The three Rs of RFID: Rewards, risk and ROI* [Online]. Available at Technology-Evaluation.com [Accessed]

Radjoum, N. (2005). IBM delivers innovation—On demand. *Trends* 2.

Rajagopalan, S., S. S. Heragu, and D. Taylor. (2004). A Lagrangian relaxation approach to solving the integrated pick-up/drop-off point selection and AGV flow-path problem. *Applied Mathematical Modeling* 28:735–750.

Ravi, R., and A. Sinha. (2006). Approximation algorithms for problems combining facility location and network design. *Operations Research* 54(1):73–81.

Rykowski, J. (2006). Management of information changes by the use of software agents. *Cybernetics and Systems* 37(2–3):229–259.

Sabri, E. H., and B. M. Beamon. (2000). A multi-objective approach to simultaneous strategic and operational planning in supply chain design. *OMEGA* 28(5):581–598.

Santoso, T., S. Ahmed, M. Goetschalckx, and A. Shapiro. (2005). A stochastic programming approach for supply chain network design under uncertainty. *European Journal of Operational Research* 167(1):96–115.

Sarmiento, A. M., and R. Nagi, (1999). A review of integrated analysis of production-distribution systems. *IIE Transactions* 31(11):1061–1074.

Shen, Z. J. M. (2005). Multi-commodity supply chain design problem. *IIE Transactions* 37(8):753–762.

Shukla, C. S., and Chen, F. F. (1996). The state of the art in intelligent real-time FMS control: A comprehensive survey. *Journal of Intelligent Manufacturing* 7:441–455.

Silwa, C., and B. Brewin. (2004). RFID test Wal-Mart suppliers. *Computer World*, 5 April.

Smith, S. F. (1994). OPIS: a methodology and architecture for reactive scheduling. In *Intelligent scheduling*. Edited by M. Zweben and M. S. Fox. San Francisco: Morgan Kaufmann Publishers.

Sullivan, L., and B. Bacheldor. (2004). RFID reality check. *Information Week*, 5 April.

Syam, S. S. (2002). A model and methodologies for the location problem with logistical components. *Computers & Operations Research* 29(9):1173–1193.

Szelke, E., and R. M. Kerr. (1994). Knowledge-based reactive scheduling. *Production Planning and Control* 5(2):124–145.

Szelke, E., and L. Monostori. (1999). Reactive scheduling in real time production control. In *Modeling manufacturing systems: from aggregate planning to real time control*. Edited by P. Brandimarte and A. Villa. New York: Springer.

Talluri, S., and R. C. Baker. (2002). A multi-phase mathematical programming approach for effective supply chain design. *European Journal of Operational Research* 141(3):544–558.

Tang, J. F., K. L. Yung, and W. Hi. (2004). Heuristics-based integrated decisions for logistics network systems. *Journal of Manufacturing Systems* 23(1):1–13.

Tawegoum, R., E. Castelain, and J. C. Gentina. (1994). Hierarchical and dynamic production control in flexible manufacturing systems. *Robotics and Computer-Integrated Manufacturing* 11(4):327–334.

Teo, C. P., and J. Shu. (2004). Warehouse-retailer network design problem. *Operations Research* 52(3):396–408.

Van den Berg, J. P. (1999). A literature survey on planning and control of warehousing systems. *IIE Transactions* 31:751–762.

Zhao, J., S. T. S. Bukkapatnam, and M. M. Dessouky. (2003). Distributed architecture for real-time coordination of bus holding in transit networks. *IEEE Transactions on Intelligent Transportation Systems* 4(1):43–51.

10 RFID Supply Chain Planning Levels

> In preparing for battle I have always found that plans are useless, but planning is indispensable.
>
> **—Dwight D. Eisenhower, thirty-fourth president**
> **of the United States, 1953–1961 (1890–1969)**

INTRODUCTION

In the following section, we demonstrate the RFID logistics application framework. In Figure 10.1 the squares represent strategic, intermediary, and tactical planning phases. The left side of the diagram demonstrates the research and assessments performed at the different planning stages, which include supply chain network design decisions, transportation policies, and inventory control policies. The decision flow indicates that oftentimes decisions are made using top-down decision policies.

The right side of the diagram represents the validation and applications at these levels, which include facility location optimization decisions, transportation optimization, and inventory management. The information flow indicates that optimization takes place in a bottom-up manner given that actual or real-world data has to be used as opposed to abstract scenarios and at the base level the real information has to flow from operations for executive management to make optimized decisions.

RFID SUPPORTS SUPPLY CHAIN PLANNING AND OPERATIONAL OPTIMIZATION

The problems encountered in the design and operations of complex logistics networks need to be solved at three levels: tactical, intermediary, and strategic. At a strategic level, a company must answer numerous design questions such as:

- How many facilities need to be built or leased
- Where to build or lease them
- The customers served by a facility
- What segments of the transportation network to outsource to third-party logistics (TPL) companies
- What segments to retain in-house
- How many trucks to own, etc.

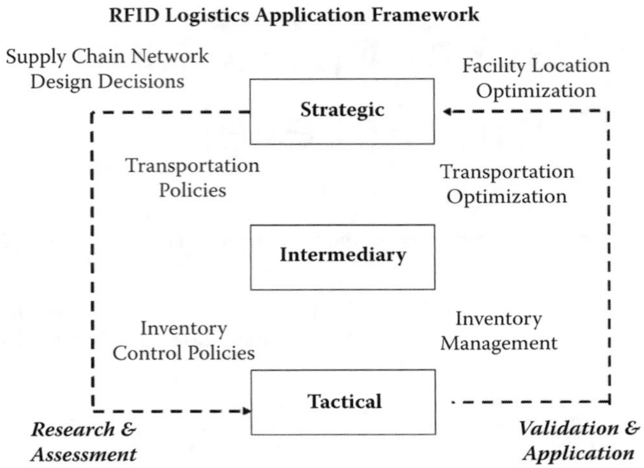

RFID Logistics Application Framework

FIGURE 10.1   RFID logistics application framework.

Because these factors are continuously changing, the company also must determine at an intermediate-term and short-term (tactical) level:

- How many and what transshipment points to operate
- How many trucks to maintain
- Driver staffing requirements, route selection, inventory positions, reorder points, etc.

Different operations may seek to minimize their cost, or maximize their profit, and pass on inefficiencies to the next operation. For example, in our framework, a warehouse manager making a tactical-level decision may seek to minimize receiving labor and create a large queue of inbound trailers (an intermediate-level decision) to wait for unloading. Also, a transportation manager (intermediate) may set trailer load plans that require each trailer to occupy a facility dock door, inevitably creating the need for a larger facility (strategic-level decision). The bullwhip effect on inventory is demonstrated by excess inventory in warehouses (tactical) due to lack of confidence in forecasts given by corporate sales (strategic). We now review the levels in more detail.

TACTICAL LEVEL

At the tactical level, using real-time data provided by RFID systems will mean on-demand availability of the most current information. Most pundits suggest that there will be a major impact on dynamic inventory replenishment for manufacturing and warehousing operations. The use of RFID as a closed-loop passive system has been discussed in earlier chapters. The ability for information to be used in an open system that provides information throughout the different levels provides unique opportunities.

As information captured is integrated into an open system, external and internal disturbances can be evaluated. Internal disturbance are caused by breakdowns in company-managed assets; external disturbance are caused by factors beyond the organization control such as hurricane, major snowstorm, tornado, earthquake, significant disruptions in fuel supply, and so on.

Due to the fact that current information is available on demand, it is possible to develop intelligent agent-based, real-time decision support systems to dynamically realign supply chain planning, such as adjusting the transportation network or opening temporary facilities. We explore tactical-level topics in other chapters, which include inventory basics and warehousing more extensively.

INTERMEDIATE-LEVEL PROBLEMS

Intermediate-level planning is commonly associated with the level of transportation planning. The main effect is for RFID real-time capabilities to reorganize transportation operations. We introduce transportation in the supply chain in the next section to provide background. As we explain the use of RFID for transportation at the intermediate level and facility location planning at the strategic levels, we provide general information about transportation basics and measurement in this section and facility location planning and measurement in the strategic level sections. We provide basic information that is described in most senior-level undergraduate or first year logistics or industrial engineering programs. We provide some high-level summaries from two texts (Chopra and Meindl 2007; Johnson et al. 1998) commonly used in operations management and industrial engineering curriculum.

TRANSPORTATION STRATEGY

RFID technologies have been utilized in transportation as far back as the 1970s. Mostly, active and semi-active technologies have been used in container tracking, trailer weigh stations, and tollbooth plazas. As these technologies continue to develop, the opportunity to reduce transportation costs may allow companies to become more profitable. In most supply chains, transportation is crucial in customer responsiveness and operational efficiency. Faster transportation allows a supply chain to be more responsive but reduces its efficiency. The transportation mode a company uses may affect the inventory management strategies and facility locations in the supply chain. The role of transportation in a company's competitive strategy is determined by the key customers. Customers who demand a high level of responsiveness and are willing to pay for the responsiveness allow a company to use transportation responsively. On the other hand, if key customers are price sensitive, then the company can use transportation techniques such as combining freight (pooling of inventory) to lower the costs. Though this cost reduction may be at the expense of customer responsiveness, it may support the business strategy. Given the necessity to fit the business strategy, companies may use transportation to increase responsiveness or efficiency. Companies seek to maximize productivity and profitability by finding the right balance between the two strategies.

Transportation Decisions

The real-time aspects of RFID may allow for faster, more effective transportation decisions. The transportation network design includes decisions about transportation modes, locations, and routes for shipping, decisions such as whether transportation routes from a manufacturer will be direct to the customer (commonly called direct ship) or the inventory will go through intermediate consolidation points. Design decisions also include whether multiple manufacturing suppliers and customer deliveries will be included on a transportation schedule or not. Also, companies must decide on the set of transportation modes that will be used.

Transportation Mode

The mode of transportation describes how product is moved from one location in the transportation network to another. Companies can choose between air, truck, rail, sea, and pipeline as modes of transport for products. Each mode has different characteristics with respect to the speed, size of shipments (parcels, cases, pallet, full trucks, railcar, and containers), cost of shipping, and flexibility that lead companies to choose one particular mode over the others. Typical measurements for transportation operations include the following metrics:

- Inbound transportation cost is the cost of bringing product into a facility as a percentage of sales or cost of goods sold (COGS). Cost can be measured per unit brought in but is typically included in COGS. It is useful to separate this cost by supplier. Historically, many companies minimized the effects of transportation cost and measured it as a percentage of sales costs.
- Inbound shipment size measures the number of units or dollars in each incoming shipment at a facility. Many operations use peak or median calculations depending on how operations determine manpower planning forecasts.
- Inbound transportation cost per shipment measures the transportation cost of each incoming delivery. Along with the incoming shipment size, the metric identifies opportunities for greater economies of scale in inbound transportation.
- Outbound transportation cost measures the cost of sending product out of a facility to the customer. Cost should be measured per unit shipped, oftentimes measured as a percentage of sales. It is useful to separate this metric by customer.
- Outbound shipment size measures the number of units or dollars on each outbound shipment at a facility.
- Outbound transportation cost per shipment measures the transportation cost of each outgoing delivery.
- Mode utilization measures how often a transportation mode is being utilized. A cost analysis is used to evaluate whether there is a more profitable mode.

Intermediate-Level Summary

In transportation planning, decisions must be made about the trade-off between the cost of transporting a given product in the most cost-effective manner against delivering at the faster pace to meet customer responsiveness. Using fast modes of transportation such as air instead of ground transportation increases responsiveness but has a higher transportation cost. This higher transportation cost supports just-in-time inventory policies that reduce inventory carrying costs. A cost analysis should be performed to determine which strategy provides the largest cost reduction advantage.

STRATEGIC LEVEL

RFID affects strategic-level planning in the form of location of facilities. The impact of RFID technologies is envisioned to create a large reduction of inventory and labor such that the number of facilities can be reduced. Models for dynamically erecting temporary buildings and portable facilities are based on demand shifts. The previous concepts of open-loop nesting of automatic data capture technologies with RFID and effective communication would support these types of operations. From a closed-loop perspective, this idea can be achieved on a smaller scale with the common passive RFID EPC protocols that are being standardized and accepted. The open-loop concept may be achieved in the future with this standardization and adoption of protocols. This type of mobile supply chain is the future using RFID technologies.

We provide a brief overview of facilities planning and consideration next.

FACILITIES STRATEGY

Facilities strategies include the locations to or from which the inventory is transported, including within a facility where inventory can be transformed into another state during manufacturing, stored in warehousing, and selected for customers in order fulfillment operations. External facilities determine how to profitably fulfill customer orders using transportation and effective inventory location.

Strategies such as using economies of scale when a product is manufactured or stored in only one location increase efficiency through centralization. The cost savings may reduce responsiveness, as many of a company's customers may be located far from the production facility. On the other hand, locating facilities close to customers increases the number of facilities needed and consequently reduces efficiency.

FACILITIES DECISIONS

Decisions regarding facilities are discussed next.

Facility Function

Production facilities designs are based on whether they accommodate production operations that are dedicated or a combination of multiple products. Flexible designs can accommodate many types of products but are often less efficient, whereas facilities designed for dedicated products are more efficient. Designs also distinguish whether a facility will support a product focus or a functional focus. A product-focused facility considers functions such as fabrication and assembly when producing a single product.

Warehouses and distribution centers (DC) must design facilities to accommodate a cross-docking or storage strategy. Cross-docking facilities design accommodate inbound trucks from suppliers being unloaded, broken down into smaller lots, and reloaded onto outgoing store-bound trucks. For storage facilities design decisions about reserve storage, primary picking location, and replenishment from reserve storage to primary pick location must be made.

Location

Facility location is commonly a trade-off between whether to centralize in order to gain economies of scale or to decentralize to become more responsive by being closer to the customer. Economic factors including quality of workers, cost of workers, cost of facility, availability of infrastructure, proximity to customers, the location of that firm's other facilities, tax effects, and other strategic factors are important prior to final decisions.

Capacity

Facility capacity determines flexibility and response to wide swings in the demand. Excess capacity will likely be less efficient per unit of product it produces than one with high utilization; however, facilities with excess capacity will have the ability to respond to demand fluctuations. Common metrics include:

- Capacity is the maximum amount a facility can store or process.
- Utilization is the percentage of capacity that is currently being used in the facility.
- Production cycle time is the time required to process a unit if there are no delays at any stage.
- Actual average cycle time is the average actual time taken for all units processed over a specified duration such as a week or a month.
- Cycle time efficiency is the ratio of the theoretical flow time to the actual average flow time.
- Product variety is the number of products processes in a facility.

Top 80/20 analysis is the percentage of total volume processed by a facility that comes from the top 20 percent of SKUs or customers. An 80/20 outcome in which the top 20 percent contribute 80 percent of the volume indicates likely benefits from focusing the facility where separate processes are used to process the top 20 percent and the remaining 80 percent. This is generally referred to as Pareto analysis.

- Process downtime is the percentage of time that the facility was processing units, being set up to process units, unavailable because it was down, or idle because it had no units to process.
- Average production batch size is the average quantity produced in each production batch.
- Production service level is the percentage of production orders completed on time and in full.

RFID BEST PRACTICES FOR SUCCESS

In this chapter we have reviewed many insights and concepts that will allow the logistics, industrial engineer, and operations manager to understand the opportunities and challenges with using RFID technologies. Some of the best practices for implementing systems include:

- Understanding the need for implementation
- Mandates and compliance with customer
- Strategic cost reductions
- Performing a SWOT analysis to review integration into company operations

STRENGTHS, WEAKNESSES, OPPORTUNITIES, AND THREATS

Identify the process and operation that RFID implementation will be most cost-effective. Generally, the higher up the supply chain that it is implemented the more cost-effective it will be, and the greater the complexity of the implementation.

The most cost-effective process is as follows:

1. Create a prototype implementation in the identified operation
2. Test and evaluate the prototype
3. Improve the prototype
4. Retest the prototype
5. Roll out the RFID system to operations

In the next chapter we suggest implementing steps two through five using a design for Six Sigma research approach.

SUMMARY

We describe how RFID supports information in the supply chain by enabling visibility. This visibility enhances supply partners' abilities to optimize inventory, orders, raw materials, and delivery points. Auto-ID technologies such as RFID standardized into a common RFID nomenclature created by standardized technology protocols will provide large supply chain savings.

We introduce a planning structure that provides opportunities at different levels to reduce inventory costs with more effective labor policies, more effective scheduling, and the reduction of expensive assets such as facilities transportation containers. The ability for RFID to provide timely information and visibility into the supply chain is based on three aspects of RFID technologies that include automatic data capture, real-time information, and real-time location status. This information can be used by the industrial engineer to provide successful RFID initiatives.

REFERENCES AND SUGGESTED READINGS

Chopra, S., and P. Meindl. (2007). Supply chain management strategy, planning, and operation. 2d ed. Upper Saddle River, N.J.: Prentice Hall.

Johnson, J. C., D. F. Wood, D. L. Wardlow, and P. R. Murphy, Jr. (1999). *Contemporary logistics*, 7th ed. Upper Saddle River, N.J.: Prentice Hall.

Part 3

RFID Implementation and Management

INTRODUCTION

This part of the book deals with the actual process of implementing an RFID system. The section begins with a discussion of project management to insure that the project is implemented effectively. Next, specific implementation strategies and tactics are discussed. Lastly, we discuss engineering economics issues with respect to RFID implementations.

SECTION CONTENTS

RFID Project Management
Implementing RFID Systems
The Engineering Economics of RFID

11 RFID Project Management

INTRODUCTION

In adopting an RFID system, the temptation to follow the "slap and ship" approach can be overwhelming. While this approach may undoubtedly be successful for a few organizations, most organizations would do better otherwise. The unique aspects of each organization's process really demands additional RFID implementation project planning to help insure success. The implementation of RFID also presents considerations above and beyond the normal project planning process. The fundamental reason behind the additional difficulties is that RFID systems can represent a dramatic change in how the organization functions. In situations like this not only must the implementation be properly planned with respect to the project planning process, but the issue of new technology acceptance must also be addressed.

To put all of these issues in perspective, the RFID implementation project process will be divided into two separate sections. In the first section, we will briefly discuss the general principles of the project management process. In the section, we will provide specific guidance on planning the implementation of an RFID system for a number of different types of scenarios. Readers who are familiar with basic project management issues may wish to advance to the RFID project implementation section.

RFID PROJECT SELECTION

Organizations contemplating implementing RFID projects may be doing so for two basic reasons. The first compelling reason to adopt RFID technology is as a response to a specific mandate. In recent years, both the U.S. Department of Defense and large retailers such as Wal-Mart have mandated the use of RFID technology to enhance their logistical train. In cases such as these, there is but little choice for the organization to implement RFID technology as the mandate requires. However, for other organizations, the choice of implementing RFID technology may begin with the selection of a specific pilot project to gain experience with the technology. Depending on the success and utility of the project, RFID technology may be expanded into other areas. Yet the question remains as to which specific RFID project should be selected for pilot purposes. To help resolve this question, the following section touches briefly on a few project management concepts associated with project selection.

PROJECT SELECTION MODELS AND FACTORS

In order to rationally and consistently select an RFID project, the organization must select what is known as a project selection model. The project selection model is a means by which the organization can rank competing processes for the application of RFID technology. Project selection models generally contain a set of factors. It is through evaluating these individual factors via the model that the organization selects the projects. The choice of factors is unique to the organization but, in general, many organizations utilize factors associated with:

- Production issues
- Financial issues
- Personnel issues
- Marketing issues

The project selection models in which these factors are examined can be broadly classified as either nonnumeric or numeric models. Nonnumeric models, as the name suggests, do not specifically utilize values to determine the ranking of projects. Numeric models, on the other hand, rely exclusively on values for the ranking of projects.

NONNUMERIC PROJECT SELECTION MODELS

Nonnumeric project selection models are generally older and simpler than numeric project selection models. However, this is not meant to imply that nonnumeric models are not necessarily useful. They should, however, be closely scrutinized to determine whether or not their use is appropriate or desired. Common nonnumeric project selection models include:

- The sacred cow
- Operating necessity
- Competive necessity
- Comparative models

The Sacred Cow

The basis for the sacred cow is that some high-level management individual has decided that it is appropriate for the organization to apply RFID technology to a particular process. Sacred cow projects are difficult to deal with since challenging ill-thought-out, unsuccessful projects may be difficult. Often the only way to terminate a sacred cow implementation is when the champion either leaves the organization or the champion's interest turns to other application areas.

Operating Necessity

The operating necessity model is based on the fact that the organization might have to adopt an RFID project in order to keep the organization functioning on a daily basis. This might occur in the case of internal tracking of manufactured assemblies.

In order to prevent products from being assembled incorrectly, the organization may select one RFID project over another.

Competitive Necessity

The competitive necessity model is the nonnumeric project selection model that is most likely to be encountered in RFID applications. In fact, this type of model is not all that dissimilar to that associated with mandates. In other words, in order to continue to be competitive in a certain marketplace, the organization selects RFID projects according to what will allow it to survive. This means that an end-user retail-based RFID application might take precedence over an internal manufacturing RFID project.

Comparative Models

Comparative project selection models are typically used to compare RFID projects that do not have directly comparable project selection factors. For example, one RFID project may have great significance to the production process. Another RFID project may be needed to properly fulfill outgoing orders. In order to select among these types of projects, an organization may appoint an evaluating committee. The responsibility of the committee is to progressively break down the various projects with respect to importance of the organization. The top-level screen may lump projects into not important, somewhat important, and very important. Each category is then looked into in greater detail and is subsequently rescreened into additional categories. Eventually, only a very few projects are accepted as sufficiently important to be implemented.

NUMERIC PROJECT SELECTION MODELS

In comparison to nonnumeric models, numeric project selection models are new and more complicated. Numeric models can be broadly classified as those that rely on profit-based data and those that require some sort of scoring mechanism. Simple profit-based models include:

- Payback time
- Average rate of return

Note that because RFID projects do not necessarily make money, but save money, the following descriptions have been modified to make the general models more applicable to RFID projects.

Payback Time

Payback time selection models are based on the amount of time the project takes to recover the amount of capital invested in the project. The measure of performance is in years. This value is obtained simply by dividing the capital invested by the amount of money that the project is expected to save on an annual basis. The determination of the amount of investment is relatively straightforward. Similarly, the organization can determine the amount of money saved by examining savings in labor costs and error resolution. The equation for determining the payback time is

$$\text{Payback} = \frac{\text{Initial investment}}{\text{Savings}}$$

This means for an RFID project that initially costs \$100,000, the payback period will be four years if on the average a savings of \$25,000 will be realized each year.

$$4 \text{ year payback} = \frac{\$100,000 \text{ initial investment}}{\$25,000 \text{ annual savings}}$$

With this model, the payback period or time is in the same units as the savings. For example, if the savings are projected on an annual basis, the payback time will be in years. Organizations will generally gravitate toward the selection of projects that have relatively short payback periods. Thus, projects that can be completed that have relatively low initial investments or high savings will normally be selected.

Average Rate of Return

The average rate of return model is used to determine which models yield the best investment. Sometimes the average rate of return is compared to how much the organization may yield in comparison to investing the project funds outside of the organization. Generally speaking, those projects with the greatest average rate of return will be selected for implementation. The equation of the average rate of return (ARR) is

$$\text{ARR} = \frac{\text{Average savings}}{\text{Initial investment}}$$

In this case, our \$100,000 RFID project would yield a 25 percent average rate of return:

$$25\% \text{ ARR} = \frac{\$25,000 \text{ Average savings}}{\$100,000 \text{ Initial investment}}$$

A distinct disadvantage of both the payback and average rate of return models, as well as many other financial models, is their inability to incorporate nonnumeric project selection considerations. Thus, these models could potentially only favor projects that look good on paper. No consideration is included to take into account issues such as competitive necessity.

To help address this lack of flexibility, numeric project selection models based on scoring methods were developed. As previously discussed, these models require the identification of scoring factors. These can include both nonnumeric and numeric scoring factors. In the RFID context, scoring factors could include, but are not limited to, issues such as the difficulty of the implementation, labor savings and error reduction as a result of the implementation, and the probability of successful implementation. Common scoring models include:

- Unweighted 0–1
- Unweighted scoring
- Weighted scoring
- Constrained weighted scoring

Unweighted 0–1

In the unweighted 0–1 scoring model, each candidate RFID application is scored as a 0 or 1 for each factor that is to be considered. The total score for all of the factors is then totaled and compared against all other RFID application candidates. Mathematically, the model appears as:

$$\text{Project score} = \sum_{i=1}^{n} \text{Factor value}_i$$

Where:

i = to n factors used to evaluate the project

Factor value = 0 or 1 for each factor i

Note that this model has the distinct disadvantage of being only able to assign a 0 or a 1 to each factor. This model also suffers from the limitation that every factor is considered as of equal importance. In reality, some factors may be more important for the organization than others. Due to these limitations, this model is not normally recommended for use.

Unweighted Scoring

To overcome the 0–1 limitation of the unweighted 0–1 model, the scoring model may be utilized. This model replaces the 0–1 value with a value on some scale between 0 and a top value. Typically, the scale will be between 0 and 5, 0 and 7, or 0 and 10. The summed value of the score will indicate how well the project candidate fulfills the project selection factor. This is mathematically represented in the following equation.

$$\text{Project score} = \sum_{i=1}^{n} \text{Factor score}_i$$

Where:

i = 1 to n factors used to evaluate the project

Factor score = 0 to x for each factor i

This scoring model overcomes the 0–1 limitation, but it still considers each factor as of equal importance. To overcome this limitation we have the weighted scoring model.

Weighted Scoring
The weighted scoring model includes both the ability to numerically score project selection factors as well as consider that the project selection factors may be of different levels of importance. To incorporate this consideration, the weighted scoring model includes a factor weighting component. Normally, this component will be assigned a value between 0 and 1. It is multiplied by the project selection factor score and summed. This is illustrated in the following equation.

$$\text{Project score} = \sum_{i=1}^{n} \text{Factor weight}_i \times \text{Factor score}_i$$

Where:
  $i = 1$ to n factors used to evaluate the project
  Factor weight = 0 to 1 for each factor i
  Factor score = 0 to x for each factor i

While the weighted scoring model is a great improvement over the previous numeric scoring models, it does still suffer from one limitation. In some cases, it must be necessary for a given project to receive a minimum score on a particular project selection factor. If the project scores below the minimum value, some mechanism must be incorporated to insure that the final project score is less competitive than projects that are otherwise completely qualified.

Constrained Weighted Scoring
The constrained weighted scoring model can be incorporated in two different manners. In the first implementation, only the specific factor for the project is given a 0 value if the factor score is below the limit and a 1 if it is above the limit. This is represented in the following manner:

$$\text{Project score} = \sum_{i=1}^{n} \text{Factor weight}_i \times \text{Factor score}_i \times \text{Factor constraint}_i$$

Where:
  $i = 1$ to n factors used to evaluate the project
  Factor weight = 0 to 1 for each factor i
  Factor score = 0 to x for each factor i
  Factor constraint = 0 or 1 for each factor i

This implementation will normally yield a non-zero score even if the project is unacceptable in one or more factors. However, it is likely that the final score is significantly lower than other projects that do not have any unacceptable factor scores.

Another method of incorporating constraint into the above project selection model is to score any model that has any unsatisfactory factor scores as a complete

0. This would effectively eliminate any projects that are unsatisfactory in any manner. Mathematically, this could be represented as:

$$\text{Project score} = \text{Factor constraint} \times \sum_{i=1}^{n} \text{Factor weight}_i \times \text{Factor score}_i$$

Where:
   $i = 1$ to n factors used to evaluate the project
   Factor weight = 0 to 1 for each factor i
   Factor score = 0 to x for each factor i
   Factor constraint = 0 if any factor i score is unacceptable, otherwise 1

The constrained weighted scoring model represents the most sophisticated of the reasonably easily implemented numeric project selection models. It has the advantage of being able to incorporate both subjective factors such as competitive necessity as well as financial performance such as payback time and rate of return.

RFID PROJECT PARAMETERS

Provided that the organization has decided to properly proceed with the RFID project, a comprehensive project management plan must be developed. An RFID project plan will enable the project manager to properly manage the project with respect to time, cost, and technical performance. The time parameter refers to the schedule allocated to the RFID implementation project. The cost parameter is the budget associated with the project. Lastly, the technical performance refers to the ability of the project to meet the required needs.

The three project parameters are frequently depicted as a triangle, with each parameter being represented by one side. The significance of modeling the project as a triangle is that any two of the three legs or parameters can seriously impact the outcome of the third. For example, if the project falls behind schedule and the same level of technical performance is required, in order to finish on schedule, the budget must be increased. Similarly, if the project needs to be completed before the scheduled finish and the same level of technical performance is required, the budget must also be increased. In both of these cases, if the budget is not increased, and the schedule must be maintained or finished early, the technical performance of the system must be compromised. This is a particularly dangerous situation, since the failure to achieve the proper level of technical performance may seriously compromise the original purpose of the project.

The same effect is realized with respect to the budget. If the budget for the project is reduced, the technical performance may have to be sacrificed. Alternatively, fewer resources could be assigned to the project, resulting in a longer completion time.

As a final comment on the project parameter triangle, the effects of the technical performance leg can be considered. If the technical specifications of the system are constantly beng revised through engineering change orders, either the completion time or the budget must be increased. In such situations, sometimes both the time and the cost of the project are increased.

RFID IMPLEMENTATION LIFE CYCLE

Many projects such as RFID implementation projects follow a general project life cycle. In the case of technological implementations such as RFID systems, the cycle follows four phases. These include conceptual, planning, installation, and startup phases. These phases are illustrated in Figure 11.1.

CONCEPTUAL PHASE

In the conceptual phase, the organization is determining the basic objectives of the implementation project. This includes specifying what benefits the organization hopes to achieve by successfully executing the project.

PLANNING PHASE

In the planning phase, the project manager is creating an outline for implementing the project. This includes as a minimum developing a work breakdown structure (WBS), a linear responsibility chart (LRC), and a Gantt chart. The work breakdown structure is a division of project tasks into increasingly detailed activities called *work packages*. The linear responsibility chart specifies who participates and to what degree for each work package. Lastly, the Gantt chart details the length and relationships between each work package. Each of these planning tools will be discussed in further detail.

INSTALLATION PHASE

In the installation phase, the organization begins by identifying and acquiring all of the hardware and software necessary to implement the RFID project. The installation phase continues by physically positioning all of the hardware and software in place.

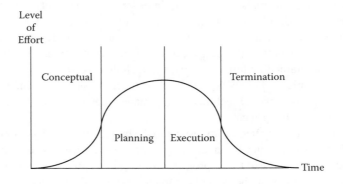

FIGURE 11.1   RFID project life cycle.

Startup Phase

In the startup phase, the organization is going through the process of testing and debugging the installed hardware and software. The startup phase is completed when the hardware and software are functioning properly. At this point, the project manager completely turns the project over to operational personnel.

RFID PROJECT MANAGER

The concept of the project manager cannot be discounted. As the primary individual responsible for the project, the project manager is largely responsible for the success or failure of the RFID implementation project. The success or failure of the project may depend on the cooperation of a variety of resources that the project manager may not necessarily have direct authority over.

RFID Project Manager Authority

Authority is defined as the power to command others to act or not to act. With respect to project management, there are two different types of authority. The first type is de jure authority. This type of authority is that awarded by some official organizational document. De jure authority gives the RFID project manager the legal power to acquire and utilize organizational resources. This type of authority would typically be held by an engineering or production manager.

The second type of authority is de facto authority. This type of authority is based on an individual's personal knowledge or skills related to a particular task. De facto authority depends on other individuals to comply out of respect for the individual's unique knowledge or skills. This type of authority is typically the kind of authority held by some sort of analyst or engineer.

The RFID project manager may have either de jure, de facto, or both types of authority. However, the most likely scenario is that the project manager is not specifically a manager but an engineer who must undertake the RFID implementation project. In this case, as an engineer without specific de jure authority, the engineer must take particular care in project management, as he will not have the power to command others to act or not to act. In other words, the engineer is more likely to have to use his de facto authority and interpersonal skills to gain the cooperation of the different individuals involved at different levels and phases of the RFID implementation project.

RFID Project Manager Functions

The project manager has five basic functions. These include planning, organizing, motivating, directing, and controlling.

Planning

This RFID project manager function is primarily performed during the planning phase of the implementation. As previously discussed, it involves creating an outline for implementing the project. This includes the work breakdown structure and the Gantt chart.

Organizing

Organizing involves the identification and acquisition of project resources. It most specifically includes identifying and arranging for the personnel that will be involved in the system design, specification, installation, and startup processes. The organizing function also includes the development of the linear responsibility chart.

Motivating

The project manager motivating function involves providing the environment necessary to obtain the desired performance from the project team members. Classical motivation theory includes work by Maslow and Herzberg.

Maslow's Theory

According to Maslow's theory, people are motivated by a tendency to fulfill unfulfilled needs according to a hierarchical list. At the bottom of the list are basic physiological needs. These are followed by safety and security. In the modern world, this is analogous to receiving adequate pay and benefits. Next is relatedness and belongingness with respect to coworkers. Fourth is the need for esteem. This includes self-esteem and esteem from others. Last is what is known as self-actualization. This means that the individual is primarily motivated by a need to fulfill themselves by maximizing their potential with respect to individual performance.

The way that this theory works is that individuals start at the lowest level. They progress to the next level in terms of need importance only when the current level has been satisfied. Upper levels beyond the current level hold no motivating value to the individual. For example, if an individual is mired in the safety and security level because his pay is inadequate, offering rewards that generate higher levels of self-esteem are not motivating. Similarly, if the individual is receiving adequate pay but cannot relate to his coworkers, offering the opportunity to reach his intellectual potential would not have a motivating effect.

What this theory means to the RFID project manager is that he will have to identify what level of the hierarchy each individual on the project team is on. By offering or arranging for rewards or opportunity at that level, the project manager can best motivate his team members.

Herzberg's Theory

Herzberg's theory involves classifying motivating factors into intrinsic and extrinsic motivators. Intrinsic motivators are more internal to the specific job. Examples of intrinsic motivators are

- Work deemed as important
- Sense of accomplishment
- Responsibility
- Recognition

Extrinsic motivators are external to the job itself. They are more related to the context in which the job is performed. These include:

- Pay
- Benefits
- Working conditions

The significance of this motivation theory is that the extrinsic factors relate to the level of job dissatisfaction, whereas the intrinsic factors relate to the level of job satisfaction. The absence of extrinsic factors produces a worker with high job dissatisfaction, but their presence only results in low job dissatisfaction. However, the presence of intrinsic factors results in a worker with high satisfaction. The absence of intrinsic rewards results in low job satisfaction. In order to have a highly motivated team member, it is necessary to have the presence of both extrinsic and intrinsic factors. However, even if strong intrinsic factors are present, you can still have a highly dissatisfied team member. With this theory, the RFID project manager must make an effort to insure the presence of both extrinsic and intrinsic factors in order to obtain maximum satisfaction and, hopefully, performance from his team members.

Directing

The directing function involves proving leadership to the RFID project implementation team. Leadership is frequently defined as an individual's ability to influence the behavior of others to achieve a specific objective. Directing is a particularly important project manager function because the RFID project manager will not necessarily have de jure authority over the RFID project team members. Many texts have been written on both general leadership and leadership associated with high-technology projects. For the purposes of this book, we will review only a few leadership theories.

Situational Leadership Theory
Situational leadership theory is founded on the concept that the project manager's leadership style should be based on the personnel situation surrounding the project. More specifically, the project personnel are evaluated with respect to ability and willingness.

With the first parameter, the personnel are categorized as being either able or unable. Able personnel have both the necessary intelligence and training to perform their responsibilities. Unable personnel are either missing the necessary intelligence or training or perhaps both. With an RFID project, we would have to assume that all of the engineers on the project have sufficient native intelligence to contribute to the project. However, as the RFID technology may be new to the engineers, they might not have had the necessary training.

Similarly with the second parameter, the personnel are categorized as being either willing or unwilling. Willing personnel are motivated to perform their responsibilities. Unwilling personnel are obviously not interested in completing their job duties. Obviously, the RFID project manager would prefer to have mostly willing project team members. However, part of the inherent project management process is the possible assignment of not necessarily willing team members. In some cases, the team members may have been taken from projects in which they had more interest. In other cases, the team members may not be familiar with RFID technology and therefore less interested in an RFID implementation.

The two personnel parameters result in a total of four different possible combinations of project personnel. These are:

- Able and willing
- Able but unwilling
- Unable but willing
- Unable and unwilling

Most project managers would naturally hope to obtain the able and willing team members. This would present the easiest but most unlikely of any of the four situations. In the able but unwilling personnel, the duty of the project manager is to find ways to motivate the project team members. In the unable but willing personnel situation, the project manager must seek ways of bringing the team members up to the necessary technical standards. If the team members have the intellectual and physical capacity, then just the necessary training is required. However, it is possible that team members simply do not have the ability to perform the job no matter how motivated that they are. In the unfortunate unable and unwilling personnel situation, the project manager is in serious trouble. In this case, there is a significant possibility of project failure.

Depending on the individual combination of parameters, the most successful project manager will adapt his leadership style.

- Able and willing; use delegating style
- Able but unwilling; use participating style
- Unable but willing; use selling style
- Unable and unwilling; use telling style

With the delegating style, the team members are able and willing. This means that the RFID project manager can take more of a coaching and assisting role with the project. With the participating style, the team members are able but unwilling. For this situation, the RFID project manager must encourage the sharing of ideas and authority. This will create an atmosphere of ownership, which will help the team members buy into the project. The selling style is used when the team members are unable but willing. In this case, the RFID project manager must explain in more detail what must be done, since the team members do not have the necessary knowledge in order to perform their responsibilities. Lastly, with the telling style, the team members will be unable and unwilling. As with the selling style, with the telling style, the RFID project manager must explicitly direct the team members to do specific tasks. Since the workers are also unwilling, the RFID project manager must also expend significant effort in following up with respect to project progress and completion.

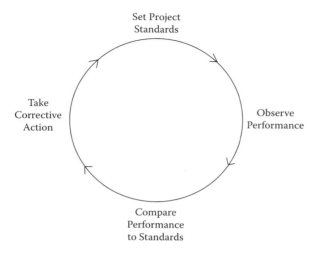

FIGURE 11.2   RFID project control cycle.

Controlling

The control function is essential to the successful completion of the project. This function involves the establishment of specific performance standards, the observation of performance, comparing the observed performance to performance standards, and taking corrective action. This process is then repeated as necessary for each significant work package. The control function is most often illustrated as a control cycle as shown in Figure 11.2.

DEVELOPING THE PROJECT PLAN

The project planning process at a minimum consists of developing a work breakdown structure (WBS), a linear responsibility chart (LRC), and a Gantt chart.

WORK BREAKDOWN STRUCTURE

A work breakdown structure (WBS) is a successively lower division of project tasks into subtasks. On the first or topmost level, the WBS might consist of only a few of the steps outlined in this book. How many lower levels to use in the project plan is at the discretion of the project manager. However, for the WBS to be meaningful, it is likely to require at least two levels. Table 11.1 illustrates a basic two-level WBS for an RFID project.

If a third level were utilized, it would be annotated with a second digit. For example a particular type of equipment specification might be represented by the number 4.1.1, Identify RFID tags. Another type of equipment specification would be represented by 4.1.2, Identify RFID reader.

TABLE 11.1
Work Breakdown Structure

WBS	Activity
Problem formulation	
Orientation	
Problem statement	
Objectives	
Project planning	
Work breakdown structure	
Linear responsibility chart	
Gantt chart	
System definition	
Identify RFID components requirements	
Identify layout of RFID system	
Equipment specification	
Identify specific equipment that meets system needs	
Acquire identified equipment	
Pilot implementation	
Installation of pilot system	
Testing and debugging	
Full-scale implementation	
Installation of full system	
Testing and debugging	
Operator training	

The level of planning in some projects is so detailed that the division of tasks into subtasks continues until the point at which a single work package is reached. A work package is a discrete unit of work for which authority and responsibility can be assigned.

LINEAR RESPONSIBILITY CHART

Most business entities utilize an organizational chart to some extent. Even though a trendy organization may deny the existence of such a chart, there will still be some sort of organizational framework in place. These charts will depict a hierarchical relationship between different organizational divisions and personnel. While these types of charts may be of some value, an RFID project is in need of a type of chart that illustrates the relationship between an activity on the WBS and the different individuals involved in the project.

This type of chart is commonly known as a linear responsibility chart (LRC). The LRC shows who participates in each activity and to what degree. For example, there may be a number of individuals involved in collecting data, but only one individual holds primary responsibility for completing the activity. The LRC can be superimposed on the existing WBS as an *x* axis going horizontally across the chart. Across the top, each individual's name or title is listed. There is an intersection between the vertical WBS tasks and the horizontal project personnel designations. At each of these intersections, the project manager can place a code corresponding to the individuals' level of participation. Although the RFID implementation project manager may choose any codes, the following codes are commonly employed.

P = Primary Responsibility
S = Secondary Responsibility
W = Worker
A = Approval
R = Review

Primary responsibility means that the individual has the primary authority and responsibility for completing that work package. Secondary responsibility is assigned as a backup to the individual with primary responsibility. If utilized in the chart, W means that the individual is to assist the primary responsibility individual with completing the task. Approval involves going over the end results of the task and providing feedback to the primary responsibility individual. Review, if utilized, may involve that individual reviewing the results for possible effects on other ongoing activities. Not all tasks are so complex that both a primary and secondary responsibility individual are required. In addition, if an individual is not involved in a particular task at all, that intersection is simply left blank.

Table 11.2 illustrates the use of a LRC with the previously existing WBS. Note how, in this case, the engineering manager wants to approve everything. Engineer 1 is mostly responsible for planning and control issues. Engineer 2 is good at installing hardware. Engineer 3 must be junior to engineers 1 and 2 as well as a skilled trainer.

GANTT CHART

A Gantt chart illustrates the duration and relationship between different project activities. The duration of individual tasks is represented by horizontal bars. The relationships between activities are illustrated by connecting lines with arrows between the dependent activities. With an RFID project, the Gantt chart can be appended to the right of the LRC or interchanged with the LRC if presentation space is at a premium. This enables the RFID project manager to identify the task, individuals involved, duration, and task relationships at a glance.

Project tasks may have what are known as relationships. These are connections between the tasks that dictate what sequences must be observed between a preceding task and a succeeding task. Common relationships include:

- Finish to start
- Start to start
- Finish to finish

TABLE 11.2

Linear Responsibility Chart

WBS	Activity	Eng. Mgr.	Eng. 1	Eng. 2	Eng. 3
Problem formulation					
Orientation					
Problem statement					
Objectives					
Project planning					
Work breakdown structure					
Linear responsibility chart					
Gantt chart					
System definition					
Identify RFID components requirements					
Identify layout of RFID system					
Equipment specification					
Identify specific equipment that meets system needs					
Acquire identified equipment					
Pilot implementation					
Installation of pilot system					
Testing and debugging					
Full-scale implementation					
Installation of full system					
Testing and debugging					
Operator training					

Finish to Start Relationship

The most common relationship is the finish to start relationship. In the finish to start relationship, it is necessary for the preceding task to finish before the succeeding task may start. This type of relationship occurs in an RFID project when attempting to test the system. For example, in order to perform a startup test of the system, it is necessary to first install both the hardware and the software.

Under most circumstances, the only way to reduce the overall time for a finish to start predecessor and a successor is to reduce the individual time of either the predecessor or successor or both. If the tasks could be performed in parallel, then the relationship would not be finish to start in the first place. A finish to start relationship is represented by an arrow that leaves the rightmost part of the predecessor and enters the leftmost part of the successor.

Start to Start Relationship

Less common than the finish to start relationship is the start to start relationship. The start to start relationship means that the predecessor and the successor must start at the same time. This sort of situation may occur when a single previous process splits into two different tasks that must be worked on simultaneously. In an RFID project, this type of relationship can appear when the RFID hardware components are identified. The RFID tags, readers, and antennas can be ordered simultaneously. It will often be desirable to begin working on a number of tasks as soon as possible, but it is not absolutely necessary to have any start to start relationships. The start to start relationship is represented by two or more arrows feeding into the leading edge of the Gantt chart task bars.

Finish to Finish Relationship

A finish to finish relationship between a predecessor and a successor is found when both tasks are desired to be completed at the same time. This means that if the tasks are of different duration, then the longer duration task must be started before the shorter duration task. The finish to finish relationship is most often found in situations where there is some sort of limited life associated with different processes that must be combined in a following task at the same time. This situation is not necessarily going to exist in an RFID project. The finish to finish relationship is represented by two arrows exiting the Gantt chart task bars.

LAGS

A possible variation to the above relationships is the concept of a lag. A lag is a required time period between the predecessor and the successor. For example, it may be desirable to begin testing the functioning of RFID tags as soon as possible after acquiring the tags. In order to begin the testing, it is necessary to actually have the tags to test. However, all of the tags may not necessarily be available for testing at the same time due to shipment issues. In this situation, the project manager may decide that it is more important to wait for all of the tags to arrive before beginning testing. Thus, for project planning purposes there could be a small lag between these two tasks. Similarly, it would be expected that the tag testing processes would finish somewhat behind the tag acquisition process.

COMPRESSING AND CRASHING PROJECTS

A natural question both during the planning phase and also during the project execution is "How can the project be compressed?" This question can arise as a result of a requirement to move on to another phase in the overall project or when the project begins to slip behind schedule. An extreme case of compression is known as *crashing* the projects. This is an analysis of how quickly the project can be completed without respect to cost. In other words, crashing the project optimizes the time parameter of the project at the expense of resource utilization.

Crashing projects is only effective if the activities that are crashed are on what is known as the critical path. The critical path is the link of activities that represents the minimum amount of time that the project can be completed. This means that if the project manager crashes activities not on the critical path, only the length of that activity will be shortened, not the length of the overall project.

Whether the project manager is simply interested in compressing the project time or crashing the project, the approach is similar. The general objective is to attempt to sequence as many tasks as possible at the same time or in parallel with each other. Since a number of tasks in the RFID project process are in whole or in part independent of each other, it is possible to perform significant project compression without affecting the quality of the project. On the other hand, some RFID project tasks simply cannot be significantly compressed because it is necessary to have the predecessor complete before the successor can begin.

As a final warning with respect to crashing RFID projects, the project manager must ensure that the significant increase in effort and expense does not go to waste. When critical activities are crashed, other activities become critical. This means that in order to continue compressing or crashing the project, the project manager must be aware of the entire picture, not just the single activity that he wishes to shorten.

Typical RFID project tasks that can be compressed are

- Acquisition of hardware and software
- Testing of RFID tags
- Installation of hardware and software

Compressing the Acquisition of Hardware and Software

RFID hardware and software are not yet in the commodity stage. This means that the acquisition of RFID hardware and software may require the project manager to obtain tags or other components from either the manufacturer or a distributor. As can be imagined, the supply chain for these RFID items themselves may be in need of attention. Significant project time may be hidden in the delivery times of RFID hardware and software. By being willing to incur significantly higher shipment costs, the RFID project manager may compress or crash the time associated with the acquisition of hardware and software. One of the few advantages of compressing the RFID project from this perspective is that there are no additional internal resource costs to expediting the shipment of hardware and software.

Compressing the Testing of RFID Tags

The testing of RFID tags is perhaps the most easily compressed or crashed task that the RFID project manager will encounter. Here it is a simple matter of devoting the necessary resources to assist the original technicians and engineers. Unlike the more complicated processes of installing RFID hardware and software described next, fewer resource problems are likely to arise. Compressing the testing of tags is also beneficial for the entire project because the need for additional or different tags will be identified earlier.

Compressing the Installation of Hardware and Software

Compressing the installation of hardware and software will necessitate an increase in either internal or external resources. Since these processes will take a fixed number of man-hours, the RFID project manager can either allocate additional internal technical and engineering support or acquire additional outside resources. While this approach may seem initially attractive to the RFID project manager, the concept of the "mythical man month" must be considered. This concept revolves around the phenomenon that adding a particular percentage of additional workers does not necessarily translate into that much more productivity. The reason behind this is that a significant amount of the original workforce may be needed to bring the new team members up to speed and the new team members themselves may not necessarily have the required training to become immediately productive.

RFID Project Tasks that Cannot or Should Not Be Compressed

An RFID implementation project task should never be compressed or crashed when there is a significant possibility that it or a related task would compromise the technical performance of the project. Typical RFID project tasks that should not be compressed are

- Hardware and software selection
- Pilot testing

Hardware and Software Selection

The RFID project manager should avoid compressing the hardware and software selection process. This is primarily due to the fact that the success or failure of the project may ride on correct decisions with respect to the specifications and suitability of the hardware and software. Making bad decisions at this point could easily result in problems that are not identifiable until much further into the project. At that point, it may be impossible to take corrective action and still successfully complete the project with respect to time, cost, and technical performance. A typical example would be deciding to acquire a system that is not capable of functioning properly with a specific type of product due to radio frequency transmission issues. By the time this is realized in a pilot implementation, the project manager has already configured the pilot system. Thus, a bad decision made during the hardware and software selection process could easily send the project back to the beginning.

Avoid Compressing Pilot Testing

The RFID project manager may decide that it would be beneficial to conduct a pilot test implementation prior to wide operational deployment. If this is the case, the RFID project manager should attempt to avoid compressing or crashing the pilot implementation. The original purpose of the pilot implementation is likely to learn from equipment acquisition, installation, and startup mistakes prior to full implementation. If sufficient time is not allowed to permit this process to be performed, the full-scale implementation may be put in danger. This would essentially be the same as not having a pilot implementation to begin with. There are probably few cases in recorded history where a full-scale implementation was more rapidly and effectively debugged than a smaller pilot implementation.

12 Implementing RFID Systems

> Words without actions are the assassins of idealism.
>
> **—Herbert Hoover, U.S. mining engineer and politician (1874–1964)**

INTRODUCTION

The above quote describes what most people like to do with RFID; that is, theorize about the benefits. Taking action and implementing a system is considered risky and oftentimes very difficult. We hope to provide some strategies in this chapter that will assist in implementing RFID.

In this chapter we discuss

- How RFID needs to be tested in prototype environment
- Introduction of Design for Six Sigma Research (DFSSR) for RFID testing
- How to execute DFSSR to test and evaluate prototypes
- Other methods for testing RFID environments

Recommended steps for a proactive implementation of RFID systems include:

- Make the ROI case for RFID
- Choose the right RFID technology
- Anticipate RFID technical problems
- Manage the Information Technology (IT) infrastructure issues
- Data management concerns
- Integration with back-end applications
- Leverage pilot project learning experiences

MAKE THE ROI CASE FOR RFID

This first step appears to be a logical step for implementing any technology, including RFID. The return-on-investment (ROI) analysis is commonly utilized to justify capital investments in such costly systems. Due to the fact that mandates are driving suppliers to use passive RFID technologies, many cost justifications are not performed prior to implementation. The mandates have made RFID implementation into a cost of doing business as opposed to simply a justified business expense. At a minimum, cost justifications should be made to evaluate the lost value of implementing an RFID solution or when the investment may eventually pay for itself.

CHOOSE THE RIGHT RFID TECHNOLOGY

Radio frequency identification (RFID) has been put into practice within industry for a number of years. To better assess its potential applications and implementation, this paper presents an approach called Design for Six Sigma (DFSS). DFSS has many applications, including creating real-world warehouse testing environments, measuring and analyzing the implementation of RFID technology, and developing and optimizing the conditions for the most efficient readability. Finally, DFSS can be used to validate RFID technological principles and draw conclusions under this real circumstance.

RFID has been called the bar code of the next generation. It is currently in use with applications ranging from libraries to tollbooth e-passes. The greatest advantage in RFID systems, which are composed of an interrogator (reader) and transponders (tags), is that they do not require a line-of-sight between the reader and the tags. Currently, thousands of items are tracked by manually updated databases or line-of-sight bar code scans that scan one item at a time. With an RFID system in place, entire bags of items affixed with RFID tags can be audited in seconds without ever having to open the bag.

RFID System Details

RFID systems consist of an interrogator (also referred to as a reader) and transponders, or tags. In other words, the tag can be hidden or imbedded within the item and the item will still be identified. In an RFID system, the antenna of the reader emits radio signals. The signals are received by the tag's antenna, which can be powered via a battery or by the radio frequency energy from the reader's pulse. The tags respond with a unique code, which is preprogrammed in the tag's microchip. After the reader antenna receives and decodes the signal, the antenna sends the information to a computer via a standard interface; this information is accessed through a database. Since RFID systems do not require a line of sight between the tag and the reader, a Space Station crewmember could potentially initiate a reader in the general vicinity of a cargo transfer lab that is full of tagged items and record an accurate count of all items within the bag in seconds. In this chapter, we will use a simulated warehouse as an environment for DFSSR techniques.

Six Sigma Methodology

With the advantages illustrated above, a series of experiments and tests will be conducted by the RFID Supply Chain Lab (RfSCL) lab at the University of Nebraska—Lincoln. A blend of methodologies will help the RfSCL lab use information to better develop a solution that best meets the needs of customers. The methodology used in this chapter is the Integrated Design for Six Sigma (DFSS; Breyfogle 2003). DMADO (De-may-doh) is the acronym for Design, Measure, Analyze, Develop, and Optimize (Breyfogle 2003). The planning function is categorized as defining the objectives and determining the correct measurement parameters. The predictive functions are analyzing viable options, designing experiments that lead to the development, identifying gaps, reanalyzing options based on performance, and creating a final design that meets the stated objectives. The performing functions are optimizing the performance of the design and verifying that the prototype is operational. This new approach to research will help bridge the gap between academic organizations and industry. The experiments and analysis will be conducted following the order of scientific methodology.

3P's THEORETICAL MODEL

In this chapter we introduce a research framework, Design for Six Sigma Research (DFSSR), that is based on a common operational prototype theme that requires development teams to plan, predict, and perform. The idea of using 3P's is catchy and has been used for science education and project management. These are referenced as Web sites in the literature review. The novelty of using 3P's in this research is that this memorable pneumatic is an effective communication tool to encapsulate our DFSSR framework. For RFID technology to better serve industrial applications, we need to conduct a series of experiments to validate the principle of facility layout of RFID into real case scenarios. The Six Sigma methodology helps us build a scientific procedure and make sure that it is the optimum layout for real warehouse scenarios. We use this framework so that operations can identify the status of projects and investigate the detailed processes within the framework. The DFSSR process steps are organized within the 3P framework as shown in Figure 12.1. The results or lessons learned can be used to effectively implement the technology in this environment. Further, the compiled lessons learned can be used to determine the best practices for implementations in the future. The methodology allows for the defining of the correct prototype environment, RFID subsystem testing, and integrated system testing for the prototype environment.

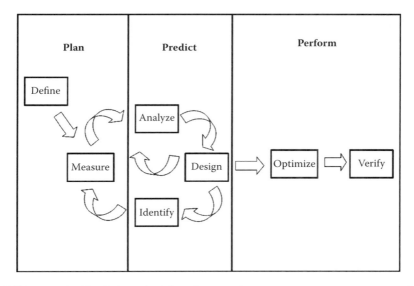

FIGURE 12.1   DFSSR 3P's methodology framework.

Plan

In this phase, we need to identify the critical path for both information and material flow. As a beginning of the planning phase, the first thing to be done is to define the problem in a real case; for example, what type of product do they use for inventory? What is the frequency of transportation they have every day? That is all related to our test design for a warehouse.

Define

In the define phase it is necessary to compile the real environmental requirements into the test parameter. This makes it necessary to show the theoretical model in the design and analyze phases as an explanation and foundation for our future experiments. In this step, we describe facility layout processes based on input data, an understanding of the roles and relationships between activities, a material flow analysis, and an activity relationship analysis. The defining step is shown in the first phase: plan. The clear material flow should be identified in this step as a basis of the predict and perform steps. Figure 12.2 shows us a clear view of this thought process.

Measure

Multi-objective RF warehouse architecture is the overall RFID warehouse implementing system. It includes three main parts: an RFID edge layer, an RFID physical layer, and an enterprise integration network. The RFID physical layer is the connection of the other two layers. The RFID system is designed to process streams of tags, or sensor data, coming from one or more readers. The edge layer has the capability to filter and aggregate data prior to sending it to a requesting application. For example, an action (tag read) is triggered when the object moves or a new object comes into the reader's view. The RFID edge servers filter and collect the tag data at each individual site and send it over the Internet to the third layer—the enterprise integration layer. The localized data is identified by moving actions and stationary actions separately. This difference divides the usage of RFID antenna into two types of equipment: one is a fixed reader for warehouse portal door, and another is a

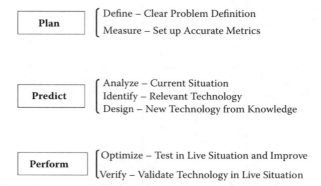

FIGURE 12.2   3P's thought process.

mobile reader for tracking inventory. The fundamental tenet of the warehouse portal distribution system is that it must be able to accommodate changes that may occur on a network. The portal devices provide real-time positioning access capabilities to user communities, as well as the abilty to deliver and search personal data. It allows external customers and partners secure access to data.

We can now divide the RFID warehouse system into three parts as discussed before: the physical layer, the logic layer, and the system integration layer. Each layer has different components depending on what functions the RFID system needs. By understanding the flow in the warehouse, we can determine the types of tags and antennas needed.

In short, RFID implementation in any process has two or three layers. The physical layer produces log events for RF sensors during process executions. The logic layer records the log events and related data including filter and integrated functions. The analysis of the physical layer activity has been discussed in facility layout research. Previous research with RFID facility layout does not include data flow as a factor that influences the RFID warehouse efficiency and performance.

Predict

In this phase, the major issue is to analyze the outcome and process of our RFID operation. As we know, the results of experiments or tests are important for the company who wants to implement RFID; the situation may vary for each company. Combined with the real environment and site requirements, the test should be conducted in appropriate and cost-effective ways.

Analyze

One of the design components of the RFID warehouse layout is the data flow through the distribution process. This is included in the experimental design phase. The goal of such an activity is to define the input and output data in order to confirm the efficiency of data flow and its physical flow. Data standards can be smoothly exchanged within the supply chain because the data is already formatted and organized. The work flow and data flow are both generated by the production flow from the physical layer to the logical layer. All the data chosen through the distribution process are generated by RFID equipment including the tags on each pallet or the antenna on the portal. Therefore, the location of the RFID equipment is influential on the accuracy of the distribution process that forms the individual data flow according to the work flow. The location of the RFID antenna, also called a sensor, will be discussed later.

Design

According to our analysis of site environment and data types, we choose to use passive tags as our technology in a warehouse, which means low cost but high volume information flow.

First, sensor refers to a device that is connected, via network or RF communication medium, to other sensor devices in the network. The location of the sensors in the warehouse relate to either its environment or its data traffic flow, which is detected by a fixed antenna on the portal door. Similarly, the data flow will be employed by sensors specifically in the picking entrance portal and the distributing portal. Therefore, the data traffic through the two portal doors and its layout will be considered in this chapter. Other communications between the nodes in the warehouse will be discussed in a future work. In order to measure the accuracy and efficiency of RFID performance in the warehouse, we are using a ratio to evaluate the relationship of performance and efficiency of RFID This is discussed again later in the text in the systematic layout planning chapter. This is σ, which equals the simple relationship between input and output data and will be related to a regression analysis to show fair performance.

$$\sigma_r = \alpha_I / \beta_o \tag{1}$$

Where:

σ_r = ratio; α_I = input; β_o = output

However, this ratio only gives an average performance for RFID readability. The components of the input require the precise data to evaluate the environment and performance. However, we measured the benchmark of the performance used to compare the different input data and data flow. For example, the different amounts of work flow reflect the different data flows in the warehouse, but the benchmark gives us reliable data to measure different warehouse environments and work flows. In the next stage, the optimize step, we will use a case study to illustrate our theory explained in the design and analyze phases.

Perform

The last phase of our study will be perform, after previous experiments and design applications. The next stage is to prove the feasibility of our design by using design of experiment (DOE) and optimize the system performance according to the current configurations.

Optimize

Based on our theoretical model, we will conduct experiments following the order of the optimum facility layout and cost-effective equipment. As a major part of statistical analysis in Six Sigma methodology, we use DOE as a possible improvement through process. In DOE the effects of several independent factors (variables) can be considered simultaneously in one experiment without evaluating all possible combinations of factor levels. For experiment 1, two independent variables (factors) and one dependent variable were used. The two independent variables include the tag replacement and the number of antennas. The dependent variable was the readability of the tags. The observed results of the experiment had an effect on the independent variable.

$$\text{Readability} = f\left(\text{TP, AN}\right) \tag{2}$$

Where:
  TP: Tag placement
  AN: Antenna number

For experiment 2, we needed to regulate some of the variables until the results achieved full-read efficiency. This was done to satisfy the customer's requirement of 100 percent readability. The model of the experiment is

$$\text{Readability} = f\left(\text{AP, PP}\right) \tag{3}$$

Where:
  AP: antenna's position
  PP: portal's position. Factors and levels

When executing a full factorial experiment, a response is obtained for all possible combinations of the experiment. Because of the large number of possible combinations in full factorial experiments, two-level factorial experiments are frequently utilized. Experiment 1 was a two-factor, two-level experiment. As described in Table 12.1, a total of four trials were needed to address all assigned combinations of the factor levels.

TABLE 12.1
Factorial Design

Factors: 2	Replicates: 10
Base runs: 4	Total runs: 40
Base blocks: 1	Total blocks:1
Number of levels: 2, 2	

The specific situations to which a DOE is applied will affect how factors and levels are chosen. Factor levels also can take different forms. In this experiment, levels are quantitative. Experiment 1 should allow for a systematic observation of a particular behavior under controlled circumstances.

Therefore, two principles were conducted in the experiment as below:

- Tag placement: top, side
- Number of antennas: One antenna and two antennas (on each side of portal; two antennas were only used in one trial within the experiment).

For experiment 2, in order to test the readability of the tags and metrics performance, the same trials were performed as experiment 1, with the following variables:

- Position of antennas: We installed two antennas at the same height on each side and at two different heights (three feet, five feet).
- The distance between each side of the portal (five feet, seven feet)

The standardized timescale was thirty seconds in consideration of limited real-world data acquisition times. All of the specifications were conducted ten times with three different replacements of tags and ten items in each trial. The experiment factors and levels are summarized in Table 12.2.

TABLE 12.2
Experiment Factors and Level

		Levels	
Factors and Designations		(1)	(2)
Experiment 1	A1: Tag Placement (TA)	Top	Side
	B1: AntennaNumber (AN)	1	2
Experiment 2	A2: Antenna's Position (AP)	Horizontal	Non-horizontal
	B2: Portal's Distance (PD)	5 feet	7 feet

Verify

We have several ways to optimize the current layout design to improve the reading accuracy. For experiment 1, the placement of the tags on the pallet or item can be classified in three ways: top, front, and side. The performance of each classification is different. To sum up, the best position of a tag on an item in this study was on the side (face to the antennas) given the results of our polarization and magnetic field conditions. The performance of the antennas and tags is totally different with these three classifications. Compared with the other two classifications results, the readability of the tags when on the side can be up to 60 percent of full satisfaction. This classification is still not very satisfying. We also determined that a significant change occurred when the number of antennas was varied. We ran the experiment using one antenna with ten items first. The readability of the tags was only 80 percent compared with almost 100 percent when using two antennas (average 96 percent). The read rate graph is shown in Figure 12.3.

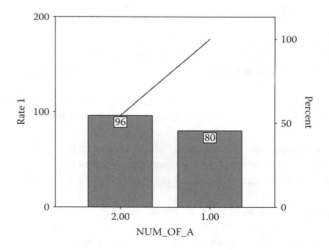

FIGURE 12.3 Read rate graph.

For experiment 2, the influence of the variable tag placement in the model is the same as in experiment 1. The antenna position had different effects on the two experiments. The experiment hypothesized that the antenna, when placed in different horizontal planes, would have a positive influence on readability. The non-horizontal antenna showed better results when distance between antennas increased. For example, the experiment conducted from five feet to seven feet demonstrated better results at seven feet than at five feet. The portal dock's position is an important factor that has an influence on reading accuracy, especially in experiment 2. The hypothesis was that the shorter the distance, the better the read efficiency. The experiment simulated real-world circumstances and was designed for two hypothesized cases. The distance between each side of the portal must be five feet with the antenna on the same horizontal line and the distance between readers can be up to seven feet with differing heights. Therefore, the objective of the experiment was to verify the hypothesis regarding whether the performance of readability would be better with nonhorizontal line orientation. If the hypothesis were proved to be true, the improvement on the antenna reading efficiency would increase by varying the height of the two antennas when other factors are fixed.

Finally, the results of the experiment supported the above hypothesis. We identified the normal distance between each side as seven feet, but the optimum and effective distance was approximately five feet. The factors of distance between each side and the nonhorizontal antenna have an influence on the effectiveness of readability.

CONCLUSION

The reaction time of the antenna on the tags was almost the same in these two cases. It can be determined that readability can achieve a full-read expectation when performed under the specifications given below:

- The full-read range is three to five feet when antennas are fixed at the same horizontal line on each side of portal.
- The full-read range is six to eight feet when the antennas are fixed with different heights on each side of portal.
- The full-read requirement needs to have the tags on the sides of items or facing toward the antennas.

Frequency, distances and angles, type of tag, location and replacement, influences of moisture, metals, and pallet patterns all played a part in the readability of the tags. The effective reading distance was analyzed in MATLAB (6.0, release 13) for visualizing the results and provided documents for future research. The data points on the graph showed random variation, but the visualization graph gives a clue that the most effective scale for the antenna is between two and three feet around the middle line. See Figure 12.4 and Figure 12.5. The bar on the right side indicates the read rate, which is based on our experiment specification of ten tags per pallet. The read rate can be reached at 90 percent or better.

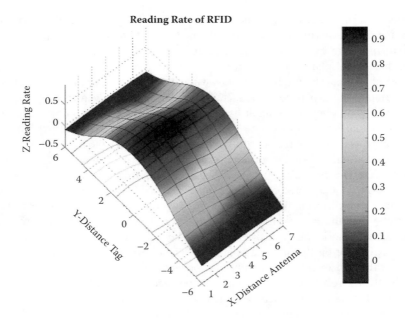

FIGURE 12.4   3-D graph for effective reading rate.

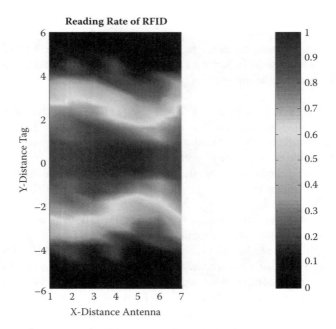

FIGURE 12.5   2-D graph for effective reading scale.

To sum up, the total conditions for receiving greater than 90 percent readability include several considerations as below:

- The placement of tags
- The distance between antennas (if there is more than one antenna)
- Appropriate stop-by time when going through the portal (at least three seconds)
- The change of the position of the antenna when other limitations are fixed

Using Six Sigma methodology increases the efficiency of test procedures and validates the influence of real warehouse case layout scenarios.

REFERENCES

Breyfogle, F. (2003). *Implementing Six Sigma: Smarter solutions using statistical methods.* 2nd ed. New York: John Wiley & Sons.

ADDITIONAL REFERENCES

Banerjee, P., Y. Zhou, and B. Montreuel. (1997). Genetically assisted optimization of cell layout and material flow path skeleton. *IIE Transactions* 29(4):277–291.

Carbon, T. A. (2000). Measuring efficiency of semiconductor manufacturing operations using data envelopment analysis (DEA). Paper presented at the IEEE SEMI Advanced Semiconductor Manufacturing Conference.

Foster, T. S. (2003). *Managing quality: An integrative approach.* 2d ed. New York: Prentice Hall.

Gaukler, G. M., Ö. ÖZer, and W. H. Hausman. (2006). RFID and order progress information: Improved dynamic emergency ordering policies. 10 July.

Gleixner, S., G. Young, L. Vanasupa, Y. Dessouky, E. Allen, and D. Parent. (2002). Teaching design of experiments and statistical analysis of data through laboratory experiments. *Frontiers in Education* 1, 6–9.

Gotsman, C., and Y. Koren. (2005). Distributed graph layout for sensor networks. *Lecture Notes in Computer Science* 3383.

Kleijnen, J. P. C. (1995). Sensitivity analysis and optimization in simulation: Design of experiments and case studies. Proceedings – Winter Simulation Conference 133–140.

Lee, Y. M., F. Cheng, and Y. T. Leung. (2004). Exploring the impact of RFID on supply chain dynamics. Proceedings – Winter Simulation Conference.

Pan, J., G. Tonkay, and A. Quintero. (1999). Screen printing process design of experiments for fine line printing of thick film ceramic substrates. *Journal of Electronics Manufacturing* 9(3):203–213.

Penttila, K., L. Sydeimo, and M. Kivikoski. (2004). Performance development of a high-speed automatic object identification using passive WID technology. Paper presented at the International Conference on Robotics & Automation.

Rao, K. V. S., P. V. Nikitin, and S. F. Lam. (2005). Antenna design for UHF RFID tags: A review and a practical application. *IEEE Transactions on Antennas and Propagation* 53(12):3870–3876.

Tompkins, J. A., J. A. White, Y. A. Bozer, E. H. Frazelle, J. M. A. Tanchoco, and J. Trevino. (1996). *Facility planning.* 2d ed. New York: John Wiley & Sons.

Wehking, K.-H., F. Seeger, and S. Kummer. (2006). RFID transponders: Link between information and material flows. How reliable are identification procedures? *Logistics Journal.*
April 1–14, 2006.
Zhang, Y., J. Liu, and F. Zhao. (2006). Information-directed routing in sensor networks using
real-time reinforcement learning. *Combinatorial Optimization in Communication Networks.* Springer Science & Business Media, 259–288.

SUGGESTED RESOURCES

Other references to the 3P methodologies available at www.bioquest.org/index3ps.html
[Accessed August 30, 2007].
Plan, prepare, perform. The 3 P's of success [Online]. Available at www.brevilleseminars.
com/html/the_three_p_s.html [Accessed August 30, 2007].
3 P's to doing it right: Prioritize, plan, proceed [Online]. Available at www.goto-silicon-val-
ley.com/column/jeff-colvin/3p.shtml [Accessed August 30, 2007].
*3-P's methodology the "three P's of science": Problem posing, problem solving, and peer per-
suasion* [Online]. Available at www.wv-hsta.org/TeacherInfo/club_exp_3a.htm [Accessed
August 30, 2007].

13 The Engineering Economics of RFID

INTRODUCTION

In order to ensure cost-effective production of specialized products, many companies use calibrated tools. Failure to use the proper calibrated tool can result in scrap and rework. This inefficiency results in events such as audit costs, higher labor costs, and loss of customer trust that translates into lost sales. Further, customers often sue companies that produce defective parts that cause injuries. These events not only produce negative publicity for the companies but may result in costly lawsuit settlements.

Calibrated tools are essential to producing quality products and should be efficiently tracked for optimal labor productivity. However, this practice is not always demonstrated. In this study, the observed company's management attributes financial losses each year to lost or stolen calibrated tools. A stolen tool is considered a lost tool for this analysis. Defective parts due to using noncalibrated tools can trigger facility audits by customers as specified in contractual arrangements. Consequently, failed audits may result in a contract fine if an operator is found to be using a noncalibrated tool.

In addition to the cost of an operator using a noncalibrated tool in production, there are also the costs of losing calibrated tools. First, there is the cost of the tool itself if the tool is never found. Second, there is the cost of the lost labor time spent searching for the tool. And finally, the lost production time if the tool is needed immediately in production. We suggest that these latter costs could be alleviated by the use of radio frequency identification (RFID), which can provide real-time tracking of calibrated tools.

RFID can be used in an asset management system, such as those supported by enterprise resource planning (ERP) systems. Asset management systems should locate assets individually, allow for locating the correct assets at the correct time, and provide information about each individual asset and the physical status of the asset.

These uses are the foundation of RFID systems. A tag is placed on each asset that carries the information of the individual item. These tags contain an antenna that allows information to be transmitted at the frequency identified by the reader. Readers are located throughout the production facility in coordination with their reading distance abilities. Software is used to capture the information transmitted to the reader. The reader sends the data to the inventory management system, which allows for parts to be tracked and located throughout the production facility.

PROBLEM STATEMENT

The fundamental question for this study is will implementing an RFID-based system reduce some of the costs of poor quality incurred due to lost calibrated tools? This analysis focuses on the labor costs, audit costs, and management time needed for implementing an RFID system. This chapter does not address lost quality due to other factors that management felt were not related problems that RFID could solve. These include training, wrong tool usage, and gauge precision. These are valid reasons for loss of quality but are not explicitly related to the tracking of lost tools.

This chapter formulates a cost analysis of implementing an RFID system to track calibrated tools throughout a production facility. By comparing two different scenarios, the best plan of action is defined (Evans, Zhang, and Vogt 2004). The net present value is used to evaluate an RFID system implementation. The goal of a new system is to save the company money with increased traceability. The RFID system put in place must provide savings greater than the cost to implement and be innovative in nature so as to put the company ahead in the industry.

BACKGROUND

An armament and technical products manufacturing facility that has no current tracking system in place is analyzed. Increased costs due to audits, rework, and customer dissatisfaction have been identified by management as costs incurred by using the wrong tools or a noncalibrated tool. In order to place more control over the practice of wrong tool usage due to the loss of calibrated tools, the company evaluated an RFID tracking system. The facility has approximately 132,000 square feet and two hundred total employees. Management personnel and production personnel costs are $40 per hour and $20 per hour, respectively, including indirect costs. Approximately two thousand calibrated tools are utilized in production.

A dedicated staff has the responsibility of calibrating and supplying the tools to the production workers. The communication between the production floor and calibration staff on the location of tools was identified as a problem; there was no effective tool tracking. Therefore, calibrated tools were difficult to find when needed and little feedback was available to production supervisors when production operators were unable to find a tool. This lack of feedback led to operators either looking for the tools or using the incorrect tool. The costs associated with using the incorrect tools including labor, scrap, rework, and failed audits are evaluated in this chapter.

COST JUSTIFICATION

This study presents two scenarios. The first scenario is the doing nothing option or the company maintains the status quo. This scenario describes the baseline costs for the study. Scenario two demonstrates the costs of implementing the RFID system over a five-year period.

SCENARIO 1: BASELINE

The first option the company has in regards to tracking its calibrated tools is to maintain the status quo, which we consider the baseline. This suggests that the costs the company is incurring will remain unchanged over the five-year period considered. In order to show the total cost, each cost is considered separately. These costs include audit costs, rework costs, scrap costs, management costs, and customer service costs.

Audit Costs

External auditors periodically review processes and procedures at the company. These audits include governmental audits and environmental audits. This study focuses on the audits that review the products created from calibrated tools. For each of these auditors that visit the plant, there is a cost to the company. The initial audit is always obligatory; therefore, the cost of the first audit is not considered. However, problems identified during the initial audit can lead to an additional audit for production areas that do not pass inspection. These secondary audit costs create additional company efforts such as management and operator time for communications about failed audits, delayed contracts, and possibly layoffs due to lost contracts.

There may be one or two more secondary audits throughout the year that would not have been needed previously. In order to estimate the cost of an additional audit, conditional probability trees are utilized to assess the probability of the company needing a second, third, or fourth audit. The probabilities utilized were established through management interviews. Due to company privacy issues, this study does not display the histograms or show the distributions of the number of occurrences of error. Instead, only the distribution probabilities are shown in Figure 13.1 as conditional probability trees.

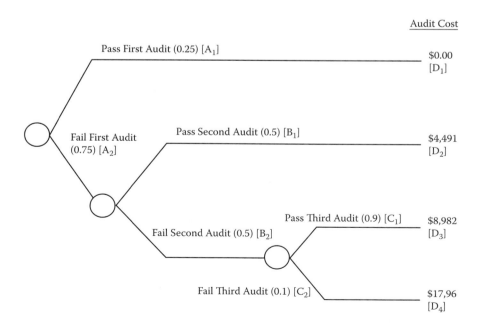

FIGURE 13.1   Audit conditional probability tree.

The expected value of the audit cost E (Xi) is given as a function derived from the decision tree. The following equation will be in this study for the audit cost calculations.

$$\text{✗} \; E(Xi) = A1D1 + A2B1D2 + A2B2C1D3 + A2B2C2D4 \tag{1}$$

Xi is the audit cost of contract i. For the audit cost calculation, an additional penalty is given if the third audit is not passed, represented as D4 in equation (1). The given cost is twice the cost of passing the third audit. This cost was included due to the additional cost of special efforts made by the company when an audit fails three times.

The costs include auditor labor and travel expenses. Each auditor is conservatively estimated to earn $25 per hour with 33 percent benefits or a total cost of approximately $33 per hour. Each audit takes approximately three days, and the auditors work eight hours daily. Thus, the average number of hours worked per audit is twenty-four hours. Overall, the personnel cost for an audit team with three members is $2,376 per audit.

In addition to the costs for the auditors, travel expenses were included. Travel expenses include air travel, lodging, and food. Given an audit team of three auditors, the total cost for airline tickets is $900 ($300 per airline ticket). Next, the audit team lodging and food cost were $100 per night for a hotel room and $35 a day for food over three days, such that the cost for three auditors would be $1,215. These costs are summarized in Table 13.1.

TABLE 13.1

Audit Costs

Audit Cost Elements per Audit	Scenario 1 ($)
Auditor	2,376
Travel	900
Lodging and food	1,215
Total cost	4,491

The total cost per audit is approximately $4,491. The expected value for an audit with the given probability of failure is estimated to be $5,389.20.

$$E(X1) = (.25)(\$0) + (.75)(.5)(\$4,491) + (.9)(.5)(.75)(\$8,982)$$

$$+ (.1)(.5)(.75)(\$17,964) = \$5,389.20 \tag{2}$$

A total of twenty-seven current company contracts were audited the previous year. The possible savings that can be achieved from audit reduction is the product of the expected audit cost and the number of audits. We use a conservative estimate of reducing the cost of twenty audits for a total cost savings for audit of $107,820.

REWORK COSTS

Another cost to consider is rework cost. Throughout this study, the company analyzed did not have data available to individually measure the different causes of rework, specifically due to a missing calibrated tool. Management estimates that 90 percent of defects were reworked and the other 10 percent become scrap. The previous year's total defects were 3,800 including defects in the final product and in subassemblies. Given a fraction defective of 0.90, we conservatively estimate that 3,420 defects were reworked. Rework included such things as retooling in order to fix

TABLE 13.2
Annual Rework Costs

Rework Cost Elements	Scenario 1
Defects to rework	3,420
Rework hours	27,360
Operator cost	$20/hr
Total cost	$547,200

the defect, complete rework of a part, or fixing a broken piece. Management interviews support an average of eight hours per defect reworked. A production worker makes approximately $15 per hour plus 33 percent benefits, which equates to a total cost of $20 per hour for a production worker. Therefore, with 3,420 defects per year reworked, eight hours lost per rework, and $20 per hour per operator, the estimate average total rework cost per year is approximately $547,200.

SCRAP COSTS

The estimated scrap cost was calculated by taking the median price of the final product and multiplying by a factor of 0.72. This factor was used because the profit and transportation costs were estimated to be 28 percent of final product price. Other costs such as management, warehousing, and labor were inclusive in the cost factor.

Parts at this company range from a price of $400 to $200,000 per part. There are approximately 2,346 parts manufactured each year. These are the final products produced to be sold in the market. The median price was estimated at $50,300 and the cost is estimated at $36,216.

Currently 380 defects are scrapped each year. We conservatively estimate that 10 percent of these defects are related to calibrated tools. We use this conservative estimate due to the fact that though the defects may result in a scrapped assembly, it may not result in a scrapped product. It is estimated that thirty-eight products are scrapped per year. Therefore, the final estimated cost of scrap is $1,376,208.

TABLE 13.3
Annual Scrap Costs

Scrap Cost Elements	Scenario 1
Cost per product	$36,216
Scrapped products	38
Total cost	$1,376,208

MANAGEMENT COSTS

Management costs were estimated as a percentage of total management time. Currently there are five managers directly involved with the results of audits and other problems that arise from the production floor. Given the number of managers, there are 2,080 hours of potential work time in a year for each manager or a total time for the five managers of 10,400 hours per year. The percentage of total time utilized to address audit concerns and production floor problems were 5 percent. Of this 5 percent, we assume that a minimum of 50 percent of this time or 2.5 percent of total time is dedicated to working with problems of

TABLE 13.4
Annual Management Costs

Management Cost Elements	Scenario 1
Hours per year	2,080
# Managers	5
5% Total work time	520 hours
Hourly cost	$39.90/hr
Total cost	$20,748,

rework and scrap. This percentage is a conservative estimate. The total time per year for five managers is 520 hours. Finally, the hourly cost per manager was determined to be $30 per hour with 33 percent benefits. Benefits increase the cost per manager to $40 per hour. The cost of management per year in regard to audits and production performance was found to be $20,748 per year.

Customer Service Costs

The customer service cost considers the risk of losing the customer or contract. Conservatively, this chapter only considers the potential loss of a portion of a contract, not the loss of the complete contract. This cost would be incurred if defective parts were distributed to the customer or the customer was unsatisfied with the service of the company. The customer may either cancel or reduce the contract at the end of the contract period. Due to this risk, the range of contract sales values were considered. Contracts could potentially range from $1,000 to $11.8 million. The conditional probability trees consider the reduction of a contract due to a defect reaching the customer and consider that, after two occurrences, the contract would be canceled. All these probabilities were considered in the conditional probability trees in Figure 13.2.

The second conditional probability tree utilized in this chapter was for deriving the function for the expected customer service cost E(Yj).

$$E(Yj) = A1D1 + A2B1C1D2 + A2B2C2D3 + A2B2C3D4 + A2B2C4D5 \quad (3)$$

Equation (2) describes the expected customer service cost calculations. Yj represents customer service cost for contract j. The conditional probability tree was based on the following assumptions from estimates of past occurrences. First, it was estimated that a minor defect on a first occurrence would cause the customer to reduce its contract by 10 percent. However, a major defect would cause the customer

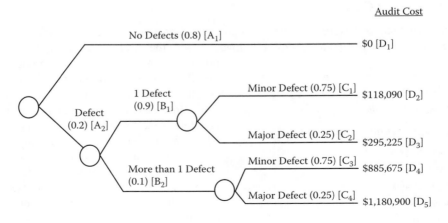

FIGURE 13.2   Customer service conditional probability tree.

to reduce its contract by 25 percent. If a minor defect was found by a customer for a second time or more, the customer was estimated to reduce its contract by 75 percent, but if the defect was major, the customer was likely to seek another company to do business with. Therefore, the company could potentially lose the entire contract on a second major defect. This penalty cost is given as D5 in equation (3). The penalty cost is quantified as the cost of completely losing value of an expected contract.

In order to complete the conditional probability tree, an expected value of the contract price needed to be found. The smallest contract was considered to be 90 percent of the total contracts, with 10 percent being the contract of $11.8 million. This gave a weighted average contract of $1,180,900 as calculated below.

$$(\$1,000)(.9) + (\$11,800,000)(.1) = \$1,180,900 \qquad (4)$$

These conditional probability tree calculations are demonstrated in Figure 13.2. The conditional probability tree was collapsed in order to find an expected cost for customer service, $48,417.

$$E(Y2) = (.8)(\$0) + (.75)(.9)(.2)(\$118,090) + (.25)(.9)(.2)(\$295,225)$$

$$+ (.75)(.1)(.2)(\$885,675) + (.25)(.1)(.2)(\$1,180,900) = \$48,417 \qquad (5)$$

Many assumptions were made with the inclusion of the customer service cost. However, it is a risk that the company takes every time it ships a product. Therefore, this cost needed to be included. This estimation has some limitations. The main one to note would be the lack of numerous occurrences. This cost was estimated on the assumption of one occurrence per year. The company is a government contractor and has lost no more than five contracts over the last five years to other plants, though audit costs have risen. This may be a low or high estimate and must be considered by any other companies looking into this model. Overall, this expected value fits this company well.

TOTAL ANNUAL COST

The total costs for scenario 1 are outlined in Table 13.5. The total cost is approximately $2.1 million dollars per year. The implementation cost of scenario 1 was zero due to the fact it is the baseline system, which was no change in the current system.

TABLE 13.5
Total Annual Cost Scenario 1

Cost Elements	Scenario 1 ($)
Audit	107,820
Rework	547,200
Scrap	1,376,208
Management	20,748
Customer service (contracts lost)	48,417
Implementation	0
Total cost	2,100,393

SCENARIO 2: RFID IMPLEMENTATION

The second scenario evaluates the cost of implementing an RFID system to track calibrated tools. This implementation would be the greatest cost to the company for this scenario, as will be seen. In addition to the implementation cost, there will be a maintenance cost each year to keep the system in good working condition. Also taken into consideration with scenario 2 is the cost reduction linked to the implementation of the RFID system.

TAG COSTS

Tags are the transponders that carry the information in an RFID system. Passive RFID tag costs can range from forty to eighty cents (United States Department of Defense 2004). Through this study, passive class 1 labels were used. These tags cost approximately seventy-five cents each. In order to implement the system, all two thousand calibrated tools would be tagged. The tags would be used to store and pass data between systems devices, in this case the tag and the reader. The estimated total tag cost is $1,500.

The cost of the tags will also include a yearly replacement of the same amount of $1,500 due to the annual replacement cost of tags. This cost will be discounted to the present value using net present value analysis shown later in this chapter. The tags will have the ability to be programmed with such information as the unique tool number, type of tool, planned location, current location, and next scheduled tool calibration.

TABLE 13.6
Annual Tag Costs

Tag Cost Elements	Scenario 2
Cost per passive tag	$0.75
Number of tags	2000
Total cost	$1,500

READER COSTS

The reader is used to communicate with the RFID tags through electromagnetic waves. The information is relayed from the tag to the reader. There are both portable readers and fixed readers in the market today (Nobel 2004). In this case, the company would be using fixed readers placed at strategic locations throughout the plant. Considering that there are numerous rooms in the plant, fifteen readers would be needed. All exits to the outside would be covered with a reader, as well as other locations within the plant. Each reader would cost the company approximately $5,000. Therefore, the initial cost of the readers would be approximately $75,000.

In addition to the readers, fifteen antennas would be purchased to boost the signal sent from the readers to the tags at various locations within the plant. A spectrum analyzer was used to conduct a site survey in order to determine the number of antennas that would be used in this environment. The antennas would be used at ingress and egress locations to provide optimal data capture of RFID tags.

These antennas would be used in areas where transmission through the material may be an issue. By adding antennas in these areas, the entire plant could be covered by the RFID network in order for all tags to be read when needed. An inventory search can be

TABLE 13.7
Annual Reader Costs

Reader Cost Elements	Scenario 2 ($)
Readers	75,000
Antennas	7,500
Total cost	82,500

initiated at any time by activating the readers and antennas. The search would identify tools that were missing from the plant. There would be no readers placed within the offices. Therefore, engineering or tooling staff would need to confirm that they were moving a calibrated tool to an office in order to prevent alarming the system. Each antenna costs approximately $500 dollars, for a total cost of $7,500. Therefore, the total cost of the readers and antennae is $82,500. The installation cost is included in the implementation cost for the RFID system analyzed later in this chapter.

SOFTWARE COSTS

The final component of the RFID system is the middleware software. This software serves as a traffic cop to send the correct data to the enterprise resource planning (ERP) system currently in place at the company. This software typically costs approximately $25,000 and includes the cost of upgrades for up to three to five years. Currently the company purchases the tags and readers from a supplier that will include the supplier's software, commonly termed *edgewear*. The cost of integration between the reader's edgewear, middleware software, and ERP are considered to be the typical software cost. Another consideration when purchasing the middleware is that the software platforms must be compatible with the current ERP system. Possible costs include interface programmers in such languages as C, C-sharp, and C++, which can be as high as $200 per hour and the costs can exceed $50,000 for this type of software integration. For this study we conservatively estimate a cost of $25,000.

IMPLEMENTATION COSTS

We estimate implementation cost by assuming that two technical personnel are assigned the task to implement the RFID system over six months. These technical personnel cost $33 per hour fully burdened. Over six months (assume twenty work days per month) and assuming an eight-hour work day, these two employees would work a total of 960 hours. This cost is $31,680 per technical personnel or $63,360 for implementation of an RFID system over a facility of 132,000 square feet.

INVESTMENT FOR SCENARIO 2

The total cost for year 1 of the second scenario is shown in Table 13.8. There is estimated to be a cost of approximately $172,360 for implementation of the RFID system.

In addition to the implementation costs of year 1, there will also be a yearly maintenance cost. This includes replacing the tags and the labor needed to perform this task. The cost to replace the tags will be considered to remain the same over the five years this study analyzes. Therefore, the cost of the replacing two thousand tags will be $1,500. The time of this project is estimated to take approximately two minutes

TABLE 13.8

Initial investment Scenario 2

Cost Elements for Year 1	Scenario 2 ($)
Tags	1,500
Readers	82,500
Software	25,000
Implementation	63,360
Total cost	172,360

TABLE 13.9
Annual Maintenance Cost

Maintenance Cost Elements	Scenario 2 ($)
Tag replacement	1,500
Labor	1,334
Total cost	2,834

TABLE 13.10
Total Annual Cost Comparison

Cost Elements	Scenario 1 ($)	Scenario 2 ($)	% Cost Reduction
Audit	107,820	87,334	19
Rework	547,200	432,288	21
Scrap	1,376,208	1,114,728	19
Management	20,748	17,013	18
Customer service (contracts lost)	48,417	39,218	19
Total cost per year	2,100,393	1,690,582	20

per tool to both find the tool and replace the tag. With more than two thousand tools it will take four thousand minutes, or sixty-seven hours. Employees performing this task will be making $15 hour. After 33 percent benefits were added to this labor cost, the personnel cost rose to $20 per hour. This brings the labor cost of maintenance to $1,334 per year and total costs to $2,834 as shown in Table 13.9.

Next we consider the change in costs per year that were incurred in scenario 1. This study estimated a reduction of 20 percent of total cost based on time studies of labor, audits, and rework (see Table 13.10). Therefore, the company would still be incurring $1,690,582 per year. This translates into a savings of $409,811.

NET PRESENT VALUE COMPARISON

We use a net present value analysis to compare the two alternatives. The assumptions applied here are that the cash flows are deterministic and that they occur at the end of each period of time analyzed.

The discount rate used in this study is considered as the current rate of inflation of 4 percent. This value makes the analysis more conservative and the conclusions more clear. The time period used is a five-year period, which is the minimum considered by the company to compare the two projects. In this comparison there is no salvage value. A further study analyzing the variability of the elements that compose the costs will be presented on the sensitivity analysis part. Cash flow diagrams for each scenario are shown in Figure 13.3.

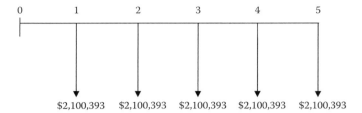

FIGURE 13.3   Scenario 1 cash flow diagram.

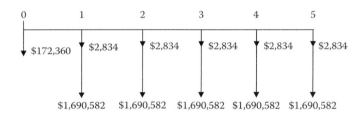

FIGURE 13.4   Scenario 2 cash flow diagram.

The above cash flow diagram (Figure 13.3) illustrates the costs and returns of scenario one. When brought to present value, the total net present worth is approximately $9.3 million, demonstrated using equation (6):

$$PW(4\%) = \$0 + \$2,100,393(P/A, 4\%, 5) = \$2,100,393(4.452)$$
$$= \$9,350,949 \sim \$9.3 \text{ million} \tag{6}$$

The cash flow diagram shown in Figure 13.4 illustrates the costs of scenario 2. In this scenario, the net present value was approximately $7.7 million, as seen in equation (7).

$$PW(4\%) = \$172,360 + (\$1,262,077 + \$2,834)(P/A, 4\%, 5)$$
$$= \$172,360 + \$1,690,582(4.452) = \$7,698,831 \sim \$7.7 \text{ million} \tag{7}$$

COMPARISON

From the results of the net present value analysis above, RFID will provide an economic benefit to the company. The difference in the two net present values is approximately $1.6 million. Due to this difference in the net present values as well as the initial savings, RFID would be a good choice for the company to pursue.

SENSITIVITY ANALYSIS

In order to justify the results of this study further, a sensitivity analysis was developed. This was done in order to justify the study and compensate for the large amounts of variability in the variables.

The term *sensitivity analysis* examines how uncertainty of the variables that compose the cash flows can influence the recommended decisions. The sources of uncertainty can be due to measurement error, unclear specification, or volatility of the future. The techniques used in this model are the spiderplot and the tornado diagram. The spiderplot has the advantage of showing the impact of each cash flow's uncertainty on the present worth of the project and also makes a comparison between the individual variables' influence easier. A spiderplot should contain the limits of uncertainty for each cash flow element, the impact of each element on the PW, and the identification of each element that might change the recommendation (Eschenbach 2003).

The tornado diagram, on other hand, is to be used when a summary of the economic performance of the variables on the present worth is needed. This chart shows the variables that have the most influence on the present worth in descending order. This makes the diagram have a tornado shape. Normally this analysis assumes that the variables are statistically independent (Eschenbach, 2006), which is the case.

The lower and upper limits used in this case were estimated based on rules of thumb as taken by Eschenbach (2003) and are demonstrated in Table 13.11. As we are dealing with two mutually exclusive scenarios, the sensitivity analysis was created using the differences between the present worths of the two scenarios.

All calculations used to construct the spiderplot used the present value of equation (3). Table 13.12 summarizes those results and detailed calculations are shown in Appendix A.

We utilized this data to construct a spiderplot that demonstrates the effect on each variable when the other variables remain constant.

From Figure 13.5 it can be seen that the factors that account for most of the variability between the two scenarios are yearly costs. The minimum difference of PW between the two scenarios is obtained when the number of periods is set to its lower limit.

To summarize the relative sensitivities of each variable a tornado diagram (Figure 13.6) was then created with this proposal. This diagram shows the variability accounted for by each factor in descending order. From this chart the influence of each variable on the present worth can be seen.

From the above sensitivity analysis, this study shows that even with variability added into the model, there remains a substantial benefit in implementing an RFID system. This can be seen in reviewing both sets of calculations. If variability were to

TABLE 13.11
Limits of Variables

Variable	Scenario 1	Scenario 2	Lower Limit (%)	Upper Limit (%)
Investment	—	$172,360	80	115
Yearly cost	$2,100,393	$1,690,582	60	120
Maintenance cost	—	$2,834	75	120
i	4%	4%	95	115
N	5	5	75	150

TABLE 13.12
Values of Limits

%	Investment ($)	Yearly Cost ($)	Maintenance Cost ($)	i ($)	N ($)
60		909,667			
75		1,183,328	1,642,584		1,219,228
80	1,673,902	1,274,548	1,641,953		1,304,924
95	1,648,048	1,548,209	1,640,060	1,649,654	1,557,029
100	1,639,430	1,639,430	1,639,430	1,639,430	1,639,430
115	1,613,576	1,913,091	1,637,537	1,609,292	1,881,838
120		2,004,311	1,636,906		1,961,070
150					2,420,484

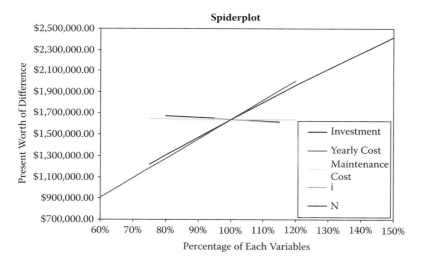

FIGURE 13.5   Spiderplot of PW of difference of the two scenarios.

place the yearly cost for scenario 1 to 60 percent of its value, there would still be a benefit of implementing an RFID system of approximately $700,000. Even these savings would be very cost-effective to a company. Therefore the study further justifies, on a more technical level, taking into account the reality of variability in the study.

LIMITATIONS

In this study there were several limitations. The cost of scrap is associated with not using a calibrated tool. Scrap costs can be further associated with inadequate training, improper workstation design, and other nonproductive practices. In order to limit this study to the impact of lost tools, we made the simplifying assumption that 10 percent of scrap was associated with using the wrong tool due to lack of

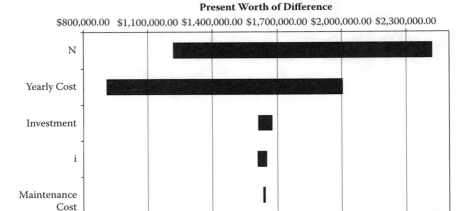

FIGURE 13.6   Tornado diagram.

availability of the correct calibrated tool. The cost to upgrade the RFID systems is not included in this analysis due to the fact this will probably happen after five years, which exceeds our cost time horizon.

Finally, the high-level time study that yielded a projected 20 percent labor reduction due to RFID implementations has a significant effect on the study. Though managers were comfortable with these savings estimates, a more detailed time study was recommended by the researchers.

CONCLUSIONS

This approach has outlined the current costs to the company of using noncalibrated tools. These costs have the potential to be reduced by implementing an RFID system to track the calibrated tools. With this technological advance, the company has the potential to use RFID in other areas besides calibrated tools. This could lead to other savings. This study outlined the cost of implementing an RFID system as well as the cost to maintain this type of system. We utilized the net present value analysis in order to evaluate the costs and benefits of RFID. The net present value analysis showed the difference between a do-nothing scenario and the scenario in which we implement RFID. The results demonstrated a savings of approximately $1.3 million if the RFID system is implemented. The savings, therefore, would be significant to the company and a good investment for the future.

REFERENCES

Eschenbach, T. G. (2003). *Engineering economy: Applying theory to practice.* 2d ed. Oxford, UK: Oxford University Press.

Eschenbach, T. G. (2006). Technical note: Constructing tornado diagrams with spreadsheets. *The Engineering Economist* 51(2):195–204.

Evans, J. L., D. Zhang, and N. Vogt. (2004). Investment analysis for automotive electronics manufacturing: A case study. *The Engineering Economist* 49:159–183.

Nobel, C. (2004). Sun, Sybase, IBM tackle RFID. *eWeek* 21:14–16.
United States Department of Defense. (2004). *United States Department of Defense suppliers' passive RFID information guide.* Version 9.0. http://www.acq.osd.mil/log/rfid/DoD_Suppliers_Passive_RFID_Information_Guide_v9.pdf. Accessed August 30, 2007.

ADDITIONAL REFERENCES

Blanchard, B. (1992). *Logistics of engineering and management.* 2d ed. Englewood Cliffs, NJ: Prentice Hall.
Clemen, R. T. (1996). *Making hard decisions.* 2d ed. Pacific Grove, CA: Duxbury Press.
Collins, J. (2004). New two-frequency RFID system. *RFID Journal.* September 1, 2004, 1105. http://www.rfidjournal.com/article/articleview/1105/1/1/, accessed August 30, 2007.
Eschenbach, T. G. (1989). *Cases in engineering economy.* New York: Wiley.
Hazen, G. B. (2003). A new perspective on multiple internal rates of return. *The Engineering Economist* 48:31–51.
IDTachEx. (2004). *The need for total asset visibility.* Cambridge: Far Field House.
Kaliski, B. (2004). RFID blocker tags. *Dr. Dobb's Journal, Boulder,* 29(9). September 2004, pp. 42–45.
RFID Wizards, Inc. (2003). *RFID equipment test results manufacturing.* RFID Wizards, Inc.

APPENDIX 13.1

INVESTMENT

$$PWFC, 80\%(4\%) = \$2,100,393(P/A, 4\%, 5) - (80\%)(\$172,360)$$
$$+ (\$1,690,582 + \$2,834)(P/A, 4\%, 5) = \$1,673,902$$

$$PWFC, 95\%(4\%) = \$2,100,393 (P/A, 4\%, 5) - (95\%)(\$172,360)$$
$$+ (\$1,690,582 + \$2,834)(P/A, 4\%, 5) = \$1,648,048$$

$$PWFC, 100\%(4\%) = \$2,100,393 (P/A, 4\%, 5) - (100\%)(\$172,360)$$
$$+ (\$1,690,582 + \$2,834)(P/A, 4\%, 5) = \$1,639,430$$

$$PWFC, 115\%(4\%) = \$2,100,393 (P/A, 4\%, 5) - (115\%)(\$172,360)$$
$$+ (\$1,690,582 + \$2,834)(P/A, 4\%, 5) = \$1,613,576$$

YEARLY COST

$$PWYC, 60\%(4\%) = (60\%)(\$2,100,393)(P/A, 4\%, 5) - (\$172,360)$$
$$+ (60\%)(\$1,690,582 + \$2,834)(P/A, 4\%, 5) = \$909,668$$

$$PWYC, 75\%(4\%) = (75\%)(\$2,100,393)(P/A, 4\%, 5) - (\$172,360)$$
$$+ (75\%)(\$1,690,582 + \$2,834)(P/A, 4\%, 5) = \$1,183,328$$

$$PWYC, 80\%(4\%) = (80\%)(\$2,100,393)(P/A, 4\%, 5) - (\$172,360)$$
$$+ (80\%)(\$1,690,582 + \$2,834)(P/A, 4\%, 5) = \$1,274,549$$

$$PWYC, 95\%(4\%) = (95\%)(\$2,100,393)(P/A, 4\%, 5) - (\$172,360)$$
$$+ (95\%)(\$1,690,582 + \$2,834)(P/A, 4\%, 5) = \$1,548,210$$

$$PWYC, 100\%(4\%) = (100\%)(\$2,100,393)(P/A, 4\%, 5) - (\$172,360)$$
$$+ (100\%)(\$1,690,582 + \$2,834)(P/A, 4\%, 5) = \$ 1,639,430$$

$$PWYC, 115\%(4\%) = (115\%)(\$2,100,393)(P/A, 4\%, 5) - (\$172,360)$$
$$+ (115\%)(\$1,690,582 + \$2,834)(P/A, 4\%, 5) = \$1,913,091$$

$$PWYC, 120\%(4\%) = (120\%)(\$2,100,393)(P/A, 4\%, 5) - (\$172,360)$$
$$+ (120\%)(\$11,690,582 + \$2,834)(P/A, 4\%, 5) = \$2,004,311$$

MAINTENANCE COST

$$PWMC, 75\%(4\%) = (\$2,100,393)(P/A, 4\%, 5) - (\$172,360)$$
$$+ [\$1,690,582 + (\$2,834)(75\%)](P/A, 4\%, 5) = \$1,642,584$$

$$PWMC, 80\%(4\%) = (\$2,100,393)(P/A, 4\%, 5) - (\$172,360)$$
$$+ [\$1,690,582 + (\$2,834)(80\%)](P/A, 4\%, 5) = \$1,641,953$$

$$PWMC, 95\%(4\%) = (\$2,100,393)(P/A, 4\%, 5) - (\$172,360)$$
$$+ [\$1,690,582 + (\$2,834)(95\%)](P/A, 4\%, 5) = \$1,640,060$$

$$PWMC, 100\%(4\%) = (\$2,100,393)(P/A, 4\%, 5) - (\$172,360)$$
$$+ [\$1,690,582 + (\$2,834)(100\%)](P/A, 4\%, 5) = \$1,639,430$$

$$PWMC, 115\%(4\%) = (\$2,100,393)(P/A, 4\%, 5) - (\$172,360)$$
$$+ [\$1,690,582 + (\$2,834)(155\%)](P/A, 4\%, 5) = \$1,637,537$$

$$PWMC, 120\%(4\%) = (\$2,100,393)(P/A, 4\%, 5) - (\$172,360)$$
$$+ [\$1,690,582 + (\$2,834)(120\%)](P/A, 4\%, 5) = \$1,636,906$$

DISCOUNT RATE (i)

$$PWi, 95\%[(95\%)(4\%)] = (\$2,100,393)[P/A, (95\%)(4\%), 5] - (\$172,360)$$
$$+ (\$1,690,582 + \$2,834)[P/A, (95\%)(4\%), 5] = \$1,649,654$$

$$PWi, 100\%[(100\%)(4\%)] = (\$2,100,393)[P/A, (100\%)(4\%), 5] - (\$172,360)$$
$$+ (\$1,690,582 + \$2,834)[P/A, (100\%)(4\%), 5] = \$1,639,430$$

$$PWi, 155\%[(115\%)(4\%)] = (\$2,100,393)[P/A, (115\%)(4\%), 5] - (\$172,360)$$
$$+ (\$1,690,582 + \$2,834)[P/A, (115\%)(4\%), 5] = \$1,609,292$$

Number of Periods (N)

PWN, 75%(4%) = ($2,100,393)[P/A, 4%, (75%)(5)] − ($172,360)
+ ($1,690,582 + $2,834)[P/A, 4%, (75%)(5)] = $1,219,228

PWN, 80%(4%) = ($2,100,393)[P/A, 4%, (80%)(5)] − ($172,360)
+ ($1,690,582 + $2,834)[P/A, 4%, (80%)(5)] = $1,304,924

PWN, 95%(4%) = ($2,100,393)[P/A, 4%, (95%)(5)] − ($172,360)
+ ($1,690,582 + $2,834)[P/A, 4%, (95%)(5)] = $1,557,029

PWN, 100%(4%) = ($2,100,393)[P/A, 4%, (100%)(5)] − ($172,360)
+ ($1,690,582 + $2,834)[P/A, 4%, (100%)(5)] = $1,639,430

PWN, 115%(4%) = ($2,100,393)[P/A, 4%, (115%)(5)] − ($172,360)
+ ($1,690,582 + $2,834)[P/A, 4%, (115%)(5)] = $1,881,838

PWN, 120%(4%) = ($2,100,393)[P/A, 4%, (120%)(5)] − ($172,360)
+ ($1,690,582 + $2,834)[P/A, 4%, (120%)(5)] = $1,961,070

PWN, 150%(4%) = ($2,100,393)[P/A, 4%, (150%)(5)] − ($172,360)
+ ($1,690,582 + $2,834)[P/A, 4%, (150%)(5)] = $2,420,484

Part 4

RFID Application Overviews

INTRODUCTION

In this section, we identify and discuss a large number of current and possible future RFID applications. In each chapter, both the RFID technology and the application issues are presented.

SECTION CONTENTS

Animal Tracking RFID Applications
Credit Device RFID Applications
Secure Document RFID Applications
DOD RFID and Wireless Communications Initiatives
Entertainment RFID Applications
Evaluating RFID Solutions for Health Care Improvement
RFID Applications in Libraries
Marine RFID Security Applications
Inventory Tracking on International Space Station Using RFID Technology
Individual Sport Competition RFID Applications
Surgical RFID Technology Applications
Tollway RFID Applications
RFID Transportation Systems Applications
Marine Terminal RFID Applications
RFID Uses in Warehousing

14 Animal Tracking RFID Applications

INTRODUCTION

One of the earliest uses of RFID technology is in the area of animal tracking. Animal tracking includes the placement of RFID tags on both wild and domestic animals. In the case of wild animals, RFID tags can be used to determine the migratory and spawning patterns of captured, released, and then recaptured animals. This is particularly important in the case of near-extinct species. Domestic animal applications include both livestock and pets. In the case of livestock intended for consumption, the animal is likely to be tagged due to health issues. This has become increasingly important due to reoccurring animal epidemics and bioterrorism issues. In the pet industry, exotic animals, particularly breeders, may be tagged due to their rarity or expense. Family pets may also be tagged due to sentimental value. Some countries such as Thailand have already required that pets be tagged. In this chapter, we will discuss:

- Tag placement methods
- Animal RFID technology
- Livestock tracking standards
- Related human applications

TAG PLACEMENT METHODS

The method of RFID tag placement is somewhat dependent on the type of animal that is to be tagged. Both external and internal tagging methods may be employed. The following parameters generally determine what method of tagging is to be utilized:

- The size of the animal
- The presence of a previously existing external tag
- Aesthetic considerations

SIZE OF THE ANIMAL

As would be expected, larger animals provide more flexibility than smaller animals in tagging. Flexibility is increased from both the standpoint of tag size and tag positioning. Despite the increasing miniaturization of RFID technology, larger tags still generally have greater capabilities and range than smaller tags. Since larger animals can obviously handle larger sized tags, more flexibility is possible than with smaller animals.

Larger animals also have the advantage over smaller animals in the number of possible tag positions. Large domestic animals such as cattle can be easily externally tagged in a large number of places without restricting the animal's normal activity. In contrast, for example, smaller animals such as exotic birds are very limited in the number of places that a tag could be placed without interfering with the animal's flight abilities.

Larger animals would also be expected to have an advantage over smaller animals with respect to the implantation of internal RFID tags. The implantation of RFID tags in domestic pets such as dogs and cats has become a routine operation in virtually any veterinarian's office. However, the same operation in an exotic bird is a riskier operation requiring more specialized techniques.

THE PRESENCE OF A PREVIOUSLY EXISTING EXTERNAL TAG

The fact that the size of the animal lends itself to the use of an external tag does not necessarily mean that one currently exists. Other considerations may be in place that drive the presence of a previously existing external tag. For example, many domestic animals are already required by law to possess other non-RFID-based tags. These include tags for licensing and vaccinations. Domestic animals may also already have tags due to inventory purposes. Existing tags may come in the form of a semi-permanent metal plate that attaches to a collar. These plates are semipermanent in the sense that they may need to be removed and replaced with new tags on a periodic basis. An example of this type of tag is one that is used for rabies vaccinations. These typically expire over a period of three years. In this case, a suitable mounting platform already exists. The most appropriate means of positioning the tag would be on the collar.

Another type of previously existing external tag is a permanent object that is directly attached to some part of the animal. One example is the metal plate that is crimped onto livestock ears. This identification tag can be associated with a database containing the livestock's breeding and veterinary record. In the event that the type of tag used is sufficiently large, the RFID tag circuitry can be piggybacked onto the existing tag or the tag can be redesigned to include the RFID chip. This would be the preferred approach with the types of tags used for domestic animals such as

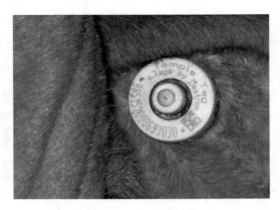

FIGURE 14.1   External RFID tags.

FIGURE 14.2   Exotic bird identification ring.

cattle that are intended for consumption. Figure 14.1 illustrates a number of external disk RFID tags.

Another example of the presence of a previously existing tag is the small metal ring placed around one leg of a domestic exotic bird. The ring typically contains stamped data related to the bird's breeder. In this case, the previously existing tag is unsuitable for modification due to its small size. Similarly, the ring is too small to have an RFID tag attached to it in the same manner as a dog or cat's collar. In this case, even though there is an existing tag or sorts, it cannot be utilized to externally add an RFID tag. Figure 14.2 illustrates a typical exotic bird breeder's ring.

NATURAL AND AESTHETIC CONSIDERATIONS

Yet two more considerations when determining the type of placement are natural and aesthetic considerations. Natural considerations are primarily associated with wild animals that are tracked in the wild for migratory or breeding purposes. The major issue here is that the tag should not have the potential to cause harm to the animal. This would be a distinct possibility in the case of an externally positioned tag, particularly if any type of collar were utilized. For this reason, internally positioned RFID tags would be preferred.

Aesthetic considerations would be more of interest with domestic animals that are considered pets. In this case, the pet owner would be interested in tracking his pet in the event that the pet became lost but would not want to alter the aesthetics of the animal. The necessity to track the animal is much less that that of a domestic animal intended for human consumption. The performance requirements that may necessitate the use of an external tag are greatly reduced. In the event that the pet were lost and taken to an animal control facility, it is standard procedure to scan the animal for RFID chips. Since the practice is to scan between the shoulders of the animal, a functioning chip is likely to be detected. Existing system practices mean that the use of an implanted RFID tag would be most appropriate in this situation.

EXTERNAL VERSUS INTERNAL TAG PLACEMENT

The following sections detail the methods as well as the advantages and disadvantages of both external and internal placement methods.

EXTERNAL TAG PLACEMENT

As previously discussed, the larger the RFID tag, the greater the capabilities and interrogation range. Since only very small RFID tags can be implanted, more capable systems require external tags. Two general approaches can be taken to external tag placement. In the first approach, the RFID tag can be attached to either a new or existing collar normally attached to the animal's neck. In this case, the tagging is in the same manner as a rabies or registration tag.

The alternative approach is to externally attach the RFID chip to some part of the animal's body. In some cases, the chip can be piggybacked onto an existing conventional tag. A typical example is an RFID tag that is affixed to the animal's ear. Cow RFID eartags are currently available for approximately $2.25 a piece.

Regardless of the placement method of the external tag, this approach has several advantages over internally placed tags. These include:

- Less tagging trauma to the animal
- Greater ease in maintainability
- Lower initial cost

Less tagging trauma is an obvious advantage since it is not necessary to anesthetize the animal when externally attaching the RFID tag to a collar. Greater maintainability is obtained since a malfunctioning tag or a tag that needs to be changed can be replaced without surgical intervention. Lastly, an external tag-based system is likely to be less expensive since the tags can be installed without the use of veterinary personnel.

External tag based systems do have a few disadvantages. These include:

- Increased possibility of tag damage or loss
- Wider and varying environmental operating conditions

Because the tags are externally positioned, the possibility exists that the tags may become damaged during the course of the animal's natural behavior. For example, an animal with a collar-based tag may lose or damage the tag while moving through brush. Livestock also periodically scratch themselves against fences and fence posts. This provides another opportunity to lose or damage the tag.

Increased variance in environmental conditions is also a concern since the tag may need to operate in both high temperatures and low temperatures during different seasons. In addition, the tag will be exposed to moisture from the rain. The tag must also be able to withstand UV radiation, which can attack the exposed RFID tag.

INTERNAL TAG PLACEMENT

Internal tag placement involves the insertion of the tag somewhere within the animal's carcass. Tags currently exist on the market that can be biologically inserted. In

FIGURE 14.3   Internal RFID tag.

addition, the tags are designed to be able to function under the environmental conditions of being inserted internally in the animal. The tags are the size of a grain of rice. Field testing indicates that animals do not experience rejection issues from the RFID tag. Figure 14.3 illustrates in internal RFID tag.

In permanent but reversible operations, the implantation process consists of injecting the tag under the skin or fur of the animal. Placed in this manner, the tag will only have to transmit and receive through a small layer of biological tissue. This greatly enhances the readability of the tag compared to other forms of surgical implantation or even ingestion. If necessary, it is far easier to remove the tag in the event that it malfunctions or needs to be updated.

The advantages and disadvantages of the internal placement of tags are generally the opposite of externally placed tags. Advantages include:

- Increased protection from damage
- More stable operating environment

Because the tag is internally positioned in the animal, it is obviously less likely to sustain damage due to the animal's normal behavior. The internal positioning also provides a more stable operating environment than an external tag. Despite fluctuations in ambient temperature, the internal body temperature of the animal is likely to remain relatively consistent.

Disadvantages include:

- Increased trauma to the animal
- Increased initial cost
- More expensive maintenance

The major disadvantage is the necessity to have the RFID tags implanted by a veterinarian. This adds some additional expense and inconvenience to the process that would not be experienced with the use of an external tag. In a single application as would be the case with a domestic pet, this is not a serious issue. However, the tagging of a large number of animals intended for human consumption may present a more difficult problem. In the event of tag malfunction, implanted tags present a more serious issue. Once again, specialized personnel will be required to safely remove the malfunctioning tag and replace it with one that is operating normally.

The issue of where the tag is implanted in the animal may also cause problems. In some past applications, the tag has been implanted in the vicinity of the animal's hoof. Positioning the tag in this manner increases the probability of tagging accidents with large animals. Internal tag positioning in the animal's hoof may also dictate the design of the RFID antenna portals. The relatively modest range of implanted RFID chips requires that these types of systems use antennas buried underground. This

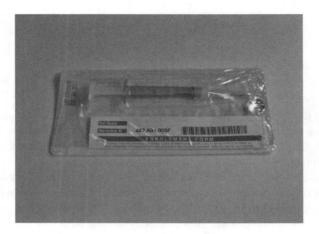

FIGURE 14.4   Implantable RFID tag and injector.

introduces additional issues that will be discussed in the antenna portal section of this chapter.

ANIMAL RFID TECHNOLOGY

Special injection apparatus is available for implanting RFID tags. Figure 14.4 illustrates one widely used system.

EXISTING SYSTEMS FOR DOMESTIC FOOD-RELATED ANIMALS

One relatively well-tested RFID system for cattle is manufactured by Valley Ag Software of Tulare, California. Their Dairy Comp 305 system consists of a small handheld computer, a twenty-four-inch-long antenna wand, and associated software. The system can be networked with a central database using wireless technology. The system price is approximately $4,500. The read range of this system is approximately fifteen inches. One difficulty has been identified with the system's modest range. This is dependent on the location of the tag. It has been discovered by users that eartags can make reads more difficult. The movement of the cow's head during the read time can result in misreads. This may require that the cows head be temporarily immobilized in order to obtain successful reads.

EXISTING SYSTEMS FOR DOMESTIC PETS

The use of RFID tags for domestic pets has become widespread. This process is commonly referred to as *microchipping.* Any area is likely to have a number of veterinarians who are capable of performing this process. The general RFID tagging process consists of implanting the rice grain–sized chip between the animal's shoulder blades with a special sterile injector. It is thought to be no more painful to the animal than a vaccination shot. Aside from the hospital visit, the price for the implantation process and the chip is approximately $50. An additional cost is the registration of the RFID tag identification number with a database service. Currently at least three companies are manufacturing chips for this purpose. These include HomeAgain, AVID, and Trovan. The scanner that is currently in vogue is the handheld Digital Angel World Scan Reader. This reader can identify the chips manufactured by HomeAgain, AVID, and Trovan, which operate in the 125- to 128-kHz radio frequency range.

Once the missing pet is scanned by the animal control or veterinarian, the RFID tag number can then be matched with the information maintained by the database service. The database service contacts the pet's owner once the tag has been matched. An example of one of these services is HomeAgain. This service is technically referred to as a *pet recovery database*. It is available twenty-four hours a day, 365 days a year by both telephone and the Internet. At the end of 2006, HomeAgain claimed to have over 3.7 million registered pets. Almost 330,000 pets are also claimed to have been recovered. The one-time database registration fee was $17.50 in 2006.

ANIMAL ANTENNA READERS AND PORTALS

The selection of a reader or a portal for animal tracking applications is greatly dependent on the following parameters:

- Nature of the application
- Position of the tag on the animal
- Frequency of required reads

Nature of the Application

The nature of the application involves how the RFID system is going to be used. For example, the use of RFID tags in a research-related catch-and-release animal tracking program would necessitate the use of a handheld reader. Animal tags would be expected to be read at different locations throughout the tracking area. It would be impossible to set up a permanent antenna portal.

Similarly, in the case of dairy cow tracking, it may be necessary to assign specific cows to specific milking stalls. The only way to determine if the correct cow is in the correct stall would be to perform the read in each stall. This would necessitate the installation and maintenance of an impossibly large number of antennas, which may defeat the purpose of the RFID system in the first place. In applications of this type, it would be most appropriate to use a portable reader going from stall to stall.

Conversely, if cattle intended for consumption were to be tracked using RFID technology, a different approach would be necessary. In this case, it might only be required to know the approximate location of each cow at a given time. Here, a limited number of antenna portals could be employed. There would be no necessity for a manned portable reader. As each cow passes through a specific portal, the central database would be automatically updated. Cows could even be segregated according to medical requirements as they pass through chutes.

Position of the Tag on the Animal

Positioning of the tag on the animal can affect both the choice of reader and, in the case of an antenna portal, the installation of the portal. One of the design principles of an RFID system is to minimize the variability of reads by positioning the tags in a consistent manner. This increases the probability of good reads because the position of the antennas can be tuned in relationship with the tags. If consistent positioning of the tag on the animal can be achieved, then the other source of variability if the movement of the animal itself.

Since the RFID tag is most likely to be passive, the limited range of the tag must also be taken into consideration. High-volume applications such as those involving meat cattle frequently use the above-the-hoof position for implanted tags. The relatively consistent positioning of the hooves allows for fixed antennas to be mounted low on control gates above the ground. Some sites have also been successful in positioning antennas horizontal to the animal's movement underneath the surface of the ground. In this case, the reduction in the interrogation zone as a result of burying the antenna must be carefully investigated.

However, if the position of the tag is such that the likely movement of the animal will be outside of a fixed interrogation zone, the RFID developer must consider the use of a portable reader. Other than increasing the range of the RFID tag and antenna, this is the only way to achieve reliable reads. This, of course, necessitates an individual to operate the reader. This is not so much of a problem if the individual is already present. But it should not be necessary to add another individual just to operate the portable reader. If this is the case, significant thought should be invested in developing alternative solutions.

Frequency of Required Reads

The frequency of required reads will also impact on the choice of either a portable reader or an antenna portal. A small number of reads like that experienced in an animal control facility or a veterinary hospital would dictate the use of an inexpensive installation free portable reader. Conversely, any operation requiring a high-volume, rapid read would preclude individual scanning of the animals with a portable reader. The meat cattle location application, for example, would definitely require a set of fixed antenna portals.

LIVESTOCK TRACKING STANDARDS

Due to various livestock health issues, European consumers have become increasing concerned about the origin of various meat products. As a result, the European Council of Ministers instituted a law based on ISO standard 11784/85 for sheep and goats. Currently, this law is optional, but it will become compulsory. By 2008, member nations with 600,000 animals or more must establish a central database for these animals. Nations with less than 600,000 do not need to comply, unless the animals are used in trade within the European Union.

With this system in place, authorities will be able to track the origin of any meat product that has been found to be contaminated. Contaminated livestock that have not yet been processed can then be treated or destroyed as necessary. Equally important, other contaminated meat products can be traced through the supply chain and tested and removed prior to consumption by customers.

Royal Philips Electronics has pioneered livestock RFID systems. They have currently implemented systems in Spain and Italy. In the Spanish system, a HITAG S RFID chip is implanted above the livestock's hoof. The movement of the cattle was tracked though buried antennas. In the Italian system, the RFID chip was integrated with the livestock's previously existing eartag. This system tracked the animal's food, veterinary, and transportation data from the animal's origin to sale. This can be considered as tracking from pen to pot.

In the Unites States, Tri-National Livestock Health and Identification Consortium was formed in 2005 through a voluntary program developed by the U.S. Department of Agriculture. This program was primarily implemented with breeders in the states of Arizona, Colorado, and New Mexico. Like the European efforts, this pilot project is intended to track livestock that could threaten the food supply. The intention of this program is to ultimately track all types of livestock, not just those intended for consumption.

The adoption of livestock tracking systems is yet another application that will feed the future development of RFID technology in general. There is a potential of one billion new tags needed each year to supply the livestock RFID industry. Volume of this size cannot but help reduce the cost of RFID technology.

RELATED HUMAN APPLICATIONS

In 2004, the U.S. Federal Drug Administration began approving human RFID implants previously used only in the animal tracking industry. The approval of the RFID implants has raised a storm of debate. Proponents such as Applied Digital Solutions claim that the use of human RFID chipping has great medical and security advantages to the individual. On the other hand, opponents believe that human applications are a further erosion of personal privacy. There cannot be any guarantee of the security of data obtained though RFID systems. This debate is likely to continue for some time into the future. In the meanwhile, we will examine what are likely to be future human RFID applications.

The success of RFID animal tracking applications naturally leads one to consider the use of RFID technology to track human beings. Applications that immediately come to mind include law enforcement corrections systems. In this type of application, prisoners would be implanted with an RFID chip and antenna portals would be placed around different parts of the prison. With existing technology, the prison management information system would be able to determine the approximate location of every prisoner 24/7.

SUMMARY

In this chapter, we presented information pertaining to RFID animal tracking applications. As we have seen, animal tracking applications are one of the most developed areas of RFID technology. These include wildlife tracking, domestic animals intended for consumption, and domestic pets. Many off-the-shelf systems currently exist that can be successfully applied to individual applications. The design of an animal RFID tracking system consists of determining where to position the predominately passive tags and what type of reader or antenna portal is to be utilized. The increasingly widespread use of RFID technology in animal tracking is contributing greatly to lowering the cost of the technology. This same animal tracking technology can be utilized for tracking human beings. However, the use of this technology will not be without significant political discussion or ramifications.

CHAPTER QUESTIONS

1. Why is it necessary to implant the RFID tag near the surface of the animal's fur or skin?
2. Why is it important to track livestock used for consumption?
3. What is the industry standard position for RFID tags in domestic pets?
4. Under what conditions would a portable RFID tag reader be preferable to a fixed antenna portal in animal tracking applications?

ADDITIONAL REFERENCES

Available at http://www.siamrfid.com/doc/Animal%20RFID%20Tag.doc [Accessed August 30, 2007].
Available at http://www.rfidnews.org/weblog/2004/02/26/rfid-aids-european-animal-disease-control.php [Accessed August 30, 2007].
Available at http://www.infowars.com/articles/ps/rfid_az_start_animal_tag_program.htm [Accessed August 30, 2007].
Available at http://www.infowars.com/articles/bb/fda_approves_human_rfid_implants.htm [Accessed August 30, 2007].
Available at http://www.altagenetics.com/English/whatsnew/20060627HighTechRFID.htm [Accessed August 30, 2007].
Available at http://www.homeagainid.com/index.cfm [Accessed August 30, 2007].
Available at http://www.trovan.com/productsuni.htm [Accessed August 30, 2007].

15 Credit Device RFID Applications

INTRODUCTION

One RFID application that is currently struggling for acceptance is use in the credit card industry. Initial pilot programs involving the use of RFID technology in credit cards began as early as 2003. As of the fall of 2006, RFID credit card applications were still not widely adopted despite significant efforts on the part of a number of credit card companies and banking institutions. For example, only approximately 1 percent of the one billion MasterCards currently utilize its widely advertised PayPass card system. Despite this low utilization rate, MasterCard is not the only credit card company investing heavily in contactless cards. Visa's equivalent card program is marketed as the Visa Wave. Similarly, American Express's program is known as Express Pay. These programs are generically referred to as *contactless payment systems*. The systems are contactless in the sense that, if functioning properly, the card does not need to be passed through a magnetic stripe reader.

Most of the public resistance to RFID credit card applications appears to stem from security- and privacy-related fears. A number of states in the United States have gone so far as to establish legislation requiring items with RFID tags to be prominently labeled as such. In this case, users have a natural fear that unauthorized scanning or reading of RFID cards may occur. Public perception is that both credit card fraud and identify theft will result. Whether or not the credit card industry will be able to overcome these fears and the resulting resistance is an issue outside of the scope of this chapter. Instead, we will concentrate on the description of the currently available systems.

FORM FACTORS

The most common form factor for contactless cards is the typical credit card form factor. The RFID circuitry is typically embedded on the back of the card. In many cases, it is necessary to provide additional markings on the contactless card to distinguish it from a conventional magnetic stripe card. This is because contactless cards also possess a magnetic stripe as a backup to the RFID chip. In the case of the Visa Wave card, a small transmission symbol is printed on both the front and the back of the card to indicate that it is a Wave contactless card. A Visa Wave contactless card symbol is illustrated in the Figure 15.1 (Visawave, online).

The use of RFID technology in credit card applications is not specifically limited to credit cards. A number of other form factors may also be used. It is anticipated that one of the more common form factors will be the RFID enabled key fob (Mastercard Pay

219

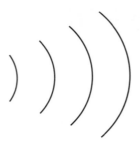

FIGURE 15.1 Visa Wave contactless card symbol.

FIGURE 15.2 RFID credit key fob.

Pass, online). In this case, the RFID circuitry is embedded within the protective plastic of the fob. Thus, the fob form factor is likely to provide superior protection to the RFID circuitry over the credit card form factor. However, unlike the conventional credit card form, key fobs do not have a magnetic stripe backup. This means that if either the RFID reader or the key fob is experiencing technical difficulties, an alternate form of payment will be required. An example of one of these is illustrated in Figure 15.2.

In the future, it is likely that the credit card companies will embed the RFID chip in other form factors. This means that one day, individuals may be able to select the form factor of their own choosing. Form factors could include previously existing personal items such as rings or pendants. The choice of individual form factors also includes the possibility of human implantation; RFID chips have been approved by the Food and Drug Administration (FDA) for implantation. This would mean that the purchaser would only have to position a finger or hand in the interrogation zone of the RFID point-of-sale reader.

GENERAL TRANSACTION PROCESS

Contactless cards are linked to credit and debit accounts in exactly the same manner as conventional magnetic stripe cards. The only difference is in the method of initiating the payment. With conventional magnetic stripe cards, the user must pass the card through or insert the card into the magnetic stripe reader. This may be performed by either the user or the vendor. In contrast, the contactless card is positioned near the RFID reader. Once in the reader's interrogation zone, the contactless card will respond with the appropriate identification and account number information. An advantage of the contactless card in this respect is that under normal circumstances the card does not need to leave the user's hand. Obviously, this means that it is less likely that the user will forget to retrieve his contactless card than a conventional magnetic stripe card.

As with the use of a conventional magnetic stripe card, some information feedback may be provided to the user through the reader's display system. However, unlike a conventional magnetic stripe card that is physically passed by the user through a reader, no physical feedback is present when a contactless card is utilized. To mitigate this lack of physical feedback, some contactless card programs are promoting a tapping action as part of the transaction process. This involves physically tapping the reader with the contactless card. If the contactless card is close enough to tap the reader, it is likely to be inside the reader's interrogation zone.

To further help overcome the lack of physical feedback, some readers now provide feedback visually and audibly. A sequence of flashing lights and tones indicates that the transaction has been performed successfully. Additional information on the operation of typical point-of-sale RFID readers is provided in the section on RFID readers.

Pilot studies involving contactless cards indicate that twenty seconds can be saved over individual transactions in comparison to cash purchases (O'Connor, 2005). However, these are not necessarily valid comparisons because a significant percentage of contactless card users would probably be using magnetic stripe cards versus cash anyway. The reduction in transaction time between use of a contactless card and a conventional credit card would likely be much less than twenty seconds.

Contrary to claims otherwise, the use of a contactless card does not necessarily mean that the individual would not have to sign for the purchase. Users would still be required to sign for purchases according to the retail store policy. In fact, in cases where users would not need to sign for purchases with contactless cards, they would not have to sign with conventional credit cards either. Typical examples of this are when the purchase is less than $25.

A real advantage to the use of contactless credit cards is that they are not completely dependent on a magnetic stripe to complete the transaction. Since the card is contactless, there is reduced likelihood that the magnetic stripe will become nonfunctional due to damage caused by repeated use. The passive RFID circuitry utilized in the contactless card does not have a specific limited operational life. To the credit card company, this means that fewer replacement cards will have to be manufactured and issued. To the user, it means that there may be less transaction frustration, as least from the standpoint of a worn magnetic stripe. Users would also be less likely to request new cards.

STANDARDS

The serious security and privacy issues associated with contactless cards have led to the adoption of the International Standards Organization air interface protocol 14443. ISO 14443 specifies both an encryption algorithm and very short read ranges. The use of very short read ranges limits the ability of unauthorized readers to scan a contactless card. In the event that a contactless card is read, the encryption algorithm is intended to prevent the identification and account number information from being decoded.

Despite these assurances, the security of RFID contactless cards is still in question by many (Farivar, 2006). Recently, in a demonstration for the *New York Times*, a security organization was able to easily capture and decode a University of Massachusetts computer science professor's contactless credit card. The computer science professor, Dr. Kevin Fu, was part of a university consortium funded by the National Science Foundation dedicated to researching RFID security and privacy issues.

Studies and demonstrations of this type essentially mean that it is possible under the correct circumstances for contactless cards to be compromised. Even with the short-range specifications of ISO 14443, contactless cards in wallets in jacket or pants pockets could be easily scanned by unauthorized individuals with concealed

FIGURE 15.3   Point-of-sale RFID reader.

RFID readers. Unfortunately, if the range of the antenna in the contactless card RFID chip is further reduced, difficulties may arise with the use of authorized point-of-sale readers.

An amusing development to the security issue is that some discussion is now underway concerning the development of RFID-blocking wallets and purses. As the name suggests, these devices incorporate materials to prevent the contactless card from receiving unauthorized interrogation signals or responding back to the unauthorized reader. In the event that contactless cards do become widely accepted, you can expect that wallets and purses will be prominently marketed as RFID secure.

CREDIT CARD RFID READERS

In order to utilize contactless cards, the merchant must have an RFID reader. These operate at 13.56 MHz. Many convenience store chains such as 7-Eleven and Sheetz have begun purchasing readers. However, there are approximately 200 million potential retailers in the United States alone. This means that significant deployment of point-of-sale readers must be performed prior to contactless cards becoming as widely used as conventional magnetic stripe readers.

Figure 15.3 illustrates a typical point-of-sale RFID reader. Point-of-sale RFID readers of this type typically have a range of four inches or less. Note the set of colored LEDs positioned across the top of the reader. When the reader has successfully interrogated the contactless card, the LEDs light in sequence from left to right, confirming the transaction. There may also be an audible tone as additional confirmation of the transaction completion. Note that when readers of this type are used, the purchaser will have to separately obtain a receipt to confirm the price of the goods that have been purchased. In contrast, most magnetic stripe readers have a digital display indicating the price of each item and the total purchase amount.

SUMMARY

In this section, we discussed the use of RFID technology for credit card applications. Although contactless RFID credit cards have been available for a number of years, public acceptance has been limited. Limited acceptance can be attributed to the public's understanding that RFID signals can be intercepted. Demonstrations as recently as the winter of 2006 support these perceptions. Some comments have even been made to the effect that with a contactless card, you might as well be wearing your name and credit card number on the back of your shirt.

Aside from overcoming negative perceptions, before this technology is accepted it must also become more widely distributed. Unlike many other application areas where a widespread RFID infrastructure does not need to be in place, in the retail industry the opposite is true. A substantial percentage of retail establishments must install RFID readers before it can become widely accepted.

CHAPTER QUESTIONS

1. What two measures have been taken by the credit card industry to help prevent contactless credit card theft?
2. What forms of feedback are used to provide customers with an indication of a successful contactless card read?
3. Why might the transaction time savings indicated by pilot studies for contactless cards not necessarily valid?

ADDITIONAL REFERENCES

Farivar, C. *Researchers hack RFID credit cards* [Online]. Available at http://www.engadget. com/2006/10/23/researchers-hack-rfid-credit-cards-big-surprise/ [Accessed 2007].
Mastercard Pay Pass [Online.] Available at www.paypass.com [Accessed 2007].
O'Conner, M. C. (2005). Chase offers contactless cards in a blink. *RFID Journal* [Online]. Available at http://www.rfidjournal.com/article/articleview/1615/1/1/ [Accessed 2007].
Visa wave [Online]. Available at http://usa.visa.com/personal/cards/contactless/index.html?it= cl%2Fpersonal%2Fcards%2Findex%2Ehtml|%2Fimg%2Fgold_arrow%2Egif [Accessed 2007].

16 Secure Document RFID Applications

INTRODUCTION

Perhaps the most sensitive RFID application to date involves the use of RFID technology with government passports. The issuance of the U.S. E-passport began on August 14, 2006. E-passports contain the same information as conventional passports but also include an RFID chip in the rear cover of the passport. Since the first E-passports were issued, a great deal of public criticism has arisen. Some tests by independent parties indicate that it is possible to overcome the built-in security and privacy measures incorporated into E-passports (Miller, 2006; Ricker, 2006; Schneider, 2005). However, whether or not these potential weaknesses can be illegally exploited by illegal aliens and terrorist groups has yet to be determined. In this chapter, we will begin with a basic description of how the E-passport functions and continue with a discussion of security issues.

BASIC PASSPORT BACKGROUND

Passports are issued by virtually all nations. They are usually required for identification purposes for entry into most nations. The few exceptions to this requirement that do exist are slowly being eliminated. For example, the Intelligence Reform and Terrorism Prevention Act of 2004 required the U.S. Department of Homeland Security and the U.S. State Department to develop and implement a plan whereby all travelers need a document such as a passport for identification purposes on entry into the United States. As a result of the act, since January 23, 2007, all persons, including U.S. citizens traveling by air, are required to have a passport or similar documentation for entry from Mexico and the Caribbean. As early as January 1, 2008, these requirements may be extended to both land and sea (U.S. Department of State, 2007).

The passport currently being issued by the Department of State is the E-passport. The significant identification data page inside the passport is illustrated in Figure 16.1.

Note that the page contains a photograph, the passport number, the individual's name, date of birth, birthplace, sex, and passport issue and expiration dates. The E-passport also contains an RFID chip on the inside back cover of the passport. The inside back cover is illustrated in Figure 16.2.

Since the passport issuing period is ten years, it will be a number of years before all of the passports in circulation will be required to be renewed. Until then, it is anticipated that all of the non-E-passports in circulation will continue to be valid.

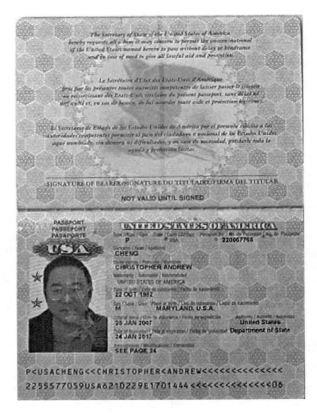

FIGURE 16.1   Photograph page of E-passport.

E-PASSPORT RFID CHIP

The E-passport RFID chip contains 64K of encrypted data. Publicly accessible sources indicate that the chip holds the same information that is available on the picture page of the E-passport. As we stated earlier, this includes the passport number, the individual's name, date of birth, birthplace, sex, and passport issue and expiration dates. The chip also includes a digital photograph of the passport holder. The presence of the digital photograph allows for the possibility of incorporating biometric identification systems at some future point in time. This means that an individual may be digitally scanned at the point of entry. The real-time scan would then be biometrically compared to the digital photo contained in the RFID chip. The exact contents of the chip are governed by the International Civil Aviation Organization, which we discuss in the next section.

INTERNATIONAL CIVIL AVIATION ORGANIZATION (ICAO) PROTOCOL

The E-passport follows the standards indicated by the International Civil Aviation Organization. These standards are available from their Web site at www.icao.int/

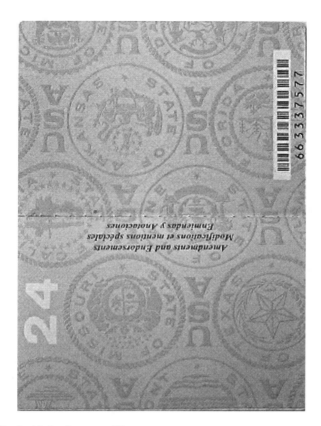

FIGURE 16.2 Inside back cover of E-passport.

mrtd/download/technical.cfm. One of the significant components of this protocol is that the E-passport is only supposed to be readable from very short distances. This is officially reported as four inches. However, there are some claims that E-passports can be read as far as a few feet away. The unauthorized reading of passports by unknown individuals has been termed *skimming*.

To combat successful skimming, the U.S. State Department has incorporated a multilayered security system to help prevent the unauthorized access of E-passport data. The first layer of protection consists of electronic shielding built into the cover of the E-passport. This is intended to block signals from any RFID readers attempting to energize the E-passport and read the resulting signal.

The second level of security is what is known as *basic access control*. This begins with a sequence of machine-readable characters physically printed on the E-passport. This sequence of numbers is an encryption key. When the passport control officer scans the E-passport, the RFID reader uses the encryption key to communicate and decode the data from the RFID chip. In theory, this means that the only way to obtain and decode the data on the E-passport is to first open up the passport and obtain the encryption key.

Critics of the basic access control system are not so optimistic. In the summer of 2006, German hackers succeeded in successfully accessing ICAO-based passport data. By reading the publicly available ICAO documents, the hacker determined that the encryption key was based on information contained on the passport photo page. The hacker was then able to crack an electronic passport and download the information to a smart memory card. By inserting the smart card into a physical passport, the hacker was able to present different physical and RFID passports.

An additional security measure used with E-passports is known as a *public key infrastructure*, or PKI. The mechanics behind the PKI are beyond the scope of this chapter. However, it should be understood that the purpose of the PKI is to help insure that the data in the E-passport RFID chip cannot be altered. It is in essence a digital signature. In the event that the data is altered, the digital signature created with the PKI will indicate that tampering has occurred. For the individual, this also means that any change in name or other data will require that an entirely new passport be obtained. To help minimize the potential burden to citizens, the U.S. Department of State is allowing new passports to be obtained without charge for one year.

Another security problem associated with E-passports is known as *eavesdropping*. This is the electronic monitoring of the signals between the RFID reader and the E-passport. The possibility of this was demonstrated in February 2006 when a group of Dutch hackers successfully eavesdropped on an RFID transmission and within two hours had successfully decrypted a digitized fingerprint, photograph, and other text information from an E-passport. Since the Dutch E-passport is based on the ICAO standards, it is presumed that this may also be performed on other ICAO standards–based E-passports. The current government response to this potential weakness is to maintain electronic eavesdropping detection equipment at ports of entry.

OTHER DEVELOPMENTS

Late in 2006, the Department of State announced the possibility of augmenting E-passports with a passport card. The passport card is intended to simplify travel between the United States, Mexico, Canada, and the Caribbean. Like the E-passport, the passport card will incorporate an RFID chip. However, at this time, the passport card is not expected to incorporate personal information in the same manner as the E-passport. Instead, the passport card will be linked to a central database that contains the individual's photograph and biographical data. The passport card will also be more convenient and significantly cheaper to acquire than an E-passport.

DEPLOYMENT

It will likely be some time in the future before E-passports outnumber the number the conventional passports in circulation. In addition to replacing the conventional passports with E-passports, the port of entry facilities must also have the optical scanners and RFID readers that the E-passport RFID chips need to operate. As this equipment is installed, the access lanes will be marked with the special international E-passport symbol illustrated in Figure 16.3. This will allow travelers to properly

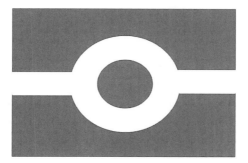

FIGURE 16.3   E-passport lane symbol.

take advantage of the increased capabilities of their E-passports. It is expected that this will help speed the processing of travelers.

SUMMARY

The use of E-passports offers potentially faster processing of individuals through port of entry facilities. Faster processing is possible because the same information that is available on the picture page of the passport is also stored in the RFID chip. When the passport is optically scanned, the RFID chip transmits this information to the control point. The immigration agent can then check the passport record against immigration records and watch lists.

The technology inherent in RFID chips has led to a number of concerns with respect to the data security of E-passports based on the ICAO standards. Independent tests have indicated that RFID E-passport data can be both cloned and eavesdropped on by unauthorized parties. However, the issuance of E-passports is still proceeding. Proponents of the use of E-passports dismiss these security concerns, stating that the use of RFID technology is intended as an additional security measure rather than as a replacement to the function of a conventional non-RFID passport.

REFERENCES

International Civil Aviation Organization Protocol. [Online]. Available at www.icao.int/mrtd/download/technical.cfm [Accessed 2007].

Miller, P. *German hackers clone RFID passports* [Online]. Available at http://www.engadget.com/2006/08/03/german-hackers-clone-rfid-e-passports/ [Accessed 2007].

Ricker, T. *Dutch RFID e-passport cracked—U.S. next* [Online]. Available at http://www.engadget.com/2006/02/03/dutch-rfid-e-passport-cracked-us-next/ [Accessed 2007].

Schneider, B. *RFID passport security revisited* [Online]. Available at http://www.schneier.com/blog/archives/2005/08/rfid_passport_s_1.html [Accessed 2007].

U.S. Department of State. *Frequently asked questions* [Online]. Available at http://travel.state.gov/passport/eppt/eppt_2788.html#One [Accessed 2007].

17 DOD RFID and Wireless Communications Initiatives

INTRODUCTION

The Department of Defense (DOD) has some specific requirements for transmission of data, in particular in the RFID arena. All automatic identification technology (AIT) devices pose frequency problems for DOD, as they are a global force that can be deployed literally anywhere in the world at a moment's notice. Most global commercial companies also have this problem, in that if they are shipping around the world, they must have prior approval for the frequencies that they use for their devices. Unlike most commercial companies that maintain worldwide operations, the additional problem for DOD when they deploy into an area of operations (AoR) is that of fixed infrastructure. Since the DOD normally deploys into war situations, the fixed infrastructure on the ground has been eliminated prior to forces moving in. This causes many additional problems, because almost all AIT devices require power and communications to allow them to function within the business process.

DOD has used active RFID and satellite tracking devices for several years and has managed to incorporate these capabilities into their logistics business process and integrate them into their systems as enablers that allow for better visibility, communications, and command and control.

Passive RFID (pRFID) is a fairly new technology and DOD is in the process of working through where this technology will fit into its logistics business processes. At this time it is thought that inventory is one area where it fits best, but the tags will need to be much cheaper and smaller for use on individual items required for this process.

In July 2004, the Office of the Secretary of Defense for Acquisition, Technology and Logistics (OSD, AT&L), issued policy requiring that "Components will immediately resource and implement the use of high data capacity active RFID in the DoD operational environment." In this same policy, the OSD, AT&L stated "DoD will use and require its suppliers to use EPC Class 0 and Class 1 tags readers and complementary devices" (Wynne, 2004). In November 2005, the final Defense Federal Acquisition Regulation (DFAR) clause was approved and posted, making it mandatory for any contract signed after that date to include passive RFID tags on shipments at the case and pallet level. Consolidated shipments require active RFID at the pallet/container level.

By 2002, the Central Command (CENTCOM) commander released a message requesting that 100 percent of all items moving into, through, and/or out of the CENTCOM AoR be tagged to enable asset tracking. Polices and instructions such as these have promoted the use of these AIT devices.

THE PAST

In every major deployment during the twentieth century, DOD has been plagued by the inability to easily identify the contents of shipping containers entering a theater of operations. This was never more evident than in operations Desert Shield and Desert Storm when thousands of containers has to be opened, inventoried, resealed, and then reinserted into the transportation system. This was necessary because soldiers could not identify their contents. As a result, in fiscal year 1995, the Total Distribution Program Action Plan was developed and approved by the vice chief of staff of the army to resolve supply and distribution problems that surfaced during the first Gulf War. Since 1993, the army has been pursuing the use of active Radio Frequency Identification (RFID) tags to gain "in the-box-visibility" for both deploying equipment and sustainment stocks. In the early years, tag use was limited to demonstrations in places such as Haiti and Macedonia. However, in November/December 1995, approximately 35 percent of all of deployed items were tagged for the U.S. Army, Europe's (USAREUR), deployment to Bosnia as part of the North Atlantic Treaty Organization's implementation force/stabilization force (IFOR/SFOR). Jumping ahead to the spring of 1999, approximately 70 percent of all items moved for the Kosovo force were tagged. Both the Army Reserve (USAR) and Eighth United States Army received RFID tagged sustainment stocks from both of the Defense Logistics Agency depots on the United States' East and West Coasts. More currently, in 2001 approximately 85 percent of unit equipment shipped from installations around the world and sustainment stocks from Defense Logistics Agency (DLA) that flowed into Operation Enduring Freedom were shipped with RFID tags.

THE PRESENT

Due to the CENTCOM Commander message in 2002, over 95 percent of equipment flowing into Operation Iraqi Freedom (OIF) have active RFID tags attached. This allows for the automated receipt of supplies, nodal in-transit visibility, and an electronic manifest on the outside of shipping containers.

As you can clearly see, RFID has become an important part of today's total asset visibility plan and has gained momentum in its use. Active RFID tags require fixed infrastructure, which enables nodal in-transit visibility. The best visibility that this capability can provide is a good fix on where the equipment was last detected, not necessarily where it is currently located. Even with the robust active RFID infrastructure currently in place (over three thousand sites around the globe), immediate asset visibility is not possible when deploying into austere environments. The fastest that the army and DOD has been able to set up the needed fixed RFID infrastructure in an austere environment is approximately three weeks. By that time, under normal operational tempo for an ongoing operation in the deployment stage, combat equipment and supplies have already moved through the intermediate support base (ISB). This leaves the RFID infrastructure to play catch-up, which of course never happens until much later in the engagement.

Likewise, the fixed infrastructure adds additional material to an already overburdened support system. Power is required for the RFID interrogator and the computer, which collects the data and provides it to the ITV servers via a communications link. RFID also requires communications (phone, local area network, and/or satellite) to report the location and asset information collected by the interrogator/computer. Contractor logistics support (CLS) is required to install and maintain this fixed infrastructure, which adds to the security burden of area commanders. Power, communications, and CLS are not always available when and where they are needed, in particular during the beginning stages of a deployment. Lessons learned from Operation Enduring Freedom and Operation Iraqi Freedom show that the best we can ever expect from the current RFID capability, as technically efficient as it is, is to know where the supplies and equipment were, not what they are.

THE FUTURE

Although active RFID has become much more in demand, the technology has virtually not changed in the last decade. The first step in creating the next generation of RFID tagging systems for asset tracking was taking three commercial off-the-shelf products and integrating them into one, thus creating a new enhanced capability. RFID integrated with satellite communications and a global positioning system results in a single device that can overcome the "where is it now?" asset tracking problem. This new capability was prototyped in 2005 and was called the *third generation radio frequency identification with satellite communications*. It has the potential to provide the DOD with the promise of unprecedented on-demand supply and equipment in-transit visibility without fixed infrastructure. These new tags maintain all of the current capabilities of their predecessor tags and allow for true, up-to-the-moment global asset tracking via satellite and GPS.

3G RFID w/SATCOM would be particularly useful in the beginning stages of a deployment, when combatant commanders, joint task force, and other commanders find that their asset management information needs are most critical for assessing their combat effectiveness. Commanders under these circumstances require near real-time and on-demand visibility.

The results from this prototype were very promising, and a follow-on project has begun with a second prototype. This project, called *next generation wireless communications* (NGWC), will use the results from the initial prototype and expand those with additional wireless capabilities. In particular, self-forming, self-healing mesh networks are being looked at as a possible capability to enhance the in-transit visibility capability. Using this mesh network, the tags will be able to communicate among themselves, with one or more of the tags, as appropriate, taking on the mission of obtaining and passing the data for all of the tags either via an RFID interrogator when one is available or a wireless communications device when the RFID network is not available. These wireless devices can be one of several technologies that the DOD currently has in use.

An 802.11 WiFi capability that is available from the tactical to the operational levels of today's military is one possibility. This wireless local area network (LAN), called the *combat-service-support automated information systems interface* (CAISI), has been fielded to most logistics units in OIF/OEF and is scheduled to continue fielding to tactical army units until all are equipped. This LAN capability could accept the signal from an 802.11-enabled RFID tag just as an RFID interrogator does today. In addition, in the OIF/OEF AORs, the CAISI system is hooked into combat service support very small aperture terminal (CSS-VSAT), which allows for long-haul worldwide transmission of data.

This CCS-VSAT capability takes advantage of commercial off-the-shelf capabilities that continue to be expanded across DOD in all domains in order to expand the bandwidth. This expansion of the DOD bandwidth is one of three recommendations from a 2003 report "The Global Wired and Wireless Communications Infrastructure." This report recommended that DOD logisticians expand their bandwidth, ensure that the current and near term bandwidth capabilities be used more effectively by using compression tools, and make sure that requirements for future systems take both into account as they are being brought on-line.

Iridium satellite is another capability that is being explored as a possible means to pass data from the NGWC tags. This global satellite capability has been well documented over the past five to seven years by several independent evaluations and prototype tests and fielded capabilities, in particular by the U.S. government. Iridium claims to be the "only two-way coverage to include all the worlds ocean's and polar regions." This low Earth orbit satellite (LEOS) network of 60-plus satellites is truly global, and with DOD already owning a downlink Earth-bound hub, which is located in Hawaii, is a good choice for DOD users with low bandwidth requirements. This capability was used during the first prototype effort and is being used with the NGWC tag as well. It is a relatively inexpensive choice for transfer of small data packets, which is all that is required of the tags.

Cellular communications is another possibility that is being researched. The one shortfall with this technology is that there is no current worldwide standard. It is widely believed that there are over eighty different cellular formats worldwide, making it difficult to attempt a single point of entry for DOD, which is again an organization that can be deployed anywhere on the globe at a moments notice. To know which of the formats to choose would be very difficult, if not impossible. Therefore, DOD has opted to look at those formats that are most widely used around the world. CDMA/TDMA and GSM are two such formats that are being closely scrutinized at this time.

CONCLUSIONS

For the past decade the army has been using active RFID technology to gain asset visibility. Today's capability provides information on where the equipment was, not where it is. Additional RFID infrastructure is needed, which will likely increase the burden on an already taxed support system. pRFID and other future AIT devices will be added to this repertoire to add to the already abundant visibility within DOD logistics. The pursuit of total asset visibility remains a critical element in achieving focused logistics and sense and respond logistics concepts. 3G RFID with SATCOM took a huge step forward in accomplishing these requirements. NGWC will continue along this path and provide a future capability for DOD logistics. When combined with pRFID for inventory, the total AIT system will provide total asset visibility across the strategic, operational, and tactical domains. 3G RFID tags provided the foothold and NGWC will continue along this path to unprecedented in-transit visibility while potentially reducing or eliminating the current fixed infrastructure. This increased total asset visibility will enable the modernization of theater distribution and will be a key tool in connecting the logistics plans.

REFERENCE

Wynne, Michael W., Radio Frequency Identification Policy, Defense AI&L, The Undersecretary of Defense, Washington, D.C.: July 30, 2003.

18 Entertainment RFID Applications

INTRODUCTION

Recreational entertainment facilities are another up-and-coming area of RFID application. These include amusement parks, water parks, ski resorts, and concerts. All of these types of entertainment facilities are characterized by a large volume of customers proceeding through a series of processes. While some processes such as payment for entry are mandatory, other processes such as individual attractions are not. Most if not all of these processes are characterized by some sort of queue system. In each of these queue systems, the customer must wait in one or more lines until one or more resources such as a ticket seller or an attraction operator is available.

Examples of processes that the customers may undergo include:

- Payment on entrance of the facility
- Payment for special activities not included in the base entrance price
- Recreational activities themselves
- Concessions
- Souvenirs

In the following sections, we will initially examine both conventional approaches and approaches that utilize RFID technology. Next, we will discuss particular aspects of specific entertainment facilities that make RFID systems superior. The chapter will finish with a summary and a set of chapter questions.

CONVENTIONAL APPROACHES

In recent years, customer tracking has been accomplished through the use of a variety of wristbands and access cards. These systems are relatively inexpensive and easy to implement.

WRISTBANDS

Wristbands are usually narrow strips of vinyl or plastic that are positioned around the customer's wrist. They usually incorporate some sort of tab or button device to both secure the wristband and to prevent a user from removing the wrist band and transferring it to another customer. Wristbands are generally considered disposable. That is, after their limited period of use, they are expected to be discarded. Fortunately, most wristbands are made of plastic and are of low cost.

Wristbands can be implemented by the entertainment facility at a number of different technology levels. At the most basic level, wristbands can be color coded to control patron access. The color code can allow access to specific attractions within the facility or can indicate other information such as the patron's age. A date or some sort of pattern or logo associated with the facility or event may also be imprinted on the wristband.

In these most basic applications, the establishment has little more than the opportunity to make a physical count of the number of wristbands sold. If an attraction operator is checking for access, they may also manually tally the number of patrons who visit their attraction. Sometimes this is performed by banded customers proceeding through a turnstile. At periodic intervals or at the end of the day, the number indicated on the turnstile is recorded for later analysis.

The amount of information that can be obtained from this most simple system is quite limited. If the customer counts are rigorously maintained, the facility may at best determine the average number of individual attractions that customers visit. However, there is no capability to determine how many attractions any given individual customer visits. Nor is much data available to determine the pattern of attraction visits. It is entirely possible that a number of customers frequent a select number of attractions multiple times. Another disadvantage is associated with the customer themselves. Some customers will undoubtedly find the use of a wristband to be inconvenient, uncomfortable, or distracting.

At a more sophisticated level, the wristbands may also have a bar code. This is achieved by providing a specific space on the wristband for printing the bar code. Bar codes may be printed in batches on-site using a special printer. This allows the facility to determine which type of bar code and numbering scheme will best suit its purposes. If desired, each wristband can be assigned a unique bar code. Each patron is then assigned a particular bar code upon entry. Since each patron is uniquely identified, the bar code can be easily integrated with the facility's information and financial system.

At the individual attractions, the attraction operators can scan the bar code on the customer's wristband. Access is provided by electronically matching the bar code with the attraction requirements in a number of manners. At the lowest level of technological implementation, the operator would use a handheld scanner that verifies the eligibility of the bar code. In more sophisticated applications, the scanner would be networked with the facility's information system for verification. It is even possible to mechanically link a physical barrier system to the bar code system. In this case, it may be possible to reduce the number of attendants to a particular attraction.

A particular advantage of this more sophisticated type of approach is that the information system can track when and how many times a particular customer proceeds through the scanning station of a specific attraction. This makes it possible to perform more advanced statistical analysis of customer behavior than basic wristbands.

FIGURE 18.1   Simple wristband.

FIGURE 18.2   Barcode wristband.

FIGURE 18.3   Tab wristband.

Bar code wristbands are not without their own disadvantages. One major disadvantage to any barcode wristband is the requirement that the bar code be visually accessible for scanning. This means that the customer may have to pull back any jacket or shirt sleeve that may be covering the bar code. Another disadvantage is the possibility of the bar code becoming damaged. This is a weakness of almost any bar code. Abrasion to the wristband bar code may degrade the pattern of bars and spaces. If the damage is sufficiently serious, the bar code scanner will not be able to properly read the bar code. The final disadvantage is the same as with basic wristbands. Some customers will object to the wristbands from a comfort point of view.

A final type of wristband may also include tear-off tags built into the wristband itself. These types of wristbands may be used with or without bar codes. The principal attraction of the tear-off tab wristband is that they can be used to limit the number of attractions visited or concessions consumed by the customer. In this case, the pattern of attraction visits or concessions consumed can be monitored, not from the customer perspective, but from the attraction or concession perspective.

ACCESS CARDS

Access cards are a second type of common or conventionally utilized means of monitoring customers in entertainment venues. As with wristbands, access cards come in a variety of technologies. Perhaps the most common conventional access card uses either a bar code imprinted on the card or a magnetic stripe identifying the card. With both of these technologies, the card is uniquely identified to the central database. To access a particular attraction, the access card is either scanned in the same manner as a bar code wristband or inserted into a magnetic card reader.

The bar code–based access card has the same liability as the bar code wristband. If the bar code is damaged, it may prevent successful reads. The bar code–based card must also be presented for reading. If the card is not externally secured to the customer, it will be necessary to access the card each time it is utilized. This can have a detrimental effect on the efficient operation of the attraction. The same liability is present with the use of a magnetic stripe–based card. The magnetic stripe–based card also has the additional liability of needing to be run through the card reader. The card cannot even be secured to the customer in the same manner as a bar code card could be with a neck lanyard.

Access cards have the advantage over conventional wristbands in that financial data can be linked to the cards. In this respect, the card can operate in the same manner as either a charge card or a prepaid credit card. In the case of a charge card, the purchases made with the card are linked to a master account for later settlement. In the case of a prepaid card, the level of available funds is reduced by each purchase.

RFID WRISTBANDS AND TAGS

The visual and physical limitations of conventional and bar code wristbands and bar code and magnetic cards can be overcome with the use of either RFID wristbands or RFID cards. Passive RFID chips are sufficiently small in size to actually be affixed to either a conventional wristband or a wristband with a bar code. Since the wristband is still basically a wristband, color codes and printed information may be utilized in addition to the RFID chip.

In practice, the use of the RFID wristband is similar to that of the bar code wristband. To obtain access, the RFID wristband is interrogated as the customer passes through each attraction's access point. As long as the antenna successfully reads the tag, the customer can proceed unhampered. Only when the tag cannot be read is it necessary for the attendant to become involved. The ability to not interact directly with the customer allows the attraction to have a much greater customer throughput. Thus, the same benefits seen in the warehouse can be seen in the entertainment facility. The only difference is the material being tagged.

Another great opportunity made possible through the use of RFID wristbands is present at the exit of the attraction. Rather than using a turnstile to keep track of departing customers, the facility can use an exit antenna portal. Not having to restrict customer departure to this type of bottleneck can also be expected to improve overall customer throughput. In addition, the departure of the specific customer is recorded. Thus, the facility has the opportunity to record both the entry and the exit of the customer.

RFID wristbands do not suffer from many of the limitations of either basic, bar code, or tear-off wristbands. As we have seen from previous chapters, the visual requirement of these other technologies is overcome by RFID. This means that even though an RFID wristband may be covered by the customer's clothing, the wristband will still be able communicate with the facility's information system.

Another advantage of the RFID wristband is that the band does not have to be oriented in a particular manner. In contrast, bar code wristbands require either the customer's arm or the reader to be oriented to the other. Delays due to positioning are eliminated with the RFID wristband. This allows the facility to increase the throughput of customers at any access point.

Lastly, the RFID wristband is less subject to possible damage due to abrasion. This is, of course, a serious issue with bar code wristbands. Thus, in normal use, with RFID wristbands, higher levels of read reliability can be expected than with bar code wristbands.

The same capabilities that are available with either the bar code or magnetic stripe technologies are also available. Thus, the facility will be able to control attraction access as well as track individual customers' marketing behaviors. The RFID wristband can also be integrated into the facility's information system for transactions involving finances. Some organizations are currently marketing RFID kiosks to

FIGURE 18.4   RFID wristband.

facilities with these operations. These kiosks can be used by patrons to reload money
to the RFID wristband from credit cards, debit cards, or even cash. Figure 18.4 illustrates an RFID wristband.

GENERAL ADVANTAGES TO RFID WRISTBANDS TO ENTERTAINMENT FACILITIES

The following sections describe the additional advantages and disadvantages that
RFID wristbands and tags can offer to entertainment facilities. These include:

- Resource distribution
- Marketing behavior
- Patron locating
- Patron restricting
- Medical records
- Locker access

RESOURCE DISTRIBUTION

The tracking of customer movement is important for both immediate and long-term
information purposes. In the immediate term, tracking customers allows the facility
operators to shift resources to maximize customer service. For example, in a water
park, the facility management may shift attendants from less popular attractions to
more popular attractions. This will allow for an increase in throughput in the more
popular attractions while maintaining a satisfactory level of service in the less popular attractions. Alternatively, the facility management could allocate floater operators as the demand dictates.

MARKETING BEHAVIOR

In the previous sections, reference was made to tracking various aspects of customer
marketing behavior. In this section, we will define these benefits more specifically.
Long-term benefits of automatic data collection allow park management to study the
patterns of behavior of the customers. More specifically, the arrival, departure, and
travel data for the attractions can be used in conjunction with simulation analysis. Simulation analysis consists of building a mathematical model that represents the behavior
of the facility. The effects of different operating policies and resource allocation decisions can be determined in compressed time without altering the actual system.

The simulation analysis can help with future capital decisions. Obviously, the
facility executives and managers will want to invest more heavily in the attractions
that are the most popular. Similarly, unpopular attractions may be considered for

elimination. The same information can be easily incorporated in marketing campaigns for the facility.

Patron Locating

Patron tracking is another important benefit inherent in the use of RFID technology in entertainment facilities. This benefit is of particular importance since most of the entertainment facilities that we discuss in this chapter include families as their patrons. Aside from the always possible lost child scenario, many families split up due to differences in entertainment interests. The ability to easily regroup at lunchtime or the end of the day is obvious.

As we already know, each time a patron requests access to a particular attraction, the RFID tag is scanned. Thus, to determine the last known location of a particular patron all that is needed is access to the database that records the RFID reads. The database will indicate all of the attractions the patron visited and the time that the patron visited the attraction. This will allow the facility management to determine the patron's pattern of movement. If the facility has also chosen to utilize exit antenna portals, the facility can determine whether a patron is still inside a particular attraction. To go one step further, it is also possible to contain a particular patron within the attraction. All that is needed is to remove the authorization for that RFID number to exit the attraction. The same principle can also be utilized to contain an individual within the next attraction entered. On a larger scale, the patron could also be prevented from leaving a section of the facility or the entire facility itself. There are limitations to this approach. For example, if the patron has exited the last attraction, the problem of locating the current position of the patron becomes somewhat more complex.

To enhance the ability of the information system to locate patrons within the facility, tracking portals can be positioned throughout the facility in addition to the normal attraction RFID antennas. As the patrons proceed through the entertainment facility, the central information system database can record their movements.

Patron Restriction

Patron restriction involves preventing particular types of patrons from accessing certain components of the facility. Restriction can be based on different levels of paid access or age. In the case of paid access, some facilities offer customers priority treatment for additional cost. Typically known as preferred or VIP levels, these customers are allowed to either jump to the head of a queue or have a separate queue from the regular customers. By utilizing special RFID numbers, only the preferred customers will be allowed access to these advantages.

The other type of access restriction involves age. Some of the facility's attractions would only be accessible, for example, to patrons over the age of eighteen. This would help prevent minors from being able to enter concessions that serve alcohol or purchase alcohol from vendors within the facility. The age restriction could also apply to amusement type attractions. On one end, customers who are too young to enter attractions without adult supervision could be denied entry, while customers who are too old to enter child-related activities could also be excluded.

MEDICAL RECORDS

Patrons with special medical conditions will appreciate the presence of RFID wristbands. Many individual attractions are posted with signs advising patrons with particular medical conditions not to engage in the attraction. Even though the facility may provide these warnings, some patrons may still inadvertently participate in an unsuitable activity. If special medical conditions are determined at the time of entry, the RFID system can alert the attraction personnel that it may not be wise to permit the customer to participate.

There are also post–medical incident advantages to the use of RFID wristbands. The facility's information system can updated with the patron's medical information. In the event of a serious medical situation, the facility personnel will be able to access the individual's medical information even if the patron is unconscious. This is performed by simply interrogating the patron's RFID wristband with a portable reader. The reader can then advise the personnel providing assistance as to identification and special medical conditions of the individual. This additional and immediately available information can make the difference between life and death for potentially serious medical situations.

LOCKER ACCESS

Many entertainment sites offer facilities for the patrons to secure personal items that are not immediately needed. These include lockers for clothing, equipment, and food. Typically, patrons will have to stand in line to purchase a key to a locker. When they want to open or close the locker, they will have to access the key. In the case of families, when any one individual wants to access the locker, he has to locate the individual with the key. Lastly, when they are ready to leave the park, patrons have to stand in line to turn in the key. In the intervening period, the patrons may lose the key. This will cause additional delays in order to verify that the locker is actually assigned to the patron. The key may also be stolen or found by another individual who will be able to successfully access the locker. In the event that a key cannot be recovered, the entertainment facility will have to rekey the locker. In the meantime, it will be unavailable for use.

The entire locker process can be greatly streamlined though the use of RFID wristbands. On entrance to the facility, the patron can purchase use of a locker at the time that the RFID wristband is assigned. Since the issuance of the locker is performed at this time, the patron will not have to stand in a separate locker key line in the locker area. Since the locker is assigned to the RFID wristband, there is no key to lose or have stolen. The lockers can be set to automatically open and close. This is useful in the event that there is nowhere to place personal items while otherwise fumbling for a key. The patron is also assured that the contents of the locker are secure. Unlike physical keys, single lockers may also have multiple users. Having multiple RFID wristbands assigned to a single locker allows any of the authorized individuals the opportunity to access the locker.

Of course there is no key to have to turn in at the end of the patron's visit to the entertainment facility. The patron does not have to wait in yet another line to turn in the key to the locker. As the patron exits the park, the RFID database is updated that the locker is available for use by another patron.

While there are numerous advantages to the customer, the entertainment facility also benefits greatly. To the entertainment facility, this means that fewer staff, if any, are required to supervise locker area. Since there are no keys to lose, the maintenance staff does not need to rekey lockers when keys are lost.

DISADVANTAGES TO RFID WRISTBANDS

RFID wristbands are not without some disadvantages. Some of these are inherent with any wristband. For example, the same ergonomic comfort issues that exist with any wristband also exist with RFID wristbands. The comfort issues have been addressed to some extent by using more flexible or softer base materials and rounded corners. However, it can be expected that a small percentage of customers will still resist the use of any type of wristband for personal reasons.

Other disadvantages to RFID wristbands are related to RFID technology itself. While the cost of RFID technology is constantly decreasing, the use of RFID wristbands will still be more expensive that the use of conventional wristbands. Not only is there the investment in the wristbands but also the additional infrastructure related to the information technology system. Some temporary entertainment events in multiuse facilities may determine that the use of this technology does not provide a sufficient cost–benefit ratio.

SPECIFIC BENEFITS TO ENTERTAINMENT APPLICATION AREAS

In this section we will examine specific benefits to the major types of entertainment facilities. These include

- Amusement parks
- Water parks
- Ski resorts
- Special events

AMUSEMENT PARKS

Most of the advantages and disadvantages to using RFID wristbands apply to amusement parks. As we have discussed, these facilities have an outer perimeter through which the patrons must pay to enter. Once inside the facility, the patrons may select which attraction to visit. If each attraction contains an entrance and an exit RFID antenna portal, the facility will be able to both track and locate the patrons.

With respect to amusement parks, RFID wristbands have special significance to patron restriction. Certain rides such as roller coasters are not designed for use by children less than a certain size. There may actually be serious safety issues in that small children may be able to slip under the restraint bars. The height restrictions are typically posted at the path leading to the ride's access gate. Patrons may spend a significant amount of time waiting in the ride's line before being turned away by the ride's operator.

To prevent ride operators from being pressured by either the children or their parents, facility managers can utilize RFID wristband technology. At the time of the band purchase, the salesperson can assess the child's height and program restriction codes for use with the wristband. When a child of insufficient height attempts to partake in a restricted ride, the system can interrogate the wristband for height suitability. Since many of the rides are different, different height restrictions can be programmed into each rides access gate.

WATER PARKS

The unique aspect to water parks is obviously the presence of water. This means that the RFID wristband will be subject to both water spray and immersion. Since the type of RFID wristband that most likely to be utilized is passive, this is not necessarily a serious issue. Since the passive RFID wristband does not need to contain its own power source, the integrated circuitry can be permanently sealed at the factory. What the facility must insure is that any markings on the wristband, include any bar codes, are printed with waterproof ink. If this is not the case, the markings or the bar codes cannot be expected to survive the environment.

The locker advantages of RFID wristbands previously described in this chapter are of specific interest to water parks. While other types of facilities may not utilize lockers, water park patrons need lockers to hold towels, dry clothes, street shoes, purses, and wallets. Since one family may utilize the same locker, the idea of multiple authorized RFID wristbands makes increasing sense from a customer accessibility standpoint.

The use of RFID wristbands with concession credits is also of interest to water parks. Water parks cannot issue food tickets in the same manner as other activities. Any paper-based ticket would not survive long in this environment. What usually happens is that water park patrons carry a small amount of cash on their person and leave their wallets or purses in the locker. After a short period of time, it is obvious that the currency will become waterlogged. During the next transaction, the patron will pay with the wet currency. This is not a problem from the perspective that the money is not still good; it is, however, a problem for the water park when counting and otherwise processing money at the end of the day.

SKI RESORTS

Ski resorts are another type of entertainment facility that can make good use of the advantages offered by RFID technology. The obvious uses of RFID in ski resorts are lift identification tags. The conventional approach is to issue a paper or cardboard tag, which is affixed to the skier's apparel. To prevent reuse by multiple individuals, the tags are attached by clips or wire that cannot be removed without being destroyed. In most cases, the tag is attached to the zipper pull on the skier's outer jacket. The tag typically has the date of use and a color code that corresponds to the type of lift pass. Resorts often sell lift passes by the week, day, and for either morning or afternoon. Visual checks by the lift operators determine the eligibility of the patron to access the lift facilities. This presents significant problems should the skier change his jacket or put on an additional jacket. In either case, the conventional tag may no longer be present or visible.

With an RFID tag, the tag need not be affixed to the skier. In fact, it may be possible for the skier to keep the tag anywhere on their person. This includes underneath outer ski jackets or bibs. Thus, RFID ski lift tags have the distinct advantage of not needing to be visible to the personnel controlling the lift. Only when a valid tag cannot be detected does the lift operator need to become involved.

SPECIAL EVENTS

Special events are those events defined as not having permanent facilities or events that only occur during a specific period of the year. Typical examples of special events are:

- Concerts
- Fairs
- Rallies

In each of these special events, an entrance ticket is required. The entrance ticket is either purchased in advance or purchased directly outside of the access gates. Concessions are typically handled by purchasing additional tickets for either food or drinks. Concession tickets or coins are usually available at the outside entrance ticket booth and at special booths throughout the event location. Vendors can only sell concession tickets and cannot sell event tickets themselves. Depending on the type of food, different numbers of tickets may be necessary. The concession tickets are in essence a form of internal currency. The only type of transaction that can be made for cash once a patron has entered the facility is one involving souvenirs. This is because of the variance in price between souvenir items.

Although these are one- or two-day events, it is still beneficial for the event organizers to consider the use of RFID technology. The activated nontransferable RFID wristband is issued in place of the entrance ticket. Admission ticket counterfeiting is impossible. The RFID wristband can be loaded with any number of food credits in the same manner as conventional concession tickets would be purchased. On entry, access is gained through the control point and the event attendees are free to purchase desired concessions with the preloaded concession credits. Because the concession credits are programmed into the RFID wristband, it is virtually impossible to acquire concessions without paying, as would be possible with forged tickets or counterfeit coins.

As with conventional concession tickets, any unused concession credits are forfeit. This allows the event organizers to maximize the concession revenue, albeit at the expense of the event patrons. An added benefit to the event organizers is that unused concession credits cannot be discarded as could be conventional concession tickets. This would be expected to help reduce the litter cleanup requirement at the end of the event.

It is possible that some special event operators will resist the use of RFID wristbands. It is not the cost of the wristbands that is likely to generate resistance. What will cause resistance is the cost associated with previously unneeded antenna portals and handheld readers or scanners. However, it may be possible for either the multi-purpose facility to invest in this technology or for the technology to be made available through a third-party organization.

SUMMARY

In this chapter, we first examined some of the current conventional technologies that are being utilized for entertainment-related facilities. We then presented the concept of utilizing RFID wristbands for these types of operations. Both the advantages and disadvantages of utilizing RFID wristbands over existing methods were examined. Many of the same benefits found in the warehouse environment are directly translatable to patron management. We then examined a few specific advantages to using RFID technology, in particular types of entertainment facilities. As we can see, from multiple viewpoints, RFID technology has indisputable advantages with respect to amusement parks, water parks, and special events. Through the use of RFID technology, entertainment facilities can not only provide improved customer service but also reduce operating costs.

CHAPTER QUESTIONS

1. What special advantages do RFID wristbands have that make them more suitable than conventional means of patron management for water parks?
2. Why might some special event organizations resist the use of RFID wristband technology?
3. Why does RFID wristband technology make an amusement park less legally liable?
4. Why is the use of RFID wristbands more advantageous to a family that needs to obtain locker access?

19 Evaluating RFID Solutions for Health Care Improvement

Jinxiang Pei and Erick C. Jones

INTRODUCTION

Three major trends will potentially result in unforeseen impacts on the health care system if they are not fully addressed. First of all, as the baby boomers continue to age, the group aged fifty-five to sixty-four will increase by 36 percent or 10.4 million people, more than any other group over the 2004–2014 time period (http://stats.bls.gov/home.htm). The aging population will critically request fast and safe services from the health care system. Secondly, a shortage of qualified health care personnel will challenge the safe and quick medical services. Thirdly, medical lawsuits generated by manual errors will pose a negative influence on health care services. However, the "new" health care system can minimize the impacts by making an investment in the emerging wireless RFID technology. The RFID solutions are at hand through the current wireless network, RFID technology, and connected medical devices.

A resistance to the new technologies by health care personnel will accompany the information technology investment in the health care industry. Realizing the conflicting objectives, the Food and Drug Administration (FDA) endorsed RFID technology for itemized pharmaceuticals. The key FDA drivers are patient safety from counterfeit drugs, product recalls, and solidifying the integrity and accountability of the wholesale drug distributor supply chain. It is estimated that over the next ten years the required IT investment in health care could be $78 billion. We are expected to see the flourish of new information technologies, including RFID and wireless technology, in the health care industry.

RFID: THE EMERGING TECHNOLOGY

Radio frequency identification (RFID), the technology of tomorrow, is here today. In fact, over a billion tags were in use worldwide by June of 2005, yielding benefits from livestock tracking to vehicle immobilization. This is such a huge number that it begs one question: Why are we still calling RFID an emerging technology? All radio frequency identification systems consist of four main components, as seen in Figure 19.1.

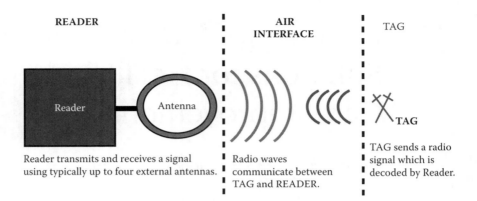

FIGURE 19.1   RFID system blocks.

- An RFID tag
- An RFID reader
- An air interface for wireless, aka radio, communications
- A processing system

Adding of collateral building blocks such as edgeware, middleware, and IT systems forms powerful networks capable of creating and delivering powerful RFID visibility. This vision of RFID will serve to form the next generation of the Internet.

COMPREHENSIVE RFID APPLICATION SYSTEM IN HEALTH CARE

There are different RFID systems that can be implemented into health care applications. Each system has its own benefits and drawbacks that need to be addressed before embarking on a final solution. For instance, the passive RFID system may be tailored to the drug supply chain because it requires item-level tagging for safety considerations. In this section, we will propose the comprehensive network shown in Figure 19.2, in which RFID could help to improve health care services.

DRUG SUPPLY CHAIN NETWORK

Counterfeiting is one of the most critical issues facing the pharmaceutical industry today. Adoption of RFID hardware and software throughout the pharmaceutical industry, as can be seen in Figure 19.3, is about to explode. This is spurred on by the push from industry organizations such as the U.S. Food and Drug Administration (FDA) to implement RFID tags to combat sales of fake drugs.

There is strong business concern about the item-level RFID tagging due to patient safety. Taking the read range, form factor, and global standards into consideration, the HF 13.56-MHz passive RFID system will be the best choice for the pharmaceutical supply chain. The current problem with this system is the bigger form factor of the HF tags compared to the size of pharmaceutical bottles.

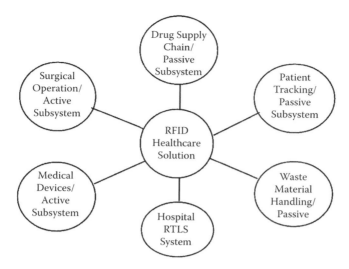

FIGURE 19.2 Comprehensive RFID applications in health care.

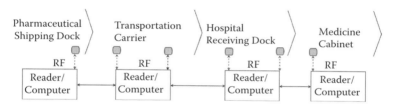

FIGURE 19.3 RFID solution for the pharmaceutical supply chain.

The benefits and efficiency of integrating RFID into the pharmaceutical supply chain are

- Due to the uniqueness of the RFID tag ID, we can create the electronic pedigree for the pharmaceuticals shipped from the suppliers to the hospitals, and even to the medicine cabinet. This characteristic will help to prevent pharmaceutical counterfeiting.
- The real-time information will help hospitals to reduce the safety stock. The replenishment order could be sent to the suppliers when the amount drops below the reorder point. At the same time, this will result in fewer, more accurate transactions.
- Using RFID across the pharmaceutical supply chain, health care personnel could recognize drug information, such as formal name, dosage, and expiration dates. Moreover, the data could be used to compare with the physician prescription, providing information to physicians and nurses immediately.
- The system will be able to help nursing staff equipped with Palm Pilot readers to distribute medicine to the right person at the right time.

POINT-OF-CARE PASSIVE SYSTEM/PATIENT MANAGEMENT

The mobile tracking system uses the cheap UHF passive tag. It can be used for patient wristbands at point of care to verify the patient information.

The benefits of patient management are

- Optimizing the flow of patients through analysis of historical data
- Monitoring wait times and medical staff performance per patient
- Reducing lost or misdirected patients; alert and alarm on these conditions
- Patient safety—right medication, right procedure

Patient management is similar to asset management. RFID systems can directly communicate the patient's location, status, and medical records to the hospital's information systems. Using a combination of passive (ISO-15693 patient wristbands; PDC) and active technologies, a health care provider can capture information and monitor the patient. Passive tags work best for a point-of-care scanning application. An active/real-time location systems (RTLS) badge can monitor patients' movements more closely than a passive tag. An active/WiFi-based tag can be reused by multiple patients, reducing the cost per use to an equal or lower cost than the cost of a passive solution.

ACTIVE SYSTEM/HOSPITAL RTLS SYSTEM/ASSET TRACKING

An effective hospital information system should have the ability to account for and locate tagged assets throughout a facility and be able to capture movement information for review and optimization. The main focus is to be able to find assets.

Most active systems use a zonal deployment strategy to gain asset location information. The tags are usually simple beacon devices that transmit an ID and some state information (movement detection, tamper) with each message. These periodic tag messages are collected by a series of readers that are deployed throughout a facility. These readers are tuned to intercept the tag's transmitted information at a certain distance. Active system installations require labor-intensive reader configuration and are usually hard-wired throughout the building. Additionally, meta-location information needs to be captured regarding the location of each reader and the different processes within the environment. Figure 19.4 shows blue rectangles representing the zones and the green ellipses demonstrate the perimeters of the tag reading area.

COMBINED RFID SYSTEM/SURGICAL OPERATION

In the emergency room setting, the surgical operation incurs many processes as shown in Figure 19.5, including personnel notification/patient preparation, instrument tracking, documentation/chart preparation, and so on. A successful surgical operation requires close cooperation among all these jobs. RFID could provide solutions for the coordination. Here, the RFID system includes both passive and active systems, even needs the handheld system to complement. Today, handheld devices are used for two main types of applications:

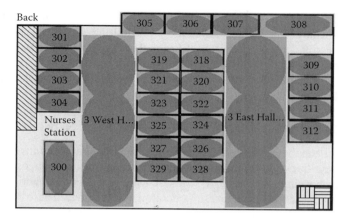

FIGURE 19.4 Active zonal approach for a hospital floor.

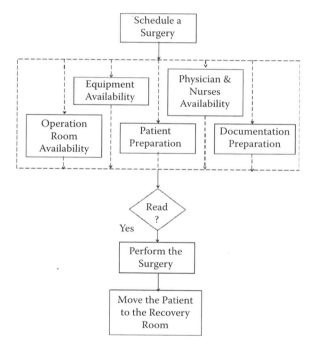

FIGURE 19.5 Surgical operation RFID procedure.

- Point-of-care capture—Utilizing both handheld devices and inexpensive passive RFID wristbands, hospital staffs are able to employ the handheld device to capture point-of-care actions. The information obtained from these devices can than be transmitted from the point-of-care to the hospital's network. Handheld devices can also receive information from the hospital's information systems. Examples of this type of information are patient charts, medication scheduling, and billing. Handheld technology saves significant time and reduces hospital staff paperwork errors.

• Inventory search—In any of the above tracking and location systems, using a handheld application allows personnel to quickly locate items and conduct item-level mobile inventory.

COST AND PERFORMANCE ANALYSIS OF THE COMPREHENSIVE NETWORK

With surgical supplies among the highest expenses in the hospital inventory, accurate instrument tracking becomes very important. Lost instruments can cost a five hundred–bed hospital an average of $200,000+ per year. Instrumentation issues are among the ten most frequent causes of operating room delays. These delays, due to incorrectly assembled or unavailable instrument sets, cost about $1,000 per hour.

To determine asset location, an active tag solution is preferable, or a passive tag system, where there are many readers located near the assets. On the other hand, due to economies and logistics, a passive solution should be sufficient for over 80 percent of the applications/volume. In this scenario, readers will either be in a storage cabinet (smart shelves) or a storage room or available as handheld readers, portal readers throughout doorways, and so on. The value of constant asset visibility and location must be assessed for each application. One may want active tagging for a specialized piece of equipment that is used by many departments and transported between locations. When designing the RFID systems for your health care service, consideration of the trade-off between the system installation and implementation and system performance is required, as shown in Figure 19.6.

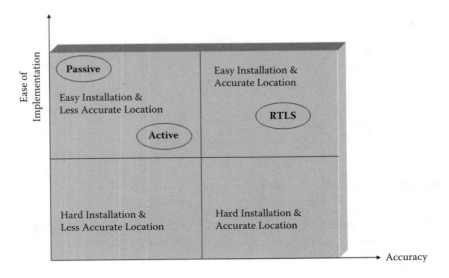

FIGURE 19.6   System parameter matrix.

TABLE 19.1
SWOT Analysis of Different RFID Systems

	Passive	Active	RTLS

Strengths	Most proven technology
	Lowest cost RFID option
	Most tags are writable
	Storing additional
	  patient and drug
	  information
		Read range up to 300 feet
		Small reading units, easier to
		  tune and install
		More industrial to reuse tags
		Proven technology
			Better location
			  information than
			  active systems

Weaknesses	Read range (13.56 MHz
	  is one foot with a
	  handheld device)
	Expensive readers
	Reader's setup: not user
	  friendly
	Read rates are difficult to
	  get to 100%
		Battery lifetime
		Cost compared to passive
		Lack of ability to get granular
		  location data
		No set frequency standard for
		  hospital environment
			2–3 times more
			  expensive than
			  active systems
			Precision installation
			  needed
			TDOA systems
			  generate phantom
			  signals

Opportunities	Mixing technologies to
	  form new solutions:
	  tools that capture
	  information in a different
	  way
	Continued technology
	  breakthroughs
		Identify and integrate technology
		  into an active solution
		Find new ways to reduce costs
			When integrated into
			  other technologies,
			  it becomes a
			  standard

Threats	Other short-range
	  technologies can be
	  lower cost and either
	  match or add to the
	  functionality
	  (SandTracker)
	Other RFID technologies
	  drop prices to compete
		Higher end systems see
		  significant price drop that make
		  it a better alternative
		New tag innovations release
		  providing similar benefits
		Power Paper has a
		  battery-powered passive tag that
		  can be read for up to 50 feet.
		  The battery lasts for years at
		  one tenth the cost.
			As a proprietary
			  system, client
			  married to vendor

For evaluating the RFID solutions in health care services, the SWOT analysis in Table 19.1 shows us the cost and performance comparison of the different RFID systems by which health care providers could improve their services.

CONCLUSIONS

The health care industry will witness the maturation of RFID technology over the following years. There are five areas of potential growth for health care asset tracking applications when combined with passive and wireless tracking systems solutions: asset tracking (passive and active). Such solutions can be used in pharmaceutical tracking and high-valued instrument tracking; as well as real-time location systems (RTLS). RTLS could be applied to accurate high-valued asset tracking; remote patient monitoring; staff mobility and alerts; rental item tracking (RTLS); record/document tracking (passive); and hazardous materials tracking (passive and active).

At the same time, there are many key obstacles to the implementation of a tracking system. The RFID system cost will become a primary consideration when looking for health care solutions. Security and privacy will still be an issue. However, it could be compensated if the technology becomes a part of our life in the future. Technology and standards sometimes develop separately and need be addressed systematically at some point. With frequent new hardware technology introduction at lower cost, RFID hardware is critically challenged by other substitutive technologies; for example, lightweight handheld devices and tablet use is expected to grow. In addition, RFID system setup and management is work-intensive due to the power use and battery life.

ADDITIONAL REFERENCES

Clampitt, H. G., D. Galarde, M. Hendricks, M. Johnson, A. De La Serna, and S. Smith. (2006). *The RFID certification textbook*. 2d ed. Houston, Tex.: PWD Group.

Sangwan, R. S., R. G. Qiu, and D. Jessen. (2005). Using RFID tags for tracking patients, charts and medical equipment within an integrated health delivery network. *Networking, Sensing and Control, 2005 IEEE Conference on* 1070–1074.

Sokol, B. RFID & emerging technologies market guide to healthcare. Fast Track Technologies Ltd. http://www.fasttrackrfid.com/marketingmanual.php?id=VMW. Accessed August 29, 2007.

Wang, S.-W., W.-H. Chen, C.-S. Ong, L. Liu, and Y.-W. C. (2006). RFID application in hospitals: A case study on a demonstration RFID project in a Taiwan hospital. *Proceedings of the 39th Hawaii International Conference on System Sciences* (HICSS'06), Track 8, 2006, p. 184a.

Wu, F., F. Kuo, L.-W. Liu. (2005). The application of RFID on drug safety of inpatient nursing healthcare. *ICEC'05* 8:85–92.

20 RFID Applications in Libraries

INTRODUCTION

The RFID library is a set of functions to dialog with RFID devices. It can take advantages of RFID technology to show automation and security issues in circulation and shelf inventory applications. The driver for today's libraries to adopt RFID is the need to increase efficiency and reduce cost. Automation and self-service can help all sizes of libraries toward achieving these aims, and RFID has the added advantage that it can also provide security for the range of different media offered in libraries.

In this project, the applications of RFID in a library system and supply chain are compared and contrasted. The basic components of a typical RFID-based library system are presented. Two mimic experiments will be conducted in the RFID Supply Chain Lab (RfSCL) at the University of Nebraska — Lincoln. One focuses on the patron self-check-in and check-out service. The other is shelf inventory and maintenance. An extended discussion will be given based on the test results. Moreover, the privacy and security issues related to an RFID-based library system are discussed in this chapter.

EXISTING APPLICATIONS

RFID technology has several advantages over the current bar code systems being used at libraries worldwide. The use of RFID in libraries promises to save time and allow more efficient and effective operations than the bar code systems. However, there are some issues to resolve before libraries can feel confident in adopting the new technology, such as cost, lack of standardization, and security concerns. Many papers talk about the security issue with the RFID application in libraries and the cost problems, as discussed next.

Singh, Brar, and Fong (2006) present the state of RFID applications in libraries. In this research, the authors first analyze the basic components of RFID system and demonstrate the features of RFID libraries system. They point out that RFID integration in libraries makes it possible to inventory hundreds and thousands of books in one day instead of a month. Moreover, the RFID technology helps to facilitate the check-out and check-in process automatically. This paper also summarizes the responses of twenty-nine libraries that participated in the survey conducted by the authors.

According to the survey, approximately 35 percent of libraries had already migrated to RFID-based libraries and of the remaining 65 percent, 90 percent that had not were considering the migration or in the process of migrating to an

RFID-based system. For those libraries that had already moved to an RFID-based system, the responding libraries reported a significant reduction in both check-in and check-out times and processes. Those libraries that had not migrated cited average conversion cost of $502,917 as a concern. The average conversion time from a bar code–based system to an RFID-enabled system was 11.18 months.

Kern (2004) presents the basic components of a typical RFID library system. The RFID technology could be used for book identification, self check-out, anti-theft control, inventory control, and sorting and conveying of library books and AV materials. These applications can lead to significant savings in labor costs, enhance customer service, and lower book theft and can provide a constant record update of media collections.

In Kern's (2004) paper, the author demonstrates the technical features of a RFID library system. Moreover, a list of criteria is provided to assess the different RFID systems. Three examples out of twenty-six RFID installations in library systems in Europe are discussed. The author points out the availability of the nonproprietary RFID chips with the ISO Standard 15693. The new RFID technology helps to standardize the RFID among the vendors.

Molnar and Wagner (2004) discuss the current deployment of RFID technology in library systems. Comparing with the application of RFID in supply chain, the author proposes that an RFID library could be the first major step toward item-level tagging instead of case- or pallet-level tagging because the library system requires item-level identification. Then the potential privacy problem and anti-theft issues related to an RFID library system are shown and modeled. This paper gives a general schema for building private authentication with work logarithmic in the number of tags, given a scheme with linear work as a subprotocol. A simple schema that provides security against a passive eavesdropper using XOR alone, without pseudo-random functions or other heavy crypto operations, is also discussed in this paper.

BACKGROUND

RFID creates a new generation of libraries in order to relocate capital and labor and increase the efficiency of circulation process and information sharing. Regardless of the collection size or the type of library, all these aspects are dramatically optimized with radio frequency identification (RFID). The common evaluations of an RFID system in every industry are automation, labor reduction, and efficiency improvement, whereas the pitfalls of RFID are high costs and immature technology. Although more and more RFID companies are improving on the performance of specific RFID applications, the advantages and disadvantages should still be presented.

ADVANTAGES OF RFID LIBRARY SYSTEMS

- Rapid and simplified patron charging — The use of RFID reduces the amount of time required to perform circulation operations. The most significant time savings are attributable to the fact that information can be read from RFID tags much faster than from bar codes.

- High-speed inventory — A unique advantage of RFID systems is their ability to scan books on the shelves without tipping them out or removing them. A handheld inventory reader can be moved rapidly across a shelf of books to read all of the unique identification information. Using wireless technology, it is possible not only to update the inventory but also to identify items which are out of proper order.
- Elimination or alleviation of repetitive strain injuries among librarians — The non-line-of-sight property of the RFID technology could help to reduce repetitive work for librarians. This means that RFID allows self-check-out of materials with the tag embedded.
- Reduction of material cost and handing — One label, instead of two or more, is required for one book in an RFID-based system. As much as 1 KB of information could be written into the tag. The antitheft digit could be incorporated into the tag, without a separate label put into the book as in a bar code system.

DISADVANTAGES OF RFID SYSTEM

- High cost — The major disadvantage of RFID technology is its cost. The high capital requirement is the greatest difficulty for most private or common libraries. Compared with the traditional bar code system, the update fee is the big issue that should be considered.
- Privacy concern and other security issues — The implementation of RFID in libraries raises concerns about patrons' privacy because the wireless item tagging may pose a threat to the patron if the information is exposed to an outside source.

RFID SUPPLY CHAINS AND LIBRARIES

Most of the applications of RFID focus on supply chain and logistics management. RFID efforts focus on consumer products and retail efforts to optimize processes in the distribution and fulfillment aspects in the supply chain. A lot of companies have now started to implement RFID technology into their business process. "Wal-Mart has tapped RFID as the technology that will help them limit out-of-stocks, allow supply chain visibility in real or 'near-real' time, and reduce costs and labor" (Liard, 2004).

RFID systems are used in about 20 million books worldwide. In the United States, there are about sixty libraries with approximately 10 million books using this technology. The booming development of the RFID industry is also expanding the RFID library implementation rapidly. Wireless technology gives the RFID library many opportunities to improve library automation. As we can see, the major trend of the RFID library system is to spread around the world. Information automation and wireless communication force RFID technology through the library and circulation process on toward the consideration of cost and labor aspects.

TABLE 20.1
Comparison of RFID in Logistics and the Library

RFID	Standard	Vendor	Tag Type	Application
Library	ISO 15693	Checkpoint Inc.	ISO 15693/18000-3	Circulation
	SIP2 protocol	Bibliotheca Inc.	Mode 1	Inventory
	ISO18000-3	3M	Checkpoint WORM	
Logistics	EPC Class 0, Class 1	SAVI Tech.	EPC Class 1	Facility location
	EPC Class 1, Gen2	Symbol Inc.	13.56 MHz	Transportation
	ISO 18000-6	Alien Tech.	EPC Class 1	Asset tracking
			915 MHz	Inventory

As can be seen from Table 20.1, the applications of RFID in library and logistics are very different in standards, tags and readers, vendors, etc. The standard of RFID may vary from industry to industry. The International Organization for Standardization (ISO) and EPC Global have been very active in developing RFID standards. Tags in libraries are all 13.56 MHz and in the shape of smart labels. Those in the supply chain are very versatile and developed. The vendors in libraries have their own proprietary standards over the international standards.

Another important issue of RFID in libraries is that profit is not the main concern when measuring success. What the Return on Investment (ROI) in implanting RFID in libraries fails to take into account is user satisfaction. Self-check-out could be seen by users as a mere shifting of the burden of check-out from the libraries to the users themselves. The RFID application in libraries is more challenging.

APPLICATION OF RFID IN LIBRARIES

THE BASIC COMPONENTS OF A TYPICAL RFID-BASED LIBRARY SYSTEM

The most important application of RFID in libraries is to speed up the circulation through patron self-service. It is possible to inventory hundreds and thousands of books by RFID technology in one day instead of a month. The RFID technology could also help the librarians to keep better inventory as well as find misplaced media in the library.

The way the book is tracked using RFID technology is shown in Figure 20.1. When the book first comes into the library, it will get a library number and be input into the library main database. The RFID tag will also bear the number, which is programmed into the chip. The RFID number is then linked to the database. The book will then be put on the shelf and will be active in the circulation system. The patron can then check out the book. After the book is returned to the library, the librarian can take inventory by means of a handheld reader (inventory wand). The reader may also be used to find misplaced books.

The RFID-based library consists of the following basic components: sensor gates, self-check-out station, and staff center. These components are partly independent and could also be added into other options in the future.

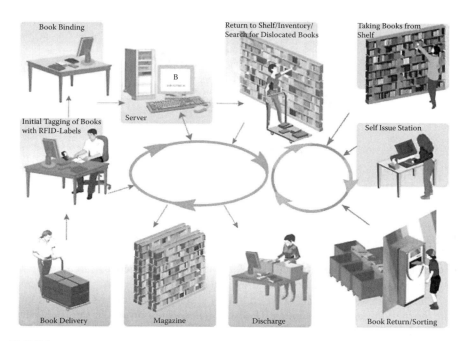

FIGURE 20.1 The way the book is tracked using RFID technology in library system.

- Sensor gates — The sensor gate has two options. When the sensor gate is not interfaced with the system database, it only checks the antitheft digit, which only shows whether the book is checked out or not. On the other hand, the sensor gate could identify the specific information of the book that is being checked out.
- Self–check-out station — The patron self-check-out station is similar to the check-out station in a bar code system. But it is faster and easier to use because the materials do not have to be carefully put in a template under the RFID technology.
- Staff service center — The other option for the patron to check out materials is to turn to the staff service center. A staff workstation at the circulation desk could help patrons check out items.
- Other options — For larger size libraries, the RFID-based system may contain other components, like the sorting system as shown in Figure 20.2. The sorter can help the libraries to eliminate the discharge and sorting function by combing with the book drop readers. The sorters include the conveyors, which move the materials and as many as two hundred bins.

DISCUSSION ABOUT ANTITHEFT AND PRIVACY ISSUES

Driven by the wide application of RFID in supply chain, libraries have started to implant RFID into their system. However, unlike the supply chain sector, libraries require item-level tagging. This gives rise to the privacy issue related to the reader habit and history record. Several vulnerabilities have been discovered in today's

FIGURE 20.2   Sorting equipment in libraries.

RFID library system. For example, the lack of access control allows easy tracking of people and books. The collision-avoidance protocol used in an RFID library system does not conceal tag identity and poor key management practices threaten the tag security. In this project, we do not address the security issue.

The good news for an RFID-based library system is that it helps to easily eliminate the theft threat. By implanting RFID technology in libraries, the tag could carry the antitheft digit as one part of the tag information without one more strip embedded in the book. When the patrons walk over the sensor gate with the tagged book, the system will check the antitheft digit or interface with main database.

COST AND BENEFITS OF INTEGRATING RFID INTO EXISTING LIBRARY SYSTEMS

From the survey, a large percentage of libraries that have not adopted the RFID technology are mainly concerned with the cost issue. It is difficult to get representative pricing structures, as the requirements vary significantly between the libraries. But the following estimation is possible: considering that the price for a label is $0.55 at 100,000 pieces plus the additional equipment cost, a small size library would have to invest about $150,000 in total. The cost may range ranged from $113,000 to $1.2 million, with the average cost being $502,917.

The libraries that have adopted the RFID technology have commented on a significant reduction in both check-in and check-out times and processes, as can be shown in Figure 20.3 and Figure 20.4. According to Checkpoint, an RFID vendor, the system processes twenty items per second, and libraries can realize as much as 75 percent reduction in handling time after installing their intelligent library system. One key benefit of an RFID-based system as far as circulation is concerned is that it combines it with Electronic Article Surveillance (EAS). The security bit in a tag replaces the security strip needed with the bar code approach, and items can be moved in or out of the premises without performing two separate steps.

EXPERIMENTS AND RESULTS

The application of RFID in a supply chain focuses on 915-MHz EPC Class 0 and Class 1 tags, and EPC Class 1 13.56-MHz tags have different applications,

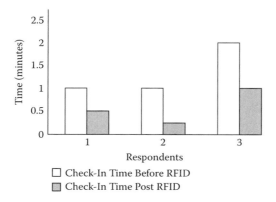

FIGURE 20.3   Average check-in times prior to and post-RFID.

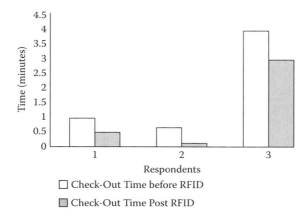

FIGURE 20.4   Average check-out times prior to and post-RFID.

like security access. The 13.56-MHz tags used by libraries are different from the 915-MHz tags considered for supply chain applications. First, the bandwidth available to 13.56-MHz tags is strictly limited by regulations in the United States, the European Union, and Japan. Second, the read range of 13.56-MHz tags is much less than that of 915-MHz tags. As a result, RF air interface protocols, such as collision avoidance, differ between 915-MHz and 13.56-MHz tags.

EXPERIMENT DESIGN

In this project, we are going to do two experiments in the RfSCL lab at the University of Nebraska — Lincoln (UNL). The first experiment is to compare the check-out speed between traditional bar code system and RFID-based system. In this experiment, we imitate the self-check-out process in the library circulation environment. We measure the times for self-check-out and then compare them with those we conducted in the engineering library at UNL. The RFID equipment we used in this experiment is Alien Gen 2 fixed reader with the Alien gateway edgeware. In the meantime, we utilized the 915-MHz Alien squiggle tags embedded in the back cover of the books. The second experiment is to demonstrate how an RFID handheld reader could help the librarians to keep better inventory. We used the Symbol Handheld reader MC906 R in this experiment.

Patron Self-Check-Out Experiment

Check-out could occur at either a service center or a special self-check-out machine that allows patrons to check out their own books. In both cases, the RFID tag is read and the association between patron ID number and book could be looked up in the bibliographic database; the status of the book is then changed to checked out in the bibliographic database. Later, when the book is checked in, the tag is read again and the bibliographic database is updated. We compare the process time of checking out ten books between bar code and RFID systems, as shown in Figure 20.5. The results accord with the survey outcomes mentioned above. The process times are reduced by approximately half in the RFID case.

Handheld Reader for Shelf Inventory and Maintenance

The promise of RFID is to dramatically reduce the time and effort of taking inventory. A handheld reader makes quick and easy work of shelf management activities like finding missing and out-of-order books.

The line-of-sight system, for example, the bar code system, requires that each book must be tipped out far enough to read the bar code if the tag is on an outside cover or removed from the shelf if the book must be opened to access the bar code. Unlike the bar code, the RFID technology allows the reader to work alongside the shelves and pick up all the individual signals from the books. In this experiment, we try to find out how accurate RFID could help to manage the inventory and how it can help to locate a specific misplaced book in the book shelf with twenty-five books. Then we compare RFID with the manually looking for a particular book. Generally, the inventory accuracy was about 80 percent in our experiment. Taking

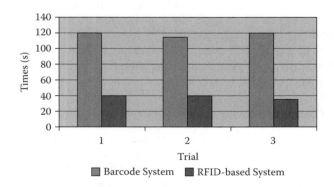

FIGURE 20.5 Comparison between check-out times.

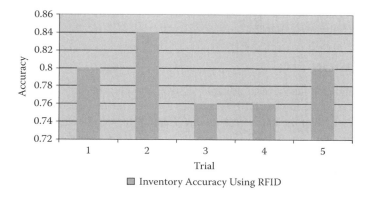

FIGURE 20.6 Inventory management using RFID.

the improper tag type and equipment into consideration, RFID is more accurate than manual inventory procedures without considering the significant time reduction in the process, as demonstrated in Figure 20.6. Additionally, it takes no time to locate the particular misplaced book in our case since the total volume is small compared to the volume of the entire library.

EXPERIMENT DISCUSSION

During the experiments, we found that reading multiple tags at the same time is theoretically easy and practically difficult. In theory, the RFID technology allows for twenty items to be read simultaneously. However, the spatial placement of tags is a significant factor in successful readings, as can be shown in Figure 20.7. Subsequently, we come down to tag reading individually. Even in this case, the RFID-based

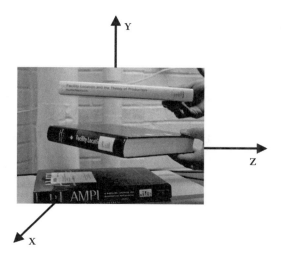

FIGURE 20.7 Spatial placement of the tags embedded in the books.

system still performs much better than a bar code system. Further experiments on multitag reading are expected.

CONCLUSION

RFID technology has several advantages over the current bar code systems being used at libraries worldwide. RFID promises to save time and operate more efficiently and effectively than the bar code systems. Some of the compensations of RFID over a bar code system are that RFID tags can be used for security as well as for status control, thereby eliminating the need to attach security strips to library items; RFID systems make self-check-out faster and easier for library patrons; and RFID portable readers can take inventory by just being passed slowly along the library shelves, without having to handle each item individually. RFID vendors, however, need to resolve some issues before libraries feel confident in adopting them. In the forefront are issues such as cost, lack of standardization among vendors, and privacy.

REFERENCES

Kern, C. (2004). Radio-frequency identification for security and media circulation in libraries. *The Electronic Library* 22(4):317–324.
Liard, Michael J. RFID in the Supply Chain: The Wal-Mart Factor, Circuits Assembly, Venture Development Corp., January 1, 2004. http://www.allbusiness.com/technology/databases/740316-1.html. Accessed August 30, 2007.
Molnar, D., and D. Wagner. (2004). Radio-frequency-identification for security and media circulation in libraries. Paper read at CCS'04, 25–29 October, Washington, D.C.
Singh, J., N. Brar, and C. Fong. (2006). The state of RFID applications in libraries. *Information Technology and Libraries* 25(1):24–32.

ADDITIONAL REFERENCES

Clampitt, H. G. (2006). *RFID certification textbook*. 1st ed. Houston, Tex.: PWD Group.
Finkenzeller, K. (2003). *RFID handbook: Fundamentals and applications in contactless smart cards and identification*. 2d ed. Hoboken, N.J.: Wiley.
Shahid, S. Md. (2005). Use of RFID technology in libraries: A new approach to circulation, tracking, inventorying, and security of library materials. University of Jammu, India, http://www.digitalcommons.unl.edu/libphilprac/62/
Yuan, K. H., A. C. Hong, M. Ang, and G. S. Peng. (Oct. 2002). Unmanned library: An intelligent robotic books retrieval & return system utilizing RFID tags. National University of Singapore, Systems, Man, and Cybernetics, 2002 IEEE International Conference, Vol. 4, p. 5, IEEE SMC TA2R1.

21 Marine RFID Security Applications

INTRODUCTION

While RFID systems are beginning to be used widely in land-based logistics systems, their use is much less developed in marine applications. Marine applications that are currently in existence focus primarily on the tracking of shipping containers on cargo freighters. In these types of applications, active RFID tags can be used for both customs and storage location purposes in the same manner as more conventional land-based applications.

However, RFID systems both now and in the future have great potential for application with respect to marine security–related systems. These include, among others, registration tag and illegal vessel identification applications. Registration tag applications can be used to track the movement of both recreational and commercial vessels. Illegal vessel identification applications include the tagging of suspect vessels at sea for subsequent apprehension by law enforcement authorities at coastal ports. Prior to examining these two potential applications, it will be first necessary to address special hardware and infrastructure considerations that are necessary in order for an RFID system to operate reliably in the marine environment.

SPECIAL RFID HARDWARE CONSIDERATIONS

The marine environment in general presents more demanding requirements on RFID systems than those typically found in warehouse environments. These include the obvious increase in exposure to moisture and corrosive agents such as salt. Additional demands are placed on the equipment due to the constant motion encountered at sea. Sophisticated electronics such as those found in RFID tags are notorious for failing in the marine environment. RFID tags, antennas, and readers can expect to suffer the same fate, if not properly hardened for these types of applications.

Hardening the RFID tag is specifically required in the following areas:

- Housing water resistance
- Circuit board hardening
- Shock resistance

WATER RESISTANCE AND WATER RESISTANCE RATINGS

A special hardware modification that is necessary in the marine environment involves the sealing of the instrument housing from moisture. All electronics specifically designed for the marine environment are specifically protected with rubber gaskets.

TABLE 21.1
JIS Rating Requirements

JIS Rating	Description
0	No special protection
1	Vertically dripping water will have no harmful effect (drip resistant 1)
2	Dripping water at an angle up to 15 degrees from vertical will have no harmful effect (drip resistant 2)
3	Falling rain at an angle up to 60 degrees from vertical will have no harmful effect (rain resistant)
4	Splashing water from any direction will have no harmful effect (splash resistant)
5	Direct jetting water from any direction will have no harmful effect (jet resistant)
6	Direct jetting water from any direction will not enter the enclosure (water tight)
7	Water will not enter the enclosure when it is immersed in water under defined conditions (immersion resistant)
8	The equipment is usable for continuous submersion in water under specified pressure (submersible)

Source: JIS standard water resistance, JIS Scale, http://www.hy-com.com/jis.htm

In this respect, passive tags that can be permanently sealed have a distinct advantage over active tags that require a replaceable or rechargeable battery. The tag's battery compartment presents an additional weak point with respect to maintaining any level of water resistance. Not only will the battery compartment need to be gasketed, but provisions must also be made to secure the cover to the main housing. This will normally be performed with captive bolts. Compare these requirements with a non-marine-grade electronics, which will have simple ungasketed, snap-on covers.

The use of a properly secured gasketed design will help maintain the integrity of not only the battery compartment but all of the other electronics as well. The complete ability of electronics to function in the marine environment with respect to water is typically rated according to the Japanese Industrial Standard for Water Resistance. Table 21.1 illustrates the different levels of ratings for electronics.

Higher end marine electronics are currently rated under the Japanese Industrial Standard JIS-7 for immersion of thirty minutes at a depth of one meter. Whether or not this level of water resistance will be needed for RFID tags depends on the exact nature of the application. Applications where the tag is sheltered, such as in the vessel's engine compartment, need not have a JIS-7 rating. However, applications where the tag is either on the deck or attached to the side of the hull will definitely require JIS-7 if the tag is to survive more than minimal use. As with other JIS-7 electronics, RFID tags with JIS-7 rating will obviously be more expensive to design and manufacture than those with lower ratings. However, as has been observed with other RFID tags, volume use will be expected to lower per unit pricing.

CIRCUIT BOARD HARDENING

In the event that the outer housing of either a passive or an active RFID tag is compromised, it is important that the circuitry is properly hardened. This will not only increase the length of operating time after compromise but will allow the possibility of refurbishing a potentially expensive tag.

Proper hardening for the circuit board includes, but is not limited to, the use of special waterproof coatings. These will help reduce the possibility of corrosion on both the circuit board itself and on the components mounted on the circuit board. The composition of the circuit board is also an issue. Less stable circuit board materials may swell with the absorption of water. If this occurs, circuit reliability may be compromised. Thus, the use of more water resistant phenolic-based circuit boards is preferred over less expensive paper-based circuit boards.

SHOCK RESISTANCE

Another special requirement that marine applications may place on RFID equipment involves shock resistance. In situations where the RFID tag is affixed to the hull of the vessel, the tags must be able to withstand water intrusion as well as the constant pounding of waves on the vessel's hull. In other situations where the RFID tag may be more protected, it will still have to be able withstand the acceleration and deceleration effects of the vessel while it is underway.

UV PROTECTION

A final consideration when selecting or designing marine security RFID systems is the issue of ultraviolet radiation. Constant, direct exposure to the sun is a major cause of many types of marine systems failures. The UV rays received directly from the sun are also augmented by UV rays that reflect off of the water's surface. The end result is that many components that do not specifically incorporate UV stabilizers are much more likely to suffer premature deaths. In particular, the outer housings of RFID tags will become less structurally sound. The housings may then crack or become brittle. Water intrusion or some other sort of failure is soon to follow. This consideration makes it imperative that not only the tags but also the rest of the exposed system be protected from UV damage.

RFID TAG POSITIONING

Just as with inventory type applications, the positioning of the RFID tag circuitry is of significant consequence for the application. In the automotive industry some discussion has revolved around the use of RFID tags embedded into the engine system. The primary purpose of this tagging is to assist with stolen vehicles. The same concept could be applied to marine engines. One question that may arise is how to prevent the end user from disconnecting the RFID tag. While this question may present considerable debate, at least one solution is to hard-wire the RFID tag into the electrical system of the engine. If the RFID tag is deliberately disabled, so may be the engine system. The topic of tag positioning is further discussed in the applications section of this chapter.

Marine Portals

Just as inventory passes through a series of specific portals, most commercial and recreational vessels pass through specific narrow navigational areas. These include jetty entrances, channels, the mouths of rivers and bays, bridge underpasses, and even marina breakwaters as illustrated in Figure 21.1 and Figure 21.2.

These areas are typically marked with navigational aids. Navigational aids include both fixed channel markers on metal stakes or wooden pilings and floating buoys of various sizes. Many of these navigational aids are powered. Power is required to either illuminate the navigational aids at night or allow the navigational aid to emit a sound signal such as a foghorn. A common approach to providing this

FIGURE 21.1   Channel entrance.

FIGURE 21.2   Bridge underpass.

FIGURE 21.3   Typical navigational channel marker.

power is to have a bank of batteries that is recharged during the hours of daylight by an array of solar panels. Figure 21.3 illustrates typical navigational channel markers. Note the battery box mounted to the left on top of the platform. The recharging solar panel array can also be observed on the back side of the platform.

Figure 21.4 illustrates a typical navigational buoy. Larger versions of these types of buoys have the same power and recharging capabilities as with the navigational channel marker.

These navigational aids offer an attractive previously existing infrastructure from which the system of RFID portals can be initially based. The navigational aids are already positioned in the ideal locations to construct a system of portals and the RFID systems can tap into the existing navigational aid power sources. This approach could easily minimize the cost of initially deploying the RFID system.

However, the existing system need not be constrained only to previously existing navigational aids. The RFID portals may be enlarged or entirely new portals can be easily constructed through the placement of new dedicated floating RFID buoys. Dedicated RFID buoys have the distinct advantage of being positioned as necessary for maximum effectiveness without disturbing the existing navigational aid system. They also allow the system operators to more easily remove and replace buoys for maintenance and repair.

Both modified navigational aids and RFID-specific buoys will ultimately have to transmit the RFID tag identification to a reader on land. If the transmission is non-satellite-based, the nearest law enforcement agency will obviously have to possess an antenna system to receive this information. This type of technology is

FIGURE 21.4   Typical navigational buoy.

currently in use today with the NOAA weather buoys operated offshore. Given the necessary components for operating an RFID portal, Figure 21.5 and Figure 21.6 illustrate what modified navigational aid markers and platforms might look like.

FIGURE 21.5   Modified navigational and RFID platform portal.

FIGURE 21.6   Modified navigational and RFID marker portal.

Antenna Mounting

One significant performance consideration concerning the implementation of an RFID system pertains to the mounting of the RFID antennas. In land-based operations, the platform on which the antenna is mounted is level and static. In this case, static refers to the stationary positioning of the antenna with respect to the horizon. For marine RFID applications where a fixed navigational aid is used as the portal antenna mount, the application is similar. This is the case when, for example, a piling or tower is used as the mount. Unless the antenna experiences a collision with a vessel, the antenna will maintain a level and static orientation. While this is the more desirable approach, it is only possible when the depth of the water is relatively shallow.

In marine applications where the depth of the water requires that the RFID portal antenna be mounted on a floating navigational buoy, antenna mounting considerations become somewhat more complicated. The same is true for an RFID antenna mounted on a vessel. In both cases, the antenna platform is subject to wave action. This means that the orientation of the interrogation zone of the RFID antenna will be constantly changing. Since many RFID systems require a certain period to successfully acquire a signal, this could present a significant performance issue.

In similar situations with other electronic systems such as radar and GPS, their antennas have been positioned on gimballing mounts. These mounts typically pivot on one or two axes. This allows the antenna to maintain a more horizontal position

FIGURE 21.7   Gimballing mount.

with respect to the horizon. To prevent uncontrolled movement with respect to the horizon, these systems typically contain some sort of dampening mechanism. Successful approaches to date include hydraulic and friction adjustable systems. In any event, the use of similar gimballing mounts for the RFID system as illustrated in Figure 21.7 can be expected to help address this difference between land- and sea-based antenna systems.

Other Considerations

The list of items previously presented is by no means comprehensive. There are many other considerations that must be taken into account when implementing a marine RFID system. Some of these have yet to be discovered. However, one that is obvious is associated with the movement of vessel-mounted tags relative to antenna portals. In land-based systems, this is usually not an issue since the tags move on a relatively stable two-dimensional grid. In contrast with a marine applications, the vessel and the portal may be moving on as many as six different axes. These include the usual x and y planes. It also includes the z plane as well as pitch, roll, and yaw. Pitch is rotational movement up and down. Roll is rotational movement around the direction of movement. Lastly, yaw is rotational movement around the z axis. This may come into play because the vessel-mounted tag is constantly changing orientation with respect to the antenna portal. The antenna portal, if mounted on a floating platform, may also be experiencing the same type of movement at the same time. The combination of the vessel mounted tag and the antenna portal may make acquisition of a good read more difficult than that of an equivalent land-based system.

While not all of the RFID technology necessary for successful marine applications may currently exist, the reader can rest assured that the need for such applications can drive the development of both modified and new technology.

MARINE RFID SECURITY APPLICATIONS

As previously identified future marine RFID applications include:

* Vessel registration tag applications
* Hostile vessel identification

In the following section, we will discuss the major issues involved in each of these applications.

VESSEL REGISTRATION TAG APPLICATIONS

One of the most promising marine security applications involves the use of RFID tags on both recreational and commercial vessels for registration and identification purposes. All recreational vessels are required to be registered. For example, in the state of Texas, any engine-powered vessel must be reregistered every two years. Currently, the tag consists of a waterproof preprinted vinyl square with the registration information printed on the face of the tag as illustrated in Figure 21.8.

FIGURE 21.8   Vessel registration tag.

A recreational vessel RFID tag could either be a passive or an active tag. Obviously, the passive tag would have the advantage of not needing an internal power source. However, the current level of RFID passive tag range may be unsuitable. The use of active tags is not as limiting as it might first appear. Since the registration must be renewed on a periodic basis, the tag's power source would only need to last that long.

As with conventional visual tags, the RFID recreational vessel tags could be mounted on the relatively narrow forward section of the hull of the vessel. This would provide a relatively unimpeded position for the RFID tag to transmit to the portal sensors. Placement of the tag elsewhere might result in signal degradation due to other components on the vessel.

SCANNING RECREATIONAL VESSEL RFID TAGS

The use of RFID-integrated registration tags would allow marine law enforcement officers to rapidly scan tags without having to visually observe or record the registration tag. This is particularly important, because the auditing of registered vessels at the dock could easily be performed from a vessel on the water. Since the RFID tag would not necessarily need to be visually acquired, it would not matter whether the vessel was docked bow or stern to. All tag reads could be achieved by simply passing between sets of docks. In the event that a vessel is not available for tag reads, the vessels could also be scanned by law enforcement officers by walking down marina docks. Again, it would not matter if the vessel were docked bow or stern to.

Recreational vessels underway could also be easily scanned by personnel positioned on a law enforcement vessel. The law enforcement vessel could be positioned alongside any commonly traversed channel. Tag reads could also be made while patrolling navigable bodies of water. As the recreational vessels come into the interrogation zone, the antenna will acquire the tag signal. The tag identification can then be matched in the vessel registration database.

In this application, RFID systems display their non-visual-dependent acquisition advantages. The law enforcement vessel and the recreational vessel could meet bow to bow, bow to stern, port to starboard, or starboard to port. Some of these meeting situations could make it difficult if not impossible for a visual based tag to be successfully acquired. For example, in a pursuit scenario, the law enforcement vessel will be coming up from astern the evading vessel. Since most registration tags are positioned near the bow of the vessel, there would be no way for law enforcement personnel to be able to visually acquire the registration tag. The only other information that may be available is the name of the vessel on the stern of the hull. There is no legal requirement to display the same name on the stern of the vessel as that entered in the state registration or the USCG documentation data base. In contrast, in any of these situations, as long as the RFID signal can be acquired, it does not matter what type of meeting situation is present.

Reliable recreational vessel tag reads can also be achieved when difficult sea or weather conditions are present. Salt spray or waves can easily obscure a visually based tag. Similarly, driving rain can prevent law enforcement personnel from visually acquiring a tag even if there is no spray or waves present. Under these conditions, identification is possible when visual observation is impossible.

Vessels without readable RFID signals could be stopped in the same manner that land-based law enforcement officers stop vehicles for out of date registration tags. During the stop, the law enforcement officials could examine the cause of the failure of the RFID tag. If the tag was deliberately deactivated, the law enforcement officials could take appropriate action. On the other hand, if the tag failure were simply an electronic issue, a summons could be issued to have the tag replaced.

Although the previous discussion has focused on recreational vessels, the same concepts are applicable to commercial vessels. All commercial vessels are normally examined on an annual basis as part of the United States Coast Guard certification inspection. The primary purpose of this inspection is to ensure the safety and seaworthiness of the vessel. As part of this inspection, the USCG can examine the RFID tag for serviceability.

STOLEN VESSEL IDENTIFICATION

Another potential application for RFID in the marine environment is the identification and subsequent recovery of stolen vessels. In this situation, the report of stolen vessels could be maintained in a central law enforcement database. As each vessel proceeds through existing marine RFID portals, the tag identification is automatically captured and compared to the centralized list of stolen vessels. A match triggers an alert to the local law enforcement agency, which can then pursue the stolen vessel according to its operating policy.

In a stolen vessel RFID application, the most effective type of tag would be one linked to the propulsion engine. In order to navigate among through the RFID portals, the vessel's engine would most likely be running. The tag can tap into the engine's electrical system to ensure that electrical power is present in order for the active tag to operate. Whether or not the tag can be designed so that it must also be operational in order for the engine to operate is a more serious question. This might present objectionable safety concerns in the event that the tag becomes inoperative. If this is not a concern, the approach could be taken one step further. In this case, an integrated tag could also receive a signal to deliberately disable the engine.

An RFID system of this type holds special interest to antiterrorism concerns. Land vehicles used in illegal operations are usually stolen to prevent traceability back to the terrorist's infrastructure. It is equally likely that a vessel used in waterborne terrorist activity is stolen. If this is the case, then the stolen vessel RFID system offers an additional layer or opportunity to help prevent terrorist attacks like that executed on the USS *Cole* in 2000.

Hostile Vessel Identification

A third potential application for RFID in the marine environment is the apprehension of potentially hostile vessels. In this case we are talking about vessels suspected of being engaged in terrorist activities, drug smuggling, or illegal alien trafficking. The apprehension of any of these three types of vessels can easily lead to a lethal situation. Even in cases where less-than-lethal force has been applied, death has resulted from an accidental chain of events. RFID approaches are inherently far less than lethal than even less-than-lethal approaches.

In a non-lethal type situation, law enforcement authorities will want to identify a suspect vessel for eventual search and/or seizure. However, in some cases, law enforcement personnel may be able to initially identify a suspect vessel at sea but will not be able to maintain contact with the vessel. This situation occurs in particular whenever a suspect vessel is encountered by aircraft. With limited fuel capacity or poor weather, the aircraft cannot stay on station until a surface resource is able to reach the location of the suspect vessel. The end result is that the initial contact with the suspect vessel is broken. The suspect vessel may then change course after the initial contact. With the change in course, the suspect vessel may then proceed to any one of a number of ports. Unless some mechanism is present to detect the suspect vessel, it may proceed unimpeded at the port of entry. Once actually in the port, the suspect vessel may then become lost among the other legitimate commercial and recreational vessels.

In hostile vessel scenarios of this type, weather conditions may make it impossible to visually identify the vessel while it is underway. Attempts to visually identify the vessel would be further complicated by any contact made during the hours of darkness. If the vessel did have a registration RFID tag system aboard as described in the previous section, the contact aircraft still might not be able to get within the interrogation zone. Any RFID system that the vessel has may also have been deliberately disabled.

In these situations, what is needed is a system that can first be easily deployed by the aircraft making contact. Second, it must be able to alert the authorities to the presence of the vessel in any one of many ports at a later date. Third, the system must not be able to be easily removed by the hostile vessel. These three requirements are easily fulfilled through the use of specifically designed RFID systems.

RFID CHAFF

These types of RFID systems operate on the same principle as radar chaff. In this case, a large number of small RFID tags are utilized in place of radar reflective strips of metal. As the law enforcement plane or helicopter passes over the suspected hostile vessel, a payload of RFID tags is deployed. The tags rain down on the vessel in the same manner as radar chaff.

Vessels that have been marked with the RFID tags in this manner will obviously attempt to remove the tags. However, like chaff, completely sanitizing the vessel of the RFID tags will prove to be a difficult if not impossible task. As long at least one tag remains on the vessel, it will be at risk of being detected as it passes through the interrogation zone of the marine portal at the port of entry.

Since the tag's identification can be linked back to their deployment, the shore-based law enforcement agencies can be alerted to not only the presence of the suspect vessel but also the circumstances under which the vessel was marked by the tags. Once the local law enforcement personnel are alerted, the search for the vessel can be reactivated.

SUMMARY

In this chapter, we have investigated some of the issues associated with implementing marine security RFID applications. Many of the advantages that RFID systems possess in land-based applications are transferable to these types of marine applications. The use of RFID systems for marine security applications introduces issues unique to the marine environment. Whereas normal RFID tags and antennas are satisfactory for their intended purpose, the electronics must be hardened for marine use. The nonstationary nature of marine applications also requires that special consideration be given to antenna mounting in certain circumstances.

Some of the technological aspects necessary for the successful implementation of RFID systems for these applications may need further development. For example, can sufficiently powerful RFID tags be produced at a low enough cost to be utilized in place of conventional registration tags? Similarly, can the range of RFID reader antennas be increased sufficiently for use between any existing navigational aid devices? These are issues that may or may or may not present barriers to the use of RFID systems in these marine security applications. However, as normal land-based RFID technology becomes more powerful and sophisticated, these enhancements will also benefit marine security applications.

CHAPTER QUESTIONS

1. What special considerations need to be considered when adapting or designing RFID tags for the marine environment?
2. How can the cost of deploying a marine portal system be reduced?
3. Why do RFID systems have a distinct advantage over existing recreational vessel registration tags?
4. What special communications equipment may be necessary for mobile RFID systems operating far offshore?
5. Why might the technology to implement marine registration systems need to be further developed?

22 Inventory Tracking on International Space Station Using RFID Technology

Erick C. Jones, Tim Farnham, Xiaofei Gao, Amy L. Schellhase

INTRODUCTION

Radio frequency identification (RFID) has been called the next-generation bar code, but it is already widely in use with current applications ranging from libraries to toll booth e-passes. The greatest advantage in RFID systems, which are composed of an interrogator (reader) and transponders (tags), is that they do not require a line of sight between the reader and the tags. Successful application of this technology could revolutionize today's bar code–based inventory system aboard the international space station, in which thousands of items are kept track of with manual database updates or line-of-sight bar code scans, one item at a time. With an RFID system in place, entire bags of items affixed with RFID tags could be audited in seconds without ever having to open the bag, saving both astronaut and ground support time. Such a system will be essential for efficient logistic support of future lunar and Mars base operations.

The current inventory management system (IMS) has been successful in keeping track of 96.84 percent of more than eight thousand items on the Space Station, and is used to locate hardware required in the crew's daily activities, audit consumables to ensure adequate resupply, and plan future stowage locations. In an RFID system, the antenna of the reader emits radio signals. The signals are received by the tag's antenna, which can be powered via a battery or by the radio frequency energy from the reader's pulse. The tags respond with a unique code, which is preprogrammed into the tag's microchip. After the reader antenna receives and decodes the signal, the antenna sends the information to a computer via a standard interface; this information is accessed through a database. Since RFID systems do not require a line of sight between the tag and the reader, a Space Station crew member could potentially wave the reader in the general vicinity of a cargo transfer tab that is full of tagged items and record an accurate count of all items within that bag in seconds. Less time spent on logistics means more time for crew members to conduct science activities. With better predictions of what the crew uses and at what rate, the ground can plan resupply missions more efficiently and accurately to ensure that food and other essential supplies are delivered to the Space Station. In addition, without launching excess supplies, more space can be allocated to payloads and critical hardware.

PLAN

With the advantages we illustrated above, the series of experiments and tests will be conducted by the Radio Frequency Identification RFID Suply Chain Lab (RfSCL) at the University of Nebraska — Lincoln. The blend of methodologies helped the RfSCL lab use information received by customers (NASA and Barrios) to better develop a solution that best meet the needs of these two organizations. Integrated Design for Six Sigma (DFSS) uses the Plan, Predict, and Perform methodology typically used in research but couples it with DFSS (Breyfogle, 2003). DMADO (De-may-doh) is the acronym for Design, Measure, Analyze, Develop, Optimize (Breyfogle, 2003). This new approach to research will help bridge the gap between academic organizations and industry. The experiments and analysis will be conducted following the order of scientific methodology as a thought process.

DEFINE PROBLEM STATEMENT

The International Space Station (ISS) currently uses bar codes to audit and control inventory onboard. However, recent events have uncovered a need to improve the current system. During a routine audit, it was discovered that supplies of food were less than the goals of the project that were given by Barrios project director Amy Schellhase. These objectives were to test commercially available off-the-shelf (COTS) RFID hardware and develop possible inventory management solutions for the ISS. The project was not to exceed six months and deliver a final recommendation on hardware to implement and processes to develop. NASA estimates the cost of an astronaut in space is one million dollars per day. This makes a manual inventory count very costly. Previous projects have looked into astronauts scanning their items as they are used. However, this would cause an incremental labor cost for every item scanned. On average, an astronaut uses fifty consumable items per day. This extra ten seconds per manual scan with a bar code reader or other such devices would add $5,787 per day per astronaut in labor alone. The station normally contains three or four crew members at any given time, making the total labor cost exceed $20,000 per day, almost $7.3 million dollars per year. Currently, astronauts spend one week every six months taking inventory. This current cost of labor is $22.4 million dollars per year. With the combination of customer requirements and technical requirements of the project, a house of quality (HOQ) was constructed. Table 22.1 shows how the HOQ was constructed. The HOQ shows the main criteria that any implementation should focus on. The three top criteria are accurate inventory, low crew interaction, and low infrastructure. Because the implementation requirements are not known, the "basement" of the house was not included in the initial analysis but was used during testing.

- Test requirements: One of the last steps in the define phase was to define test requirements by compiling a list of all forms of tests that needed to be performed and determine the metrics for which to test. For example,

TABLE 22.1
House of Quality

Interactions (roof), correlations between Design Requirements:

- Time to Inventory: −1
- Cost of Development: −1, −1
- Time of Development: −1, −1, 2
- Cost of Implementation: −1, −1, 1, 1
- Time of Implementation: −1, −1, −1, −1, −1
- Life Expectancy of Tags: −1, −1, −1, , −1
- Life Expectancy of Reader: −1, −1, −1, −1
- Power Life of Reader (Recharging): −2, −2, , , −2, −1
- Range of Tag: −2, −2, , , , 1
- Size of Tag: −2, −2, , , , −1, , , −2

Customer Requirements		Readability of Tags in Environment	Time to Inventory	Cost of Development	Time of Development	Cost of Implementation	Time of Implementation	Life Expectancy of Tags	Life Expectancy of Reader	Power Life of Reader (Recharging)	Range of Tage	Size of Tage		
		X	N	N	N	N	N	X	X	X	T	N		
Accurate inventory	5	9	3	9	9	3	3	9	9	3	9	1	335	27.92%
Low crew interaction	5	3	9	9	9	3	9	1	3	3	3		260	21.67%
Low infrastructure	4	3	3	3		9	9		3	3	3	1	148	12.33%
Radiation proof	5	9		3	3	3							90	7.50%
Low power requirements	3		3	3	3	3	3	3	3	3	9	1	102	8.50%
Durability	4	9	3	3	1				3	1			80	6.67%
Non-intrusive (to packing)	3	3	3	3	3	3	1	3			9	9	111	9.25%
Short implementation time	2	1	3	3	9	9	9				3		74	6.17%

for interference testing, signal strength and read rate were used. For range testing, distance and orientation to antennae were parameters. For read rate, reads per second were used. A key concern with the use if RFID tags is interference with the surrounding environment. Preliminary tests were used to define key elements that needed to be further tested to best understand how RFID tags could be used.

- Define hardware vendors: Selection criteria for vendors related directly to customer (NASA/Barrios) demand. Critical issues were longevity of vendor, such that it would be difficult to switch vendors should one vendor discontinue service for any reason. Another key issue was the vendor's ability to get tags on a regular basis and have the ability to deliver tags when needed.

MEASURE

The test was conducted in a real-world, "noisy" environment, which means radio noise is caused by but not limited to telecommunication towers, motor vehicles, miscellaneous electrical devices, and ambient radio signals from television and radio transmission towers nearby.

- Read range: The read range test determined the approximate range of each system of RFID tags. This metric is very important because of the nature of RFIS systems. It is a limiting factor of what types of procedures can be implemented on a per tag basis.
- Orientation sensitivity: For some tags, as the orientation of the tag to the reader changed, the read range changed. We referred to this phenomenon as *orientation sensitivity*. After documenting this factor, a test was developed for quantifying the sensitivity. Table 22.2 shows the data collected.
- Reading accuracy: Reading accuracy is defined as scanned tags properly transferring their information. This test ensured that all tags, reader, and anticollision logarithms work properly.

PREDICT

In predict phase, we analyze the results and design the reasonable solution according to the available conditions. With the limitation of reading range and accuracy of the reading test, we could use the experiment result for future research.

$$99.9\% \; \text{Range}_{\text{System}} =$$
$$\min(\mu_{0°} - Z_{.005}\sigma_{0°}, \mu_{30°} - Z_{.005}\sigma_{30°}, \mu_{60°} - Z_{.005}\sigma_{60°}, \mu_{90°} - Z_{.005}\sigma_{90°}) \tag{1}$$

ANALYZE

Using the data gathered in the measure phase, statistics were then used to determine the actual range of the tags. Using the customer specification of 99.9 percent accuracy, we formulated what range would give 99.9 percent accuracy. This was done by separating the factorial data by tag angle and RFID system. Descriptive statistics were then applied to each group of data and then used to predict the 99.9 percent read range, as demonstrated in equation (1). Table 22.3 shows the data with the calculations for equation (1).

Using an analysis of variance on the average (ANOVA), the significance of each factor was analyzed. Table 22.4 is the ANOVA summary. As indicated by the p-values obtained from the data, all three of the main effects' cofactors were significant, as were the interactions between floor angle and polarization and floor angle and tag angle. Polarization and tag angle as well as the interaction between all three factors were less significant.

Table 22.2
Polarization Test Data

Interval	R0, A0	R45, A0	R90, A0	R0, A30	R45, A30	R90, A30	R0, A45	R45, A45	R990, A4	R0, A6	R45, A
1 Antennae											
1	14.8	15.17	16.3	29.29	25.09	25.19	19.28	21.7	22.39	0	14.02
2	14.8	15.27	16.28	29.42	25.23	25.31	19.06	21.65	22.35	0	13.92
3	14.6	15.04	16.25	29.22	25.5	24.96	19.45	21.6	22.37	0	14.45
4	14.75	14.87	16.27	28.68	25.37	25.59	18.91	21.52	22.47	0	14.83
5	14.74	15.19	16.32	28.78	25.27	25.43	18.96	21.52	22.53	0	14.31
2 Antennae, Polarized											
1	29.77	28.76	26.76	14.04	12.45	21.27	16.26	12.83	12.84	0	0
2	29.32	28.89	26.64	13.94	12.46	31.21	16.05	12.87	13.27	0	0
3	29.39	28.01	27.33	14.2	12.37	31.09	16.01	12.75	13.71	0	0
4	28.96	27.78	27.2	14.15	12.45	31.18	16.33	12.58	13.48	0	0
5	29.45	28.03	27.3	14.03	12.64	31.42	16.28	12.92	13.02	0	0
2 Antennae, Non-Polarized											
1	19.51	16.25	19.17	23.05	25.45	21.26	11.17	19.06	22.59	0.56	10.29
2	20	16.34	18.09	23.06	25.67	21.14	11.27	19.32	22.46	0.52	10.09

TABLE 22.3
Read Range Analysis

Trial/Angle	Marix 4x4				Matrix 2x2				Alien — SamSys			
	0	30	60	90	0	30	60	90	0	30	60	90
1	12.50	16.00	15.00	16.00	9.00	5.50	6.00	7.00	5.50	5.00	4.50	4.50
2	12.50	16.00	15.00	16.50	9.00	5.50	6.00	7.00	5.50	5.50	4.50	4.50
3	12.50	16.00	16.00	16.00	9.00	5.50	6.00	6.00	5.50	5.50	4.50	4.00
4	12.50	16.00	16.00	16.00	9.00	5.50	6.00	6.00	5.50	5.50	5.00	4.00
5	12.50	16.00	16.00	16.00	8.00	5.50	6.00	6.00	5.50	5.00	5.00	4.50
6	12.50	16.00	16.00	16.00	8.00	6.00	6.00	7.00	5.50	5.00	4.50	4.50
7	12.50	16.00	16.00	16.00	8.00	5.50	6.00	7.00	5.50	5.00	5.00	4.50
8	12.50	16.00	16.50	16.00	8.00	5.50	6.00	7.00	5.00	5.00	4.50	4.50
9	12.50	16.00	16.00	16.00	8.00	5.50	6.00	6.00	5.50	5.00	5.50	4.50
10	12.50	16.00	16.00	16.50	8.00	5.00	6.00	6.00	5.00	5.00	5.00	4.00
Mean	12.5	16.0	15.9	16.1	8.4	5.5	6.0	6.6	5.4	5.2	4.8	4.4
StDev	0.0	0.0	0.5	0.2	0.5	0.2	0.0	0.5	0.2	0.2	0.3	0.2
Z	3.1	3.1	3.1	3.1	3.1	3.1	3.1	3.1	3.1	3.1	3.1	3.1
99.9% Range	12.5	16.0	14.4	15.4	6.8	4.8	6.0	5.0	4.7	4.4	3.7	3.6
Min Range	**12.50**				**4.77**				**3.60**			

Read accuracy showed 100 percent readability. This test was conducted by verifying that the tag number received by the computer was the tag that was scanned. This test was conducted by placing twenty tags in a CTB with crumpled paper and Styrofoam. The bag was then shaken and scanned for ten seconds. All tags were read properly throughout the twenty-scan study.

DESIGN

According to the analysis of the experiment data, we could get a systematic overview of our system configuration under certain circumstances. In the next step of our predict phase, the goal will be to design the appropriate RFID system compatible with current technology and human resources.

- Smart shelf: The smart shelf system integrates shelving hardware with RFID antennas. This system would have dual capabilities. The main function of the smart shelf is accurate inventory. However, the system also has the capability to locate items onboard the ISS. The unique infrastructure for this system would consist of blanketing the storage areas with mats that act as RFID antennae. These antennae read passively tagged consumable items and report their location within a couple feet (see Figure 22.1).

FIGURE 22.1   Smart shelf diagram.

TABLE 22.4
Delphi Decision Matrix of RFID Hardware Configuration

		Weight	System			
			Sensor	Door Tracking	Waste Tracking	Smart Shelf
Factors	Infrastructure	3	7	4	9	5
	Intervention	3	9	9	9	9
	Reliability	2	8	8	7	9
	Location	1	9	7	5	9
	Development	1	5	8	7	5
			78	70	80	74

		Weight	Tag				
			Alien	Matrics 4x4	Matrics 2x2	RF Code	SAVI
Factors	Ability toget tags	2	10	8	7	8	6
	Size/Shape	2	7	7	9	8	3
	Read distance	2	6	9	7	7	7
	Durability	2	9	9	9	9	10
	Ease of tagging	1	6	10	9	7	1
	Cost	1	10	10	10	4	2
			80	86	83	75	55

- Door tracking: Door tracking is a system that tracks tagged items as they move through the ISS. This system allows for accurate item quantities to be recorded by recording when items were moved from storage and into trash areas. Location of items can also be found with this system by a query that reports which module an item is located in.

- Waste tracking: Waste tracking is a unique form of inventory management because it measures items and quantities used instead of scanning the station for inventory. This concept exploits the centralization of waste on the ISS and therefore uses fewer infrastructures and less power then other systems. It also has the possibility of avoiding misreads due to interference or background reflection. The process begins on the ground with packaging like items in bags. For the purpose of this report we will use thirty-six razor cartridges. Because a typical launch will consist of two to four bags of these cartridges, all of one bag will be used before another bag is opened. Once one bag of razors is used and the Ziploc® bag is thrown away, the system registers that thirty-six razors have been used and need to be replenished during the next launch.
- Sensor active tag (SAT): The sensor active tag system has the potential to be the ideal inventory management system for ISS. Key functions of the SAT system are that it can query consumables onboard the ISS on a regular schedule as well as locate items onboard the ISS. These audits can keep the ground crew constantly aware of which items are being used on a daily basis. An SAT is an active tag that can read passive tags. These SAT devices are placed inside CTBs and periodically scan the contents and transmit the data to the central IMS software. SATs can also be equipped to help the crew locate the bag by audible methods.

PERFORM

The last phase of our study will be perform, after previous experiments and design applications. The next stage is to prove the feasibility of our design by using decision matrix and optimize the system cost according to the current configurations.

OPTIMIZE

To determine which application to implement, a Delphi decision matrix was used. This organized the different applications to the customers needs and ranked the equipment and the proposed systems.

The decision matrix in Table 22.4 shows that the matrices 4 by 4 tags used with the waste tracking inventory method would work best.

VERIFY

To verify the system configuration and implement RFID system successfully, we need to conduct cost analysis for individual case, in this study; we take the common cases that RFID cost on installation, maintenance, and other related costs. There will be several costs associated with the implementation of the RFID waste tracking system. Table 22.5 outlines all of the costs associated with the system.

The incremental costs of the WTS are in three parts as well. Table 22.6 outlines all the incremental costs. The return on the investment can be seen in Table 22.7. This shows the annual savings of $20.4 million EBIT over three years.

TABLE 22.5	
Fixed Costs for WTS	
Readers	$75,000.00
Software	$100,000.00
Installation	$4,500,000.00
	$4,675,000.0

TABLE 22.6	
Annual Incremental Costs for WTS	
Tags	$15,000.00
Ground crew labor	$300,000.00
Maintenance	$150,000.00
	$465,000.0

TABLE 22.7
Annual Savings for WTS

Year	Fixed Cost	Annual Cost	Annual Savings	Annual Return
1	$4,675,000.00	$465.000.00	$22,400,000.00	$17,260,000.00
2		$465.000.00	$22,400,000.00	$39,195,000.00
3		$465.000.00	$22,400,000.00	$61,130,000.00

CONCLUSION

RFID has the ability to help streamline the ISS inventory management systems. With less time spent on inventorying consumable items, they will be able to do more research then before. The initial cost of almost $5 million dollars is returned in the first year with the labor savings.

REFERENCE

Breyfogle, F. W. (2003). *Implementing Six Sigma*. 2d ed. Hoboken, N.J.: Wiley.

ADDITIONAL REFERENCES

Carbon, T. A. (2000). Measuring efficiency of semiconductor manufacturing operations using data envelopment analysis (DEA). Paper read at the IEEE SEMI Advanced Semiconductor Manufacturing Conference.

Carreau, M. (Dec. 10, 2004). Space station crew endures food shortage. *Houston Chronicle*, http://www.chron.com/disp/story.mpl/space/iss/2940602.html.

Gotsman, C., and Y. Koren. (2005). Distributed graph layout for sensor networks. *Lecture Notes in Computer Science* 3383.

Tompkins, J. A., J. A. White, Y. A. Bozer, E. H. Frazelle, J. M. A. Tanchoco, and J. Trevino. (1996). *Facility planning*. 2nd ed. John Wiley & Sons.

Wehking, K.-H., F. Seeger, and S. Kummer. (2006). RFID transponders: Link between information and material flows. How reliable are identification procedures? *Logistics Journal*.

Zhang, Y., J. Liu, and F. Zhao. (2006). Information-directed routing in sensor networks using real-time reinforcement learning. *Combinatorial Optimization in Communication Networks*, 2006, Springer Science & Business Media, 259–288.

23 Individual Sport Competition RFID Applications

INTRODUCTION

Yet another application that has found use for RFID technology is the competitive sports industry. RFID technology has actually been used in some individual competitive sports such as running as early as 1994. In that year, the passive RFID ChampionChip was utilized in the Berlin marathon. Since then, RFID chips have been used in cycling, skating, and even triatholon competitions.

The use of RFID technology in these types of events is particularly advantageous because competition race committees need to process large volumes of competitors in relatively short periods of time. For example, in a marathon race, there may be hundreds or even thousands of runners at the start of the race. Though the numbers of competitors passing though the checkpoints at the same time will diminish over the course, each individual competitor still needs an accurate time record.

Unlike bar codes or digital video records, RFID technology has the capability of being able to record the large volume of competitors nearly simultaneously. As competitors enter the antenna portal, the powering and transmission of the RFID chip and subsequent receipt of the signal is measured in milliseconds. Depending on the number of RFID readers in position, the time records for large numbers of competitors can be read at the same time.

For the purposes of illustration, in this chapter we will initially focus our discussion of RFID technology on individual running type sports competitions. These include normal distance running, marathons, and walking events. However, the same technology is similar for other sports competitions such as cycling and skating.

APPLICATION CONSIDERATIONS

The use of RFID tags in individual sports competition is dependent on the organizing committee. Some organizing committees may accept compatible competitor-owned RFID chips; other committees may require competitors to use race-specific chips.

The use of compatible competitor-owned RFID chips reduces the logistical costs to the organizing committee. However, other problems may be introduced. Unfortunately, a common problem is that before the race, competitors using their own chips must ensure that their tag's identification number is properly associated with their entry. If the competitor fails to do so, there is no way that the committee can properly record his start, splits, or finishes.

The race committee can require competitors to utilize the organizations RFID chips. This has the advantage of insuring that each competitor's tag identification number is properly recorded. However, the purchase of the anticipated number of RFID tags plus a reserve for a particular competition can significantly add to the operating costs of the event.

The cost of the event also depends on how the organizing committee intends to set up the RFID technology. RFID tags can be used to record any combination of individual starts, splits and checkpoints, and finishes.

The exact choice of RFID tag reading may also be a function of the funding available to the race committee. Obviously, the most expensive system will be one that uses RFID tags to record the start, a number of splits or checkpoints, and the finish. There must be reader antenna systems positioned at each of these locations. In addition, if the data are to be centrally recorded, additional networking hardware will be required. This type of system will actually produce the most accurate type of performance data. The net time resulting from the difference between the finish and the start can be precisely calculated for each competitor. Competitors can also utilize the split times for race analysis and future training. Similarly, race organizers can utilize the checkpoint times to insure that competitors have negotiated the entire course in realistic times. This approach virtually eliminates the possibility of competitors cheating, as has happened with many competitions in the past.

On the other end of the spectrum, to minimize costs, some race committees will limit themselves to a conventional start, no splits or checkpoints, and only an RFID-enabled finish. In these types of applications, the level of technology is greatly reduced. It is possible to use a single reader and a local computer system.

TAGS

The dominant tag in the individual sporting event arena is the ChampionChip. This is a 134-KHz passive RFID tag and specialized housing. The specialized housing is designed to enable the chip to be securely fastened to the laces of a shoe or an arm or ankle band.

As a passive tag, the ChampionChip is dependent on the reader antenna to energize the chip's circuitry. When energized, the tag transmits its unique identification code. The ChampionChip identification code consists of seven digits. Some characters are not used. However, generally speaking, the first two digits are alphabetical characters, the third digit is numeric, and the fourth through seventh digits can be either numeric or alphabetical.

Figure 23.1 illustrates both the ChampionChip's tag and housing.

As can be seen from the illustration, the actual passive RFID tag is the small cylindrical capsule. The antenna and the circuitry can be observed. The

FIGURE 23.1   ChampionChip RFID tag.

RFID tag is by necessity waterproof. It is normally held inside the mounting unit, which in turn is attached to shoelaces or an arm or ankle band. Different styles and colors are also available; however, the RFID tag is universal.

MOUNTING CONSIDERATIONS

Despite increasingly robust components, some consideration must be made to protect the RFID chip from damage. RFID chips are sufficiently robust to absorb the shock received from being mounted on the top of footwear. The chip housing is typically secured with the shoelaces. In this position, the shock and possible damage to the RFID chip is mitigated by the shoe's padding. Figure 23.2 illustrates a Champion-Chip affixed to a runner's shoe.

In other competitions such as triathlons, competitors will wear a variety of footwear. It would be disadvantageous for the competitor to repeatedly dismount and remount the unique RFID tag. In this case, competitors normally affix the RFID tag to some portion of clothing or a wrist or ankle band. This is illustrated in Figure 23.3.

FIGURE 23.2   RFID tag affixed to shoe.

FIGURE 23.3   Ankle band mounting.

If an area other than near the competitor's foot is selected for the chip placement, this must be taken into consideration when designing the antenna reader system. Similarly, competitors are also advised not to finish in unusual body postures such as walking on their hands, as this would be outside of the finish line's antenna's normal interrogation zone.

ANTENNA SYSTEMS

Due to the volume of reads required at potentially the same time, specially designed antenna portals may be required for individual sporting events. The most obvious requirement is that the portal must be wide enough to allow a substantial number of competitors to pass through at the same time. The other issue that drives that antenna design is the fact that short-range passive RFID chips are utilized. This means that the antenna must be relatively close to the position of the tags as they pass by.

These two design considerations have led to the development of antenna mats. The antenna structure is housed inside of the mat itself. If properly set up, competitors who step on the mat will be inside the antenna's interrogation zone. Up to four of the antenna mats illustrated in Figure 23.4 may be attached to a single reader. The use of four mats at one time effectively quadruples the width of the antenna portal.

READER SYSTEMS

In contrast to the antenna systems, the sports application reader systems are relatively conventional. The only significant difference between these and other RFID readers is the possible increased need for portability and the ability to operate under adverse environmental conditions.

The portability requirement means that the RFID reader antenna system cannot necessarily rely on AC power. In order to function in power-inaccessible areas, the

FIGURE 23.4   Antenna mat.

system must be capable of operating on DC power. This means that the system must be powered off of a battery. The battery must be capable of powering the system long enough to read the first and last finishers.

The environmental requirements mean that the system must be able to operate under various temperature and humidity conditions. Thousands of dollars are expended on even the most modest events. So competitions are not normally canceled unless really extraordinary conditions exist. Thus, for example, the RFID reader antenna system must be able to operate in the rain. Both the portability and the environmental condition requirements have been addressed through housing the system in waterproof boxes and powering the system with a battery.

Figure 23.5 and Figure 23.6 illustrate portable RFID readers.

FIGURE 23.5   Portable RFID reader.

FIGURE 23.6   Portable RFID reader.

PERFORMANCE ISSUES

A significant issue with the use of any type of RFID technology is reliability. This is not necessarily an issue with the technology itself but rather in recognition that anytime that technology is used, it may also fail. The type of technology used in individual sports competition is relatively mature passive RFID technology in which only the tag's identification number is transmitted. However, at any given time, an individual antenna reader system may experience difficulty reading an individual tag. This is a real issue with the short-range passive RFID tags typically used in sporting applications. This concern is definitely an issue since, in many cases, the positioning of the tag with respect to the antenna is not at all consistent.

For this reason, many organizing committees utilize both a primary and a secondary antenna reader system. This has the potential of reducing the probability of a bad read caused by any type of tag interference. It also provides a backup in the event that either of the two antenna reader systems fail. What it does not protect against is RFID tag malfunctions. The only way to reduce the occurrences of such problems is by assigning two or more tags to an individual competitor. Although this may seem to be an extreme measure, in most cases, individual sporting performances cannot be repeated in the same manner as improperly shipped goods can be reordered.

EXTENSIONS TO OTHER SPORTS COMPETITIONS

The basic RFID technology discussed in this chapter has so far focused on applications to individual running-type sports competitions. This same RFID technology has been adapted to other individual sports competitions such as cycling and skating.

SPECIAL CYCLING RFID CONSIDERATIONS

The same passive RFID tag that is used in running sports may also be utilized for competitive cycling. However, some modifications must be made as to how the RFID tag is positioned with respect to the competitor. In cycling, the tag cannot be attached to the competitor's shoe as with running sports. The reason for this is that the cyclist's shoe travels in a circle subscribed by the pedal. At the top of the circle, the cyclist's shoe will be the maximum distance away from the antenna mat. With the relatively short range of passive RFID tags, this position may be beyond the range of the interrogation zone of the antenna mat. If this occurs, the competitor's RFID tag will not be recorded.

To prevent no-reads of this type, the current practice is to mount the RFID tag in a holder specifically designed to be attached to some position on the actual cycle itself. The exact position does not matter as long as it fulfills two requirements. First, the metal in the bicycle frame cannot block the tag's signal. Second, the position of the tag must be as close as possible to the antenna mat. One practice is to affix the RFID tag housing to the front tire axle. This provides a consistent position with a direct line of sight to the mat.

Special Skating RFID Considerations

Special considerations must also be made when this RFID technology is utilized in skating-type events. The first consideration is that the RFID tag must be positioned so that the blade of the skate does not interfere with the RFID tag's signal. The second consideration is that with ice skating in particular, for obvious reasons, it is not possible for the skaters to skate directly over the antenna mat. Because of the short-range reads for the passive tags, reader antennas cannot be positioned on either side of the skating track. This means that an antenna mat must still be used. However, in this case, there is no alternative but to position the antenna below the ice. Testing will be required to insure that this method of antenna positioning provides reliable reads.

SUMMARY

The use of RFID technology in individual competition sporting events began in 1994. Since then, RFID technology has been used in running events as large as city marathons. The popularity of using RFID tags continues to increase as race organizers appreciate the increased timing accuracy available only through the use of this technology. Although not a primary consideration, RFID technology can also help ensure that competitors properly pass through a number of checkpoints. This eliminates the possibility of competitors improperly completing a competition route. These advantages will ensure that RFID technology continues to become increasingly widespread in the coming years. The technology is currently sufficiently widespread that many competitors have a permanent RFID chip registered to them.

QUESTIONS

1. Why is RFID technology so advantageous over bar codes and digital video for recording accurate start and finish times in sports competitions?
2. Why can RFID chips not be affixed to competitors' shoes in triathlon competitions?
3. How can the use of RFID technology help insure that the competitors complete the course properly?
4. Why is it necessary to provide both a primary and a secondary RFID system in an important sporting event?

ADDITIONAL REFERENCES

AMB Identification and Timing. [Online]. Available at http://www.amb-it.com/ [Accessed August 30, 2007].

ChampionChip. [Online]. Available at http://www.championchipusa.com [Accessed August 30, 2007].

Wyld, D. C. *Sports 2.0: A look at the future of sports in the context of RFID* [Online]. Available at http://www.thesportjournal.org/2006Journal/Vol9-No4/Wyld.asp [Accessed August 30, 2007].

24 Surgical RFID Technology Applications

A. Rogers, Erick C. Jones, D. Oleynikov

INTRODUCTION

The importance of ensuring the removal of all foreign bodies from a patient after surgery cannot be overstated. Retention of surgical instrumentation inside body tissues, most often surgical sponges, is an inconvenience for the patient at best and can lead to severe physiological consequences in extreme cases. Most operating rooms utilize a sponges, sharps, and instruments count to prevent this occurrence, but in the heat of surgical operation, especially when unforeseen circumstances occur during an operation that require emergency measures to be taken, mistakes can and do happen. These occasional mistakes in the sponge count, while rare, can result in both physical harm to the patient and damage to the surgeon via consequential malpractice suits.

The long-term objective of this research is the development of a radio frequency identification (RFID) system embedded within surgical sponges that will allow for a fast and accurate count during surgical operations. The overall objective of this system would be to eliminate errors in the sponge count by removing the human error factor and applying an automated, non-line-of-sight inventory system. RFID's power to inventory unique frequency signals for multiple items as well as the removal of the line-of-sight requirements of other technologies (e.g., bar codes) gives this technology a unique ability to meet the requirements of the surgical environment.

MATERIALS AND METHODS

A recent popular press study has estimated that as many as 1 in 100 surgeries worldwide may result in a retained surgical instrument (Gawande, 2003). When the incident results from a retained surgical sponge, the result is a generalized group of symptoms classified as gossypiboma, including development of abscess or granuloma around the sponge itself. A majority of hospitals utilize some form of sponge, sharps, and instrument count to prevent this, but no standardized method exists. In many cases, the count procedure is defined by the individual hospital and is frequently omitted in cases of emergency or transvaginal surgery or for vaginal deliveries (Gibbs and Aurbech, 2001). Any number of factors can contribute to this possibility, including but not limited to surgical packs used during fascial closure, hurried counts at the end of long operations (Zbar et al., 1998), emergency surgeries, or surgeries where complications arise over the course of the proceedings (Gawande et al., 2003).

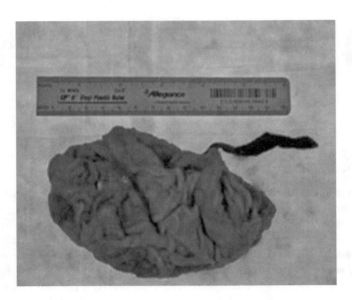

FIGURE 24.1 Extracted surgical sponge showing gossypiboma.

More recently, surgical sponges have been produced that are embedded with radio-opaque strips, allowing them to be visualized by postoperative X-ray. However, while this has reduced the instances of gossypiboma, it has not eliminated it (see Figure 24.1). In one study, three out of twenty-nine cases where X-ray was used to screen for radio-opaque sponges resulted in a false negative (Gibbs and Aurbech, 2001). More importantly, these X-rays must be performed postoperatively, meaning that any sponges discovered must be removed via a second operation, exposing the patient to an even larger degree of risk for infection or trauma.

Data regarding incidents of retained surgical instrumentation from surgery is difficult at best to discover. The Joint Commission for Accreditation for Healthcare Organizations (JCAHO) policy mentions that instances of "unintentionally retained foreign body without major permanent loss of function" do not require reporting (Gibbs and Aurbech, 2001). This leads to a gross underestimation of the incidents and incurred costs of retained surgical instruments, confounding efforts to compile numbers regarding them. Published studies list worldwide surgical instrument retention rates ranging between one in fifteen thousand operations (Emery, 2006) to as many as one in one hundred operations (Medical Malpractice Today, 2003). Of these, roughly two thirds consist of incidents of retained surgical sponges (Emery, 2006). Presentation of gossypiboma is either acute or delayed, with acute symptoms resulting in abscess or granuloma and delayed symptoms resulting typically in adhesion formation and encapsulation, resulting in a subacute intestinal obstruction months or even years after the initial operation (Zbar et al., 1998). In some extreme cases, complications have been observed including perforation of the bowel, sepsis, and, in very rare instances, death (Gawande et al., 2003).

RFID systems function by utilizing a system of individual transponders, typically referred to as tags, that emit a specific identification signal. Nearby antennas emit radio waves that are absorbed by the tag, converted to electrical energy, and then re-emitted at the tag's specific frequency (Clampitt and Jones 2006). These frequencies are then read by the antennas, creating an active inventory of each item read by the system (Bhuptani and Moradpour 2005; Shepard 2005). This inventory information is then usable by a variety of middleware applications, opening options for IMS, portal checkpoints, logistics, and access control systems.

An RFID sponge system would reduce gossypiboma by utilizing a small hand-held device to perform an automated count of inventoried sponges before, during, and after the operation, minimizing human error in surgical tool counts and allowing for immediate discovery and retrieval of surgical sponges within the peritoneum.

The first objective, testing of current RFID technology's ability to function within the requirements of an operating room setting, consisted primarily of a series of experiments involving submersion of RFID tags into body fluids (primarily water) and tests involving tag survivability after sterilization procedures (autoclave, chemical, etc.) to identify the weaknesses in the current technology as it pertains to this particular application. Once that information had been identified, the next objective was to design a prototype "smart sponge." Issues that needed to be addressed during this period included: identifying the existing RFID tag/reader combination that resulted in the desired accuracy as well as determining optimum placement of the RFID tags upon the sponge surface for optimum readability and resistance to mechanical stress. Assembly of this prototype was then tested by placing the RFID-labeled surgical sponges within the abdominal cavity of a euthanized pig cadaver and then retesting readability upon removal.

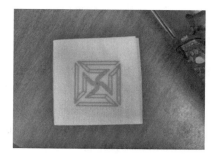

Once all of these objectives are met, the entire system will be assembled for final experimental confirmation of function and fine tuning via implementation in a simulated or actual operating theater.

FIGURE 24.2   An RFID-labeled surgical sponge.

RESULTS

Initial experimentation indicated that water would prove to be the primary obstacle to overcome for project success. While the porcine test resulted in positive read rates when the sponge was placed inside the body cavity and removed, tests involving full submersion into water proved to cause much more disruption in reads. Specifically, read range seemed to be reduced sharply as a result of full submersion and removal, along with a slight decrease in overall tag readability.

Experiments comparing performance with the sponges labeled on the exterior versus embedded inside showed a much better performance for tags on the outside of the sponge, presumably as a result of the removal of the intervening layer of liquid between reader and sponge. Additional testing demonstrated a positive correlation between this relationship and reader strength. Initial concerns arose due to the

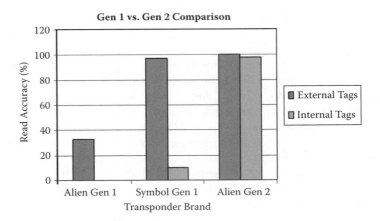

FIGURE 24.3 Comparison of results between various brands and technology levels.

possibility of separation of an RFID tag from the sponge, but further testing has shown this to be unlikely. Any weakening of the adhesive can be compensated for in later prototypes through utilization of water-resistant adhesives and/or through printing the RFID antenna directly onto the sponge itself.

Release of second generation RFID technology (Gen 2) during the testing phases of this experiment opened the possibility for utilization of more rugged RFID transponders in the smart sponge system. Gen 2 technology typically features better range along with more consistent read rate and resistance to various factors that hinder RFID read accuracy (such as water.) In actual practice, this translated into a greatly increased read accuracy, even with the tag placed inside of the sponge.

One initial goal of the project was to allow readability of the RFID tags through a patient's skin, thus allowing mobile RFID readers to be utilized to locate missing sponges within a patient's body cavity. At this time, off-the-shelf available RFID technology seems incapable of performing this function. Further experimentation during the porcine test indicated that a layer of skin was capable of disrupting tag reads completely when Gen 1 labels were applied to sponges. Unfortunately, Gen 2 tags were not available at the time of the experiment, and thus no conclusion can be drawn regarding the ability of the technology to function in this environment. In any case, X-rays taken of sponges embedded with RFID tags were clearly visible, due to the highly metallic content of the antenna inks. Thus, they should be capable of functioning for the same task as the current practice of radio-opaque labeled sponges until such time as RFID technology improves to allow for location within the patient's body cavity.

DISCUSSION

Early experimental results strongly suggest that current RFID technology is capable of performing the function of inventorying surgical sponges during an operation accurately and with minimal human error. Specifically, Gen 2 Alien Squiggle T Tags

FIGURE 24.4 A mobile RFID reader suitable for immediate application in hospital operating rooms.

have repeatedly demonstrated a 100 percent read accuracy when wet, even when submerged in water for up to an hour.

Given this data, an RFID sponge inventory system can be reasonably envisioned wherein each sponge is read entering the operating room, as it is being placed within the patient, and finally at the end of the operation itself. A list of each sponge's individual ID number would then be compared from the beginning of the operation and the end, with any discrepancies being immediately visible. With a high enough level of sophistication, this system can be fine-tuned to a level of accuracy that will preclude the manual sponge count because the automated inventory system will be more accurate and free of human bias.

The immediate reduction in gossypiboma cases would result in an increase in patient safety and efficiency in the operating room as well as a reduction in malpractice suits for the medical community at large. Any sponges that are left within a patient will be identified immediately, allowing retrieval before the surgeon closes up, thus eliminating the need to perform a second operation to retrieve the sponge. Moreover, a direct benefit would accrue for surgeons, as the operating room can be made more efficient through the elimination of the need for lengthy counts and recounts at the end of each operation. A reduction in the number of miscounts would also reduce the need to X-ray the site of the operation to locate the sponge, decreasing the amount of time spent on this tedious task as well as minimizing the patent's radiation exposure.

Once established, a similar methodology can be utilized to radiolabel other surgical instruments for similar applications. With all of the surgical tools in an operating room tagged by RFID, it will require only a small step on the part of hospital organizers to branch into an RFID-managed inventory control system, smart shelf technology, real-time location systems, and numerous other applications.

REFERENCES

Bhuptani, M., and S. Moradpour. (2005). *RFID field guide: Deploying radio frequency identification systems*. Sun Microsystems.

Clampitt, H. G., and E. C. Jones, eds. (2006). *RFID certification textbook*. Houston, Tex.: PWD Group.

Emery, G. (2006). *Emergency surgery often leaves foreign object in body* [Online]. Available at http://www.slackdavis.com/practice_article.php/news_id/argval/122/argname/practice_area/argval/Medical+Malpractice+Home Wed. Jan. 15 [Accessed August 30, 2007].

Gawande, A. A., D. M. Studdert, E. J. Orav, T. A. Brennan, and M. J. Zinner. (Jan. 16, 2003). Risk factors for retained instruments and sponges after surgery. *The New England Journal of Medicine* 348(3): 229–235.

Gibbs, V. C., and A. D. Aurbech. (2001). *Chapter 22. The retained surgical sponge* [Online]. Available at http://www.ahrq.gov/clinic/ptsafety/chap22.htm [Accessed August 30, 2007].

Medical Malpractice Today (2003). *Retained foreign bodies* [Online]. Available at http://www.medicalmalpracticetoday.com/medicalmalpracticetopic-retainedbodies.html [Accessed August 30, 2007].

Shepard, S. (2005). *RFID: Radio frequency identification*. New York: McGraw-Hill.

Zbar, A. P., Grawal, A., Saeed, I. T., Utidjian, M. R. (Dec. 1998). Gossypiboma revisited: A case report and review of the literature. *Journal of the Royal College of Surgeons of Edinbourgh* 43(6): 417–418.

25 Tollway RFID Applications

INTRODUCTION

Tollway applications constitute one of the earliest and most mature uses of RFID technology. The need for a large volume of reads and the relatively consistent positioning of the host vehicle make this process ideal for the use of RFID tags. At the current state of development, the use of RFID tags are estimated to provide a 250 to 300 percent increase in tollway throughput. This increase in performance is just one benefit. Some tollway RFID reader systems can simultaneously monitor up to eight lanes. This level of automation not only increases throughput but also lowers operational costs by being able to reduce the workforce. Some tollway authorities pass on the savings to the patrons. The Harris County Texas Tollway administration, for example, offers a 25 percent reduction in toll costs for the use of their E-ZPass system. Lastly, the use of RFID tag systems on tollways also has environmental impact. A savings of 1.2 million gallons of fuel is estimated as a result of vehicles not having to wait in line to pay tolls.

In this chapter, we will discuss:

- Tollway applications
- Tollway RFID technology
- Tollway consortiums
- New developments in tollway RFID technology
- Associated applications

TOLLWAY APPLICATIONS

To recoup construction costs and provide for ongoing operating costs, some roads require the operators of vehicles to pay a toll. These roads are commonly called tollways. Tollbooths are positioned either at regular intervals along the tollway or at exits or entrances in order to collect tolls. The operation of tollways is normally performed by a quasi-governmental agency or administration. Up until the early 1990s, tolls were generally collected by either an automatic coin machine or a human tollbooth operator. Passage through the tollbooth was controlled by either a pivoting barrier or a set of red and green lights.

The operation of tollways in general presents a number of problems to the tollway administration. First and foremost is the fact that in order to pay the toll, the vehicle must slow down and pass through the tollbooth area. This has a significant potential to disrupt the flow of the traffic from both a resource and an operational viewpoint. If insufficient personnel are available to man tollbooths, the tollbooth throughput will

FIGURE 25.1   Tollbooth with RFID antennas.

be reduced. Similarly, if any event slows the progress of vehicle operators through the tollbooth, throughput will also be compromised.

In the event that the vehicle operator does not have the correct change, the tollbooth operation time increases dramatically. In this case, the vehicle operator must proceed to a manned booth to pay for the toll and perhaps receive change and/or a receipt. In the event that a vehicle attempts to pass through the tollway without paying, automatic cameras are positioned to capture the event. The tollway administration will provide the vehicle's owner with a citation from the license plate captured in the photograph.

Beginning in the early 1990s early RFID technology was applied to various tollways around the northeastern part of the United States. The use of this type of technology is generally referred to as *electronic toll collection*, or ETC. The basic ETC RFID system consists of a vehicle-mounted RFID tag and an antenna and reader system mounted in the tollbooths. The RFID tag is usually mounted inside the vehicle somewhere near the center of the vehicle's windshield and the RFID antenna is suspended from below the booth's ceiling. A typical RFID antenna mounting in a tollbooth is illustrated in Figure 25.1.

In actual practice, most ETC tollways actually now have three different types of booths in major toll areas. The first is used exclusively by RFID tag users. These booths may or may not also contain a pivoting barrier. If there is no barrier, the tagged car may actually be able to proceed at high speed through the tollbooth. This is usually the more common of the two, since a pivoting barrier would defeat the purpose of the RFID system in the first place. The second type of booth is the exact change booth, which is exactly the same as a conventional exact change booth with the addition of the RFID antenna system. The last type of booth is the conventional manned booth. As with the RFID-enhanced exact change booth, the manned booth may also have an RFID antenna system. Both the exact change and manned booths will have either pivoting barriers or control lights. The installation of the RFID antenna system in these types of booths in addition to the ETC booth adds flexibility because the tagged vehicle will be able to use these in the event that any of the other booths are not operational or manned.

In practice, as the registered vehicle passes by the antenna interrogation zone, the tag wakes up and responds with its unique identification number. The antenna then gathers the tags signal and processes it through the reader and the host computer. The host computer ultimately matches the tag's identification number with the registered owner of the vehicle and the license plate number. The date and time of the toll is also recorded and processed.

Since vehicles that utilize ETC RFID systems do not pay as they go, some other payment method must be utilized. In most cases, ETC RFID systems require payment in advance. The payment component of the ETC RFID system is commonly maintained by the tollway administration through on-line Internet systems. Users with registered tags can access their accounts and transfer money in order to pay for tolls. A variety of schemes have been set up to perform in this manner. Some systems require the manual transfer of funds. Others automatically debit funds from another account that is linked the ETC system. ETC administrators encourage the latter by imposing a hefty fine if the vehicle operator passes through a tollbooth with insufficient funds in the ETC account.

TOLLWAY RFID TECHNOLOGY

As with a number of other RFID application areas, specific RFID technology has been developed for use in tollway applications. Specialized tollway RFID technology includes both active and passive tags and readers.

ACTIVE TOLLWAY TAGS

As with other types of active RFID tags, active tollway tags possess greater capabilities and range than passive tags. As a result, the tollway industry is currently dominated by active RFID tags. The most common active tollway RFID tag in use today is the Mark IV Industries RFID transponder. According to Mark IV Industries, approximately 18 million of their transponders are in use today. The Mark IV transponder is currently in use in New York, Pennsylvania, Virginia, Maryland, and many other states. Figure 25.2 illustrates the face of the Mark IV E-ZPass tag.

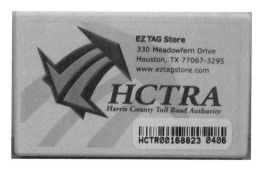

FIGURE 25.2   E-ZPass transponder.

FIGURE 25.3   EZ-Pass transponder mounted to car windshield.

The Mark IV tag is generally positioned on the inside of the windshield in the vicinity of the rearview mirror. This position helps allow for an unobstructed read by the vertically hanging RFID antenna. Figure 25.3 illustrates this mounting.

Active tags such as the Mark IV suffer from the same weaknesses of all other active RFID tags. In comparison to passive tollway tags, the active tollway tags are more expensive. Unfortunately for the vehicle operator, the increased cost of the tag is passed along. Tollway administrations that use active tags frequently pass along the expense through both a one-time processing fee and a monthly rental fee.

Another weakness of the active RFID tollway tag such as the Mark IV is the requirement to periodically replace the internal battery. The actual battery life is dependent on the number of times that the tag is used through the ETC. However, many tollway systems issue tags that are only effective for a period of three to five years. This allows the tollway authorities to ensure that the battery is likely to be functioning. Some measures have been put into place to minimize problems associated with poor reads caused by depleted batteries. After the first few times that an RFID registered vehicle operator passes through the tollway with bad reads, he is notified. If the operator does not correct the read problem, fines will ensue.

Tags like the Mark IV actually come in two different versions. The normal version is for positioning on the inside of the windshield. For this purpose, the tag is well protected from environmental concerns. However, some vehicles, as discussed in a subsequent section, cannot use internally mounted tags. For this reason, externally mountable tags are also available for use. These tags have additional protection for the circuitry that allows them to better survive exposure to the environment. These same external tags are also required for use on motorcycles where no protected area exists. The external version of the Mark IV is similar in physical appearance to the regular version of the Mark IV with the exception of an additional protective coating.

PASSIVE TOLLWAY TAGS

As previously discussed, a weakness of the active tollway tag is that each tag must be returned to the issue point every three to five years. This is necessary in order to replace the active tag's battery. In contrast, passive RFID tags have no internal

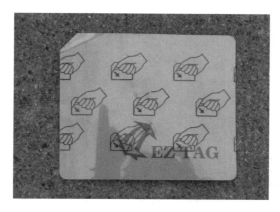

FIGURE 25.4 Windshield-based RFID tag.

FIGURE 25.5 Mounted passive E-ZPass tag.

battery. Their circuitry is powered from the radio frequency energy transmitted by the RFID system's antenna. This means that passive RFID tags utilized in ETC systems do not need to be returned for replacement. Instead of supplying a deposit and paying a monthly rental fee, passive tags are generally purchased and used for the life of the vehicle.

An example of a passive ETC windshield-based RFID tag is the Transcore eGo plus. This tag operates on 915 MHz. The tag is capable of a 31.5 foot range. This enables it to be easily used with overhead ETC RFID antenna systems. The price of the tag is approximately $10. The tag is quite low profile, being similar to an automobile registration sticker. Figure 25.4 illustrates the Transcore tag. Figure 25.5 illustrates a passive E-ZPass tag correctly mounted on the inside of a vehicle's window.

In addition to the passive tag's ability to function without battery replacement improvements include its increased aesthetics. Many vehicle operators object to the larger box-like characteristics of the active RFID tollway tag. Because the passive tollway RFID tag is virtually flat, it is much less obtrusive. Most vehicles already

FIGURE 25.6   Mark IV Badger reader.

possess a number of windshield registration stickers, so one additional sticker is not nearly as obtrusive as an active RFID tag.

The only unique limitation to passive ETC RFID tags is their durability under certain conditions. Cleaning chemicals, for example, can cause the components of the tag to separate from the tag substrate. For this reason, users are given certain precautions when installing passive tags.

TOLLWAY ANTENNA READER SYSTEMS

As illustrated in the previous figures, tollway antennas in the antenna reader systems are suspended from the roof of the tollbooth or tollway. The antennas are generally hard-wired to a central location where the reader unit is located. The reader unit in turn is linked to a host computer system that controls both the reader and the antenna.

The predominant readers are manufactured by Mark IV industries. Their readers come in a variety of grades. More sophisticated readers such as their Badger model are capable of simultaneously monitoring eight normal lanes or four high-speed lanes. The Badger model also differentiates itself by having greater high-speed acquisition capabilities. This model is claimed by Mark IV to be able to read vehicles traveling one hundred miles per hour.

One innovative approach involving tollway reader systems is the use of a solar-powered reader. All other tollway readers require AC power in order to operate. The Mark IV industries MGate unveiled in 2006 is a solar-powered portable reader system. The system is contained in a small trailer. It consists of a laptop computer, the antenna, reader, and a solar panel array. As vehicles pass by, the RFID tag is scanned and processed by the computer. The data are then transmitted through a wireless Internet connection to the host server.

The MGate system as illustrated in Figure 25.7 is particularly important in the case of situations where traffic must be rerouted from an existing system due to construction, accident, or environmental conditions. This is important because it may not be economically feasible for the tollway administration to construct a temporary reader system complete with AC power in these situations. The tollway administration may be forced to

FIGURE 25.7   M-Gate reader.

allow motorists to pass unread around the RFID readers. A specific example is when an accident blocks or restricts the tollway. Tag users may be forced to use conventional tollbooths. By converting a conventional tollbooth to a tag booth, the tollway administration can increase the traffic throughput (see Figure 25.8).

PROBLEMS WITH READS

The vast majority of vehicles do not have difficulty in being read by existing RFID antenna systems. The exception to this involves vehicles that incorporate any type of metal strip laminated within the vehicle's windshield.

FIGURE 25.8

This is most commonly encountered with radio antennas. However, windshields that also have metal heating elements may also have difficulties. Most tollway administrations keep a list of vehicles with known reading problems. For example, the New Jersey E-ZPass system includes certain vehicles manufactured by:

- Buick, Roadmaster, all years
- Cadillac, Catera, 1999–2001
- Chevrolet, Lumina and Venture, prior to 2002
- Ford, Crown Victoria, 1987–1994, Taurus prior to 1995
- Oldmobile, Silhouette, prior to 2002
- Pontiac, Trans Sport and Montana, prior to 2002
- Subaru, SVX, all years

In addition to the above lists, some other E-ZPass systems report that Audis, BMWs, and Mercedes may also have problems with windshield-mounted tags. While operators of these vehicles cannot use internal tags, they can request external tags instead. Figure 25.6 illustrates an external Mark IV badge reader used for this purpose.

MULTIPLE VEHICLE REGISTRATIONS

One problem that appears to be a persistent issue with RFID toll systems is the patron's use of the tag with multiple vehicles. This is particularly an issue with the larger active tags, which can be removed with only minor difficulty. Most E-ZPass systems are set up so that each vehicle is intended to possess its own RFID tag in the same manner as a license plate. To combat the practice of switching vehicles, many E-ZPass systems will consider the use of a different tag as a violation. The reason behind this requirement is that if the E-ZPass tag does not function correctly, the tollway cameras will record the license plate and deduct the charge amount from the operator's account. Since the tag is registered to a particular class of vehicle (i.e., semi-truck vs. car or personal truck), using the same tag on two different vehicles may result in incorrect toll charges being assessed. Since passive E-ZPass tags are permanently mounted to the windshield of a particular vehicle, multiple vehicle use is not a problem with these types of tags.

TOLLWAY CONSORTIUMS

In 1991, the E-ZPass InterAgency Group (IAG) was formed to create an interoperable tollway system in the Northeastern part of the United States. The original consortium consisted of seven independently operating toll systems including:

- The Pennsylvania Turnpike Commision
- The Port Authority of New York and New Jersey
- The New Jersey Turnpike Authority
- The New Jersey Highway Authority
- The New York Metropolitan Transportation Authority
- The New York State Thruway Authority
- The South Jersey Transportation Authority

Today, the consortium consists of twenty-two transportation agencies and port authorities spread across eleven states.

NEW DEVELOPMENTS IN TOLLWAY RFID TECHNOLOGY

One of the limitations of the current RFID technology is that the tollway system cannot automatically determine that the level of tag is appropriate for the vehicle passing through the tollway. For example, a light passenger truck passing through a tollway would be charged the same amount whether or not it was towing a trailer. In these types of cases, the tollway users are advised to pass through a conventional booth. However, as can be expected, a large number of users are likely to inadvertently pass through the RFID lane. Some violators may be identified by the tollway administration, but this is more of a hit-or-miss situation.

To more accurately exact tolls on vehicle operators, a variety of technologies are currently being developed and tested. This technology is focused at detection of the number of axles that a single vehicle and trailer combination may have. When these systems become operational, any vehicle will automatically be charged additional tolls in the event that it is towing a trailer.

ASSOCIATED APPLICATIONS

The widespread use the E-ZPass tag has led to other applications. E-ZPass Plus systems include the ability of the tag to be used with other facilities, most notably parking facilities also under government jurisdiction, including those typically found in airports and city-run convention centers.

SUMMARY

In this chapter, we presented information pertaining to the use of RFID technology with respect to toll roads. Electronic toll collection is one of the oldest and most mature uses of this technology. Originally started in 1993, ETC has seen a technological progression from active to passive RFID tags. Most of the operating issues associated with this RFID technology have been addressed. Many other applications could benefit from a brief examination of how RFID is being utilized in ETC. An additional source that readers may want to consult is the *Toll Road News*. This Web-based publication is available from www.tollroadnews.info. This Web site contains information not only on RFID applications related to tollways but also tollway information in general.

CHAPTER QUESTIONS

1. Why did tollways become one of the earliest uses of RFID technology?
2. Why is passive RFID technology replacing active RFID technology in ETC?
3. Why are ETC users not allowed to use their tags with multiple vehicles?
4. Why is it sometimes necessary to utilize external ETC RFID tags?

ADDITIONAL REFERENCES

Electronic Toll Collection (ETC), available at http://www.ivhs.com/e_toll_industry.htm [Accessed August 30, 2007].

Go Plus Sticker Tag, available at http://www.transcore.com/pdf/PP_eGo%20Plus%20Tag.pdf [Accessed August 30, 2007].

Samuel, S. *EZ-Pass radio frequency identification* [Online]. Available at http://www.fiu.edu/~ssamu003/Radio%20Frequency%20Identification%20paper.pdf [Accessed August 30, 2007].

Swedberg, C. (Nov. 17, 2006). Solar-Powered RFID Reader Measures Road Traffic. Available at http://www.rfidjournal.com/article/articleview/2830/1/1/ [Accessed August 30, 2007].

26 RFID Transportation Systems Applications

INTRODUCTION

A supply chain can be defined as the parts that are involved, directly or indirectly, in fulfilling a customer request (Chopra and Peter 2007). By this definition, it can be seen that a supply chain consists of manufacturers, warehouses, retailers, transporters, and customers. The purpose of a supply chain is to maximize the value generated for the customer; namely, maximizing the difference between the final product worth and the total expended by the supply chain to provide the product to the customer.

In order to succeed, the supply chain must be conducted to minimize the costs incurred. Supply chain management (SCM) is responsible for optimizing the flows within its operational stages which include raw materials, manufacturing, distribution, and transportation in order to minimize the total cost of the supply chain. SCM is a unification of a series of concepts about integrated business planning that can be joined together by the advances in information technology (IT) (Shapiro 2007), yet many companies have not completely taken advantage of this process.

In today's world, the competition between companies, more demanding customers, and reduced margins make the scenario more difficult for companies to succeed. In this context, SCM is an important practice for companies that want not only to keep in business but also have their results optimized and meet the clients' expectations.

Responsiveness in the supply chain has gained importance and it is a trend that apparently will dictate future decisions regarding supply chain design. According to Novack, Langley, and Rinehart (1995), the themes that will have influence on logistics on the near future are

- Strong corporate leadership will enhance logistics value through focusing on efficiency, effectiveness, and differentiation.
- Value realization requires marketing of logistics capabilities within the company and to external customers.
- Emphasis on the "scientific" aspect of logistics management in order to enhance the "art" of creating customer satisfaction.
- Enhancing logistics value through integrating product, information, and cash flows for decision-making linking external and internal processes.
- Logistics value enhanced by ownership of responsibility internally and externally to the firm.
- Focus of successful companies is to create internal value for their organizations and external value for their suppliers and customers.

From these themes, it can be seen that SCM plays and will continue to play an active role in successful companies' routines. In order to achieve better results in the supply chain and better responsiveness to customers' necessities, new techniques such as real-time inventory and dynamic supply chain need to be developed.

TRANSPORTATION IN SCM

As a supply chain driver, transportation has a large impact on customer responsiveness and operational efficiency. Faster transportation allows a supply chain to be more responsive but reduces its efficiency. The type of transportation a company uses also affects the inventory and facility locations in the supply chain. The role of transportation in a company's competitive strategy is determined by the target customers. Customers who demand a high level of responsiveness, and are willing to pay for the responsiveness, allow a company to use transportation responsively. Conversely, if the customer base is price sensitive, then the company can use transportation to lower the cost of the product at the expense of responsiveness. Because a company may use transportation to increase responsiveness or efficiency, the optimal decision for the company means finding the right balance between the two.

The transportation design is the collection of transportation modes, locations, and routes for shipping. Decisions are made on whether transportation will go from a supply source directly to the customer or through intermediate consolidation points. Design decisions also include whether multiple supply or demand points will be included in a single run or not. Also, companies must decide on the set of transportation modes that will be used.

The mode of transportation describes how product is moved from one location in the supply chain network to another. Companies can choose between air, truck, rail, sea, and pipeline as modes of transport for products. Each mode has different characteristics with respect to the speed, size of shipments (parcels, cases, pallet, full trucks, railcar, and containers), cost of shipping, and flexibility that lead companies to choose one particular mode over the others. Typical measurement for transportation operations includes the following metrics:

- Average inbound transportation cost, or the cost of bringing product into a facility as a percentage of sales or cost of goods sold (COGS). Cost can be measured per unit brought in but is typically included in COGS. It is useful to separate this cost by supplier.
- Average incoming shipment size measures the average number of units or dollars in each incoming shipment at a facility.
- Average inbound transportation cost per shipment measures the average transportation cost of each incoming delivery. Along with the incoming shipment size, the metric identifies opportunities for greater economies of scale in inbound transportation.
- Average outbound transportation cost measures the cost of sending product out of a facility to the customer. Cost should be measured per unit shipped, oftentimes measured as a percentage of sales. It is useful to separate this metric by customer.

- Average outbound shipment size measures the average number of units or dollars on each outbound shipment at a facility.
- Average outbound transportation cost per shipment measures the average transportation cost of each outgoing delivery.
- Fraction transported by mode measures the fraction of transportation (in units or dollars) using each mode of transportation. This metric can be used to estimate whether certain modes are overused or underutilized.

The fundamental trade-off for transportation is between the cost of transporting a given product (efficiency) and the speed with which that product is transported (responsiveness). Using fast modes of transport raises responsiveness and transportation cost but lowers the inventory holding cost.

INFORMATION TECHNOLOGY AND SCM

It is no surprise that IT played a big role in enabling many processes and ideas in Supply Chain Management (SCM) that seemed impossible in earlier years. The first advance was the decreasing of inventory levels by managers abandoning rules of thumb and adopting the setting of inventories based on service level desired and historical demand (Shapiro 2007). IT allowed the analysis of a great quantity of units and the process of recalculating the inventory level as the demand changed. This ability to analyze inventory needs made the companies more agile while decreasing inventory levels and increasing service levels.

Another important fact that gave a great contribution to SCM was the electronic data interchange (EDI). This technology allows the direct data interchange between companies using computers. EDI changed the relationship between the company and its customers, with its suppliers, and also with the employees. The ability of trading data almost instantly across the supply chain gave companies the ability to manipulate more up-to-date information in a shorter period of time. This reduced the need for printing and transporting papers, enabled just-in-time practices, and helped to restructure logistics supply chain relationships. Together with EDI we can also mention the importance of the Internet in global business (Johnson et al. 1999).

Artificial intelligence systems are responsible for many advances achieved by society and by SCM as well. Computers can be programmed to execute routine functions and according to the rules imposed to the computer it can be capable of behaving as an intelligent system that can execute complex activities in reduced time. This brought to logistics a much larger capacity of processing information and executing tasks. Many activities can operate without human interference and this converges to a more responsive and accurate supply chain (Johnson et al. 1999).

Some technologies, discussed later in this chapter, can be used to make real-time adjustments to the supply chain. Those adjustments could be due to many events such as manpower shortages or equipment breakdowns. For example, if a problem occurs with a truck or the road conditions change due to weather, the system, supplied with this updated information, should be able to make the necessary corrections to the transportation routes of other trucks to compensate for the truck failure.

This system would be very useful for natural disasters such as Hurricane Katrina. With real-time information, the system would reallocate transportation and production. This kind of modeling would reduce the response time for such events from months or weeks to days or even hours. This system can also be expanded to urban transportation within a city or long distances between two cities.

REAL-TIME TECHNOLOGIES

Radio frequency identification (RFID) and global positioning systems (GPS) are emerging technologies that will allow for real-time data collection to assist with decision support in SCM. RFID has a wide variety of applications. Some examples of RFID uses are library checkout stations, automatic car toll tags, animal identification tags, and inventory systems. Real-time data collected using RFID allows a supply chain to synchronize reorder points and other data. Real-time information can also be used to design and operate logistical systems on a real-time basis. GPS is currently used solely as a means to locate equipment and derive navigation directions.

An RFID system consists of a reader, tags, and an air interface. The reader, also known as an interrogator, sends out a signal through an antenna. This signal is usually in the form of an electromagnetic wave, so a direct line of sight is not needed to read the information on the tag. This is a major advantage of RFID. The signal is received by the tag and a response signal is sent back to the reader. This response signal contains a unique identifier associated with a tag. The response signal can be powered in two ways corresponding to the type of tag. Passive tags utilize the energy of the original signal to send a response signal back to the reader. Passive tags have a limited amount of energy to power the response signal. Therefore, the amount of information transmitted by a passive tag is fairly small, quite similar to the information carried in a bar code. Active and semi-active tags use energy from an attached battery to power the response signal. The use of the embedded battery allows the response signal to contain more information and travel farther. The reader receives the response signal, decodes it, and sends that information to a database. Often the information in the response signal is connected to additional information in the database.

RFID technology can be used throughout the supply chain in order to promote visibility. This visibility helps coordinate actions between entities in the supply chain. Figure 26.1 shows the relationships within the supply chain that can be affected by the implementation of the RFID technologies. An example of RFID implementation is the use of active tags for detecting tampering and monitoring security of maritime containers. Those types of tags also have the tracking advantages of RFID and can be used to improve operations management. Those tags can be seen in Figure 26.2.

GPS systems consist of a series of receivers and satellites that orbit the Earth. GPS works by calculating the distances from a receiver to a number of satellites. With each distance between a receiver and satellite, the number of possible locations is narrowed down until there is only one possible location. A receiver must calculate its distance from at least three satellites to determine a location on the surface of the Earth. However, four satellites are usually used to increase the location accuracy (Dommety and Jain 1996). This process of location would be controlled by

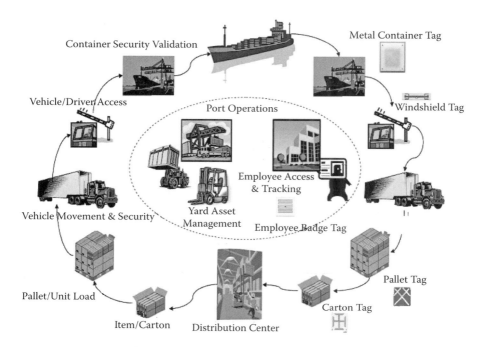

FIGURE 26.1   Integrated supply chain with RFID. (Source: SAVI Technologies.)

FIGURE 26.2   RFID container seal. (Source: SAVI Technologies.)

the positioning module of GPS system. An average GPS positioning and navigation system would also have the following modules:

- Digital map database
- Map matching
- Route planning and guidance
- Human-machine interface
- Wireless communication

There are three positioning technologies that can be used: radio wave–based positioning, dead-reckoning, and signpost. The use of GPS for navigation can have direct and indirect impacts on intelligent transportation systems. GPS navigation systems can provide information about local surroundings. Also, emergency personnel can be provided with a precise location for situations, thus reducing response times. Asset tracking is one of the most popular uses of GPS. One of the limitations of GPS is that receivers cannot communicate with satellites when indoors (Feng and Law, 2002).

RFID and GPS are radio wave–based technologies that are currently used by many organizations. RFID is primarily used in inventory and material handling processes. Tags are placed on items. When these items pass by checkpoints where readers are located, the tag is read and the appropriate action can be taken. Real-time inventory can be kept by monitoring tag reads at strategic points like loading docks. RFID can also be useful in material handling. Items on a conveyor can be diverted at the appropriate times based on the information received from the RFID tag. GPS is primarily use to track assets such as vehicles and other expensive equipment. For example, if a truck breaks down, it is possible to locate the truck and get the shipment moving again in a fraction of the time it would take with a GPS receiver.

FUTURE TECHNOLOGIES

Current applications of RFID and GPS systems have allowed for more effective tracking of inventory and assets. These technologies can be used in conjunction, but the data has to be captured and written to a database to be correlated to other tags or receivers. If these technologies can be combined to produce hybrid systems, greater gains can be achieved. One focus of research is the nesting of GPS receivers and various RFID tag types. If tags and receivers were able to communicate with one another, even more accurate real-time data collection could be achieved during transportation. This would also reduce equipment costs because fewer readers would be required. The nesting would follow the form in Figure 26.3.

If these technologies can be nested, it will allow the information in a bar code or a passive RFID tag to be collected by an active tag. This information could then be combined with the information contained within the active tag and transferred to a GPS receiver. The GPS receiver could then send not only its location but all of the information about the cargo being shipped (Reade and Lindsay 2003). A possible application of this nested technology approach would be in the railroad industry. Currently, there are two passive RFID tags attached to the sides of all railcars in the United States. In addition, most railroads use GPS receivers to track locomotives. If nesting became possible, implementation would be easy. Active tags could be used to capture the information correlated to the cargo in all of the railcars and transmit it to the GPS receiver and thus to the inventory databases.

In addition to nesting technologies, more advanced tags can be developed to allow more detailed data collection. Tags that utilize sensors to capture and write data to the tag are being developed. Some tags have been developed but are still very unreliable. These sensor tags could be used to monitor physical parameters, like temperature and humidity, as well as security parameters. The main problem

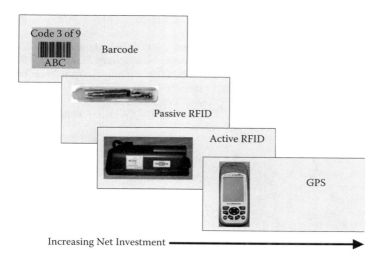

FIGURE 26.3 Nesting diagram.

faced by these passive sensor tags is the limited power supply. The sensor cannot use any energy while outside the range of the reader. Also, the amount of energy available while in read range is very small. This limits possible measurement techniques (Want 2004). With these sensor tags, perishable goods could be monitored to guard against possible safety issues. This could include salmonella outbreaks caused by frozen chicken reaching too-high temperatures for too long and medications being held at temperatures that reduce potency.

CONCLUSION

Technologies are being used to allow real-time data collection. This allows for more dynamic SCM systems that are able to adjust to varying market and environmental conditions. RFID and GPS facilitate this dynamic supply chain management. RFID allows for up-to-date inventory levels and when combined with GPS can provide a means of tracking inventory as it moves from supplier to customer through the supply chain. New technologies are being developed to further the amount of information to decision support systems for SCM.

REFERENCES

Chopra, S., and M. Peter. (2007). *Supply chain management: Strategy, planning, and operation*. N.J.: Pearson.

Dommety, G., and R. Jain. (1996). *Potential networking applications of global postitioning systems (GPS)* [Online]. Available at http://arxiv.org/abs/cs.NI/9809079 [Accessed January 2007].

Feng, S., and C. L. Law. (Sept. 2002). Assisted GPS and its impact on navigation and intelligent transportation systems. *IEEE 5th International Conference on Intelligent Transportation Systems* 926–931.

Johnson, J. C., D. F. Wood, D. L. Wardlow, and P. R. Murphy. (1999). *Contemporary logistics.*
    N.J.: Prentice Hall.
Novack, A. R., J. Langley, Jr., and L. M. Rinehart. (1995). *Creating logistics value: Themes
    for the future.* Oak Brook: Council of Logistics Management.
Reade, W., and J. D. Lindsay. (2003). *Cascading RFID tags* [Online]. Available at http://www.
    jefflindsay.com/rfid3.shtml [Accessed January 2007].
Shapiro, J. F. (2007). *Modeling the supply chain.* Belmont: Thomson.
Want, R. (2004). Enabling ubiquitous sensing with RFID. *Computer* 37:84–86.

27 Marine Terminal RFID Applications

INTRODUCTION

According to U.S. Customs and Border Protection (USCBPa), approximately 95 percent of the cargo tonnage that enters the United States comes by sea. In FY 2005, this amounted to 11 million containers (USCBPa, 2005). The Container Security Initiative (CSI) was created in 2002 to identify and examine high-risk containers prior to being loaded on vessels intended for the United States. Currently, fifty ports in foreign countries are participating in the CSI program. This covers approximately 82 percent of all cargo containers headed to the United States.

There are four foundations of the CSI program:

- Identify high-risk containers
- Prescreen and evaluate containers before they are shipped
- Use technology to prescreen containers
- Use smarter, more secure containers

TRACKING CONTAINERS

The fourth foundation is where RFID technology is being applied with respect to shipping containers. The use of RFID technology is directly covered in the Customs Trade Partnership against Terrorism program. This program is an industry-driven effort to develop a global security network from the point of origin to the point of delivery. This includes tracking across countries and different modes of transportation. Tracking and security are achieved through the mounting of RFID tags on each shipping container. The tags are monitored at each RFID-enabled facility that is linked to the global security network.

CONTAINER TAGS

The container tags used in the CSI and C-TPAT programs were developed by the Savi Corporation. The designation for these tags is ST-676. These tags are similar to the Savi ST-656 but incorporate both RFID circuitry and sensor technology. The tags include sensor technology for both security tampering and environmental monitoring. The security sensors protect the container from possible theft or terrorist-based intrusion. The security sensors monitor both light and whether or not the container doors are open or closed. The environmental sensors monitor temperature, humidity, and shock. The user can set acceptable environmental standards to the tag's memory.

These environmental sensors can help prevent spoilage or other damage to the contents of the container.

TAG OPERATION

Under normal operation, the tag sensors monitor the container. In the event that an event occurs, the type of event, time, and date is recorded in the memory. A signal is then sent to the facility RFID reader. The reader can then transmit an alert message via the Internet or telephone. The facility personnel can then investigate the cause of the alarm. In the event that the alarm was intrusion based, security personnel can be dispatched to the exact location of the container.

TAG MOUNTING

The tags are designed to be fixed to the left-hand door of ISO shipping containers without any special procedures or tools. The mounting process can be completed in seconds. It is weatherproofed to function under adverse environmental conditions. The tag itself is positioned inside the container. The antenna remains outside. The tag operates on 433 MHz. It has a range of approximately one hundred meters. The tag has a replace-

FIGURE 27.1   SAVI ST-676 container tag.

able 3.6-volt lithium battery. The battery is expected to power the tag for up to four years based on two data collection operations per day. Figure 27.1 illustrates the Savi ST-676 Container Tag.

REFERENCES

U.S. customs and border protection (2005). Maritime cargo security in the age of global terrorism [Online]. Available at http://www.customs.gov/xp/cgov/newsroom/full_text_articles/trade_prog_initiatives/cargo_security.xml [Accessed]

ADDITIONAL REFERENCES

Savi Technology. http://www.savi.com/products/SensorTag_676.pdf [Accessed].
Sullivan, L. *U.S. ports tackle security with technology* [Online]. Available at http://www.infor-mationweek.com/news/showArticle.jhtml;jsessionid=GC3RUMNDZEYDKQSNDBO CKH0CJUMEKJVN?articleID=177105452&pgno=1 [Accessed January 30, 2006].

28 RFID Uses in Warehousing

INTRODUCTION

It is important to discuss software when we describe RFID and operations such as warehousing. Since the mid-1990s warehousing and other operations have become computerized. To realize any benefit from technologies such as RFID, operations must be computerized. In this section we describe the different types of systems that allow for efficient operations. Because software and middleware are the most important pieces to an RFID solution. These packages are needed to make use of information collected by RFID technology with all the other systems operating in the warehouse: warehouse management systems (WMS), transportation management systems (TMS), event management systems (EMS), order management systems (OMS), and enterprise resource planning (ERP) systems.

The ability to capture, store, rationalize, and integrate information captured by RFID technology, including product information, location, volume, and transactional data, allows organizations to more efficiently pick/pack, ship, route, track, and distribute materials. This operational improvement can result in lower inventory levels and improved labor and equipment productivity. Integrating the information from RFID tags into an ERP system allows alerts to be sent when preset conditions have occurred such as when inventory max-min levels are realized. System standards and compatibility problems currently create an expensive software implementation process. Standards are currently being developed at EPC global.

WAREHOUSE APPLICATIONS

Manhattan Associates, the largest warehouse management system (WMS) vendor, has built their business by implementing software that allows for warehousing best practices. Bobby Collins, senior vice president of national accounts, suggests that the warehousing problems drive efficiencies and costs in most large and small companies. He explains that WMS implementations seek to drive value by solving the warehousing problems. Below are the top ten warehousing problems:

- Inventory accuracy
- Space utilization
- Picking information
- Slotting
- Order picking
- Order accuracy
- Returns

- Vendor coordination
- Performance reporting
- Strategic planning

Warehousing is a requirement of a successful business and delivers customer satisfaction. When implementing WMS systems, a standard process includes the following master planning methodology:

- Document current warehouse operations
- Determine future requirements over the planning horizon
- Identify and document deficiencies in the existing warehouse
- Identify and document alternative warehouse plans
- Qualitative and quantitative evaluation of alternatives
- Select and specify a plan
- Detail planning
- Implementation

In the following sections we provide a brief overview of relevant warehousing operations and how RFID may support improvements in these areas. Also included is an overall presentation of warehousing and warehouse management systems donated by Global Concepts on best practices for warehousing and warehouse management systems to further describe usage improving warehousing operations.

Receiving

RFID technology eliminates the need to physically check the bill of lading and/ or the packing slip during the receiving process in a warehouse. This represents a significant labor reduction and inventory accuracy improvement in most operations. RFID can alert most WMS systems to indicate whether a product requires cross-dock movement. Cross-docking is the process in which product received can be identified as immediately needed to fulfill an order and is immediate loaded into outbound trailers for fulfillment. This cross-docking process reduces the labor and time to store, replenish, pick, pack, and ship a product. The system requirement consists of a WMS interfacing with an OMS to determine whether this product is needed so that a task can be created to ship the product across the dock to the outbound dock so the order can be completed and placed on the waiting vehicle. RFID makes the identification of these types of immediate needs easily identifiable and possibly more reliable than traditional bar code scanning.

If using a conveyor receiving process or conveyor in general, RFID provides greater efficiencies by eliminating the to ensure that cases/items are placed properly on the conveyor so that the bar code can be read accurately. RFID allows accurate reads regardless of product position, resulting in fewer read errors.

Storage

RFID systems can eliminate the need to scan the bar code on the pallet and at the storage, replenishment, and picking locations for the different types of storage racks.

RFID scanners can continuously scan locations using WMS specifications and create a task from identification of inventory inaccuracies. Since the RFID tags can be read from anywhere, products and pallets do not have to be placed in specific or assigned locations. Material handling principles such as using random storage locations system, minimizing honeycombing, and replenishment to fast picking zones can be realized.

PICK/PACK

RFID readers can integrate with the WMS to validate that the correct items and amounts are picked and measure productivity in the warehouse.

SHIPPING

An RFID reader can confirm that each item is placed onto the correct outbound vehicle, which can improve the accuracy of the shipping process. This verification can be made as the product moves through the portal of the outbound dock door. RFID allows for an automatic check of the items loaded into the trailer against the bill of lading. By using RFID readers or portals at facility exits and employee areas ensures that all items leaving the building are accounted for.

RELIABILITY

The reliability of the RFID tags is a problem with many pilot implementations. Currently, RFID accuracy for Wal-Mart implementations has averaged between 70 and 75 percent. General problems with accuracy are related to multiple reads and no reads because of readers inadvertently scanning adjacent products and/or double-scanning the same product. Products containing metal or liquids will respectively reflect or absorb the signal from the RFID scanner. Metal racking systems could also pose a problem of reflected signals. Additional problems occur with data overload from the high-speed movements of products. No-reads creates a unique problem for RFID technology at the present. With bar code technology, the reader can detect that it did not read a bar code. With RFID technology, a no-read goes undetected.

IT INFRASTRUCTURE ISSUES

One of the major concerns is the potential bandwidth requirement of an RFID system capturing all the available data from every RFID tag in a given warehouse. The potential volume of information from real-time scans moving between multiple applications or every single case or pallet in a warehouse can easily overwhelm even the most robust information system. Hewlett Packard uses RFID in its facilities in Memphis, Tennessee; Chester, Virginia; and Sao Paulo, Brazil. These sites generate one to five terabytes of data a day. Therefore, organizations must analyze the potential data from an RFID tag and determine what information needs to be captured in real time and what information can wait for a batch update. The information systems also need to be robust enough to handle the speed increases associated with a successful RFID implementation. Shorter scanning intervals, faster product movements, and shorter order cycle times must be handled without sacrificing system integrity.

Other problems include the differences between storing UPC bar codes, which are 11 digits, and storing RFID serial numbers, or EPCs, which are 13 digits. The Uniform Code Council, a standards body for the retail and manufacturing industries, states that their Sunrise 2005 initiative requires all U.S and Canadian companies to be capable of scanning and processing up to fourteen-digit bar codes by January 2005.

Slap-and-ship RFID implementation is an approach in which the minimal amount of investment is made to slap tags onto a subset of outgoing shipments to comply with the current mandates. The second approach relies on larger investments to develop an internal capacity that impacts the supply chain upstream, in an effort to both comply with mandates and capture operational efficiencies from RFID.

The slap-and-ship approach is driven by the mentality that RFID is a cost of doing business due to the mandates set forth by both Wal-Mart and the DOD. Organizations employing this strategy are not looking for a short- or long-term Return on Investment (ROI) on their investment; they are only concerned with being compliant with their customers so that they are able to continue doing business. This approach oftentimes is just as costly as a well-thought-out long-term strategy to use the technology. Most pundits suggest that the second approach should be utilized in order to increase business efficiency. The next section provides some implementation examples in which the companies sought to integrate RFID into operations.

RFID WAREHOUSE IMPLEMENTATION EXAMPLES

The following are examples of RFID system implementations in various companies in different business sectors.

GILLETTE

In January 2003, Gillette bought over 500 million Class I EPC tags from Alien Technology. Gillette has been using the order to tag all pallets and cases of women's razors. Gillette worked with its WMS and TMS provider, Provia, to ensure that the RFID information can be integrated into the appropriate systems. Below is an explanation of how some companies incorporated the tags into their processes.

INTERNATIONAL PAPER

International Paper, the world's largest paper and forest products company, went live with their first fully automated RFID warehouse tracking system in August 2003. The use of clamp-truck-mounted RFID readers and proprietary tracking technology provide forklift operators information and execution tasks. The replacement of RFID portals with the use of mobile forklifts provided a better fit for RFID in operations and improved productivity.

PROCTOR & GAMBLE

Proctor & Gamble performed a project in which they used RFID at manufacturing plant in Spain to send pallets to domestic operations. Results indicated this was a cost-effective way to implement RFID tagging.

Part 5

RFID Case Studies and Research

INTRODUCTION

This section includes additional material that focuses on specific RFID case studies and research subjects. The chapters that are included are more focused on specific areas of RFID technology rather than the application overviews presented in part 4.

SECTION CONTENTS

29 RFID Research Activities in Academia

INTRODUCTION

RFID is a technology many organizations feel will change the way companies approach logistics, engineering, and manufacturing. Corporations have embraced the opportunity to use this technology and have developed and manufactured cost-effective tags over the last decade. With the development of a passive tag standard created by EPC Global, the reality of the RFID tags reaching a price that is cost-effective may be realized. In order to support the industry's need for developing the manpower and future workforce in this technology, universities such as the University of Nebraska and Oklahoma State University have added RFID to their curriculum. These universities are a part of the Center for Engineering Logistics and Distribution (CELDi), which is supported by the National Science Foundation for industry and university integrated research.

Radio frequency identification was developed in the latter part of WWII when Allied airplanes used the underlying technology to identify friend or foe aircraft. RFID technologies have been interwoven into our lives over the last thirty years with such technologies as toll tags, security chips at retailers, and animal eartags. The development of an inexpensive passive tag that utilizes a unique license plate on standards governed by EPC Global has companies excited about driving down costs in the supply chain. Wal-Mart and the Department of Defense initiated mandates for their top suppliers to use this passive technology initially by first quarter 2005 and has since extended the deadline. Because of the support of these organizations along with other top retailers, many suppliers seek to integrate this technology into their operations in a cost-efficient manner.

Academia has been criticized as slow in keeping up with relevant technologies. Some universities are seeking to change that image and prepare students, as well as develop working methods, prototypes, and discoveries that can support this emerging technology. The University of Nebraska — Lincoln is offering an RFID course in spring 2006 that offers a certified RFID supply chain manager designation, along with opportunities to work in the RFID Supply Chain Logistics Lab (RfSCL) where integrated industry research projects are implemented with such organizations as NASA and Centurian. Oklahoma State University offered an RFID course in spring 2005 and spring 2006 along with RFID research with companies such as Haliburton and the Federal Aviation Administration. These universities are part of CELDi, which includes the University of Arkansas, University of Oklahoma, University of Louisville, University of Florida — Gainsville, Texas Tech University, and LeHigh Unvirsity. These universities are working with companies on integrated

RFID research; for example, the University of Arkansas is working extensively with Wal-Mart on development of RFID technologies at their corporate headquarters in Arkansas. A more extensive look at the RFID research is given below.

CENTER FOR ENGINEERING LOGISTICS AND DISTRIBUTION

The Center for Engineering Logistics and Distribution is a multi-university, multidisciplinary National Science Foundation (NSF)-sponsored Industry/University Cooperative Research Center (I/UCRC). CELDi provides integrated solutions to logistics problems through research related to modeling, analysis, and intelligent systems technologies. Eight academic partners have joined together to merge unique research strengths that allow CELDi to surpass traditional research institutions that offer a compartmentalized approach to logistics research.

- University of Nebraska
- University of Arkansas
- Oklahoma State University
- University of Florida
- University of Louisville
- Lehigh University
- Texas Tech University
- University of Oklahoma

Radio frequency identification (RFID) is a focus area among CELDi academic partners. Each institution brings complementary expertise to the organization.

UNIVERSITY OF NEBRASKA

The University of Nebraska — Lincoln (UNL) utilizes RFID technologies for classroom projects in both undergraduate- and graduate-level curriculum. The commitment of UNL to RFID research and education is demonstrated in the existing research activities and scheduled educational activities. Existing research projects include the following:

- Evaluation and recommendation of RFID for NASA ISS consumable inventory
- Use of Design for Six Sigma to optimize RFID experiments
- Cost justification of RFID at a Department of Defense manufacturing contractor
- An integrated RFID supply chain model
- Use of RFID to monitor marathon runners
- Use of RFID to locate steel structures during construction
- Use of technologies to monitor live cattle from birth to slaughter
- Development of parent/child RFID tag
- Integration of RFID bar codes into warehouse management systems; system architecture

FIGURE 29.1 UNL NSF CELDi RFID lab conveyor system.

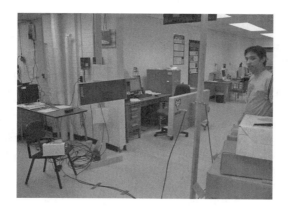

FIGURE 29.2 UNL NSF CELDi RFID lab portal system.

Figure 29.1, Figure 29.2, and Figure 29.3 illustrate a few of the UNL NSF CELDi RFID lab capabilities.

UNL is scheduled to sponsor the RFID in Logistics Engineering Course (IMSE 996) in spring 2006 and the RFID 2nd Annual Academic Symposium. Dr. Erick Jones is the site director for CELDi at UNL.

UNIVERSITY OF ARKANSAS

The University of Arkansas — Fayetteville serves as the lead institution in the CELDi consortium. The University of Arkansas is currently conducting research projects with companies and agencies that investigate the state of RFID technology and its potential for cost savings through implementation. In particular, there are projects underway to create solutions for difficult RFID applications (e.g., metal containers and liquid products).

FIGURE 29.3   UNL NSF CELDi RFID lab hardware lab.

- The Department of Industrial Engineering has adopted a departmental RFID tracking system for asset/inventory management.
- A proposal is pending to implement an RFID tracking system to perform asset/inventory management for the entire University of Arkansas — Fayetteville campus.
- The department houses a laboratory that implements RFID tracking systems and works in collaboration with the Walton College of Business's RFID Research Center.
- The RFID Research Center uses as its base of operations a lab that models a production warehouse environment in seven thousand square feet of space donated to the center by Hanna's Candles and located within Hanna's manufacturing and warehouse facility.
- The RFID Research Center is accredited by EPC Global, one of the first such facilities to be accredited worldwide, and serves as a compliance testing facility for Wal-Mart suppliers and many other companies with RFID testing needs.

OKLAHOMA STATE UNIVERSITY

Oklahoma State University is home to the COMMSEN: Sensor Networks (RFID) and Complex Manufacturing Systems Monitoring Research Lab. Dr. Satish Bukkapatnam serves as the director for this lab, which was established in 2004 at the Advanced Technology Research Center (ATRC) of Oklahoma State University in Stillwater, Oklahoma. The facility is comprised of more than one thousand square feet of space at ATRC with two Alien antennae and reader, an AWID reader with antenna, and two hundred passive tags of various form factors and other specifications. Information from an RFID reader is processed on Linux servers that house the SUN JAVA RFID Application Suite. Oracle 10i is being used as the database to store information collected from our experiments. New experimental test bays with the latest Gen 2–specific hardware and software are being set up for future applications. The current research focus is monitoring real-world complex systems by harnessing information from a network of wired and wireless sensors.

University of Florida

At the University of Florida (UF), the primary focus in RFID is rapid application prototyping. Auto-ID technologies such as RFID, machine vision, and bar code are changing at a rapid pace. UF-CELDi recognizes two opportunities to assist industry to assimilate auto-ID technologies including (1) rapid application prototyping and (2) student/employee training. Rapid application prototyping allows companies to experiment with new technologies in order to efficiently develop functional specifications for new systems. Additionally, such opportunities allow graduate students and corporate employees to gain valuable training in cutting-edge areas. A primary goal of UF-CELDi is to develop a critical mass of software/hardware talent in order to be able to serve immediate technical needs of industrial stakeholders while providing a reliable source for well trained future employees. Specific projects underway at UF include:

- Supply chain safety and security
- Computer modeling
- Manual labor productivity monitoring system (GatorPacker™)
- RFID-enabled, digital, dual time-temperature integrator development
- Package aggregation and tracking using radio frequency identification technology (RFID)

University of Louisville

The University of Louisville has proposed a consortium on identification technologies (IDTECH) to make chip-based and chipless identification technologies as pervasive as bar coding technology. The consortium will test and assess various available chip-based and chipless identification technologies and conduct benchmarking studies. It will also serve as a laboratory for demonstration of the available technologies. The consortium's goal will be to focus on numerous applications, including those pertaining to item tracking in a supply chain using RFID-tagged labels pasted on individual items or placed inside cartons and security and control of classified documents, passports, event tickets, and checks. The consortium's goal is also to test, evaluate, and benchmark various available identification technologies including, but not limited to, radio frequency, magnetic, optical, and chemical. It will help conduct feasibility studies and identify the advantages and shortcomings of the technologies in multiple applications.

In conclusion, CELDi has chosen to destroy the myth that universities are one to two years behind the industry in the training of students and research in emerging technologies. These partner universities not only are up to date on RFID technology but may be leading the charge of this emerging technology in the future. CELDi not only provides thought leadership in RFID but also in supply chain logistics, transportation, and facility location modeling. The integration of industry and academia is what is needed to keep our country as a thought leader in emerging technologies and in academics.

For more information contact the authors.

30 Optimizing RFID Portal Locations in Distribution Using Systematic Layout Planning (SLP)

Jane Silveray, Gao Fei, and Erick C. Jones

INTRODUCTION

The manufacturing facility layout design (FLD) has been discussed by a number of researchers. Continuous improvement has been achieved through the use of simulation and computer-aided programs for designing facilities in actual manufacturing and warehouse environments. However, FLD still is a complex and broad area that cuts across several specialized disciplines. Basically, the facility layout problem is to determine the most efficient arrangement of cells or functional departments subject to flow and capital constraints imposed by the original layout, management, and site requirements.

The optimum solution for these facility layout problems is not only controlled by numerical function, but more depends on the accepted baseline of the application of site and relevant requirements. Therefore, the solution for each single layout problem should not be a single solution with the optimum result based on the ratio of each function department and its weight value. Most of the research on facility layout utilizes the classical concept by either the Quadratic Assignment Problem (QAP) or a large-scale mixed-integer programming (MLP) problem (Montreuil 1990). Whereas nonlinear programming (NLP) formulations have been solved by numerical methods (Tam and Li 1991; van Camp et al. 1992), by simulated annealing (Tam 1992) or by genetic algorithm approaches (Tate and Smith 1995), mixed-integer programming (MIP) formulations have been solved by ad hoc interactive designer reasoning (Montreuil and Ratliff 1989) or by reducing the MIP to a linear programming optimization problem either by qualitative reasoning (Banerjee et al. 1992) or, once again, by ad hoc interactive designer reasoning (Montreuil et al. 1993) and by a genetic approach (Banerjee and Zhou 1995). Although integer and noninteger problems have solved complicated layout problems that are two-dimensional with flow and capital consideration, particular situations and single case problems may have to be evaluated in other ways.

RFID facility layouts with warehouse applications introduce a new type of parameter to the traditional FLD problem. The following sections illustrate the differences.

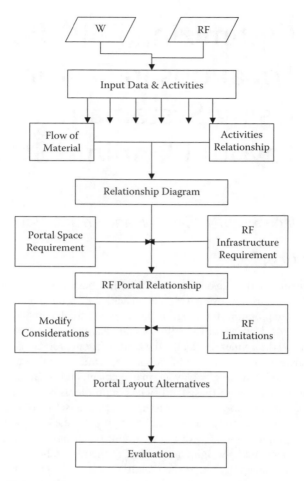

FIGURE 30.1   SLP procedure.

Muther (1979) developed a layout procedure known as *systematic layout planning* (SLP). It uses as its foundation the activity relationship chart described in the facility layout process. SLP is based on input data and an understanding of the roles and relationships between activities, a material flow analysis (from-to-chart), and an activity relationship analysis (activity relationship chart). This analysis results in a relationship diagram. The next two steps involve the determination of the amount of space to be assigned to each activity. Based on modifying considerations and practical limitations, a number of layout alternatives are developed and evaluated. The SLP procedure can be used sequentially to develop first a block layout and then a detailed layout for each planning department. The following example discusses the application of SLP with an RFID warehouse design procedure.

MODELING PROCEDURE

PHASE 1: MULTI-OBJECTIVE RF WAREHOUSE ARCHITECTURE

The overall RFID warehouse implementing system includes three main parts: RFID edge layer, RFID physical layer and enterprise integration network. The RFID physical layer is the connection of the other two layers. The RFID system is designed to process streams of tags or sensor data coming from one or more readers. The edge layer has the ability to filter and aggregate data prior to sending it to a requesting application. For example, an action (tag read) is triggered when the object moves or a new object comes into the reader's view. The RFID edge servers to filter and collect the tag data at each individual site and send it over the Internet to the third layer, the enterprise integration layer. The localized data is identified by moving actions and stationary actions separately. The moving and stationary actions divide the RFID reading type to portal door distribution process within limited range and mobile reader inventory checking. The fundamental tenet of warehouse portal distribution systems is that they must be able to accommodate changes that may occur in a network. The portal devices provide real-time positioning access capabilities to user communities, delivering and searching personal data. It allows external customer and partner accessing with data protecting and securely access.

We can now divide the RFID warehouse system into three parts as discussed before, the physical layer, the logic layer, and the system integration layer. Each layer has different components depending on what functions the RFID system needs. By understanding the flow in the warehouse we can determine the types of tag and antennas needed in the warehouse.

Basically, the RFID implementation in any process has two to three layers. The physical layer produces log events for RF sensors during process executions. The

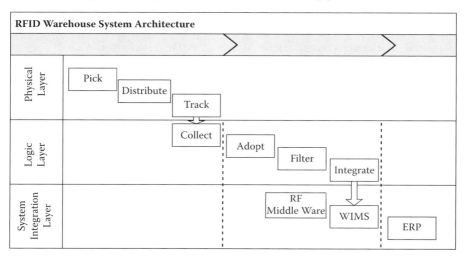

FIGURE 30.2   RFID operation in distribution process.

logic layer records the log events including filter and integrate functions. The analysis of the physical layer activity has been discussed in facility layout research. The difference between previous research on RFID facility layout and this is that the data flow should be added as a factor that influences the RFID warehouse efficiency and performance.

First, the production process has its own upstream and downstream flow. Each department and activity function has multiple interactions with the others where the layout is defined by the traditional facility layout algorithm. For any given department, the overall workflow for sites is how and where the functional part fits into it. But for RFID warehousing, the labeling function part is substituted by a two-dimensional portal door with installed antenna.

PHASE 2: DATA ENVIRONMENT ANALYSIS

The data flow through the distribution process in a warehouse is one of the design components of RFID warehouse layout. The goal of such an activity is to define the input and output data in order to confirm the efficiency of data flow and its physical flow. Data standards standardize data formats and data organization to ensure that the required data can be smoothly exchanged within the supply chain. The workflow and data flow are both generated by production flow from physical layer to logical layer. All the data, through picking to the distributing process, are generated by RFID equipment including the tags on each pallet or antenna on the portal. Therefore, the location of RFID equipment influences the accuracy of the distribution process that will form the individual data flow according to the workflow. The location of RFID antenna, or sensor, will be discussed in this chapter. First, the sensor is used to refer to a device that is connected, via network or RF communication medium, to other sensor devices in the network. The location of sensors in the warehouse relates to either its environment or data traffic flow itself, which is detected by fixed antenna on portal door. Similarly, the data flow will be employed by sensors specifically in the picking entrance portal and distributing portal. Therefore, the data traffic through two portal doors and its layout will be our considered in this chapter. We will discuss the other communication between the nodes in warehouse in future work. In order to measure the accuracy and efficiency of RFID performance in warehouse, we use a ratio to evaluate the relationship of performance and efficiency of RFID readability that is equal to the simple relationship between input and output data and will be related to regression analysis to show fair performance.

$$\sigma_r = \alpha_I/\beta_o \tag{1}$$

Where:
   σ_r = ratio
   α_I = input
   β_o = output

However, this ratio only gives an average performance for RFID readability. The components of input require the precise data to evaluate the environment and performance. But we measure the benchmark of the performance used to compare the different input data and data flow. For example, the different amounts of workflow reflect the different data flows in a warehouse, but the benchmark gives us reliable data to measure different warehouse environments and workflows.

The statistical power analysis estimates the power of the workflow to detect a meaningful effect, given product flow size, significance level, and standardized effect size. Product flow size analysis determines the product flow size required to get a significant result, given statistical power, test size, and standardized effect size. These analyses examine the sensitivity of statistical power and product flow size to other components, enabling researchers to efficiently use the research resources. According to the power of the data analysis, we know the workflow during the distribution process can be too low or too high, which will influence the capital loss for a warehouse. If sample size is too large, time and resources will be wasted, often for minimal gain. For the benchmark, we used GPOWER, high-precision power analysis software, to determine the product flow size. The inputs of GPOWER for determining the flow size in linear multiple regression model are effect size, the alpha level, power value, and the number of predictors. GPOWER uses f as a measure of effect size, which has a relationship with R (coefficient of determination; the total proportion of the dependent variable variability that is explained by predicted variables), as the following equation describes:

$$f^2 = \frac{R^2}{1 - R^2} \tag{2}$$

In this experiment, we used $f = 1.5$ ($R = 0.6$). We used alpha value (0.05), power value (0.90), and the number of predictors (4) as other three inputs. Special considerations should be addressed when setting up an RFID system with multiple interrogators that have overlapping interrogation zones. For instance, a pair of readers in a portal door interrogation zone may interrogate multiple tags in a dynamic environment.

The concept of interrogation will be abstracted as "read zone" as for the practical and real environment reason in the following content. By considering the warehouse environment requirement for RFID application in a distribution process, the portal door RF read zone will be limited in some ranges between dock equipment and RF interrogation range. The ranges of RF antenna (portal) and physical range of dock

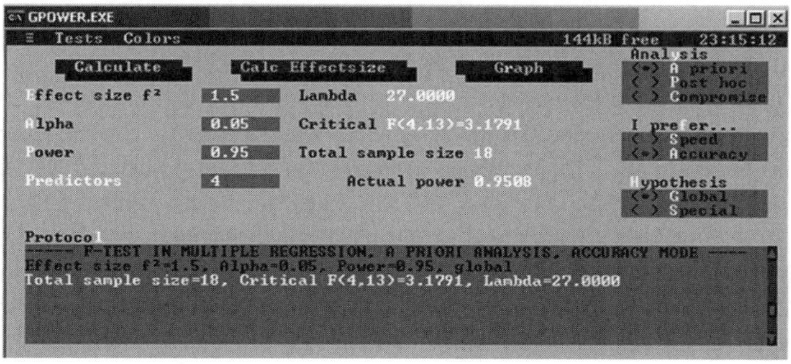

FIGURE 30.3 Results screen from GPOWER program.

door layout can be described as n – vertex graph which $G [V = (1, ..., n), E]$, and for each edge $(i,j) \in E$ its Euclidean length. Denote a 2D layout of the graph byxyer, where the coordinates of vertex i are $p_i = (x_i, y_i)$. Denote

$$dij = \|p_i - p_j\| = \sqrt{(x_i - x_j)^2 + (y_i - y_j)^2}.$$

In the non-noisy version of the problem, we know that there exists a layout of the antennas that realizes the given edge lengths (i.e., dij = lij). Our goal is then to reproduce this layout. Fortunately, there is additional information that we may exploit to eliminate spurious solutions to the layout problem — we know that the graph is a complete description of the close antennas. Consequently, the distance between each two nonadjacent antennas should be greater than some constant r, which is larger than the longest edge. This can further constrain the search space and eliminate most undesired solutions. Formally, we may pose our problem as follows:

Layout problem given a graph $G [V = (1, ..., n), E]$, and for each edge — its Euclidean length, find an optimal layout ( ) (is the location of the antenna i), which satisfies for all: $i \neq j$:

$$\|p_i - p_j\| = l_{ij} \text{ if } \langle i,j \rangle \in E \tag{3}$$

$$\|p_i - p_j\| = R \text{ if } \langle i,j \rangle \notin E \tag{4}$$

Where:

$$R = \max_{\langle i,j \rangle \in E} l_{ij}$$

An optimal layout is similar to that generated by common force-directed graph drawing algorithms that place adjacent nodes close while separating nonadjacent nodes. Therefore, we may estimate the distances between nonadjacent antennas and then give constructive suggestions to minimize the blind spot within the reachable zone.

From the graphs in Figure 30.4 and Figure 30.5, the interrogation zone from a pair of antenna gives us a visual description for the range we calculated in formulas (3) and (4). The center red zone means the high readability zone for two inches on each side of the portal door. The accuracy reduced with the increasing of the distance from tag to each side of the portal, estimating an antenna's physical coordinates according to the feature and requirement of RFID and warehouse system. The data that the antenna is reporting should be accompanied with an indication of where in space that data was reported. The bandwidth and limitations of the antenna network made it necessary for the data location coordinates of the physical location of portal door in the warehouse. In many cases, location itself gives the range of data that should be scanned. The localized area drives the location of an RFID antenna network in the warehouse. This is used to locate the items and tagged parts. The accuracy of geographic routing and graphing algorithms facilitates the next step of validating the portal in warehouse.

The design of the portal door and the layout of RFID antennas combine both frequency interrogation and physical portal length so that the tagged pallets will be tracked and the employed frequency from the antenna can record the data with moving tags.

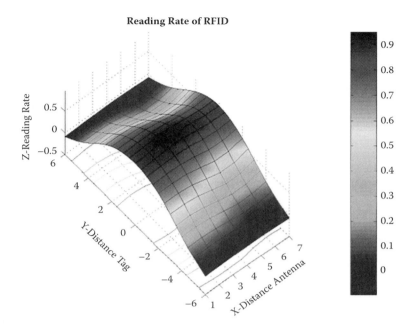

FIGURE 30.4 Dimension RF interrogation zone (effective range).

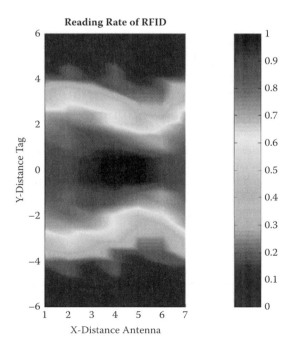

FIGURE 30.5 Dimension RF interrogation zone (effective range).

TABLE 30.1

Minimum Maneuvering Distance Between the Back of the Dock Leveler and the Beginning of the Staging Area and Recommended Dock Staging Dimensions

Equipment Used	Distance (feet)	Item	Dimensions (fddt)
None (manual)	5	Served road width	
Hand truck		One-way traffic	12
Two wheel	6	Two-way	24
Four wheel	8	Gate openings, vehicles only	
Hand lift (jack)	8	One-way traffic	16
Narrow aisle truck	10	Two-way	28
Lift truck	12	Gate openings, vehicles + pedestrians	
Tow tractor	14	One-way	22
		Two-way	34

Source: Data from Thompkins (1982).

LAYOUT IMPROVEMENT ALTERNATIVES AND NUMERICAL RESULTS

Given the aforementioned RFID constraints, the facility layout algorithm will follow the baseline model we discussed above. A qualitative algorithm is deployed to analyze the overall operational functions. The layout algorithm then develops the relationship between each operation to optimize a warehouse layout using RFID. Because of the limitation of the RFID interrogation zone, we consider this to be correlated to the RF facility layout.

COMPUTER-AIDED PROGRAM ALGORITHM APPROACH (BLOCPLAN)

The program generates and evaluates block-type layouts in response to user-supplied data. It is used for single story layouts. BLOCPLAN uses a banding procedure to develop layouts. This permits a large range of possible layouts for a problem. For a nine-department problem, the number of possible layouts is close to 20 million, and for a fifteen-department layout there are more than 2.6×10^{13} possibilities. Each department will also be rectangular in shape. The structure that holds the departments will also be rectangular in shape, and the user may select the length/width ratio of the structure.

RELATIONSHIP DATA

BLOCPLAN uses the relationship codes described by Muther (1973) in "Systematic Layout Planning." Each subprocedure we discussed in the SLP flowchart shows that the functional departments are defined by the material flow. We take one of the typical warehouses as an example. For BLOCPLAN, they use adjacencies for one type of layout analysis. We define the departments as picking/receiving, storing, inspecting, forward-picking, sorting, shipping, and dock-to-dock. The differences

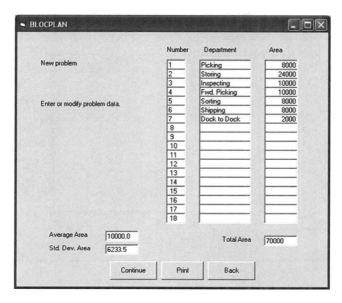

FIGURE 30.6   Layout data.

between classic warehouse layout algorithm using BLOCPLAN and RFID applied warehouse is the consideration of adjacent function zone are separated for the reason of interfaces between sensors. For instance, the picking, forward picking, shipping, and dock-to-dock zone are considerably separated according to the amount of product flow.

For this example, Figure 30.6 illustrates the departments and the square footage required for the each department. Figure 30.7 illustrates one possible solution to the given problem. This solution has a layout score of 0.87. Layout scores may

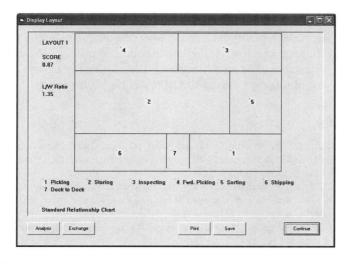

FIGURE 30.7   Layout.

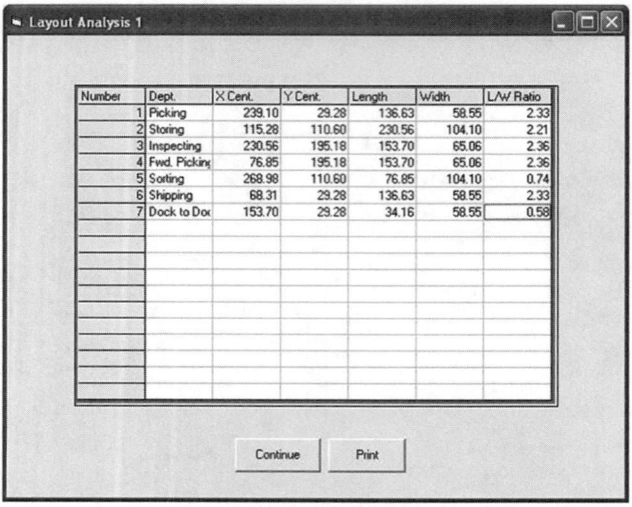

Number	Dept.	X Cent.	Y Cent.	Length	Width	L/W Ratio
1	Picking	239.10	29.28	136.63	58.55	2.33
2	Storing	115.28	110.60	230.56	104.10	2.21
3	Inspecting	230.56	195.18	153.70	65.06	2.36
4	Fwd. Pickin	76.85	195.18	153.70	65.06	2.36
5	Sorting	268.98	110.60	76.85	104.10	0.74
6	Shipping	68.31	29.28	136.63	58.55	2.33
7	Dock to Do	153.70	29.28	34.16	58.55	0.58

FIGURE 30.8 Layout analysis.

range from 0 to 1.00. Higher scores indicate greater satisfaction of the adjacency relationships specified in the problem parameters. Figure 30.8 provides additional analysis results for the solution provided in Figure 30.7. This figure provides the x and y centroids of each department along with the department's length, width, and its length/width ratio.

DISCUSSION AND CONCLUSION

The use of RFID systems in both existing and new facilities requires rethinking traditional layout approaches due to the need to take into consideration the department relationship requirements added by RFID system components. What may have previously been an optimal facility layout may no longer be optimal.

This chapter describes a layout methodology that takes an integrating multi-objective architectural approach involving data environment analysis and RFID interrogation zone optimization. The effectiveness of the resulting layouts can be evaluated using facility layout software such as BLOCPLAN for Windows.

REFERENCES

Banerjee, P., Montreuil, B., Moodie, C. L., and Kashyap, R. L. (1992). A modeling of interactive facilities layout designer reasoning using qualitative patterns. *International Journal of Production Research*, 30(3), 433–453.

Banerjee, P. and Zhou, Y. (1995). Facilities layout design optimization with single loop material flow path configuration. *International Journal of Producton Research*, 33(1),183–204.

Montreuil, B. (1990). A modeling framework for integrating layout design and flow network design, in Proceedings of the Material Handling Research Colloquium, June 19–21, Hebron, Kentucky, pp. 43–58.

Montreuil, B. and Ratliff, H. D. (1989). Utilizing cut trees as design skeletons for facility layout. *IIE Transactions*, 21(2), 136–143.

Montreuil, B., Venkatadri, U. and Ratliff, H. D. (1993). Generating a layout from a design skeleton. *IIE Transactions*, 25(1), 3–15.

Muther, R. (1973). *Systematic Layout Planning*, Von Nostrand Reinhold, New York.

Tam, K. Y. (1992). A simulated annealing algorithm for allocating space to manufacturing cells. *International Journal of Production Research*, 30(1), 63–87.

Tam, K. Y. and Li, S. G. (1991). A hierarchical approach to the facility layout problem. *International Journal of Production Research*, 29(1), 165–184.

Tate, D. M. and Smith, a. E. (1995). Unequal area facility layout using genetic search. *IIE Transactions*, 27(4), 465–472.

van Camp, D. J., Carter, M. W. and Vannelli, A. (1992). A nonlinear optimization approach for solving facility layout problems. *European Journal of Operations Research*, 57(2), 174–189.

ADDITIONAL REFERENCES

Banerjee, P., Y. Zhou, and B. Montreuel. (1997). Genetically assisted optimization of cell layout and material flow path skeleton. *IIE Transactions* 29(4):277–291.

Carbon, T. A. (2000). Measuring efficiency of semiconductor manufacturing operations using data envelopment analysis (DEA). Paper read at the IEEE SEMI Advanced Semiconductor Manufacturing Conference.

Gaukler, G. M., Ö. Özer, and W. H. Hausman. (July 10, 2006). Working Paper: Order Progress Information: Improved Dynamic Emergency Ordering Policies, Stanford University.

Gotsman, C., and Y. Koren. (2005). Distributed graph layout for sensor networks. *Lecture Notes in Computer Science* 3383.

Tompkins, J. A., J. A. White, Y. A. Bozer, E. H. Frazelle, J. M. A. Tanchoco, and J. Trevino. (1996). *Facility planning*. 2d ed. New York: John Wiley & Sons.

Wehking, K.-H., F. Seeger, and S. Kummer. (2006). RFID Transponders: Link between information and material flows. How reliable are identification procedures? *Logistics Journal*. April 2006.

Zhang, Y., J. Liu, and F. Zhao. (2006). Information-Directed Routing in Sensor Networks Using Real-Time Reinforcement Learning. *Combinatorial Optimization in Communication Networks*, 2006 Springer Science & Business Media, pp. 259–288.

31 Obsolete Inventory Reduction with Modified Carrying Cost Ratio

INTRODUCTION

This chapter considers a medical supplies and pharmaceutical inventory management problem faced by a city health and human services department and shows how inefficient warehousing can become if inventory is not periodically checked for obsolescence. The department purchases and distributes medical supplies used by service centers spread throughout the city. To support the service process, the department operates several warehouses in the city. Furthermore, the warehouses order large quantities of goods at a negotiated price and store the items until a service center places an order for a relatively smaller quantity. Then the warehouse fills the orders. If the order quantity is on hand, the items are picked by warehouse employees and delivered to the offices. If the warehouses do not have an item in stock, the item is placed on back order and is delivered when it becomes available. The department estimates that the out-of-stock inventory is very costly.

This chapter is organized in the following manner: The next section will discuss the carrying costs associated with a two-echelon supply chain inventory model. Then a one-echelon supply chain inventory model that utilizes a just-in-time (JIT) procurement will be discussed. Next we will introduce the modified carrying cost ratio model as a decision tool to evaluate which system to use in practice, followed by a case study that demonstrates the practical use of this ratio in making a decision in the aforementioned governmental operation.

THE TWO-ECHELON MODEL

In 2003, Caglar, Li, and Simchi-Levi presented a two-echelon supply chain model that we consider very useful in making cost-effective decisions about warehouse inventory levels. We utilize this model to demonstrate the current two-echelon supply chain in practice by the city department. First, we will consider a two-echelon multiconsumable goods inventory system consisting of a central distribution center and multiple customers that require service as illustrated in Figure 31.1.

Each service center office acts as a smaller warehouse. This is because they each supply many customers and maintain a stock level SCM for each item. Therefore, each office consists of a set I of n items that are used at a mean rate. When an item is used by a customer, the customer replenishes itself by taking item i from office M's

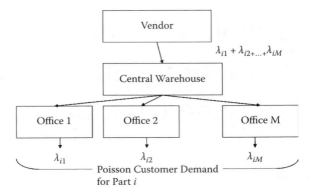

FIGURE 31.1 Two-echelon inventory chain.

supply stock if the item is in stock. If the item is not in stock, the item is back ordered and the customer has to wait for the item to become available at the office.

The goal of this chapter is to make a decision of supply chain type based on basic purchasing and holding cost information, while maintaining an average response time that will not negatively affect the customers. This may include the elimination of the central warehouse.

Using the notation in Table 31.1, a model of the cost of operating a warehouse and implementing a JIT system was derived. This information can then be used to determine if the organization benefits from operating the warehouse.

There are many operating costs associated with warehouse management. These operating costs include fixed costs such as racking, utilities, labor, vehicle fleet maintenance, property maintenance, property depreciation, and a lease or any other tied up capital. Let A_w be all periodic fixed costs that the savings of purchasing in large quantities have to justify in order to minimize the total cost of the operation. For this model, we will use annual costs.

$$A_w = \sum_{j \in J} C_{Wj} + C_{Uj} + C_{Lj} + C_{Vj} + C_{Mj} + \theta_c * V_{Wj}$$

These fixed costs in addition to item-associated costs make up the total cost of having a warehouse in operation. Many of these costs are hidden and are frequently overlooked when procurement managers decide the level of quantities to purchase. Shrinkage in the form of lost items, stolen items, or damaged items, obsolescence, and the cost of capitol on the inventory is typically among these hidden costs. These costs can be modeled as a percentage of the total inventory on hand.

THE ONE-ECHELON MODEL

The second model used for reference is the common one-echelon JIT system. JIT requires better planning of demand from customers and can sometimes make management feel uneasy about the extra procurement cost of items on a per unit basis.

TABLE 31.1
Notation for Models

Notation	Meaning
A_w	Annual fixed cost of warehouse operation
C_I	Total cost of holding inventory
C_{Lj}	Labor cost of warehouse j
C_{Uj}	Cost of utilities at office j
C_W	Lease price or depreciation and cost of capitol of warehouse
C_{Mj}	Annual property maintenance for warehouse j
$J = \{1, 2, \ldots, M\}$	Set of offices
K_j	Customer at office j
l_i	Demand rate of item i
L_{JITij}	JIT lead time for an expedited order of item i at office j
$_{ij} = K_j l_i$	Demand rate for item i at office j
$_c$	Organizationscost of capitol
$_{Oij}$	Obsolescence rate for item i at office j
$_s$	Shrinkage rate based on total inventory in system
P_{Wi}	Purchase price using warehouse system of item i
P_{JITi}	Negotiated JIT purchase price for item i
S_{ij}	Base stock level for item i at office j
SS_{ij}	Safety stock of item i at office j
SS_{ij}	Safety stock of item i at office j
VW_j	Value of warehouse j
W_{ij}	Waiting time for a customer ordering item i from office j
W_j	Waiting time for a customer ordering from office j

But there are many cases where the elimination or significant downsizing of a warehouse operation can save money without sacrificing service to the customer.

In the JIT system depicted in this model, ordered items go directly from the vendor to the office, where a smaller stock level is used versus the warehouse. One-echelon systems will differ in that there is no intermediary between the vendors and the offices (Cagler et al. 2003; Lee 2003; Wang, Cohen, and Zheng 2000). This system is shown based on a simplification of Cagler et al.'s model in Figure 31.2.

The JIT contracts that will need to be made with the vendors is established based upon demand rate λ_{ij}. We determine the expected time of backorders of item i in office j by the following:

$$W_{ij} = E\left[L\left(S_{ij}\right)\right] = \sum_{j\in J}\sum_{i\in I}\left(L_{JITij} * \left(1 - \sum_{i=0}^{SS_{ij}}\left(\frac{\lambda_{ij}L_{JITij}}{n!}\right)^n \exp\left(\lambda_{ij}L_{JITij}\right)\right)\right),$$

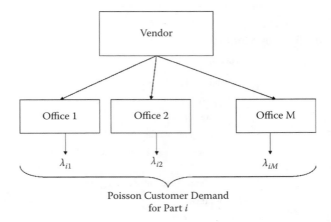

FIGURE 31.2   One-echelon inventory chain.

In this case, items are delivered to the offices at the same rate the items are being used. The symbol t_{ij} represents time between deliveries for item i at office j. Therefore, by substitution, $\lambda_{ij}t_{ij}$ is also the order quantity.

$$S_{ij} = \lambda_{ij}t_{ij} + SS_{ij}$$

Keeping the expected wait time for the customer for each system the same will allow for a comparison of costs without changing the response time to the customer.

Costs associated with the JIT system will contain all of the fixed costs of the system as well as any additional costs of requiring more service from vendors. In some instances, the unit price can remain constant by ordering a couple of large quantity orders or several small quantity orders. However, shipping rates for the smaller orders may increase. Due to this, it may be important to select vendors that are close to the offices.

After factoring in a possible increase in purchase and shipping prices, we suggest that the total cost for the JIT system will be as follows:

$$C_{JIT} = \sum_{i \in I} \sum_{j \in J} P_{JIT_i} \lambda_{ij} + C_I$$

When

$$C_I = \sum_{i \in I} \sum_{j \in J} \left(I_{ij} * \left(\theta_C + \theta_S + \theta_{Oij} \right) \right)$$

Once again, in many situations the data needed to use this optimization may not be available in the time allotted to the project. This is where our simplified carrying cost ratio model simplifies the decision to move to a two-echelon system.

THE MODIFIED CARRYING COST RATIO MODEL

The model focuses on comparing the two systems and selecting the best choice of operational model. As long as the total cost for purchasing, storing, and delivering items to the customer can be derived, we can determine which system is a better economic choice with our decision model.

The ratio simply compares the total cost of the purchased inventory to the amount of money spent holding and delivering it to the offices. This cost ratio has been developed to evaluate and analyze supply chain costs for operations relying on inventory delivery from a supplier. The purpose is to provide a methodology for determining cost incurred over the supply chain process from the time an inventory item is loaded on a truck from the original vendor to the time an operation buys or requisitions the item for use in their business. The merits of understanding these incurred costs include: (1) an understanding of the cost of each item, (2) knowledge of the cost the operation would be required to overcome, and (3) guidelines for which actions an operation can take to decrease the cost/dollar spent ratio.

We hypothesize that the cost of inventory plus the fixed costs comprises the total cost of the warehouse operation, given by the equation below.

$$\text{Total Warehouse Cost} = A_w - C_I$$

We suggest that after identifying the stock levels using the aforementioned formulas or current accounting information, the next step would be to use our ratio to determine which system is better for the operation. We present the ratio as a calculation that can be used in operations. Put simply, it is the ratio of the total cost of maintaining the inventory and the total inventory purchase price.

$$\mu_W = \frac{A_W + C_I}{\sum_{i \in I} C_{Wi}}$$

when all costs are annual.

$$\sum_{i \in I} C_{Wi} = \text{total dollars purchased}$$

The above relationship defines the total cost determined over the course of the supply chain. It combines the cost of delivering an item with the cost incurred during the process of holding that item in inventory. This equation is the ratio of warehouse cost per item to purchase price per item. This effectively demonstrates the ratio of money a supplier spends storing and shipping an item to the actual monetary investment put into each inventory item, represented by the ratio (CSystem)/CP. This ratio, when combined with holding cost, can be extremely effective in determining the efficiency of a supply chain as well as providing an indicator of the inventory turn rate for the entire system. We will later show the results of our case study using data to perform the calculation of this ratio.

TABLE 31.2
General Handling Cost

Cost Source	% of Purcchase Price
Insurance	0.25%
Storage facilities	0.25%
Taxes	0.50%
Transportation	0.50%
Handling	2.50%
Depreciation	5.00%
Interest	6.00%
Obsolescence	10.00%
	25.00%

Another benefit of this formula is that it can be used as a baseline for the financial efficiency of the operation. This unitless number is a ratio of total dollars spent maintaining inventory versus the total purchase price of all the items in the inventory.

Most JIT contracts will increase purchase prices between 15 and 25 percent. Thus, if an organization's modified carrying cost ratio is above this target, JIT one-echelon options should be considered. Table 31.2 shows a widely cited break down of holding costs associated with warehousing merchandise (Johnson 1999). If the percentages are above these baselines for any specific holding cost area, focus can be turned to that area. Some pundits suggest that in the event that the total cost for storage facilities is above the 25 percent baseline, lowering facilities costs through the elimination of facilities in conjunction with a JIT system should be recommended. We suggest the use of the carrying cost ratio as an alternative before making this type of decision.

RESULTS: CASE STUDY

This system was used in the analysis of the "City of X" health and human services (CoXHHS) department that had its own distribution network to service thirty offices. An analysis was performed to determine inefficiencies in the supply chain (slow inventory turn items, inefficient racking, etc.). This data was then used to create a cash flow analysis to determine which actions would be useful in reducing operational costs. We suggest that these methods can be beneficial in determining which actions will yield the most positive results in reducing costs and increasing net profits for an organization.

FACILITIES COSTS

The second element of the holding cost calculation involved compiling the total facilities cost for each of the warehouses involved in the operation's supply chain. This

TABLE 31.3
Facilities Cost

WHj	Labor Cost	Utilities and Supplies	Lease Cost	Facility Total Cost
WH1	123	356	0	480
WH2	30	50	78	158
WH3	26	74	0	100
WH4	26	62	0	89
WH5	12	28	0	40
Total	217	570	78	867

data are included in Table 31.3. Additionally, CoXHHS was only leasing WH 2, at a price of $78,000 a year. This incremental price was another possibility for removal, as all the other warehouse facilities were owned by the city. These problems would be an important factor in determining which actions to take in an options analysis.

PURCHASING COSTS

With facilities costs and inventory turn rates by item calculated, it was possible to proceed to a more in-depth analysis of the data. *Inventory turns* refers to the number of times per time period an item is purchased and sold. For example. a turn rate of 1.0 indicates that all inventory that was purchased during the year was ordered. The first step was to calculate an average turn rate for all items for each facility in the CoXHHS supply chain. The desired result is that each facility would have at least a turn rate of 1.0, indicating that the inventory in each warehouse was turned once a year. The results are summarized in Table 31.4.

Table 31.4 shows the only facility that demonstrated the desired average turn rate was WH 2. The other buildings, especially WH 3, featured extremely low turn rates. The most likely cause of this was the presence of vast amounts of obsolete inventory in each facility. Schnetzler, Sennheiser, and Schonsleben (2007) note that in trying to achieve lower inventories and shorter lead times, operational costs are affected.

TABLE 31.4
Purchasing Cost

Warehouse #	Turns/Year	Total Receipts
WH1	0.36	$48,065.62
WH2	2.18	$501,062.43
WH3	0.07	$34,541.00
WH4	0.49	$531,931.75
WH5	0.15	$25,475.21
Total Purchases		$1,141,076.01

These effects can be counteracted by reducing the amount of waste and obsolete inventory present in the system. The low receipts for the WH 5 show that they were not ordering any items, a fact that is consistent with its role as an intermediary building in the supply chain. Thus, their low turn rate is acceptable given the building's role. However, WH 4 and WH 1 each sent out a large number of orders but showed an unacceptably low turn rate.

THE MODIFIED CARRYING COST RATIO

The total cost incurred per item was calculated for the entire CoXHHS supply chain and compared back to the total purchase cost, resulting in the warehouse cost per dollar spent. This calculated value was also exceptionally high, netting an average of $0.97 per dollar purchased being spent to store and transport each inventory item. Lowering this ratio could be accomplished through a variety of methods including consolidating inventory, increasing efficiency by standardizing procedures and optimizing storage use, and, most importantly, through elimination of obsolete inventory items from each facility. Table 31.5 shows the calculations for the CoXHHS modified carrying cost ratio.

INVENTORY TURN ANALYSIS

The ratio showed that the facilities costs of the system were well above 25 percent of the total purchase price. So in order to eliminate facilities and implement JIT inventory turns, data were needed. Inventory turns are defined as the average number of items kept in stock divided by the annual usage of the item.

$$T = \frac{S_{ij} + S_{i0}}{\lambda_{ij}}$$

The ABC analysis compares all the items ordered and prioritizes them according to use. ABC analysis, with results, are indicated in Table 31.6. An ABC analysis evaluates the turn rates of inventory. An A mover is the fastest mover with the highest turn rate, a B mover is next, and so on. In most ABC analyses, the slower moving inventory is referred to as C and D movers. In our study, the order policy for each type of mover was set by movement category. Items that are deemed A movers were placed on continual review for reordering. B movers are reviewed quarterly.

TABLE 31.5
Carrying Cost Ratio of CoXHHS

Costs	Facilities	Shrinkage	Fleet	Sum
Annual	867	127	87	1081
Purchases	1115			1115
			i = 0.97	

TABLE 31.6
ABCD Analysis of Inventory

Category	Number of Items
A	104
B	150
C	476
D	2,262
Total	2,992

C movers are reviewed annually. Items that had an inventory turn period greater than one year were classified as D movers or obsolete inventory.

THE DECISION

After determining that the current cost ratio for the CoXHHS was above the expected 15 to 25 percent procurement cost increase, a decision was made to switch from a two-echelon system to a one-echelon system. The switch had an earning before interest and taxes of $250,000 with a return on investment of just over one year. The cost ratio was reduced from 97 to 30 percent. Ordering policies were simplified and managed by each office, eliminating the need for a centralized logistics system. However, much of the savings was due to lowering the total volume of obsolete inventory in the warehouses. This reduction in obsolete inventory produced a 75 percent reduction in racking requirements.

CONCLUSION

Many organizations operate warehouses in order to reduce costs. Oftentimes in governmental operations, if not carefully managed these warehouse operations become bloated with inventory that is no longer needed or is needed at a much lower demand. Unless managers periodically analyze the contents of their warehouses, the carrying cost of all items purchased can outweigh savings from procurement when purchasing in bulk.

In today's fast-paced business world, the time to evaluate business operations is not available, and quick decisions need to be made. This modified carrying cost ratio, based on easily found data, shows when a warehouse's operations are inefficient and not cost-effective. This model speeds up the process and thereby speeds change and cost savings in a company.

However, there are some limitations to this model. One limitation would be very large systems where JIT contracts would be too complicated. Organizations with a large service range such as a regional or larger retailers may not benefit from this ratio as is. However, for a smaller company or a city, this model can be very effective at recognizing overcapacity or inefficiencies in a supply chain.

REFERENCES

Caglar, D., C. L. Li, and C. Simchi-Levi. (2003). Two-echelon spare parts inventory system subject to a service constraint. *IIE Transactions* 36:655–666.

Johnson, J. C., Wood, D. F., Wardlow, D. L., and Murphy, P. R., Jr. (1999). *Contemporary Logistics*, 7th Edition. Upper Saddle River, NJ: Prentice Hall.

Lee, C. B. (2003). Multi-echelon inventory optomization. Evant White Paper Series. http://www.stanford.edu/group/scforum/Welcome/white%20Papers/Multi-Echelon%20%Inventory720Optimization%20-%20Evant%20white%20paper.pdf. Accessed August 30, 2007.

Schnetzler, M. J., A. Sennheiser, and P. Schonsleben. (2007). A decomposition-based approach for the development of a supply chain strategy. *International Journal of Production Economics* 105:21–42.

Wang, Y., M. A. Cohen, and Y. S. Zheng. (2000). A two-echelon repairable system with restocking-center-dependant depot replenishment lead times. *Management Science* 46:1441–1453.

ADDITIONAL REFERENCES

Graves, S. C. (1985). A multi-echelon inventory model for a repairable item with one-for-one replenishment. *Management Science* 31:1247–1256.

Muckstadt, J. A. (1973). A model for a multi-item, multi-indenture inventory system. *Management Science* 20:472–481.

Muckstadt, J. A., and L. J. Thomas. (1980). Are multi-echelon inventory methods worth implementing with low demand items? *Management Science* 26:483–494.

Sherbrooke, C. C. (1968). METRIC: A multi-echelon technique for recoverable item control. *Operations Research* 16:122–141.

Simon, R. M. (1971). Stationary properties of a two-echelon inventory model for low demands. *Operations Research* 19:761–777.

32 A Case Study of a Supply Chain Management Network Model in Government Public Works Department

Erick Jones and Josephine Ann Hain

INTRODUCTION

Technical organizations often face the challenge of aligning their supply chains. The engineering manager faces challenges in coordinating data collection and analysis efforts to evaluate the supply chain in a cost-effective manner. In some organizations it may be prudent to utilize current technical personnel to perform this analysis. Oftentimes, companies consider utilizing costly software and consultants prior to using their in-house resources. Allowing the engineering manager to utilize an internal team to provide an analysis is more cost-effective for several reasons.

- Data collected will be utilized again if consultants are deemed necessary
- The in-house team will understand the implications of solutions that the model may provide and can make adjustments for reality
- Simplified assumptions can be agreed upon by internal stakeholders
- The project will prepare personnel for change
- The project provides a cost-effective solution

Also, this study will reveal whether your supply chain network may be too complex to model using the Excel solver prior to investing in an extensive study. Though it is very important to perform supply chain analysis, many companies cannot justify the use of expensive software and consultants to perform these analyses continually. The engineering manager can provide good solutions by creating this type of study.

Previously, a project team of students and faculty from the University of Nebraska–Lincoln and material management personnel from a city located in the Southwest United States began a Six Sigma project to reduce obsolete inventory. The supply chain consisted of a network of warehouses, storerooms, suppliers, and the internal end-user, which represented the customer. During the Six Sigma process improvement study, the team determined that customer service needs were not being met, obsolete inventory was being driven by purchasing behavior, and facility costs could be reduced with facility consolidations. The team analyzed the supply chain network of the city's public works department using modeling techniques to recommend which warehouses could be consolidated. Based on recommendations, 96,000 square feet could be reduced and a gross of $3.5M would be saved over five years, not including taxes and depreciation. This represents a cost reduction of 25 percent.

BACKGROUND

An engineering manager's goal when locating facilities and allocating inventory should maximize the overall profitability of the resulting supply chain network while providing customers with adequate service. Traditionally, revenues come from the sale of product and costs arise from facilities, labor, transportation, material, and inventory holding. Ideally, profits after tariffs and taxes should be maximized when designing a supply chain network. In this scenario, the city government does not pay taxes or collect revenues, so their goals were to minimize overall operating costs and still be responsive to the customer.

Trade-offs must be made by the engineering managers during network design. For example, building many facilities to serve local markets reduces transportation costs and provides fast response time, but it increases the facility and inventory costs incurred by the firm. Engineering managers can use network design models in two different situations. First, those models are used to decide on locations where facilities will be established and the capacity assigned to each facility. Second, these models are used to assign current demand to the available facilities and identify lanes along which product will be transported. Managers must consider this decision at least on an annual demand basis: prices and tariffs change. In both cases the goal is to maximize the profit while satisfying customer needs. The following information must be available before the design decisions can be made (Chopra and Meindl 2004).

- Location of supply sources and markets
- Location of potential sites
- Demand forecast by market
- Facility, labor, and material cost by site
- Transportation costs between each pair of sites
- Inventory costs by site as well as a function of quantity
- Sales price of product in different regions
- Taxes and tariffs as product is moved between locations
- Desired response time and other service factors

Given this information, a choice of model type can be made. Previous literature highlights some general models that have differing goals. Each model has differing objectives; the models that were considered for this study were the capacitated plant location model and the gravity location model. The capacitated plant location model seeks to minimize the total cost of the current supply chain network; the problem is formulated into an integer program. The gravity location model's goal is to locate an optimal location based on cost inputs. Beyond optimization models, the engineering manager could build a simulation of their supply chain (Chang 2004).

In this study, we chose to use the capacitated plant location model (Chopra and Meindl 2004) in order to determine the minimal number of facilities that could hold inventory and meet customer demand. In our study, the city has chosen to consolidate warehouse facilities. Management is questioning whether all twelve facilities are necessary. They have assigned a supply chain team of University of Nebraska–Lincoln and city personnel to study the network for the public works operations and identify the warehouses that can be closed. The goal is to formulate the model to minimize total costs taking into account costs, taxes, and duties by location. Given that taxes and duties do not vary between various locations, and that the city does not pay taxes, the team decided to use the existing facility locations and allocate demand to the open warehouses to minimize the total cost of facilities, transportation, and inventory.

The capacitated plant location network optimization model requires the following inputs:

N = number of potential locations
M = number of demand points
D_i = annual demand from market i
K_i = potential capacity of plant i
F_i = annualized fixed cost of keeping factory i open
C_{ij} = cost of producing and shipping one unit from factory i to market j (cost includes production inventory, transportation, and duties)

and the following decision variables:

Y_i = 1 if plant is open, 0 otherwise
X_{ij} = quantity shipped from factory i to market j

The problem is formulated as the following integer program:

$$Min \left(\sum_{i=1}^{n} F_i Y_i + \sum_{i=1}^{n} \sum_{j=1}^{m} C_{ij} X_{ij} \right)$$

Subject to:

$$\sum_{i=1}^{m} X_{ij} D_{ij} \quad \text{for } j = 1, \ldots, m \tag{1}$$

$$\sum_{j=1}^{n} X_{ij} \leq K_i Y_i \quad \text{for } i = 1, \ldots, n \tag{2}$$

$$Y_i \in (0, 1) \quad \text{for } i = 1, \ldots, n \tag{3}$$

The objective function minimizes the total cost (fixed + variable) of setting up and operating the network. The constraint in equation (1) requires that the demand at each facility market be satisfied. The constraint in equation (2) states that no plant can supply more than its capacity. (Capacity is 0 if closed and K_i if it is open. The product of the terms K_iY_i captures this effect.) The constraint in equation (3) enforces that each plant is either open ($Y_i = 1$) or closed ($Y_i = 0$). The solution will identify the plants that are to be kept open, their capacity, and the allocation of regional demand to these plants. The model is solved using the Solver tool in Excel (Chopra and Meindl 2004).

NETWORK MODELING STEPS INCORPORATED INTO A SIX SIGMA SERVICE PROJECT

The typical Six Sigma DMAIC approach was used with the addition of a network model within the Analyze phase. DMAIC stands for Define, Measure, Analyze, Improve, and Control. These are the steps in a standard improvement model for a Six Sigma directed project.

DEFINE

The main work in the Define phase is for the team to complete an analysis of what the project should accomplish and to confirm their understanding with their sponsor(s). They should agree on the problem, understand the project's link to corporate strategy and its expected contribution to ROIC, agree on the project boundaries, and know what indicators or metrics will be used to evaluate success. The last two issues often prove particularly important in service environments (George 2003). The problem defined for this project was to reduce obsolete inventory.

MEASURE

One of the major advances of Six Sigma is its demand for data driven management. Most other improvement methodologies tended to derive from identifying a project into Improve without sufficient data to really understand the underlying causes of the problem. The Measure phase is Six Sigma's stage for data collection and measuring the problem. This phase is generally broken into several steps, including establish baselines, observe the process, and collect data (George 2003). The measure of success was reducing the percentage of obsolete inventory in the supply chain.

ANALYZE

The purpose of the Analyze phase is to make sense of all the information and data collected in the Measure phase. A challenge to all teams is sticking to the data, not just using their own experience and opinions to make conclusions about the root causes (George 2003). There are many tools available in the Analyze phase, including network modeling. Network models provide a rich and robust framework for combining data, relationships, and forecasts from descriptive models. They provide managers with broad and deep insights into effective plans, which are based on the company's decision options, goals, commitments, and resource constraints (Shapiro 2001). After using regression analysis and design of experiment analysis, the team chose to use supply chain optimization for a more robust solution.

The network model used within this project followed several steps, including:

1. Collect input data and establish baseline
2. Set optimization constraints
3. Run alternatives with the capacitated plant location model (Chopra and Meindl 2004)
4. Show alternatives in revenue, savings, and customer service
5. Select an alternative

These steps led to an alternative that minimized the cost of the supply chain. This alternative then directs the tasks within the Improve stage.

Improve

The sole purpose of the Improve phase is to make changes in a process that will eliminate the defects, waste, costs, etc, that are linked to the customer needs identified in the Define stage (George 2003). The Improve stage differs for every Six Sigma project. The common underlier is that the improvements should be centered on the largest issues found in the Analyze phase. The recommendations for consolidating facilities by using a more robust criterion for eliminating outdated inventory were recommended for the improvement.

Control

The purpose of Control is to make sure that any gains made will be preserved, until and unless new knowledge and data show that there is an even better way to operate the process. The team must address how to hand off what they learned to the process owner and ensure that everyone working on the process is trained in using any new, documented procedures. Six areas of Control are critical: document the improved process, turn the results into dollars, verify maintenance of gains continually, install an automatic monitoring system, pilot the implementation, and develop a control plan. Key performance indicators were identified to be tracked with statistical process control charts for the following year. This is further elaborated in the results section.

The DMAIC process with the capacitated plant location model in the Analyze phase was utilized to study the city's public works warehousing operations.

CASE DESCRIPTION

Organizational Description

The organization used for this case study is a city in the Southwest United States, public works, materials management branch (MMB). The materials management branch is responsible for the processing and coordination of all procurement and contract-related activities as well as warehousing and distribution of all general inventory items for the department.

The branch facilitates purchases ranging from pipes for restoration of sewer lines to computers and traffic signs. To promptly obtain goods and services, the department utilizes in excess of eight hundred commodity and service contracts. The branch is divided into three functional sections: procurement; contract management, and warehousing and distribution. This study was centered on the warehousing and distribution section.

The materials management branch has the responsibility for warehousing and distribution of general and automotive inventory items, from cradle-to-grave, for the department. Two central depots serve as staging locations for inventory that is distributed to a network of ten general supply warehouses, nine automotive warehouses, and many storerooms located throughout the city. The inventory consists of a variety of items; for example, pipes, valves, fittings, office and janitorial supplies, etc.

PROJECT DESCRIPTION

The MMB had been audited in previous years, and the audits identified opportunities for improvement in the warehousing operations. The audits identified excess obsolete inventory, the need to evaluate standard operating procedures, and labor productivity. Obsolete inventory is defined as inventory that has not been requested for disbursement for over one year.

The current system contains twelve warehouses and twenty-eight storerooms with an ongoing cost of $14.94M. Upon inspection, it was estimated that the warehouses have a maximum of 30 percent space utilization. The current supply chain is shown in Figure 32.1. Public works owned $10.1M of inventory within the MMB warehouses. The inventory that was deemed obsolete was valued at $3.6M, or 35 percent of the total inventory.

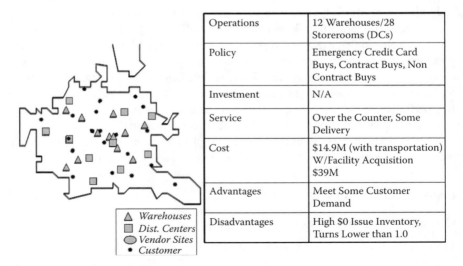

Operations	12 Warehouses/28 Storerooms (DCs)
Policy	Emergency Credit Card Buys, Contract Buys, Non Contract Buys
Investment	N/A
Service	Over the Counter, Some Delivery
Cost	$14.9M (with transportation) W/Facility Acquisition $39M
Advantages	Meet Some Customer Demand
Disadvantages	High $0 Issue Inventory, Turns Lower than 1.0

△ Warehouses
■ Dist. Centers
⬤ Vendor Sites
• Customer

FIGURE 32.1 Current supply chain description.

The modeling steps were followed to complete the analysis.

1. Collect input data and establish baseline: The current supply chain information was collected to form the input data for the network model. The inputs included costs for electricity, gas, data lines, and labor. Also, holding and transportation costs were estimated for each facility. The warehouses do not pay taxes or water costs since they are in a city building, so information as to lost water sales and lost taxes were also captured and used in the cost equations.
2. Set optimization constraints: The optimization constraints included the size limitations of each facility and the future demand at each facility. The facility size was collected from operations. The future demand on inventory was estimated to be the same as last year's value.
3. Run alternatives with the capacitated plant location model (Chopra and Meindl 2004): The costs and data that were collected in steps 1 and 2 of the modeling were input into Chopra and Meindl's model in Excel and the Solver Add-In was utilized to run alternatives of the least cost model.
4. Show alternatives in revenue, savings, and customer service: The different alternatives were then evaluated for revenue and savings with an ROI calculation assuming the project had a five-year life. The customer service provided in each alternative was evaluated by a team from operations. Savings were associated with space reduction; taxes and depreciation were associated with closing facilities. The savings for closing the facilities were limited due to the fact that the profit of selling the property was not included, only the savings of eliminating long-term leases was included. The city does not pay taxes on the property, so the savings were minimal compared to those in other industries. The team felt that this provided a conservative and acceptable estimate for cost savings in governmental operations. In other industries, the taxes, depreciation, and probability of sales profit would be estimated in potential savings.
5. Select an alternative: The optimal solution contains two warehouses, which are centrally located as shown in Figure 32.2. This gives a reduction of 96,000 square feet which translates into $3.5M over five years. This solution will increase the space utilization to 65 percent and reduce the obsolete inventory to 10 percent of the total value held within the warehouses.

As the city moves to the optimized model, the Control phase of DMAIC will keep the improvements in place and running smoothly. The metrics that are given to continue the control are the key performance indicators (KPIs) given in Table 32.1. These should be measured and tracked utilizing statistical process control (SPC). This data could then be used to repeat an optimization in the future.

LESSONS LEARNED

The lessons learned included model complexity changes and challenges and limitations that could be better met. The model complexity was chosen to reflect a first look at the supply chain and a simple optimization. A more complex model may

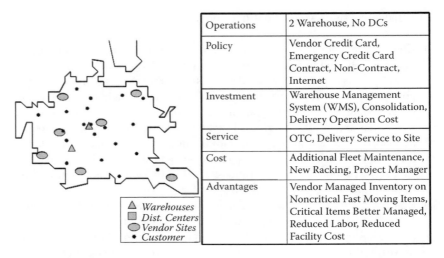

Operations	2 Warehouse, No DCs
Policy	Vendor Credit Card, Emergency Credit Card Contract, Non-Contract, Internet
Investment	Warehouse Management System (WMS), Consolidation, Delivery Operation Cost
Service	OTC, Delivery Service to Site
Cost	Additional Fleet Maintenance, New Racking, Project Manager
Advantages	Vendor Managed Inventory on Noncritical Fast Moving Items, Critical Items Better Managed, Reduced Labor, Reduced Facility Cost

△ Warehouses
▣ Dist. Centers
● Vendor Sites
• Customer

FIGURE 32.2 Optimized supply chain.

TABLE 32.1
Kay Performance Indicators

Category	Metric	Definition
Service	Turns	Annual $ issued divided by average
Service	Percent obsolete inventory	Number of commodity codes (CC) that have not been issued for over 1 year divided by the total number of CC's
Cost	Cost/pick	Total labor cost divided by total number of picks
Cost	Cost/order	Total labor cost divided by total number of orders
Asset management	Facility utilization	Number of pallet positions utilized vs. available
Future		
Transportation	Shipments/division	Track the number of deliveries to site for each division
Inventory	Velocity	Annual revenue/daily overhead
Labor	Percent productivity by area/task	Divide actual labor hours by the efficiency standard for the task and track by employee
Labor	Picks/hour	Number of pick issues and divide by pick labor hours
Purchasing	PCard spend by category	PCard spend by contract, non-contract, and emergency usage vs. total PCard spend

have been used if better original data had been available. The data that were available could not be validated because they came from the enterprise resource planning (ERP) system, which was antiquated. The model was validated with site tours and sampling for volumetric data. We note that the model is only as good as the data it is provided. A common saying is if you put garbage in to a model, you get garbage out. If a more complex model were utilized, software other than Excel would be needed in addition to consultants.

It was difficult to reach agreement between divisions on what part of the cost data can be incorporated as reduced costs. For example, the portion of overall utility costs can be equated to warehouse space versus the other uses of the buildings today, and the percentage of value can be used for holding cost because the city does not pay taxes and does not invest excess monies.

IMPLICATIONS FOR THE ENGINEERING MANAGER

An engineering manager should use this article to better understand his own first steps in supply chain optimization projects. This information should encourage the manager to begin to look at information internally, before hiring a consulting team. The first look may give a viable answer that can be implemented for increased efficiencies and savings.

An engineering manager can gather internal data and then use the methods in Excel Solver to create the appropriate supply chain model. The specific steps for using Excel can be found in different references; we recommend the steps outlined by Chopra and Meindl (2004). The engineering manager can justify many good solutions for the supply chain by further using current technical personnel. This may provide another tool for the engineering manager to justify his technical staff. If the internal team does not solve the problem, or the manager is ready for a second look at the issue, a consultant can be hired with very little cost to the company.

This study provided an overall method for performing continuous improvement projects using the Six Sigma methodology. Further, this study shows how an engineering manager can perform a supply chain analysis on current operations in the Analyze stage. The engineering manager can use this study as a guide for both.

CONCLUSIONS

This chapter details a quick and relatively inexpensive way to perform an analysis for supply chain savings opportunities. The major benefit is that you utilize internal personnel who have been already budgeted for and may have a better understanding of operations than outside consultants. Also, the initial study may be modeled using existing spreadsheets before more costly software and consulting options are explored.

The application of the Six Sigma methodology is not limited to city governments but can be duplicated in industry. This study introduced supply chain modeling as another technique that can be used in the Six Sigma methodology to help organizations improve operations. This additional technique may be considered in logistics, distribution, and other supply chain management projects that utilize transactional data to evaluate alternatives.

This simple analysis may not replace a complex supply chain analysis using some of the more advanced software that incorporates the CPLEX and ILOG modeling engines. These software companies allow for more constraints than the less powerful spreadsheets will allow. They have claimed to have 20 to 50 percent more optimized results that may translate into more cost savings. This is contingent on whether consultants can better interpret data and future business strategies and evaluate logistics networks including transportation traffic patterns.

From the case study application we identified a workable set of challenges with lessons learned that can be valuable to organizations when modeling the supply chain. The engineering manager and his team can be a valuable asset when doing both continuous improvement projects and providing valuable supply chain modeling expertise.

REFERENCES

Chang, Y. and Makatsoris, H. C. (2004). Supply Chain Modeling Using Simulation, *International Journal of Simulation*, 2(1), 24–30.

Chopra, S., and P. Meindl. (2004). *Supply chain management*. Pearson Prentice Hall.

George, M. L. (2003). *Lean Six Sigma for service*. McGraw-Hill.

Shapiro, J. F. (2001). *Modeling the supply chain*. Pacific Grove, CA: Duxbury Press.

ADDITIONAL REFERENCES

Bowersox, D. J., D. J. Closs, and M. Bixby Cooper. (2002). *Supply chain logistics management*. McGraw-Hill/Irwin.

George, M. L. (2002). *Lean Six Sigma*. McGraw-Hill.

Johnson, J. C., D. F. Wood, D. L. Wardlow, and P. R. Murphy, Jr. (1999). *Contemporary logistics*. Prentice Hall.

Kotnour, T. G., S. Barton, J. Jennings, and R. D. Bridges. (1998). Understanding and leading large-scale change at the Kennedy Space Center. *Engineering Management Journal* 10(2):17–21.

Kotnour, T. G., J. Matkovich, and R. Ellison. (1999). Establishing a change infrastructure through teams. *Engineering Management Journal* 11(3):25–30.

Leach, F. J., and J. D. Westbrook. (2000). Motivation and job satisfaction in one government and development environment. *Engineering Management Journal* 12(4):3–9.

Michealson, H. B. (1982). *How to write and publish engineering papers and reports*. iSi Press.

Turnquist, M. A., and L. K. Nozick. (2004). A nonlinear optimization model of time and resource allocation decisions in projects with uncertainty. *Engineering Management Journal* 16(1):40–49.

Vof, S., and D. L. Woodruff. (2003). *Introduction to computational optimization models for production planning in a supply chain*. Springer.

Yoon, C., and H. Makatsoris. (2004). Supply chain modeling using simulation. *International Journal of Simulation* 2(1):24–30.

33 The Future of RFID in Army Logistics

Alex Sheehan

INTRODUCTION

A key functionality in army logistics is the concept of focused logistics to provide asset visibility, rapid response, and advanced agility tailored to the continued support of forces at all levels: strategic, operational, and tactical. Solutions lie in new technology that enhance and improve logistical processes and functions in order to meet the needs of the ever transforming global force. The future army will demand near-real-time global, in-transit visibility and total asset visibility of materials, equipment, personnel, and vital supplies. A reliable, versatile, mobile, integrated wireless network is essential to attaining the desired result of total asset visibility.

BACKGROUND

During Operation Desert Storm and Operation Desert Shield, the U.S. Army sent $2 billion worth of supplies to Iraq in containers. At the end of the war, the army sent $1.6 billion worth of supplies back to the United States. This means that the army only used $400 million of supplies during the war because no system for determining the contents of each container had been developed. This lack of visibility led to millions of dollars in lost materials and decreased logistical capability. The mandate for RFID was a result of this lack of asset visibility. Over the next fifteen years, the military has spent hundreds of millions of dollars for the goal of total asset visibility. The army gradually tagged over 750,000 containers and other resources beginning with the operations in Bosnia and Somalia. The initial mandate was for "in-the-box visibility," that is, visibility of resources in a base or other area with readers or nodes, but the demands for the system grew over the subsequent years. Now, military leaders want total global resource visibility.

DISCUSSION OF RFID AND ITS ALTERNATIVES

RFID is an emerging technology that requires tremendous infrastructure and information technology support and has many reasonable uses with respect to the variety of operations the army performs. Because the capability of RFID and related areas is so broad, the military must choose the system to use carefully. The array of possibilities begins with RFID but can run the gamut of RF technology.

Cellular and GSM technologies work for many fleets of vehicles and other resources. For example, Halliburton has the second largest fleet of vehicles in the world, second only to the U.S. Army. Halliburton utilizes cellular and GSM technologies for their functions; however, because the Army traditionally works in areas with little to no infrastructure for cellular activity, it is neither cost-effective nor practical to use only the GSM technology. Other technologies that are possible include 802.11-type wireless technologies in addition to satellite technologies. The three technologies that will be discussed are the current active RFID system and two new systems developed or being developed by the military known as *Third-Generation with RFID* (3G RFID) and *Next-Generation Wireless Communication* (NGWC).

CURRENT RFID SYSTEM

The current RFID system was implemented in the early to mid-1990s and currently has 750,000 tagged objects and 1,900 readers or nodes. Current RFID is, for the most part, connected to a fixed infrastructure. An RFID tag is written with the source-generated data at the originating facility and then mounted on a transportation platform (e.g., pallet, container, vehicle). As the shipment passes through the various nodes, the tag is interrogated (read) at those instrumented nodal points along the logistics lines of communications, most notably at the strategic air and sea ports of debarkation/embarkation and at final destination supply support activities. There is a limited capability for a temporary infrastructure via the Early Entry Deployment Support Kit, at the combatant commander's direction, to read the tags and report the status. Both the fixed and temporary infrastructures require an interrogator, a personal computer, some type of communications, and electric power. This capability also allows for "stand-off, in-the-box visibility" when using a handheld interrogator to read the tags to identify what is in or on a transportation platform (e.g., pallet, container, or vehicle).

THIRD-GENERATION RFID (3G RFID)

Third-generation RFID, developed by the U.S. Army in the last two years, utilizes active RFID and satellite communication (satcom) in combination with a GPS system. The active RFID tag utilizes the current infrastructure, whereas satcom can be used anywhere in the world to locate a tag through the GPS system. This system provides nearly unlimited flexibility while providing the ability to store reasonable amounts of data concerning contents, location, and time. This visibility will enhance the army's capability to have total asset visibility.

NEXT-GENERATION WIRELESS COMMUNICATION (NGWC)

Next-generation wireless communication is now being developed by the U.S. Army with cooperation from several civilian businesses. NGWC builds on the ideas of 3G RFID by adding 802.16 wireless communication network to the 3G hardware of an active RFID tag, satcom chip, and GPS system. NGWC will have two types of tags: (1) a tag with every capability just discussed, and (2) a tag with only the active tag, GPS, and wireless network. The NGWC tag will utilize a microcontroller to coordinate which technology is suited for the location of its use. An example of the use of this technology will best demonstrate its capabilities. If a convoy of resources is going to a remote location in a country like Iraq or Afghanistan, one vehicle will have a tag with satcom while the other vehicles, containers, etc, will have the other type. The wireless network will be activated by each tag's microcontroller when the tags will send their information to the satcom capable tag to send all the information as a packet to where it was requested. This will allow the army to track resources at a cheaper price with only minimal to no reduction in visibility.

The wireless network will be different than the networks we are accustomed to for wireless Internet. Most wireless networks utilize 802.11A or 802.11B, whereas NGWC will utilize 802.16, which provides a much larger coverage area (twenty-mile radius) than an active tag can provide (three hundred yards), greater data transmission speeds, and higher levels of security.

Another benefit of NGWC is the capability to connect sensors to the tag, providing it with the capability of taking readings from digital or analog sources. Examples of the use of this feature include measuring the amount of fuel or water left in a tank, measuring fuel viscosity, or delivering messages about equipment failure, etc. This function will allow the logistics to use more of the concepts of "lean logistics." In other words, the military leaders will know when to replace, refill, or perform maintenance on vehicles or storage facilities rather than finding them in disrepair or replacing/refilling a tank or storage too often. Or, to put it technically, lean logistics will enhance war-fighting sustainability, shrink the logistics footprint, and reduce infrastructure.

ECONOMIC ANALYSIS

Because the newer systems are not in use currently, determining the economic value of each system is quite difficult. However, an excellent estimate can be concluded by evaluating several criteria. The factors that we will evaluate are the annual tag cost, maintenance cost per tag per year, and infrastructure cost per tag per year. From these costs, we will be able to calculate the total cost per year to improve the read capability by 25 percent each year as well as the benefits from this increased capability; see Table 33.1 for a summary of costs.

- Annual tag cost: The prices of tags vary greatly from active tags to tags with satcom capability. The traditional active tag costs about $70, whereas the satcom tag can cost as much as $350. All tags' costs are based on a seven-year life. The NGWC tags have a weighted average cost based on the expected amount of each tag and the projected cost of each.
- Maintenance cost: Maintenance costs are based on expected error of active tags. These repairs include database error, tag misreads, and any other tag problems. The maintenance costs are expected to be higher for the current system because of the extreme dependency on the active tags; the newer systems will not rely completely on this feature.
- Infrastructure cost: Infrastructure costs include all costs associated with implementing new nodes and data processing hardware, as well as several other factors. Because the infrastructure for the current system will be used in the proposed systems, the cost of infrastructure will increase.

TABLE 33.1
Summary of Costs

	Current ($)	3G RFID ($)	NGWC ($)
Annual tag cost (7-year life)	10	50	15
Maintenance cost per tag	20	0	0
Infrastructure cost per tag	28	38	38
Total annual cost per tag	58	88	53
Total tag cost	12,250,000	61,250,000	18,025,000
Cost to increase read capability 25%	3,951,971	364,437	107,249
Savings in lost container material	0	(50,000,000)	(50,000,000)
Savings in detention charges	0	(6,900,000)	(6,900,000)
Total system cost or benefit	16,201,971	4,714,437	(38,767,751)

- Savings in lost container material: The estimates for savings in lost container materials are ambiguous estimates at best. From expert reports and professional opinions, these projections are assumed to be within the range of possibilities.
- Savings in detention charges: Detention charges are a result of penalties fined by contractors who cannot perform their job functions due to misplaced assets and the inability to locate necessary equipment and/or personnel.

ENGINEERING ANALYSIS

Because each system is so different, analysis of the different specifications is absolutely necessary. Although comparing each system is difficult due to the variety of uses and applications, we will attempt to quantify each; see the decision matrix in Table 33.2 for reference.

- Information capability: Information capability refers to a system's capability to process data that it can gather from sensors and devices like a GPS.
- Implementation cost: Implementation cost refers to the initial capital investment required by the army to experience a significant increase in read capability.
- Maintenance cost: Maintenance cost refers to the annual investment required to sustain the readability of the system.
- Asset visibility: Asset visibility refers to the ability of military leaders to find or know where assets are at any given time.
- Ease of expansion: Ease of expansion refers to the ability of military leaders to expand the relevant system with respect investment amount, implementation time, and other requirements necessary for full implementation.
- Operations cost: Operations cost refers to the time required of contractor and military personnel to facilitate the relevant system.
- Real-time data capability: Real-time data capability refers to the capability of a system to facilitate data transference.

TABLE 33.2
System Decision Matrix

		System Decision Metric		
	Weight	Current System	3G RFID	NGWC
Information capability	2	4	6	9
Implementation cost	1	9	3	7
Maintenance cost	1	3	8	7
Asset visibility	3	2	10	8
Ease of expansion	2	1	9	8
Operations cost	1	9	3	7
Real-time data capability	3	3	8	7
		46	98	100

Each system varies in its capabilities, costs, and return on investment. The method selected to determine the best system, based on these factors, is a decision metric known as a Delphi chart. The Delphi chart utilizes a ten-point weighted scale based on seven factors. These factors have been rated as such based on collected data and expert opinion.

CONCLUSION/RECOMMENDATIONS

Each of the systems presented here can provide tremendous opportunities. However, only one of these systems can provide the information that logisticians need at a reasonable investment. The next-generation wireless communications system can provide both total asset visibility and in transit visibility. The combination of satcom capability with 802.16Wi Max wireless networks can provide numerous opportunities in addition to the current active RFID infrastructure. Currently, tags may go a year without being read, but with the ability for tags to create mesh networks this will rarely happen with NGWC. Logisticians will be able to use this information to not only manage the flow of material but to manage idle assets more effectively, giving them the ability to engineer solutions that will enable them to proactively decide why and where assets should be.

Finally, logisticians will be able to use data to provide enhanced asset management capabilities in new and innovative ways. Logisticians will also be able to consider asset management by considering issues such as warehousing, distribution, and idle or distressed cargo. A system like NGWC will provide better, tighter control over the use of transportation distribution and warehousing assets as well as infrastructure. This system is the answer to the questions of military leaders.

ADDITIONAL REFERENCES

Angeles, R. (2005). RFID technologies: Supply-chain: Applications and implementation issues. *Information Systems Management* Winter (2005): 22(1), 51–65.

Clampitt, H. G. (2006). *The RFID certification handbook*. Houston, Tex.: PWD Group.

Fee, J. (2006). Telephone conversation with the author, 26–27 April.

Fee, J., and A. Schmack. (2005). Improving RFID technology. *Army Logistician* 37:34–35.

Kohn, W., V. Brayman, and J. Littleton. (2005). Repair-control of enterprise systems using RFID sensory data. *IIE Transactions* 37: 281–290.

Ocean Systems Engineering Corporation. (2004). Business process analysis report.

Ocean Systems Engineering Corporation. (2006). Cost benefit analysis report.

Ocean Systems Engineering Corporation. (2006). Functional requirements analysis.

Ocean Systems Engineering Corporation. (2006). Technical baseline analysis.

34 RFID in Golf — Applications and Parallels

Bret Clark

INTRODUCTION

Golf is an old game that has existed for years and years. Countless amateurs have spent years practicing this craft, yet very few become truly proficient and master the game. So many golfers have failed at this monumental task, yielding to the extreme frustration that many experience. One of the many sources of this frustration is lost balls; however, one company, Radar Golf™, is attempting to eliminate this frustration for amateur players.

Radar Golf™ has introduced a new product, the Radar Golf™ System. This system uses RFID tags embedded into golf balls to help locate lost balls. The tags are located by a handheld reader operated by the golfer searching for his ball. The reader sends out radio frequency waves to the golf ball, and the ball's tag responds by bouncing a signal back to the reader. As the signal to the handheld reader increases in strength, two signs indicate that the reader is approaching the ball. The reader beeps in increasing frequency, and a liquid crystal display (LCD) on the reader indicates increasing proximity by a growing number of bars on the LCD screen.

The Radar Golf™ System proposes to allow golfers of various skill sets and abilities to increase their satisfaction from playing golf. For example, the frustrating time spent searching through tall grass for a lost ball will be eliminated. Also, the penalty for not finding a ball within the five-minute search limit will be eliminated because the ball will be found. Finally, the cost of replacing the balls should decrease because there will be fewer lost balls.

This chapter will investigate the claims of the Radar Golf™ System. The author anticipates that the system will save an average golfer a measurable amount of time on a round of golf. The time savings exhibited on the golf course will then be related to time and labor savings in an industrial setting.

TESTING AND EXPERIMENTATION

A variety of tests were performed using the Radar Golf™ System. These tests included read range, reliability, speed of play, durability, and extreme location testing. Due to time and other constraints, not all of the tests envisioned by the author were able to be completed, but sufficient testing of the product was completed.

The initial tests performed were simple tests of the read range of the reader. The company advertises that the system will work (start receiving a signal) at a range of thirty to one hundred feet, depending on elevation and terrain. Read range tests were performed at assumed ideal conditions. The terrain was flat, the weather was calm, and there were no objects to interfere with the transmission of the radio waves. Also, the testing was performed on a golf course, in an area assumed to be free of outside radio frequencies to interfere with the signal.

The author also desired to test the reliability of the system. Because metal inhibits the transmission of radio frequency waves, the author tested the impact on the performance of the system on various metal objects that could appear on a golf course. In addition, the durability of the system is a valid question. Golf balls are subject to extreme forces when struck, and they often undergo some mild compression. The technology must be able to withstand such impacts and still perform adequately. A final consideration of the system is its reliability under adverse connections. Radio frequency signals are inhibited by the presence of water; therefore, testing the system in rain would be an interesting measure. Unfortunately, the author was never able to test the system in rain. The system was tested, however, in other adverse conditions such as hills, woods, tall grass, and sand.

These initial tests were performed to simply measure the performance of the reader and the tags in the golf balls. In order to measure the overall effectiveness of the system, several test rounds of golf were played. Each round consisted of nine holes, played on the same course, and in the same order. In each case, the subject playing the holes was Chelsea Shoemaker. Miss Shoemaker played three rounds without the RFID technology and three rounds with the Radar Golf™ System.

RESULTS

The author first conducted simple tests of the read range of the product. The maximum read ranges attained by the author topped out at roughly fifty-five feet, under ideal conditions. This value falls in the range specified by the vendor, but it is not close to the maximum range given of one hundred feet.

Under ideal conditions, the system worked, but the author chose to investigate the reliability of this system. Because the system uses radio frequency waves, metal objects present an obvious barrier or impediment to the system. At one point in the testing, a ball was struck and happened to land near a metal fence, which caused both the reader and the author great difficulty in recovering the ball. The system did not locate the ball outside of thirty feet in this case because of the metal fence. To further test this idea, the ball was placed directly underneath a metal garbage container. With the metal base of the can separating the reader and the ball by less than one foot, the LCD showed only half of the bars as filled on the screen. The ball was very close to the reader, and the LCD should have displayed all bars as full because the ball was so close. However, the metal significantly blocked the signal, so that the reader gave the indication that the ball was in that direction but still some distance away. This type of scenario could present a problem if, for example, the ball ended up behind anything metal, such as a maintenance shed or a bathroom.

With respect to the durability testing, time and lack of equipment were two significant constraints hampering the testing performed. The author envisioned repeatedly striking the ball into a net with a driver, but no such driving facilities were available to the author, and there was a lack of time for such testing. It was deemed more important to test the system on the golf course and use this testing as the basis of any durability analysis. After playing fifty-four holes with one ball, the reader still located the ball from as far away as the initial test.

Although the system was never tested in a precipitous environment, the ball was subjected to other extreme locations and environments. Wooded areas and areas of tall grass provided little or no impediment to the read ranges of the system. Hilly terrain also did little to negatively affect the system, although it should be noted that few hills greater than ten to fifteen feet in height were available for such testing. The ball was tested in sand under various conditions, and it is possible for a sand trap to hinder the communication between the ball and the reader. A golf ball can potentially become buried in sand, but the ball is almost never covered completely in sand. Generally, a portion of the ball (usually at least half) will protrude from the sand if the ball becomes buried at all. In testing, the ball was placed in sand at reasonable (meaning likely to happen in a round of golf) depths, and the system performed as intended. When the ball was completely buried, the reader still received a signal. If the ball were buried too deep, the signal could be blocked, potentially by moisture in the sand; nonetheless, this is a highly unlikely occurrence, so the system is believed to be fully functional in the sand.

Given the knowledge that the system is capable of performing more or less as advertised, the author researched the direct benefits of the system. These benefits are most readily realized in the form of time saved by eliminating searching for lost balls. Each hole was timed while the subject played the six rounds, three with the system and three without. The times for each hole and for each round are summarized in Table 34.1 and Table 34.2. Table 34.3 shows the difference between the first three rounds (without RFID) and the final three rounds (with RFID).

The general trend, indicated by the lower average times with the Radar Golf™ system, was a decrease in the time it took to play a hole, which could be attributed to the new technology. The numbers 1–9 signify from which hole the time was taken, and the numbers 1–3 on the left indicate from which round the time was taken.

Without searching through every figure in the tables, a quick summary can be obtained from Table 34.3. On average, playing with Radar Golf™ can save around twelve minutes per nine holes. The problem with these results is the lack of data points, which would lead to a very large standard deviation for the average time saved per nine holes. Given more time, the author would pursue the research further, obtaining more data points to validate the given results. Knowing that the results are potentially

TABLE 34.1
Time to Play Each Hole without Radar Golf

	1	2	3	4	5	6	7	8	9	Total Min	Hours
1	12.7	8.65	13.04	15.56	15.72	6.55	12.74	9.89	14.91	109.76	1.829
2	15.2	9.55	15.09	20.16	18.68	7.36	12.39	12.04	19.34	129.81	2.164
3	13.68	8.23	14.67	14.99	15.36	6.97	15.62	10.36	18.39	118.27	1.971
	13.860	8.810	14.267	16.903	16.587	6.960	13.583	10.763	17.125	119.280	1.988

TABLE 34.2
Time to Play Each Hole with Radar Golf

	1	2	3	4	5	6	7	8	9	Total Min	Hours
1	12.4	8.36	16.24	13.69	15.02	6.57	11.29	9.92	15.06	108.55	1.809
2	13.5	8.61	11.58	14.39	14.63	7.07	11.56	9.36	15.12	105.82	1.764
3	12.58	9.36	13.64	13.54	14.35	6.89	12.36	8.92	16.83	108.47	1.808
	12.827	8.777	13.820	13.873	14.667	6.843	11.737	9.400	15.670	107.613	1.794

TABLE 34.3
Time Saved with Radar Golf

1	2	3	4	5	6	7	8	9	Total Min	Hours
0.3	0.29	−3.2	1.87	0.7	−0.02	1.45	−0.03	−0.15	1.21	0.020
1.7	0.94	3.51	5.77	4.05	0.29	0.83	2.68	4.22	23.99	0.400
1.1	−1.13	1.03	1.45	1.01	0.08	3.26	1.44	1.56	9.8	0.163
1.033	0.033	0.447	3.030	1.920	0.117	1.847	1.363	1.455	11.667	0.194

fragile and susceptible, the author believes that the conclusion that RFID can save time on the golf course is valid, based on observations from the testing period.

DISCUSSION

The initial testing proved the manufacturer's and vendor's claims to be more or less valid. The system works as advertised, although not always quite as well as they might hope. Based on a limited set of data points and some observations, using RFID can help a golfer realize savings in time. In this study, the average was twelve minutes saved for every two hours (the average time for nine holes without RFID), but it would not be unreasonable to expect saving fifteen minutes for every two hours. The reduced cycle times in golf can be compared to reduced cycle times in an industrial setting. In golf, saving time yields little financial benefit, but in a warehouse, eliminating fifteen minutes of searching time for every two hours of work is substantial. Considering four of these two-hour periods (an eight-hour work day), a company could save an hour per day of labor. The time spent searching for products would be greatly reduced or eliminated due to the RFID system. Gaining an extra hour of labor per day from even just a few employees would make a significant difference in the long run. Obviously, the connection between a golf system and a warehouse system using RFID cannot be assumed to be equal and simple, but it is reasonable to expect some amount of labor reduction due to an RFID system. For example, Wal-Mart is estimated to save over one billion dollars in labor alone due to implementing RFID.

In addition to reducing cycle times (saving labor), RFID systems can benefit inventory control systems. In golf, one of the principal ideas behind the Radar

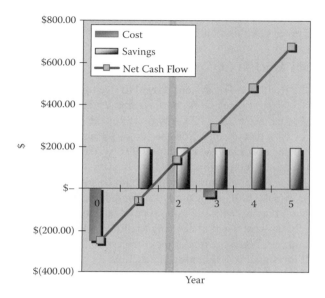

FIGURE 34.1 Cost analysis of Radar Golf™ system over five years.

Golf™ system is fewer lost balls. In economic terms, fewer lost balls means having to replace balls less frequently. In an industrial setting, the same idea applies: Fewer lost products or reducing the lost inventory means having to replace things less and less frequently, which translates to a decrease in costs. Figure 34.1 displays the yearly cash flows for a five-year period of operating the Radar Golf™ system, based on a few assumptions:

- Replacing a Titleist Pro V1 costs $4.83.
- An average of two balls is lost per round.
- An average of twenty rounds per year is played.
- The Radar Golf™ balls are replaced in year three for $39.95

The initial cost of the system at time zero is $249.95. Since two balls are lost per round and twenty rounds are played each year, approximately forty balls need to be replaced per year. This cost is eliminated due to RFID, yielding a yearly savings of $193.33, although the RFID balls are replaced in year three because they may still be lost in water.

The graph displays the trend toward positive cash flows at the end of the five-year period due to the decreased replacement costs for golf balls. The same principle could apply to inventory in any system. For example, one marine unit implemented RFID to better track its inventory. This unit was experiencing problems with lost inventory that was not truly lost but just could not be found. Using "more accurate and timely information, that one unit reduced its inventory value from $127 million to $70 million and its order backlog from 92,000 requests for supplies to 11,000" (Trebilcock 2006; online). Again, the golf example proves to be a small-scale but relevant example from which parallels to traditional RFID applications can be readily drawn. The savings from not replacing lost golf balls are minimal, but consider a high-dollar or high-value item. Would it be worth fifteen cents per item to accurately track a $10,000 piece of equipment?

CONCLUSION AND RECOMMENDATIONS

In conclusion, the Radar Golf™ system proved to live up to the vendor's claims, for the most part. The system does work, but it is not perfect and there could be some improvements. For example, the LCD only indicates the proximity to the ball based on the number of bars that are filled on the screen. What if two players are playing together and each has his or her own Radar Golf™ system? It seems that there could be some interference or confusion caused by readers receiving signals bouncing back off of both tags. One recommendation would be to use the traditional method already in place in golf. Balls are usually numbered one to four, and players make sure that if they are playing with the same type of ball, they use a different number. In this example, both players would be using the Radar Golf™ balls, but each would use a different number. When the reader picks up a signal, the display would indicate from which ball the signal is originating. This could increase the cost of the system, but given the capability of RFID systems, this type of identification would present little difficulty for a manufacturer.

More and more golf courses are becoming equipped with GPS, which is often placed in the golf cart. The screen displays the hole, the geographic features of the hole, and the location of the GPS unit on the course. The GPS system gives the golfer accurate information on distance to the pin, water, sand trap, etc. If balls with RFID tags become more popular, it would be interesting to see the two systems tied together. More readers on the course would be necessary to facilitate an RFID RTLS (Real Time Locator System), which could locate the ball, and in an idyllic world, display the position of the ball on the GPS screen of the course.

These suggestions are not possible with the current technology in the Radar Golf™ system, but that is not to say that it is without merit. As this chapter demonstrates, an RFID system in golf balls could help save golfers valuable time and reduce frustration. Additionally, fewer lost balls would lead to fewer expenses at the clubhouse on sleeves of new golf balls, saving the golfer money. These results are not earth-shattering or record-breaking as far as savings are concerned, but they do prove a valid point. The RadarGolf™ system is a small-scale but very practical example of the possible benefits to companies who implement RFID. The parallels discussed in this report are obvious enough: RFID, if it is affordable and used correctly, could save companies billions of dollars in a variety of ways.

REFERENCES

Radar Golf. (2004). [Online]. Available at http://www.radargolf.com [Accessed 25 April 2006].
Trebilcock, B. (2006). RFID on the front lines. *Modern Materials Handling*.January 2006. Accessed August 30, 2007, http://www.mmh.com/article/CA6299039.html.

ADDITIONAL REFERENCE

Pucket, D., and C. Patrick. (June 1998). Automatic identification in mining. *Mining Engineering* 50(6), 95–100.

35 Railroad Car Tracking by an RFID System to Organize Traffic Flow

Erick C. Jones, Mehmet Eren, James R. Gubbels

ABSTRACT

Existing railroad crossings impede the traffic flow during peak traveling times. Currently, signalization is used to close crossings, and many of these crossings do not have an overpass route crossing for traffic to go over the tracks. With no warning system before the actual crossing, traffic will take a route toward a crossing in which a train is passing through and traffic backups will result. This not only creates time delays for the drivers but also may create unwanted accidents. There have been many suggested warning systems to correct this issue. Radio frequency identification (RFID) is an emerging technology that has not really been considered. In comparison to other possible systems, RFID has the potential for more than just a warning system. It also can be used as a tool in supplying real-time information in a supply chain. In this study, we found that an RFID system is feasible and a definite possibility to solve the traffic backup problem as well as becoming a potential tracking system.

INTRODUCTION

Almost every driver who has come across a railroad crossing and has had to wait for the train to pass has probably wondered to themselves: what if they had been warned of the oncoming train? If they had known about it blocking their path, would they have gone another way? Since not every railroad crossing has an overpass to allow traffic to freely pass, traffic can get backed up during busy times, causing potential delays. With a warning system somewhere along their route, drivers will be able to take alternate routes and potentially save time.

Several issues can result from a traffic buildup, with safety being the largest. The Southwest Research Institute recently presented the Texas Department of Transportation TransGuide with a system design document that looked right into the heart of the subject matter. The system is called AWARD, or Advance Warning to Avoid Railroad Delays. This system would notify oncoming traffic of an oncoming train and that they would need to take an alternate route to avoid this train or expect a delay waiting for the train to pass. The system, however, does not use radio frequency identification (RFID) as a tool.

Radio frequency identification has been around for a long time, but until recently it has not really been utilized as well as it could potentially be. The *RFID Certification Textbook* (Clampitt and Jones 2006) not only talks about RFID in general, but it also gives insight as to where it could and already is used. An RFID system consists of a tag (either passive or active), a reader, an antenna, edgeware, middleware, and some sort of IT system. The RFID system can be set up to desired settings if the appropriate components are being used. In this particular case, the RFID system can be used not only to set up a warning system for oncoming traffic but also to tell what the train is carrying, where it has been, and even how fast the train is currently traveling. This is why it would be interesting to see whether an RFID system would potentially work in this particular situation. Information is invaluable to every component of a supply chain and RFID could potentially provide it readily and in real time.

Another aspect that needs some attention in this project is the traffic signalization and specifics regarding what can be done at an intersection or section of railroad. The book *Traffic Engineering* (Roess, Prassas, and McShane 2004) goes into these specifics. Although the specifics are not in great detail, they certainly are very helpful when tackling this particular task. The signalization times, design standards and regulations, and basic ideas to help create an ideal warning system are listed in this book.

When it comes to ideas on how to communicate with the drivers of the vehicles, the book *Intelligent Transportation Primer* (Institute of Transportation Engineers 2000) has a lot of good ideas. There is everything from a simply LCD display sign strategically located along the route to simply having the driver tune his or her radio to a particular radio station, which provides updates with the information drivers need. Although there are many options, RFID may limit which ones can be used and which ones cannot be used.

In the article "Safety Warning Based on Highway Sensor Networks" (Xing et al., 2005), the authors talk about a proposed system in which various sensors would be used to record and send information to inform drivers of what is happening ahead. They go on to say how and when a driver should be warned. Their proposed system is not limited to only railroad crossings but can be utilized for any traffic problem. The whole concept behind this system is not only safety but to also eliminate any unnecessary delays.

CURRENT PROBLEM

Railroad crossings cause delays in traffic. In most places, an approaching train cannot be seen from a far enough distance that drivers are able choose an alternative route. Instead, they head to the crossing and are forced to wait. In many situations, cars get trapped with no way out.

Freight trains generally have more cars and are much longer than passenger trains. Their speed tends to also be relatively low. They are the biggest part of the train network in the United States. Most freight trains have one hundred cars on average, and each car is 51.51 feet (15.70 meters). For safety purposes and certain laws, trains lower their speed when they get close to a crossing, which creates longer times for the cars to wait at the crossing. The average passing time through a crossing for freight trains is about 4.5 minutes. In some crossings this time can be up to 12 minutes due to weather and conditions of the trains.

Many railroad crossing accidents are caused by the cars and pedestrians who get to a closed railroad gate and do not obey the traffic signalization for various reasons. Nearly half of the total crossing accidents are caused at the railroad crossings that have warning devices like the stop signs, advance warning signs, and pavement markings. Many of these accidents occur when the lighting is poor and the people cannot see the train coming or they simply misjudge its location. Even with many new devices and methods being tested, accidents still regularly occur and a need for a new system is evident.

REASON FOR IMPROVEMENT

The objective of the proposed system is to provide a warning system to traffic and prevent unnecessary delays. Radio frequency identification can be used in place of other proposed systems, such as using radar sensors and underground sensors. These systems do not allow for flexibility and sometimes do not provide accurate information to the control center. Radar systems tend to be sensitive to the environment. Very cold weather or heavy rain can alter their functionality.

Radio frequency identification eliminates this issue and provides extended information to the control center. This allows the control center workers to organize the traffic flow more efficiently. In doing this, not only does it organize traffic, but it also eliminates the unwanted backups at the crossings.

Another possibility, besides being a tool in a warning system, is that RFID may be used for a nationwide railcar tracking network to follow the movement of any train equipped with an RFID system. There is also a possibility to use RFID for tracking passenger trains and for providing their expected arrivals and departures. This information can be updated on the Internet, so the people who are going to use the train will be informed by using the Web site.

Being able to track railcars in real time opens the door to better supply chain management. Information about the location of supplies or finished goods could potentially speed up the entire production process and provide better customer service. This concept is not limited to only railcar tracking. It also can be applied to trucks, airplanes, and any other means of transporting goods.

RFID tracking systems, like every system, has pluses and minuses. When all these are taken into consideration, radio frequency identification comes out on top as a great tool to solve the problem of traffic backups, considering its other potential uses.

STRATEGY

The proposed RFID system would use active tags to send and record any necessary information. Figure 35.1 shows an example of the proposed RFID system. The rest of the RFID system would need to be task-oriented and specific.

The reader, which reads the signal of the active tag mounted on the train, needs to send the tag data to the traffic signal control center. This task could be accomplished in a few different ways. First, a copper twisted pair cable line can be used to connect the reader to the control center. By using the cable, the cost would be more

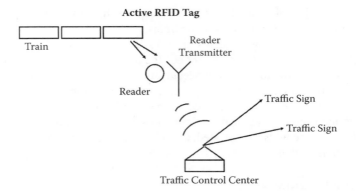

FIGURE 35.1   RFID warning system.

reasonable in the long term, in comparison to other methods. Also, communications cutoffs would be minimized due to the cable's reliability. However, this method requires setting the cable underground, which would take a lot of time, and it does not provide any flexibility for any kind of system changes if some conflict would arise.

Another possible method of communicating with the control center to consider is using a wireless technology. Bluetooth 802.11 technology is a wireless technology that connects the electronic devices wirelessly. Low required power can permit using sunlight as an energy source for this method, but because of current distance limitations of the Bluetooth 802.11 technology, it would not be suitable for this application.

This leads to another possibility, a global positioning system (GPS). The current space-based telecommunications environment is characterized by satellites orbiting the earth at various distances. The signals can be transmitted and received with GPS devices by using the satellites. This kind of communication is expensive and it requires the user to be registered in the network all the time. This potentially rules GPS out as an option for the final system design.

The final option is broadcasting the signal from the reader to the control center. A radio station uses a small portion of the radio spectrum for broadcasting audible data. Radio data systems use a portion of the unused spectrum called a *subcarrier* to transmit information. An RDS receiver receives the signal and then decodes it or translates the information to text or audio information. This makes broadcasting a feasible option for the proposed system.

METHODOLOGY

TESTING THE ACTIVE TAGS

The experiment consisted of an RF code mobile reader installed in an HP Palm Pilot, RF code active tags with a frequency of 303 MHz, and a car. The idea was to test the reader's ability to read while the tags were in motion, much like a train would be. If the tags read consistently, then the system would be feasible. The test consisted of

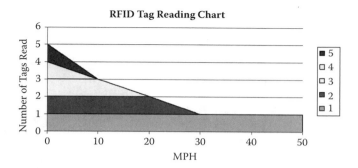

FIGURE 35.2 Tag readability graph.

five active tags placed on the car at select locations. Then the car would drive past the stationary reader and the data could be recorded for various speeds of the car.

TEST RESULTS

The car was tested at speeds of 0, 10, 20, 30, 40, and 50 miles per hour. Each time the reader would capture certain tags based upon their location and also the speed of the car. The tag placed on the nose of the car proved to be the only tag that read every single time. The tags placed on other locations read based on the speed. This can be seen in Figure 35.2. The tags were numbered 1 through 5 with Tag 1 being the tag on the nose of the car. Tags 2, 3, and 4 were placed on the car's windshield and Tag 5 was located inside the car. Since there was always one tag reading ever single test, it can be concluded that speed is not a factor and that using active tags in the system is feasible.

FINDING A PRACTICAL WAY TO SEND DATA TO THE CONTROL CENTER

As mentioned before, each RFID reader placed around the crossings needs to communicate with the traffic control center. This can be established by wire or wireless communication. In the case of placing the readers around the crossing and assuming the traffic control center is to be no more than four miles away from the reader location, a radio transmitter or radio modem would be a good solution. The fact that the readers are placed outside and they communicate with the control center in open environment with no line-of-sight requirement makes the process easier. The frequency of 458 MHz allows a communication range up to twenty kilometers in free space. A transmitter and receiver with that frequency are recommended to connect the RFID to the control center.

DETERMINING THE APPROPRIATE LAYOUT TO SET THE DEVICES

Since the connection from the reader to the control center can be made wirelessly, a certain tolerance for the distance of placing the readers must be considered. This tolerance allows the control center to organize the routes properly for specific cases.

FIGURE 35.3   Reader and crossing positions.

For the proposed system, RFID readers are to be placed about 1.5 miles away from the crossing, as illustrated in Figure 35.3.

SIMULATION RESULTS

To demonstrate a case regarding the wait time of the cars, SIMUL8 software is used. In the simulation,

> 4,000 units = one minute
> 66.667 units = one second
> Average passing time for a train = 5 minutes (default; Naik, personal communication)
> Train speed = thirty miles per hour (default)
> Average wait time for a car due to closed crossing = 3.8 min
> Average number of cars waiting = 73.6

From these results, it can be determined that each car loses 3.8 minutes depending on the time of the day, and there are approximately seventy-four cars involved this loss. Therefore, each time the crossing is closed, the average total time lost is 4.29 hours. This might not represent any variable that can be used in the calculations, but it makes sense if some of the drivers are on duty and using their working time.

Also, some accidents occur at railroad crossings. These accidents can be caused by signalization errors or drivers who do not obey the signalizations. An early warning system might be able to reduce these accidents. The idea is to divert traffic so that there are fewer backups. If traffic is diverted, there is less of a chance of an accident caused by a driver not being alert or being impatient.

Cost Analysis

The essential equipment for an RFID system is the reader and a tag. As mentioned earlier, the recommended tags need to be active, which are more expensive than passive tags. The range for active tags is $35 to $142. The tag that has the highest read range of one hundred feet is about $140. Each train requires one of these active tags.

Because of the environment, the reader has to be durable, but at the same time it should not be costly. There are many kinds of active readers in the market that cost anywhere between $1200 and $7000. The reader chosen for the proposed system costs $1480.

If we look at the average total cost for a crossing, including the other equipment required, the following are found:

- The reader: $1200–$7000
- Active tags: $35–$142
- Transmitter–receiver: $300–$800
- Electronic sign: $80–$600
- Labor: $700
- Average total for the proposed system: $4,100 (two readers, tags not included)
- Periodic cost: $350 each year (maintenance)
- Total cost for five years: $5850

If the system were to be implemented at every intersection, not including tag cost:

$$280,000 \text{ crossings} \times \$5850 = \$1,638,000,000$$

RECOMMENDATIONS

Radio frequency identification readers can be connected to up to four antennas. Taking advantage of this fact, instead of using a reader at each crossing, a reader antenna can be placed by itself at certain crossings. If two or three crossings are close enough to each other, only one reader would be necessary with the use of antennas. In this case the communication can be established via special antenna cables, which vary depending on the kind of the reader. This would in turn affect the cost analysis, depending on what gets implemented.

An alternative solution could be to connect the reader directly to the traffic signs. This system would bypass the control center. Each warning sign in this case needs to have a radio transmitter to get the information from the reader directly. Although a cheaper alternative, this solution would take away from some of the benefits that RFID could create.

CONCLUSION

An RFID-based system can replace existing sensor systems with affordable cost and more effectiveness. The proposed RFID system has the capability of sending more information about the train than basic data such as the train's speed. Prior to the exeperiment the main question had been, can the readers read tags in motion? The test results show that active tags are able to be read when they are at twice the expected speed of a passing train at an intersection. This makes the usage of RFID in a system a reality. A radio transmitter for communication between the reader and control center or directly to the electronic signs is the ideal recommendation for the proposed RFID system.

The primary concern of this study is saving time and avoiding backups. However, there is the definite possibility that the proposed system may help to prevent accidents. The total cost for the proposed system per crossing is $5,850. The system could be paid for in several ways depending on who is using it. As a warning system, if it can actually prevent accidents from happening or even save rescuers time, the potential savings begin to add up. In terms of the other possibilities, if a train can be tracked in real time, then supply chain management becomes faster. Also, RFID may be able to help increase passenger traffic on passenger trains if a person could check the train's status in real time. The possibilities are endless, and a warning system using RFID is only the beginning. The initial cost may be large, but the potential savings and usage help tip the scale back in the proposed system's favor.

REFERENCES

Clampitt, H. G., and E. C. Jones. (2006). *RFID certification textbook*. Houston, Tex.: PWD Group.

Institute of Transportation Engineers. (2000). *Intelligent transportation primer*. Library of Congress.

Roess, R. P., E. S. Prassas, and W. R. McShane. (2004). *Traffic engineering*. 2d ed. Pearson Prentice Hall.

Southwest Research Institute, Railroad delay advance warning system, 25/03/98, Texas Department of Transportation, TransGuide. http://www.transguide.dot.state.tx.us/mdi/ AWARD_VDD.pdf, accessed August 30, 2007.

Xing, K., M. Ding, X. Cheng, and S. Rotenstreich. Safety warning based on highway sensor networks. IEEE Communications Society. Vol. 4, pp. 2355–2361, 13–17 March, 2005.

ADDITIONAL REFERENCES

Coleman III, F., R. W. Eck, and E. R. Russell. Railroad-highway grade crossings, a look forward. Committee on Railroad-Highway Grade Crossings. http://onlinepubs.trb.org/ onlinepubs/millennium/00096.pdf, accessed August 30, 2007.

Siegemund, F., and C. Florkemeier. Interaction in pervasive computing settings using Bluetooth-enabled active tags and passive RFID technology together with mobile phones. Paper read at the IEEE International Conference on Pervasive Computing and Communications. http://xml.coverpages.org/Siegmund-BluetoothRFID.pdf, accessed August 30, 2007.

Singh, J. P., N. Bambos, B. Srinivasan, and D. Clawin. Wireless LAN performance under varied stress conditions in vehicular traffic scenarios. http://path.berkeley.edu/dsrc/ reading/stan.pdf, accessed August 30, 2007.

36 RFID Middleware and Web Service

Jerry Tie

ABSTRACT

Middleware, also known as RFID manager software, enables the rapid development and deployment of RFID systems. The middleware absorbs differences in various RFID tags from multiple suppliers and integrates that data, making it possible to build flexible and scalable RFID solutions. Because web services make it easier for business partners to electronically share real-time data and conduct transactions, the marriage of RFID and web services promises to be a productive union. In this work, we list some basic concepts of web services and middleware, comparing web services and EDI technology, return on investment (ROI) of implementing web services and how to measure the ROI, and list some of the recent development in the world of web services that are crucial and attempt to show incorporating them in RFID-centric networks.

INTRODUCTION

Web services are middleware based on the extensible markup language (XML), which is used primarily for business-to-business e-commerce applications. Typically, web services are reusable code that allows two or more Web-based applications to communicate with each other. The code can be used with older applications or build new ones. Web services can let Web-based applications from two different companies share data or let one company perform operations, like calculations and database searches, on another company's computer remotely over the Internet. Rather than granting a business partner direct access to its databases, a company can employ a web service that allows others to access a restricted part of its data or perform only specified operations or queries.

EDI VERSUS WEB SERVICE

Electronic data interchange (EDI) is both a technology and a service model for the trusted exchange by automated electronic means of business documentation between trading partners and between enterprises and government agencies. EDI technologies have received the benefit of twenty years of development and have reached maturity in terms of security, reliability, and accountability. In 2001, the size of the EDI market was about US\$3.7 billion, made up of services (US\$3.3 billion) and software (US\$360 million). It is a market growing at about 6 percent a year on average.

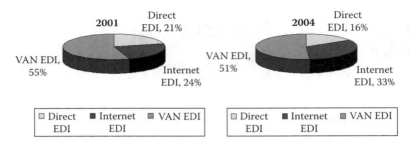

FIGURE 36.1 Predicted evolution of EDI traffic.

In the United States between 2001 and 2004, there was an increase in Internet EDI traffic, taking 33 percent share in 2004, and declines in both Value Added Network (VAN) Electronic Data Interchange (EDI) and direct EDI shares of traffic during the corresponding period.

The Internet EDI option is predicted to grow faster than direct EDI and VAN EDI. But in spite of the availability of Internet, VAN EDI and direct EDI still offer advantages when the traffic is made up of a large flow of files or documents of large files to a large number of locations or when a large investment in EDI systems has already been made.

The Internet effect has highlighted a number of constraints in the EDI model and technologies:

* The cost is based on the volume of the transactions and can carry a high surcharge.
* EDI depends on third-party connectivity (in the case of VAN EDI).
* EDI is difficult and expensive for smaller companies to use.

So, EDI is working but restricted to closed collaboration initiatives (direct and VAN). Users are face with high fees (VAN), rigid technology decisions, and systems that need to be sourced from suppliers.

Two innovations came about with the emergence of the Internet: encapsulation and real-time. Encapsulation of EDI data in XML was done using the Internet as an

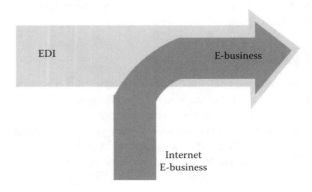

FIGURE 36.2 Convergence of EDI and E Business.

alternative transport mechanism. Real-time work extended the EDI standard in order to incorporate the support for real-time, rather than pure batch transactions. The consequence is a shift from EDI to Internet-based (XML) networks with real-time functionality, cheaper operational cost, wider reach to new customers, and a wider range of suppliers.

Web services, however, promise to simplify the electronic exchange of information. They can do this because they provide a single application program interface (API) that allows other applications on remote computers — even if those applications are written in different languages or on different operating systems — to exchange data. The data is exchanged in a XML format, usually transported using simple object access protocol (SOAP) and often transmitted over the Internet.

APPLICATIONS OF WEB SERVICES IN RFID

One of the expected applications of Web services is that they will make it easier for business partners to share real-time data about goods and conduct transactions electronically. So if a supplier ships twelve pallets of goods to a retail distribution center, the RFID tags on the pallets could be scanned automatically as they leave the supplier's loading dock. When the truck door is closed and sealed with an RFID bolt seal, scanning the bolt seal could trigger the supplier's internal system to send the retailer an advance shipping notice (ASN) automatically.

On the other end, the retailer's internal system would receive the ASN and, thanks to web services technology, be able to read it regardless of format used by the supplier's internal system. The retailer could use ASN to verify the accuracy of the shipment when it arrives and is unloaded from the truck. When the retailer scans the RFID tags on the twelve pallets arriving at the DC, the information can be compared with the information in the ASN. If the information matches up, the retailer's internal system could automatically confirm that the shipment arrived, and the supplier's system could generate and transmit an electronic invoice. The retailer can receive the invoice and start the payment process. If the information on the tags and the ASN do not match up, the web services interface could request that the supplier's internal system confirm the shipment. People would need to get involved only if the problem could not be resolved by these software agents.

WEB SERVICES RETURN ON INVESTMENT (SAMTANI AND SADHWANI, 2002)

Web services run through industry standard protocols and offer the potential of eliminating the need for proprietary hardware, software, and network protocols. Companies will be able to lower their investment costs greatly in terms of increased ROI by implementing web services.

There is no fixed model for calculating ROI of web services as of now, and the ROI in each company would greatly depend on how the technology is actually employed in solving software and business processes–related tasks. Any model used for calculating ROI should take into account the risks associated with the usage of web services.

Return on investment (ROI) is a key financial metric of the value of business investments and expenditures. It is a ratio of net benefits over costs expressed as a percentage. This formula can be expressed as:

ROI = [(Monetary Benefits (Tangible and Intangible) − Cost of Using Web

Services Technology)/Cost of Using Web Services Technology] × 100

As an example, the IT group within a company determines that there is a 10 percent increase in the automation of software development following the implementation of web services for an organization's IT project. Other data from the IT group reveal that each one percent increase in the automation of software development is equal to increased annual revenue of $25,000. Furthermore, it is known that the web services implementation will cost $75,000. For this example, ROI is calculated as follows:

[($250,000 − $75,00)/75,000] × 100 = 233%

That's $25,000 for each one percent increase, for a total of $250,000 for a 10 percent increase. This means that for every $1 invested in the web services implementation, the organization realized a net benefit of $2.33 in the form of increased revenue from the automation of software development.

There are two fundamental methodologies through which companies can conduct ROI analysis of a new technology such as web services. They are discounted cash flow analysis and payback period analysis. Before we look at both these methods, let's discuss some of the fundamental concepts behind them.

DIRECT AND INDIRECT MEASURES

Both the direct, cash flow–generating contributions of a new technology or project as well as the indirect measures valued by management should be considered when calculating the ROI.

- Discount rate or weighted average cost of capital (WACC): The discount rate, also known as the weighted average cost of capital (WACC), is the opportunity cost of capital, which is the expected rate of return that could be obtained from other projects of similar risk.
- Net present value (NPV): Net present value is the difference between the cost of an investment and the return on an investment measured in today's dollars. In other words, NPV calculations account for money's time value by discounting the future cash flow of the investment at some rate that varies with the risk of the investment. The NPV calculation determines the present value of the return and compares it to the initial investment. We calculate the present value as in the following formula:

Present Value = [Net Cash Flow for Year 1/(1 + Discount Rate)]

+ [Net Cash Flow for Year 2/(1 + Discount Rate)] × 2 + ...

+ [Net Cash Flow for Year N/(1 + discount rate)] × N

We calculate the net present value as follows:

$$NPV = \text{Initial Investment} + \text{Present Value}$$

For example, if web services technology costs $200,000 and will save (or generate return) of $50,000 per year for five years, there is a $50,000 net return on the investment. The NPV of the investment, however, is actually less than $50,000 due to time value of money.

INTERNAL RATE OF RETURN (IRR)

If there is an investment that requires and produces a number of cash flows over time, the internal rate of return is defined to be the discount rate that makes the net present value of those cash flows equal to zero. In other words, the discount rate that makes the project have a zero NPV is the IRR.

The IRR method of analyzing investment in a new technology or using a technology in a project allows a company to consider the time value of money. IRR enables you to find the interest rate that is equivalent to the dollar returns that are expected from the technology or project under consideration. Once a company knows the rate, it can compare it to the rates that it could earn by investing money in other technologies or projects or investments.

DISCOUNTED CASH FLOW ANALYSIS

In the discounted cash flow ROI analysis methodology, the expected cash flows relating to investments for a new technology or IT-related project spanning several years are discounted using an appropriate rate to determine an NPV and/or IRR. If the NPV is positive, then the project's present value exceeds its required cash outlay, and the project should be undertaken. When a project has a positive NPV, the NPV decreases as the discount rate used increases. Similarly, if the IRR is greater than the cost of capital for the company, then the project should be undertaken.

PAYBACK PERIOD ANALYSIS

In the payback period ROI analysis methodology, the period of time it takes for a new technology or IT-related project to yield enough returns to pay for the initial investment, or to break even, is considered.

ROI ANALYSIS BECOMING A NECESSITY

Return on investment for technology projects, both new and existing, is no longer a single-dimensional function of operational cost reduction. It has to account for multidimensional functions related to operational costs, changes in business activities, growth, efficiency, and productivity.

ROI analysis is gradually becoming a core requirement for the kickoff of any new project or use of new technology, as well as for measuring the success or failure of any existing project. A good ROI analysis can lead a new project or introduction of any technology to lower costs, improved business performance, and competitive advantage.

ROI and Web Services

A company should calculate the implementation and ongoing costs associated with web services, including software, hardware, system integration, and future production support expenses. These cost estimates should be carefully examined to determine the ROI for the proposed solution.

Whatever the underlying technology for which ROI is being calculated, there is always a set of business and personnel factors that have a great impact on it. We cannot stress enough the fact that technology alone will not produce the quantifiable results and benefits as projected in any ROI matrix or calculation. Several business factors, such as the speed of rollout and systems adoption rate, play a critical role in determining the final numbers.

Calculating ROI of Web Services

How do you measure the ROI of web services? Well, there is a right way and a wrong way to measure ROI. The wrong way is to measure the time representatives save in reduced paper work or in revenue the company saves by reducing the need for data entry. The right way is to measure the amount of reduction in operational and developmental costs. The ROI on web services comes from the increased operational efficiency and reduced costs that are achieved by streamlining and automating business processes, reduced application development cycle time, and increased reusability of applications in the form of services.

Factors to Be Included in ROI Calculation

The relevance and importance of each of these factors will greatly vary from company to company, application to application, and implementation to implementation. If all of these factors are considered together, however, you can get a pretty decent result from the ROI model used for web services. The factors we will look at are:

- Costs and expenses
- Technical benefits
- Business benefits

Costs and Expenses

These factors break down into the following elements:

- Hardware requirements
- Software requirements
- Training requirements
- Network bandwidth requirements
- Monitoring tools
- Operational costs and vendor consulting

Technical Benefits

These factors break down into the following elements:

- Software development automation
- Streamlining of middleware technology
- Usage of standards-based integration
- Integration with applications and business process management
- End of duplication of software code, leading to reusability

Business Benefits

These factors break down into the following elements:

- End-user productivity
- Participation in dynamic business
- Collaborative business activities
- Better and cheaper customer service

Other Benefits

There may be other direct and indirect benefits for the usage of web services, such as faster time to market, increased process efficiency, and increased efficiency through business process automation. These also have to be accounted for in the ROI calculation.

APPLYING THE ROI FORMULA

Now that we have discussed all the costs and expenses along with the technical and business benefits and risks of web services, it is time to apply the numbers to the ROI formula for web services. As presented earlier in the chapter, you can either choose the discount cash flow analysis or payback period analysis.

We will arrive at the numbers through a series of simple steps:

- Calculate the total cost of web services implementation. Sum up all the expenses.
- Determine the total savings resulting through the technical benefits listed for the usage of web services. Determine the increase in productivity, efficiency, and revenues through the business benefits of using web services. For this, traverse through points 12 to 16.
- Quantify the risks associated with the introduction and usage of web services.

The last step is to categorize the results from steps 1 through 4 under the following headings:

- Project costs including capital expenses, implementation labor, management and support, operations and contract expenses (A)
- Project benefits including net tangible benefits (B)
- Project risks quantified as potential expenses (C)

Using the formula from earlier in the article, we apply the figures as follows:

$$\text{ROI for Web Services} = (B - A - C)/(A+C) \times 100$$

The desired result for using web services is the following:

- Increased revenue
- Decreased cost
- Improved efficiency
- Higher profitability
- Shorter payback period
- Higher IRR
- Less risk

NOT THE ONLY MODEL

We should mention that this is not the only model that can or should be used to calculate and measure ROI. Each company or organization may use a different model to measure ROI, such as using a method that begins by identifying the desired economic results of web services strategy and then focuses on creating the activities necessary to achieve those results. Use the model that best fits your organization. Finally, be sure that ROI should account for phased implementation of web services technology.

XML AND PML LANGUAGE

Extensible markup language (XML) is a simple, very flexible text format derived from SGML (ISO 8879) (Agrawal et al., 1993). Originally designed to meet the challenges of large-scale electronic publishing, XML is also playing an increasingly important role in the exchange of a wide variety of data on the web and elsewhere.

The purpose of the core physical markup language (PML core) is to provide a standardized format for the exchange of data captured by the sensors in an RFID infrastructure; for example, RFID readers. This data is exchanged between the event manager and other applications. PML core provides a set of XML schemas that define the interchange format for the transmission of the data values captured.

The snippet below is a PML message sent by middleware corresponding to a TagsIn event, when a tagged item comes in view of an antenna. A similar event with a command TagOut is sent when a tagged item goes out of view of an antenna (Gupta and Srivastava, 2004).

```
<?xml version="1.0" encoding="UTF-8" standalone="yes"?>

<Sensor xmlns="urn:autoid:specification:interchange:
PMLCore:xml:schema:1">

<ns1:ID xmlns:ns1="urn:autoid:specification:universal:
Identifier:xml:schema:1">urn:epc:id:gid:1.1.3</ns1:ID>

<Observation>

<ns2:ID xmlns:ns2="urn:autoid:specification:universal:
Identifier:xml:schema:1">4</ns2:ID>
```

```
<DateTime>2006-04-07T12:35:12.758-07:00</DateTime>
<Command>TagsIn</Command>
<Tag>
<ns3:ID xmlns:ns3="urn:autoid:specification:universal:
Identifier:xml:schema:1"> urn:epc:id:gid:1.1.209 </ns3:ID>
</Tag>
</observation>
</Sensor>
```

The sensor element is the main interchange element for PML core messaging. This element is a composite element comprising the following subordinate elements:

- ID element
- One or more observation element

The sensor element captures sensor information. A sensor is any device that makes measurements and observations. Sensors in the EPC network are identified by an identifier code. The default identification scheme should be the EPC.

The ID element follows EPC as the default identification scheme to uniquely identify sensors and tags. The use of other identification scheme is supported but is not encouraged.

Each observation element contains data that are result of a measurement by a particular sensor. Each observation must be labeled with date and time. It can be equipped with a unique ID and a reference to the kind of command that was issued to make the observation. The observation element consists of the following:

- An optional ID element
- An optional command element
- Date/time element
- Zero or more data elements
- Zero or more tag elements

The date/time element captures the date and time when the observation was made. It is based on the (XSD) data type. The command element can be used to specify the command that was issued to trigger the observation. The tag element is a kind of observed value introduced with recognition of importance of automatic identifications in the EPC network. The tag represents any device that can be detected by a sensor. The tag element consists of the following elements:

- ID element
- Optional data element
- Zero or more sensor elements

All ID elements follow the EPC as the default identification scheme to uniquely identify sensors and tags.

Urn:epc:id:gid:1.1.3 is the unique ID of the reader and antenna encoded in the GID EPC scheme. A reader can have a unique EPC for each associated antennae, or if the EPC for each antennae is not specified, all antennae will inherit the reader EPC. The unique EPC for each reader-antenna is mapped to the location of the antenna and can be used to track the location of the tagged item as it is scanned by the antenna. Urn:epc:id:gid:1.1.209 is the unique EPC number of the tagged item read by the RFID represented in GID URI format (Gupta and Srivastava, 2004).

ADDITIONAL REFERENCES

Agrawal, R., T. Imielinski, and A. Swami. (1993). *Mining association rules between sets of items in large databases.* San Jose, CA: IBM Almaden Research Center. http://rakesh. agrawal-family.com/papers/sigmod93assoc.pdf, accessed August 30, 1007.
Anywhere Solutions, Inc. (2005). RFID anywhere overview. White paper. Sybase, Inc. http:// www.ianywhere.com/downloads/whitepapers/rfidanywhereoverview.pdf, accessed August 30, 2007.
Chawathe, S. S., V. Krishnamurthy, S. Ramachandran, and S. Sarma. Managing RFID data. in *Proceedings of the International Conference on Very Large Databases (VLDB),* Toronto, Canada.
Gonzalez, H., J. Han, X. Li, and D. Klabjan. Warehousing and analyzing massive RFID data sets. http://www.faculty.cs.uiuc.edu/~hanj/pdf/icde06_whrfid.pdf., accessed August 30, 2007.
Gupta, A. and Srivastava, M. Development Auto-ID Solutions using Sun Java System RFID Software, October 2004. http://java.sun.com/developer/technicalArticles/Ecommerce/ rfid/sjsrfid/RFID.html.
Papasliotis, I.-E. (Jan 2005). Mining for data and personal privacy: Reflections on an impasse, *Proceedings of the 4th International Symposium on Information and Communication Technologies,* Cape Town, South Africa.
Park, J. S., M.-S. Chen, and P. S. Yu. (1995). *An effective hash-based algorithm for Mining Association rules.* New York: IBM Thomas J. Watson Research Center.
Prabhu, B. S. and X. Su. WinRFID—A middleware for the enablement of radio frequency identification (RFID) based applications. University of California-Los Angeles, CA. http://www.wireless.ucla.edu/techreports2/UCLA-WinRFID.pdf, accessed August 30, 2007.
Samtani, G. and Sadhwani, D. Web Services Return on Investment: Working out what you're getting out of Web Services, Wednesday, August 14, 2002.
Wang, F., and P. Liu. (2005). *Temporal management of RFID data.* Proceedings of the 31st International Conference on Very Lare Databases, Industrial session: New data types and algorithms, 1128–1139. Princeton, N.J.: Siemens Corporate Research.

Part 6

RFID Related Software

INTRODUCTION

This section includes material to assist the reader with using software described in the handbook.

SECTION CONTENTS

37 Interactive RFID Training Simulator

The RFID Handbook Interactive Learning Simulator is an interactive computer program designed to assist the user in understanding basic RFID concepts. The simulator specifically incorporates animation and interactivity to reinforce the concepts of:

- What is RFID?
- How does RFID work?
- RFID components
- RFID applications

The "What is RFID?" material provides a high-level description of basic concepts of radio frequency identification. The "How does RFID work?" content describes the basic functioning and relationship of the various components that are necessary for an RFID system. The "RFID components" material provides more in-depth coverage of the individual RFID components. Lastly, the "RFID applications" sections describe how the various components work in actual use.

PROGRAM ORGANIZATION

The program is organized into three major sections. These sections may also be referred to as modes. The three modes are

- Instructional mode
- Training mode
- Evaluation mode

INSTRUCTIONAL MODE

In the instructional mode, the user is presented with computer-based instruction on the basic RFID subjects identified in the introduction section of this chapter. In each of these sections, users navigate through a series of screens that present information on specific subjects. In some cases, the subjects are sufficiently complex to require the user to go through a second layer before the actual instruction is presented. For example, in the RFID components section, users will have to select among RFID tags, RFID antennas, and RFID readers. Similarly, in the RFID applications section, users will be able to select among tollways, animal tracking, warehousing, and entertainment applications. In many of the instructional mode screens, particular subjects are presented in the form of animations. This approach helps reinforce specific RFID concepts.

RFID in Logistics: A Practical Introduction

Training Mode

The training mode is intended to be used after the user has completed the instructional mode. In the training mode, the user receives training through interactively working with:

- RFID tag components
- RFID tag selection
- RFID tag positioning
- RFID antenna positioning

In the RFID tag components section, users receive training on RFID tag components by identifying the various parts of an RFID tag. In the RFID tag selection section, users select the appropriate type of tag given specific system requirements. In the RFID tag positioning section, users are asked to position RFID tags in the correct locations on products and pallets. Lastly, in the RFID antenna positioning section, users determine where the most appropriate position is for RFID antennas in a variety of applications.

Evaluation Mode

The objective of the evaluation mode is to assess the user's level of basic RFID knowledge. Normally, the evaluation mode is intended to be used after both the instructional and training modes have been utilized. The evaluation mode consists of responding to a number of random questions by selecting one of four multiple choices. At the end of the session, the user is provided with the percentage of correct responses.

PROGRAM USE

When the simulator is launched, the user is first presented with a credits screen as illustrated in Figure 37.1.

The credits screen provides the user with the program version number. It also lists contact information in the event that users encounter difficulties or bugs with the program.

The credits screen is cleared by clicking on the ok button. The main menu then appears as illustrated in Figure 37.2.

The main menu screen provides users with a brief introduction to the use of the program. The three operating mode choices are presented at the bottom of the main menu screen. These include instructional, training, and evaluation modes. When the user clicks any of these buttons, the program will then launch that section. The main menu also has an exit button which allows the user to exit the program.

Instructional Mode

Under normal circumstances, the user will begin with the instructional mode. On entering the instructional mode, the user is presented with the screen illustrated in Figure 37.3.

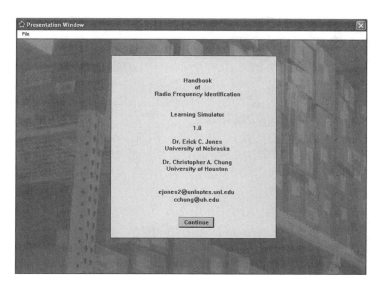

FIGURE 37.1 Credits screen.

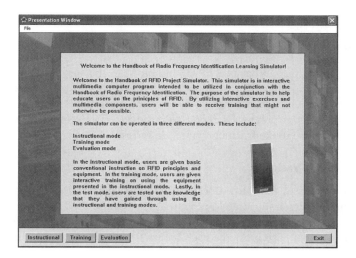

FIGURE 37.2 Main menu screen.

The instructional menu screen provides a brief description of the purpose of the instructional mode. On the menu bar at the bottom of the screen, users have the option of selecting instruction on the following topics:

- What is RFID?
- How does RFID work?
- RFID components
- RFID applications

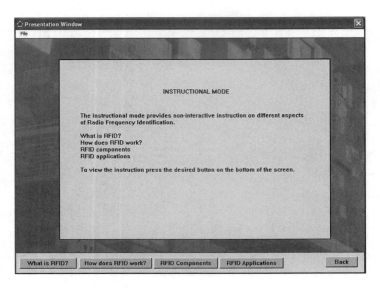

FIGURE 37.3 Instructional menu screen.

The user also has the option of pressing the back button, which returns the user to the main menu.

What Is RFID?

If the user presses the "What is RFID?" button from the instructional menu, the screen illustrated in Figure 37.4 will appear.

This screen provides a brief introduction to RFID. From this screen, the user can navigate to the next or previous screen on the subject. The user can also press the back button to return to the instructional mode screen.

How Does RFID Work?

When the user presses the "How does RFID work?" button from the instructional mode screen, the screen illustrated in Figure 37.5 appears.

From this screen, the user can navigate to the next or previous screen on the subject. The user can also press the back button to return to the instructional mode screen. A number of screens in this section are animated. This helps better explain how RFID technology works.

RFID Components

If the user presses the "RFID components" button from the instructional menu, the screen illustrated in Figure 37.6 appears. From this screen, users can elect to obtain more detailed information on:

- RFID tags
- RFID antennas
- RFID readers

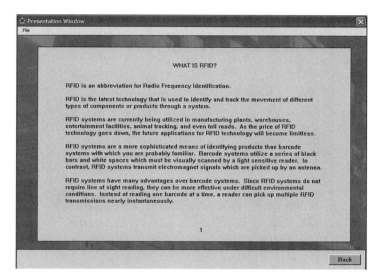

FIGURE 37.4 What is RFID? screen.

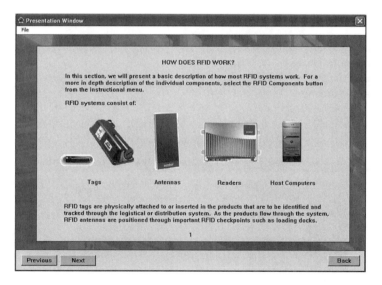

FIGURE 37.5 How does RFID work? screen.

The user can also press the back button to return to the instructional mode screen. If the user selects one of the three component buttons for further information, the program will present a series of screens on the particular component. As with many of the other instructional screens, the user may press the next and previous buttons to navigate within the information. To return to the RFID components menu, the user can press the back button.

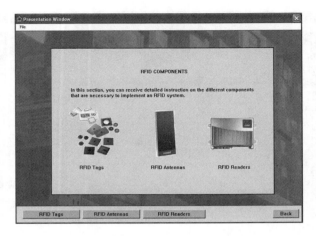

FIGURE 37.6   RFID components screen.

RFID Applications

When the user selects the "RFID applications" button from the instructional menu screen, the screen illustrated in Figure 37.7 appears. This screen allows users to further select information from the following applications:

- Tollway
- Animal tracking
- Warehousing
- Entertainment

The user can also press the back button to return to the instruction menu screen. If the user elects to receive additional instruction on one of these RFID application areas,

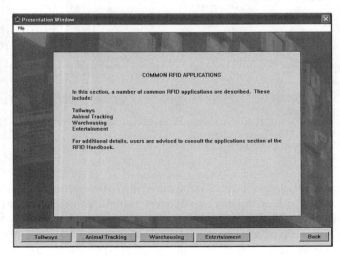

FIGURE 37.7   RFID applications.

he will enter the specific RFID application screen system. As with the previous instructional screens, the user can navigate to the next or previous screen on the subject. To return to the RFID application menu screen, the user can press the back button.

TRAINING MODE

As previously discussed, the training mode is intended to provide interactive training on the subjects covered in the instructional section of the simulator. For that reason, users should not attempt to use simulator in the training mode until all of the sections in the instructional mode have been completed.

The training mode is entered by pressing the training button from the main menu screen. When this is performed, the training mode menu screen illustrated in Figure 37.8 appears.

The training mode menu screen provides a brief description of the purpose of the training mode. The user then has the opportunity to select training on the following topics:

- RFID tag components
- RFID tag selection
- RFID tag placement
- RFID antenna placement

RFID Tag Components

If the user selects the "RFID tag components" button, a brief orientation screen will appear as illustrated in Figure 37.9.

Once the user has read the orientation screen, the program will then continue with the training and present the screen illustrated in Figure 37.10.

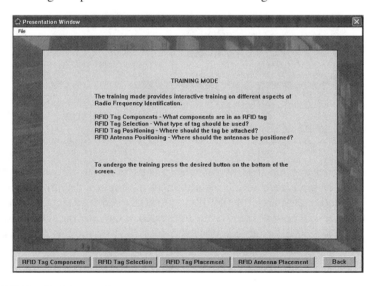

FIGURE 37.8   Training mode menu screen.

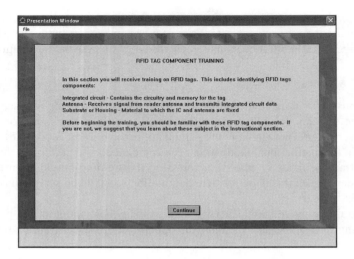

FIGURE 37.9   RFID tag component training orientation training screen.

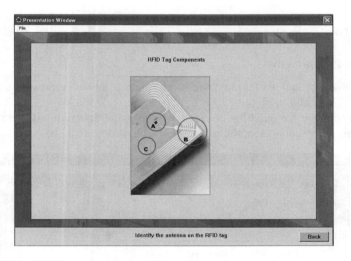

FIGURE 37.10   RFID tag component training screen.

In this screen and the next two screens, instructions are provided to the user at the bottom of the screen in the menu bar. In this figure, the program instructs the user to identify the part of the RFID tag that labels the antenna. In subsequent screens, the user will need to identify the integrated circuit and the substrate. In each of these three screens, the tag component is identified by moving the cursor over the component and clicking the mouse button. When the mouse button is clicked, another screen pops up informing the user as to whether their response was correct or incorrect. After identifying all of the parts, the user is automatically returned to the training mode menu screen.

RFID Tag Selection

When the user selects the "RFID tag selection" button, the RFID tag selection orientation screen, the screen first appears as illustrated in Figure 37.11.

When the user clears this screen, one of several tag selection screens will appear. In each of these screens, the user is presented with a question concerning which is the most appropriate type of tag to use in an application. Figure 37.12 illustrates a typical tag selection training screen.

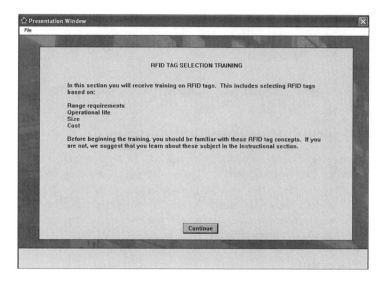

FIGURE 37.11   RFID tag selection training orientation screen.

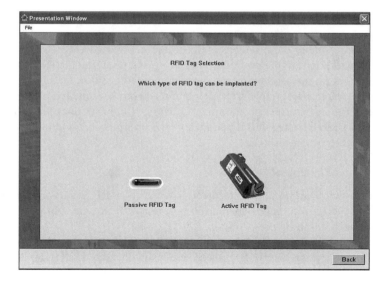

FIGURE 37.12   RFID tag selection training screen.

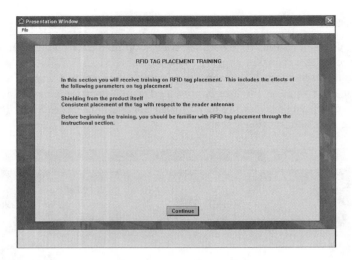

FIGURE 37.13   RFID tag placement training orientation screen.

In this case, the user is asked, "Which tag can be implanted?" The choices are between a passive tag and an active tag. The user responds to the question by clicking on the correct type of tag. After the user makes his selection, he is given feedback as to whether the selection is correct or incorrect. The program will then automatically proceed to the next question on tag selection. If the user wishes to return to the training menu, he may do so by pressing the back button at any time.

RFID Tag Placement

If the user selects the "RFID tag placement" from the training mode menu screen, the program presents a brief orientation screen discussing tag placement as illustrated in Figure 37.13.

When this screen is cleared, the program presents one of a number of screens on tag positioning. One of these screens is illustrated in Figure 37.14.

The user responds to the program by clicking and dragging the RFID tag to the correct position on the product. If the user attempts to position the tag in an incorrect position, the tag will return to its original place on the screen, and the user will be advised of their incorrect positioning of the tag. If the user does place the tag in the correct position, the tag will remain where the user placed it and the user will be informed of the correct response.

RFID Antenna Placement

As with the other training screens, if the user selects the "RFID antenna placement" button from the training mode menu, the program will present a brief orientation screen as illustrated in Figure 37.15.

After the orientation screen, the user will be asked to position a number of antennas in different applications. One of these screens is illustrated in Figure 37.16.

In this case, the program is instructing the user to position the left RFID reader antenna in the correct position to create a portal. The user responds by clicking and

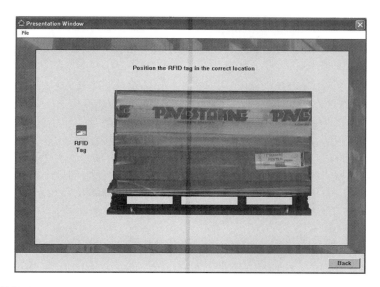

FIGURE 37.14   RFID tag placement training screen.

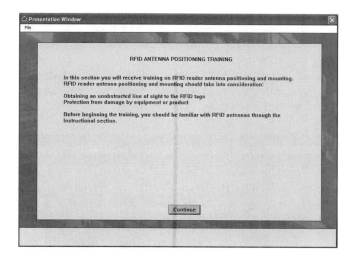

FIGURE 37.15   RFID antenna placement training orientation screen.

dragging the antenna to the correct position. If the user does not position the antenna in the correct position, the program will return the antenna to its original position on the screen and advise the user of the incorrect positioning. If the user does move the antenna in to the correct position, the left antenna will remain in the correct position and the user will be informed of the results. The program will then ask the user to position the right side antenna in the correct position in the portal. After the user has correctly positioned the current antenna or antennas, the program will proceed to the next antenna placement application.

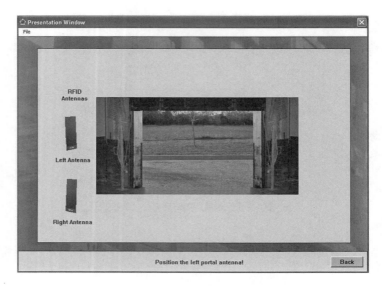

FIGURE 37.16   RFID antenna placement training screen.

A second antenna placement application screen is illustrated in Figure 37.17. In this case, we are attempting to determine the correct position to place an antenna in a tollway application. As with the previous antenna placement screen, the user needs to click and drag the antennas.

When all of the applications have been successfully completed, the program will return to the training menu. The user may also elect to return to the training menu at any time by pressing the back button.

FIGURE 37.17   Second RFID antenna placement training screen.

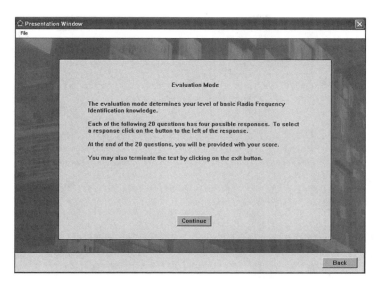

FIGURE 37.18   Evaluation mode orientation screen.

EVALUATION MODE

When the user has completed both the instructional and training modes of the simulator, it is time to evaluate the user's new RFID knowledge. The evaluation mode is
entered by pressing the evaluation button from the main menu. When this is performed, the user is presented with the evaluation mode orientation screen illustrated
in Figure 37.18.

The evaluation orientation screen describes the evaluation process. In this case,
the evaluation is based on a total of twenty questions pertaining to RFID and RFID
applications. When the user clears the evaluation mode orientation screen, the program begins the evaluation. Questions are presented in random order each time the
user is evaluated. Figure 37.19 illustrates a representative evaluation question.

The user responds to each question by clicking on the lettered box next to
the desired answer. The program then proceeds to the next question. Once all of the
questions have been presented, the program automatically scores all of the responses
and presents a scoring screen similar to that illustrated in Figure 37.20.

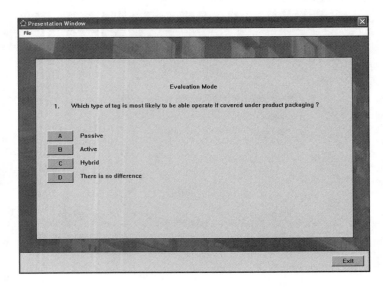

FIGURE 37.19   Representative evaluation mode question screen.

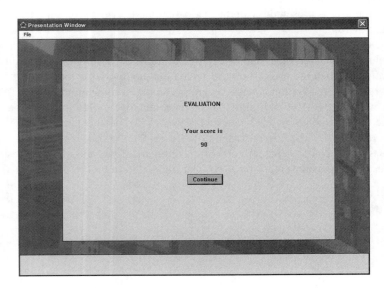

FIGURE 37.20   Evaluation mode score screen.

38 Developing Facility Layouts with BLOCPLAN for Windows

Charles E. Donaghey, Christopher A. Chung, Haiyan Kong

INTRODUCTION

In order to conduct effective RFID-integrated facility operations, not only must the RFID system be properly implemented, but the facility must also be properly laid out. Far too many organizations pay too little attention to effectively laying out their facilities. In some cases, organizations will simply adopt the facility layout used by previous tenants. In other cases, organizations have layouts because that is the way things have always been done. Both of these approaches are likely to result in less than optimal layouts. The subsequent implementation of RFID systems in less than optimal layouts can greatly limit the potential benefits of this technology.

One method of helping to improve the basic layout of any facility is to use computer-aided layout software. Software of this type helps organizations to rapidly assess a near infinite number of different possible layouts. In the case of an RFID-integrated facility, this means that layouts can be developed that take into account the adjacency compatibility of individual departments, the flow of product, and the acquisition of information through RFID systems.

The *RFID Handbook* includes a copy of the computer-aided facility layout software BLOCPLAN for reader use. The remainder of this chapter is devoted to assisting users with developing layouts with this software.

BLOCPLAN is a facility layout system that was developed in the Industrial Engineering Department of the University of Houston for PC systems.

The program generates and evaluates block-type layouts in response to user-supplied data. It is used only for single-story layouts. For multi-story or multi-facility analysis, BLOCPLAN (Multi-Story) should be utilized.

BLOCPLAN (Single-Story) uses a banding procedure to develop layouts. This permits a large range of possible layouts for a problem. For a nine-department problem, the number of possible layouts is close to 20 million, and for a fifteen-department layout there are more than 2.6×10^{13} possibilities. Each department will also be rectangular in shape. The structure that holds the departments will also be rectangular in shape, and the user may select the length/width ratio of the structure. There are several scoring procedures that may be used to evaluate a layout. The

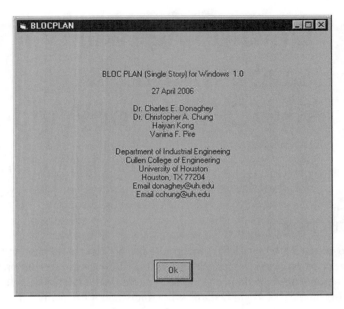

FIGURE 38.1   Credits screen for BLOCPLAN (Single-Story) for Windows.

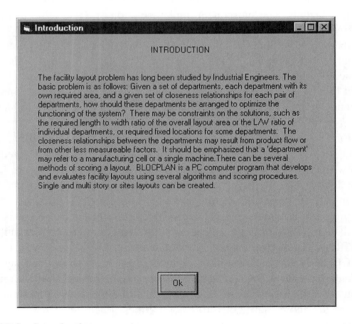

FIGURE 38.2   Introduction screen.

manual explains how the current version is used. BLOCPLAN-WIN is the name of the current Windows version of BLOCPLAN. Figure 38.1 and Figure 38.2 illustrate the opening screens where BLOCPLAN for Windows is launched.

BLOCPLAN MAIN MENU

The menu of choices in the main menu are shown in Figure 38.3. There are four menu options available to the user. The user clicks on the selection choice to cause execution of the proper option. The user may return to this main menu a number of times when working on a layout. It allows him to introduce a new problem, to modify data on the current problem, to examine single-story layouts, and to save the data on the current problem. The user can also exit from BLOCPLAN with the quit button. After a selection is made from the main menu, the user will be presented with new menus and information that pertain to the selection that has been made.

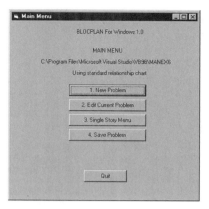

FIGURE 38.3   BLOCPLAN main menu selections.

NEW PROBLEM

If the user wants to introduce a new problem to BLOCPLAN, he uses main menu selection 1. The BLOCPLAN system will respond with the message illustrated in Figure 38.4.

Data Input

The system will first ask if a new problem is to be entered or if an existing problem is to be entered.

The user will click on his choice. If an existing problem choice is made, a list of the saved problems will be shown, and the user will click on the problem name, and the data concerning the saved problem will then be entered.

For a new problem, the screen shown in Figure 38.5 will be displayed. The user would then type in the name of each department (eight characters maximum) in the

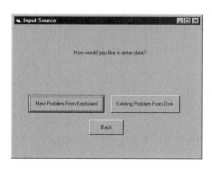

FIGURE 38.4   Problem source screen.

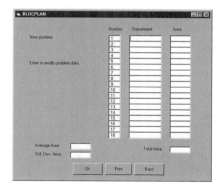

FIGURE 38.5   Department and area information screen.

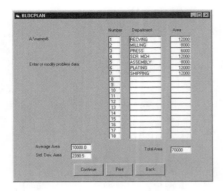

FIGURE 38.6 Example problem data.

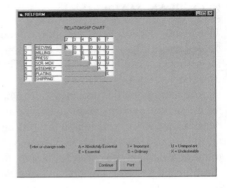

FIGURE 38.7 Relationship chart.

layout and the area of each. BLOCPLAN can handle a maximum of eighteen departments. When all departments and their areas have been entered, the user would click on the OK button.

Figure 38.6 shows this display for an example problem. The total area for all the departments, the average department area, and the standard deviation of the department areas are calculated by the system and displayed.

The user may change any data in the list of departments by simply changing the data on the screen. The cursor is placed on the screen in the proper position and the data are entered.

Relationship Data

BLOCPLAN uses the relationship codes described by Muther (1973) in *Systematic Layout Planning*. Figure 38.7 shows the screen display after the user has furnished the codes for each of the' departmental relationships. This chart is called a *relationship chart*. The bottom of the screen gives a legend of acceptable codes and their definitions. An "A" indicates that it is absolutely essential that the two departments having this code be adjacent. An "E" indicates that it is essential, etc. The "X" code indicates that it is undesirable. BLOCPLAN uses adjacencies for one type of layout analysis. Figure 38.8 gives the numeric worth of each of these codes. The user can change any of these values

The numeric worth of each department is found by summing all of the numeric codes associated with the department. For example, the press department has two "O"s and four "U"s associated it. The BLOCPAN

FIGURE 38.8 Numeric values for relationship codes.

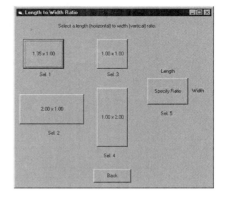

FIGURE 38.9   Numeric worth of each department.

FIGURE 38.10   Screen presented during selection of length/width ratio for layout.

numeric worth of these associations would be 2. $(2 \times 1) + (4 \times 0)$. These scores for all departments in the example are shown in Figure 38.9.

Length/Width Ratio

The ratio of the length to the width of the facility that will contain the departments can be selected by the user. Figure 38.10 shows the display that is presented that permits this selection. There are five selections given. Selections 1, 2, 3, and 4 are standard L/W ratios. Selection 1 is 1.35/1, selection 2 is 2/1, selection 3 is 1/1, and selection 4 is 1/2. The user can choose any of these by clicking on the desired selection. If the user chooses selection 5, he will be asked for the desired L/W ratio. The user inputs the desired values of the L/W ratio of the facility that will contain the departments. Once the desired ratio has been selected, BLOCPLAN will calculate the length and the width of the facility outline so that it will have the required area to contain the departments in the problem.

Material Handling Information

BLOCPLAN allows the inclusion of material handling information in the layout analysis. This information is furnished by listing moves per time period between departments into a from/to matrix. Figure 38.11 shows the format for giving material handling information. The user can change or enter new values into the matrix when it is on the screen.

Edit Current Problem Data

When the user selects main menu option 2, it indicates that he/she wishes to change the data that pertain to the current problem. The edit/adjust data menu will then be presented that contains the options that are available. Figure 38.12 shows this menu. A user may examine and/or change the department areas, the relationship information, the length-to-width ratio of the layout area, and the material handling information. He can also ask for a relationship chart that is based solely on material handling information, and he can restore the original relationship chart when needed.

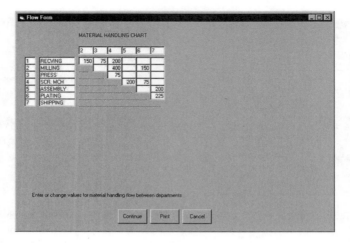

FIGURE 38.11   Screen display for entering material handling information.

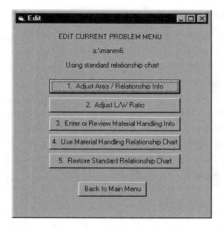

FIGURE 38.12   Edit/adjust data menu.

Adjust Area/Relationship Data

Selection 1 from the edit/adjust data menu allows the user to change the area and/or the relationship information currently in effect. After this option is selected, the display previously shown appears, and the user is allowed to change any of the department areas. This is followed by the screen displays previously illustrated in Figure 38.5, Figure 38.6, and Figure 38.7 allowing for changes in the relationship data and the score vectors. The user is then returned to the main menu previously illustrated in Figure 38.3. It should be noted that all layouts that have been previously saved may now be reviewed under this new set of area and/or relationship parameters.

Adjust Length/Width Ratio

A new L/W ratio may be established by selecting menu selection 2 from the edit/adjust data menu. When this choice is made, the display of Figure 38.10 is brought to the screen, and the user selects the desired L/W ratio. All layouts currently saved can then be reviewed with the new ratio. After the new ratio is selected, the system will return to the edit/adjust data menu.

Review Material Handling Information

The material handling information can be reviewed and changed, if desired, by using selection 3 from the edit/adjust data menu. After the selection is entered, the screen display of Figure 38.12 appears, and the user can inspect and/or modify any of the data. If there is currently no material handling information in the problem, it can be added with this selection. In this case, the screen display would have material handling data, and the user would use the "C" option to indicate that a change is required.

Use Material Handling Relationship Chart

This selection will cause BLOCPLAN to develop an alternate REL chart that is based entirely on material handling. The example problem had material handling information that is summarized in Figure 38.11. This figure shows the greatest amount of product flow is between departments 2 and 4 (four hundred unit loads). BLOCPLAN will divide this maximum flow figure by 5.0 to develop product flow values for REL codes "A" through "U". 400/5 = 80. Thus, any product flow between 321 and 400 will be assigned an "A" code. A product flow from 241 to 320 will be assigned an "E"; from 161 to 240 an "I"; from 81 to 160 an "O"; and zero to 80 a "U" code. When edit/adjust menu selection 4 is made, BLOCPLAN will make these calculations and assignments depending upon the current material handling information that has been given. It will then display the resulting REL chart. Figure 38.13 shows the REL chart that resulted for the example problem with the material handling information that is summarized in Figure 38.9 and Figure 38.10. This REL chart is now the one that BLOCPLAN will use for its scoring calculations. Any layout scores or tables that are developed will use this REL chart. The user may alter any of the REL codes that are in effect by using menu selection 1 in the edit/adjust data menu (adjust REL info). If the material handling information is changed by using selection 4 in the edit/adjust data menu, the user will have to then call on this selection again (selection 4) to cause the REL chart to reflect these changes. A message on the screen will indicate whether the material handling information is used to develop layouts.

Restore Relationship Chart

The REL chart that the user entered when creating the problem, along with any modifications that have been made to it, may be recalled from memory to replace a material handling REL chart by using this menu selection. The chart is recalled from disk and displayed on the screen. It will then be the chart that is used for scoring any layouts. The relationship chart that was used will be displayed for any tables or

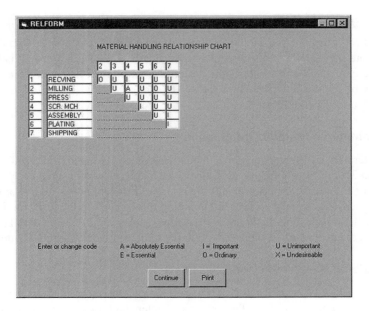

FIGURE 38.13   Material handling relationship chart.

layouts created. This REL chart is based entirely on the material handling information that is summarized in Figure 38.11. The user may make any changes desired.

Return to Main Menu

When this selection is made, the user transfers from the edit/adjust data menu and the menu shown in Figure 38.3 is placed on the screen.

SINGLE-STORY LAYOUT MENU

When the user decides that the layout is to be developed with all departments on the same level, he uses selection 3 from the main menu. After this selection is made the single-story layout menu will be displayed. This menu is shown in Figure 38.14.

Manually Insert Departments

The user can manually position departments in the layout by using this option. When it is evoked the screen display in Figure 38.15 appears.

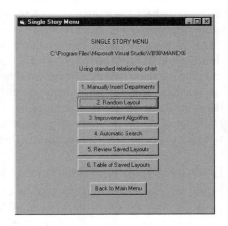

FIGURE 38.14   Single-story layout menu.

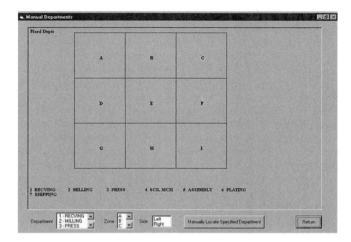

FIGURE 38.15   Screen display for manually locating departments.

BLOCPLAN provides nine zones for locating departments. These zones are designated A through I, and they are arranged in three tiers of three zones each, as can be seen in Figure 38.15. Each zone can be further divided into its left side or its right side. The layout outline for manual insertion is drawn according to the current L/W ratio. The display in Figure 38.16 is for a L/W ratio of 1/1. Suppose the user wants to place Dept. 1 (RECVING) in the upper left-hand side of the layout, and Dept. 7 (SHIPPING) next to it on the right. He would click on the RECVING choice in the department scroll at the bottom of the screen, Zone A for the zone choice, and specify that it is to be on the left side of the zone. He would then click on the "Manually Locate Specified Department" option. He would do the same thing for RECVING, placing it in Zone A on the right side. After placing these two departments, he would use the "Return" option. These two departments would be placed in those two locations for the rest of the analysis.

Adjacency Scoring

The layout display shown in Figure 38.16 is the format that BLOCPLAN uses to display a single-story layout that it has created. It has a layout score of .44 assigned to it. BLOCPLAN uses an adjacency criterion to develop this score. The departments that share a boundary in the layout are examined and the numeric values of each of their relationship codes are added. The total value of all the normalized adjacency score for the layout of Figure 38.16 is 19/43 = .44 (rounded to two places). A 1.0 would be the highest possible adjacency score.

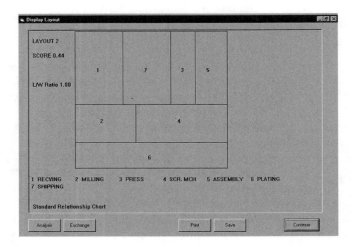

FIGURE 38.16   Screen display after departments 1 and 7 have been manually located.

Saving Layouts

Figure 38.16 also shows the options that are available to a user when a layout is created. These options are: "Save" to save a layout, "Analysis" to have a layout analysis performed, "Exchange" to exchange departments in the layout, and the "Print" option to get a hard copy of the layout being displayed. BLOCPLAN is capable of saving twenty layouts in the saved layout area in memory. When the user uses the save option, the layout currently on the screen will be stored. If there are currently twenty layouts stored when this option is used, the twentieth layout in memory will be replaced with the one currently on the screen.

Layout Analysis

A layout analysis for the layout currently on the screen will be performed when the Analysis button is pressed. There are several screen displays of information that will be displayed when this option is used. Figure 38.17 shows the first display in this sequence. The centroid of each department, along with the department's length, width, and its length/width ratio in the current layout, is given in the display.

FIGURE 38.17   Department information for layout.

The next display given in the layout analysis uses the relationship chart that was given. The adjacencies that have been satisfied in the layout are displayed in uppercase letters, and the adjacencies that have not been satisfied are displayed in lowercase.

The next screen display of information resulting from the layout analysis is shown in Figure 38.18. This screen displays the results of using another criterion

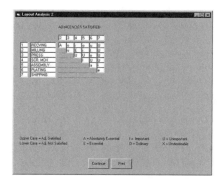

FIGURE 38.18 Adjacencies that have been satisfied for layout.

to evaluate a layout. The adjacency criterion that was discussed previously only involved departments that shared boundaries. The criterion that will now be used sums the products of the distance between each pair of departments and their corresponding relationship score. For example, from Figure 38.17 it can be seen that the centroid of department 1 is (41.78, 192.76). The centroid for department 4 is (185.20, 83.15.). Therefore, the distance between these departments, assuming rectilinear travel, is $|41.78 - 185.20| + |192.76 - 83.15|$ = 253.03 feet. The relationship matrix shows that departments 1 and 4 have an "I" relationship code, which has been assigned an equivalent score of two. Therefore, the product of the distance and the relationship score for these two departments is 253.03 × 2 = 506.06. These values are calculated and summed for each pair of departments in the layout. This sum is shown at the bottom of the screen, 7984.00. The better layouts should have a lower Rel-Dist score. BLOCPLAN normalizes this score.

BLOCPLAN will create a vector of these twenty-one distance values from the lowest to the highest. This vector **D** would be

$$\mathbf{D} = d_1, d_2, ..., d_{21}$$

A vector of the twenty-one numeric values of the relationship chart for the problem is also developed. This vector **S** would also go from the lowest to the highest.

$$\mathbf{S} = s_1, s_2, ..., s_{21}$$

A lower bound for the Rel-Dist score for the layout would be

$$\text{Lower Bound} = d_{21}s_1 + d_{20}s_2 + ... + d_1s_{21}$$

The highest value in the **D** vector is multiplied by the lowest value in the **S** vector, the next highest **D** value by the next lowest **S** value, etc. An upper bound for Rel-Dist score can be found by:

$$\text{Upper Bound} = d_1s_1 + d_2s_2 + ... + d_{21}s_{21}$$

It should be noted that these bounds may not be obtainable for a given layout, and they will vary for each layout for a given set of departments. The lower and upper bounds for the Rel-Dist score for the layout is shown on the bottom of the display in Figure 38.19. The actual distances are used in the D vector instead of the entries in the distance matrix. The entries in the distance matrix have been divided by 10 and integerized to control the size of the matrix for the display. The normalized score for

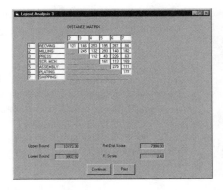

FIGURE 38.19   Screen display giving distances between departments for current layout.

this criterion is also shown in Figure 38.19. It is labeled R-SCORE and is calculated by:

R-Score = 1 − (Rel-Dist Score − Lower Bound)/(Upper Bound − Lower Bound)

For the example, the value is 1−(7,984.00 − 3,802.92)/(10,773.38 −3,802.92) or 0.40. An R-SCORE of 1.0 would be a perfect layout, and a value of zero would be the worst possible.

The last display that results from the Analysis option is shown in Figure 38.20. This is the product flow screen. If there has been no product information given for a problem, this display will not be generated. This is still another display that results from a layout analysis. It is suppressed if no product data has been supplied.

The matrix in Figure 38.20 shows the product of the unit loads and the distance between them for each pair of departments. The value has been divided by 1000 and rounded to the closest integer to control the size of the matrix. The divisor in this normalization is problem dependent. At the bottom of the screen, the total unit load distance value for the problem is shown. In this example the value is 264,853.63

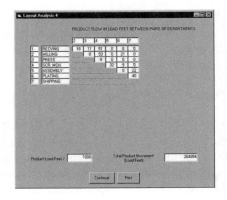

FIGURE 38.20   Screen display giving product flow information.

unit load feet. The two departments having the greatest contribution to this total are departments 2 and 4, which have approximately 53,000 unit load feet of product flow between them. This display will stay on the screen until the user depresses the "Continue" button. The layout that has just been analyzed with a layout analysis will then be returned.

Exchanging Departments

When a layout is displayed, the exchange button appears at the bottom of the screen. This allows the user to switch the locations of any two departments in the layout. When the exchanged button is pressed, the screen in Figure 38.21 appears. In this figure, the departments 7 and 1 have been entered for exchange. The exchange is executed by pressing the "Make Change" button. The layout is then updated with the change, and the resulting layout of Figure 38.22 would be displayed. This process is repeated for each set of departments to be exchanged. The total number of changes is the combinations of departments taken two at a time. For example, for seven departments the formula for the combinations is

$$= 7!/(5! \ 2!) = 21 \text{ combinations}$$

The system will make the necessary adjustments in the positioning of the other departments so that the exchange can take place. The layout will be scored and the user has the same options available that were given with a new layout.

Improvement Algorithm

The improvement algorithm operates on a layout that has been previously saved. It then successively interchanges each pair of departments in that layout and scores each resulting layout. For example, for a seven-department problem it will first automatically interchange departments 1 and 2. It will then interchange departments 1

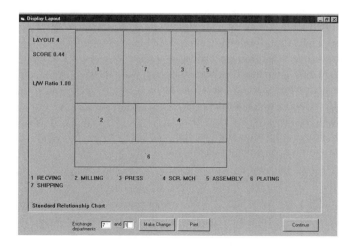

FIGURE 38.21   Exchanging departments.

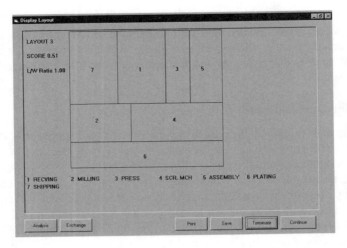

FIGURE 38.22 Layout when departments 1 and 7 have been exchanged.

and 3. The successive interchanges will be 1,2, 1,3, 1,4, ..., 1,7, 2,3, 2,4, ..., 2,7, ..., 6,7. Table 38.1 shows the total number of possible interchanges for a seven-department problem to be twenty-one. Each iteration would give a different layout with the two departments switched. The layout presented in each iteration can be saved and examined, or the process can be terminated with a "T" option.

Automatic Search

The "Automatic Search" option that is available in BLOCPLAN-WIN (Single-Story, menu selection 4) greatly simplifies this task. The procedures that an experienced BLOCPLAN user used in obtaining a good layout were studied and these procedures have been incorporated into BLOCPLAN-WIN. When this option is selected, the first prompt that the system will give asks for the number of layouts desired. The user responds with a number between 1 and 20. The layouts that result from the automatic search procedure will be stored in memory in the common saved

TABLE 38.1

Number of Iterations for Exchange/ Improvement Algorithm

Departments	Iterations
2	1
3	3
4	6
5	10
6	15
7	21
8	28
9	36
10	45
11	55
12	66
13	78
14	84
15	105
16	120
17	136
18	153

layout area. The next screen display will afford the user with the opportunity to manually locate some departments before the automatic search begins. The system

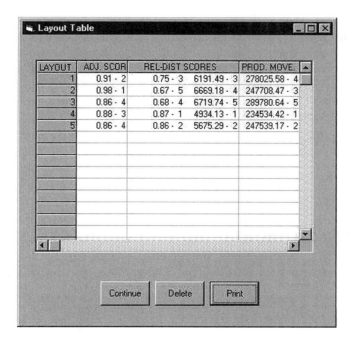

FIGURE 38.23   Resulting table of layouts after the automatic search procedure was used.

starts with an initial random seed layout and operates on this layout until it is not able to improve it. This final layout is saved. Another seed layout is created and the process is continued until the total desired layouts have been created. A table showing the information on the saved layouts is then displayed. The display in Figure 38.23 shows this table for an example problem. Five layouts have been saved, and the Adjacency Score, the Normalized and Un-Normalized Rel-Dist Score, and the Total Product Movement are shown for each of them. The rankings of each of these scores are also shown. Layout 2 has the highest adjacency score of .98, and Layout 4 has the best Rel-Dist score of .87 and the lowest Product Movement of 234,534 load feet.

Review Saved Layouts

Layouts that have previously been saved can be reviewed by using menu selection 5. When this selection is made, the screen will be cleared and the user will be asked for the starting point for the review. The user would give the number of the first layout from the previous figure that he would like to review. The specified layout will be displayed, and the user can have a layout analysis performed (option "A"), departments can be exchanged (option "E"), or he can terminate the remainder of the reviews (option "T").

Save Problem Data

In order to save a problem in memory so that it will be available at a later time, the BLOCPLAN user will select the save option in the main menu. The screen that will appear after this selection is made is used to specify the layout name. The user types the file name that is to be assigned to the problem. Any layouts or partitions that exist with the problem will be stored in memory with the problem and will be available when the problem is again loaded. As mentioned earlier, there are two problem files. These are named MANEX6 (Manual Example) and EX12, a problem with twelve departments.

Quit (Main Menu Selection)

An exit from BLOCPLAN is made when "Quit" is selected.

REFERENCE

Muther, R. (1973). *Systematic layout planning.* Cahners Books, p. 5-4.

ADDITIONAL REFERENCES

Donaghey, C. E., and H. Kong. (1999). *MHAND users manual.* University of Houston, Texas. http://www.egr.uh.edu/courses/INDE/inde6385/atbtts/tele/mhwin/manual.doc, accessed August 30, 2007.
Pire, V. F. (1989). An automated multistory layout system. Master's thesis, University of Houston,Texas.

Part 7

Other RFID Material

INTRODUCTION

In this section, we have included material that does not directly fall into any of the categories covered in parts 1 through 6.

SECTION CONTENTS

Radio Frequency Theory
End of Book Questions
Lecture Notes
References

39 Radio Frequency Theory

Any sufficiently advanced technology is indistinguishable from magic.

—**Arthur C. Clarke, English physicist and science fiction author (1917–),**
"Profiles of the Future," 1961 (Clarke's third law)

INTRODUCTION

The quote above describes how remarkable the phenomenon of information passing through the air has become. Some suggest that if were a previous generation, many people would consider RFID technologies "black magic." Currently, some opponents to RFID technologies have demonized the technology in such a way that others have described the technologies as "Big Brother," the realization of the 1997 movie *Gattaca*, in which people are stamped at birth, or, in the extreme, the end of the world as we know it. This chapter describes some of the physics of RFID technologies and hopefully will distinguish it from magic.

This section explores some of the basics of radio frequency (RF) communication, including wave propagation and electromagnetic field theory. It is useful when beginning any RFID project to understand the underlying physical properties which allow the system to operate. We have included four sections. Section 1 is common terms, section 2 is radio wave theory, section 3 is antenna theory, and section 4 is modulation. These terms are common to most introductory electrical engineering courses. We have adapted the technical description for these terms from an industry text (Clampitt 2006) that relates the theory for RFID application use and a commonly used introductory academic text (Stallings 2007).

COMMON TERMS

- Cycle: A cycle is a complete crest to crest or peak to peak movement of a wave.
- Period: A period is the time taken to complete a cycle. It is given the physics code T and measured in seconds.
- Frequency: Frequency is the number cycles in a second. It is given the physics code f and measured in Hertz (Hz). $f = 1/T$.
- Bandwidth: Bandwidth describes a range of frequencies. It equals the difference between the highest frequency and the lowest frequency of the device or application. There is a direct correlation between bandwidth and data carrying capacity. All radio frequency components are classified as being either wideband or narrowband. Bandwidth is often measured by looking

at standing wave ratio (SWR). We introduce an SWR reader in the design section of the text.

- Resistance: Resistance is the ease with which electrons flow through a conductor. Current flow is proportional to the applied voltage and inversely proportional to the value of the resistance. This is Ohm's law, and this type of resistance often is referred to as *ohmic*. It applies whether the voltage is direct current from a battery or alternating current. It is given the physics code *r* and measured in ohms.

- Reactance: Reactance is the form of resistance sensitive to the frequency. Two kinds exist: inductive and capacitive.

- Impedance: Impedance is a measure of the total opposition to current flow in an alternating current circuit, made up of two components: resistance and reactance. It is given the physics code Z and usually is represented in complex notation as $Z = R + iX$, where R is the resistance and X is the reactance.

- Decibels: Loss and gain are two fundamental concepts that affect all devices. If the signal coming out is bigger than the signal going in, the device exhibits gain. It is also known as an amplifier. If a signal coming into the device is ten times bigger than the signal going out, the gain is said to be 10 dB. The signals leaving a transmitter can be 1 billion times bigger than those going in, so the multiplication and division of these numbers can be difficult. Engineers have come up with a mathematical means to express these big numbers with a convenient notation known as *decibels*. Based on logarithms to the base 10, there are only three things you need to know:
  - Logs are always a ratio of two values and governed by the formula 10 × log (power out/power in)
  - Multiplication is the addition of logs, whereas division is the subtraction of logs. To work with this concept there are really only two dB conversions you must memorize:
    +3 dB means two times bigger
    +10 dB means ten times bigger
  - There are two corollaries you must also know (if the numbers get smaller, the dBs are negative):
    −3 dB means half the size
    −10 dB means one tenth the size
  Example:
    – If a signal experiences a gain of 8,000 times, what is the gain in dB?
    – Break up the gains into simpler figures 10 × 10 × 10 × 2 × 2 × 2
    – Replace the multiplication by the dB factors by the addition of dB
    – 8,000 = 10 db + 10 db + 10 db + 3 db + 3 db+ 3 db = 39 dB
    – If the number does not break down into factors of 2 and 10, then interpolate and you will be close enough.

- dBm: Notation represents a power level in decibels relative to one milliwatt. dBW notation represents the power level in decibels relative to 1 watt.

- dB: Notation is useful for representing gain or attenuation, where the output will always be related to the level of the input signal to a device. The input signal is either amplified or diminished by a certain factor, which is represented in decibels. Using dB notation simplifies power calculations in communications systems. For example, if the measured power at the input of an amplifier is 5 dBm and the gain of the amplifier is 20 dB, then the measured output power after the amplifier should be 5 dBm + 20 dB = 25 dBm.

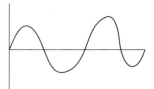

FIGURE 39.1 Signal.

- Signals: Signals fall into two categories: analog or digital. In either case, the electrical energy contained in the signal is important. An analog signal varies over time. A sine wave is an example of an analog signal. Whether it is current flowing in the air or over a wire, a sine wave signal varies in a controlled manner. The intensity of a signal is characterized by a measure of power in watts. Typically the antenna's power is referred to as ERP, or effective radiated power in watts.

- Digital signals: Commonly used in logic-processing machines such as computers. Unlike the analog signal, which varies over time, the digital signal varies in its transition from zero to one. For practical purposes, the digital signal has two states that it uses to create a pattern to represent information. It is important to understand that digital signals do not carry information over the air. Only analog signals carry information over the air. When an analog signal is used for this purpose it is referred to as a *carrier*. The process of combining digital information onto the carrier is called modulation. When a transmitter is always on, it is referred to as a *continuous wave* (CW) RF signal. When the transmitter is rapidly turned on and off, the signal is known as a *pulsed* RF signal.

- Signal phase: For alternating voltages or currents, the relative timing of the signal is important. If the two waveforms A and B represent an airborne signal arriving at an antenna in a different phase at the same time, you can dramatically affect the resultant signal. In one extreme, the waves may be added constructively to not only double the positive signal but also to double the negative signal for a total increase of +6 db, or a quadrupling of the original signal. In the other extreme, the waves may cancel each other out completely. Impedance matching, VSWR, and return-loss are factors that deal with phase shifts. Directional properties of antennas take advantage of combining signals from several directions being in phase in the desired direction and out of phase in the undesired direction.

UNITS AND PREFIXES

Common prefixes associated with RF and RFID technology are listed in Table 39.1.

WAVE THEORY

This section describes theoretical concepts that are related to RFID technology. We describe the basics of radio wave creation.

TABLE 39.1

Typical Prefixes

Prefix	Definition	Example	Notation
Milli	1/1000th	100 mHz	0.1 Hz
Kilo	1,000	10 kHz	10,000 Hz
Mega	1,000,000	915 MHz	915,000,000 Hz
Giga	1,000,000,000	2.45 GHz	2,450,000,000 Hz

ELECTROMAGNETIC WAVES

Radio frequency identification is a way to store and retrieve data through electromagnetic transmission to an RF-compatible electronic circuit. Radio transmissions use electromagnetic waves that are created when alternating currents flow through an antenna.

Electric fields are created by differences in voltage. The relationship can be described as the higher the voltage, the stronger the field. Magnetic fields are created when current flows. Also, it is known that the greater the current, the stronger the magnetic field. The difference is that electric fields exist even when current is not flowing, whereas magnetic fields exist only when current is flowing. When the two exist together, they are commonly referred to as *electromagnetic fields* (EMF).

RADIO WAVES

Radio waves are created by changing an electric current in a wire to create a magnetic field. This can be demonstrated by placing a compass very close to a wire with current flowing in it. The magnetic field will exert a force on the compass to move it from magnetic north. An electrical voltage between two points generates a field of electric force in the space between the two points. The electric field can be detected by the appropriate equipment almost as easily as the magnetic field.

Magnetic and electric fields exist because energy is temporarily transferred from the electrical circuit to the surrounding space, termed *electromagnetic radiation*. These fields of stored energy can be shown through calculation to reach an infinite distance in all directions where the concentration of energy per unit volume is always decreasing as distance from the source increases.

Mathematically, electromagnetic radiation, or EM radiation, is a combination cross-product of changing electric and magnetic fields perpendicular to each other, moving through space as a wave, effectively transporting energy and momentum. EM radiation is quantized as particles called *photons*. Any electric charge that accelerates, or any changing magnetic field, produces electromagnetic radiation. Electromagnetic information about the charge travels at the speed of light. When any wire (or other conducting object such as an antenna) conducts alternating current, EM radiation is propagated at the same frequency as the electric current. Depending on the circumstances, it may behave as waves or as particles. As a wave, it is defined by three factors:

- Velocity (the speed of light)
- Wavelength and frequency
- Amplitude

When considered particles, known as photons, each with an energy related to the frequency of the wave given by Planck's relation $E = h\nu$, where E is the energy of the photon, $h = 6.626 \times 10^{-34}$, J is Planck's constant, and ν is the frequency of the wave. EM radiation is classified by wavelength into electrical energy, radio, microwave, infrared, light, ultraviolet, X-rays, and gamma rays, all of which are part of the electromagnetic spectrum. The behavior of EM radiation depends on its wavelength. When EM radiation interacts with single atoms and molecules, its behavior depends on the amount of energy per quantum it carries. One rule is always obeyed, regardless of the circumstances. EM radiation in a vacuum always travels at the speed of light, relative to the observer, regardless of the observer's velocity. (This observation led to Albert Einstein's development of the theory of special relativity.) Radio waves used in the air interface for RFID carry information by varying amplitude and by varying frequency within a frequency band and, in the case of EPC standards for North America, must change, or hop, frequencies at a predetermined rate. When EM radiation impinges upon a conductor, it couples to the conductor, travels along it, and induces an electric current on the surface of that conductor. This effect, known as the *skin effect*, is used in antennas.

FREQUENCY SPECTRUM

The power and variance of the electromagnetic field is vital to radio's successful operation. An important concept that helps define EMF is frequency. Imagine an ocean with a series of regular waves. The frequency simply describes the number of waves per second that crest at a static point of measurement. Engineers describe this as the oscillations or cycles per second. The term *wavelength* describes the distance between the crest of one wave and the next. Hence, wavelength and frequency are related: the higher the frequency, the shorter the wavelength.

A simple analogy that explains the concept of frequency would be the following demonstration: Tie a long rope to a door handle and hold the free end. Moving it up and then down slowly will generate a single big wave; more rapid motion will generate a series of smaller waves. The length of the rope is constant; as you create more waves, you increase the frequency while making them shorter in wavelength.

Frequency is commonly known as *Hertz* in honor of radio pioneer, Heinrich Hertz. One cycle per second is 1 Hertz. The frequency of oscillations ranges from 1 Hertz to infinity, and this entire range is known as the *frequency spectrum.*

The frequency spectrum is viewed as an important resource and is coordinated with legal and political governing bodies generating a plethora of complicated rules and regulations. RFID has specific frequencies for its use. Currently they are:

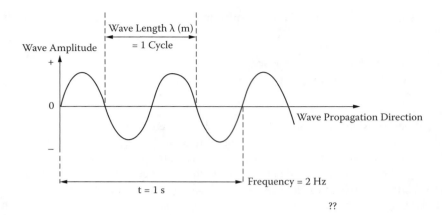

FIGURE 39.2   Frequency.

- LF (low frequency): 125 kHz, 134 kHz
- HF (high frequency): 13.56 MHz
- UHF (ultra high frequency): 868 MHz — Europe; 902 to 928 MHz — United States
- Microwave: 2.45 GHz

MEASURING POWER LOSS

To measure the amount of power loss in the system, RF engineers use the standing wave ratio (SWR), a measurement of match that represents how efficiently an RF signal is transferred from one point to another. The better the match, the less RF energy is wasted on leakage. Some key SWR values are shown in Table 39.2.

SWR may be understood by considering the voltage at various points along a cable driving a poorly matched antenna. A mismatched antenna reflects some of the incident power back toward the transmitter. Because this reflected wave is traveling in the opposite direction of the incident wave, there will be some points along the cable where the two waves are in phase and other points where the waves are out of phase (assuming a sufficiently long cable). If one could attach an RF voltmeter at these two points, the two voltages could be measured; their ratio would be the

TABLE 39.2
SWR Values

SWR	Meaning
1.0:1	Perfect match, no waste, cannot be realized in practice
1.4:1	Excellent match, very little leaking, often a design goal
2.0:1	Good match, acceptable amount of waste
10:1	Poor match, unacceptable performance

SWR. Identical results would be obtained by measuring the electrical current with an ammeter. By convention, this ratio is calculated with the higher voltage or current in the numerator so the SWR is one or greater.

To better understand the calculation, look at the following examples. Consider a 5-volt source driving a 50-ohm cable with a short on the end such that all of the power is reflected back to the source. Because the reflected wave is as big as the incident wave, there will be points at which the two voltages cancel completely and other places at which the voltage will be 10 volts. The ratio of 10/0 is infinity, the worst SWR possible. If, instead, the load were equal to 50 ohms, the characteristic impedance of the feed line, no power would be reflected and only a constant incident wave would appear at all points along the cable. The ratio of any two voltages would therefore be 1, the best SWR possible. The SWR for terminations between these two extremes may be calculated by considering the interaction of the reflected wave with the incident wave to determine the minimum and maximum voltages. The SWR is simply the ratio of the resistance of the termination and the characteristic impedance of the line. For example, a 75-ohm load will give an SWR of 1.5 when used to terminate a 50-ohm cable since 75/50 = 1.5. A 25-ohm resistor will give an SWR of 2 since 50/25 = 2.

The goal is that the impedance for the entire chain from the radio to the antenna is the same, and the standard for RFID radio equipment is an impedance of 50 ohms. If any piece of the chain fails to show 50-ohm impedance because of bad connections, incorrect antenna length, etc, the maximum power will not be transferred along the path. Instead, part or the entire wave is reflected back down the line. The amount of the wave reflected back depends on the level of the mismatch.

Smith Chart

One common way to visualize the voltage standing wave ration (VSWR) is a polar plot called the *Smith chart*. From this plot, the VSWR value, the return-loss, and the impedance for the different frequencies can be derived. Therefore, it is an important tool for understanding RF transmission paths and antennas.

The Smith chart appeared in 1939 as a graphical method of simplifying the complex math of impedance (recall that calculations involving variables of the form $[Z = R + jX]$ are needed to describe the characteristics of resistance and reactance). Although the Smith chart can look imposing, it is nothing more than a special type of two-dimensional graph, much as polar and semilog and log-log scales constitute special types of two-dimensional graphs.

Typically, the RF engineer wants to know what reflection coefficient would result from connecting a particular load impedance to a system having a given characteristic impedance. A Smith chart visually ties together the return-loss, the reflection coefficient, and VSWR for specified impedance. These are vital steps in creating an efficient air interface with an optimum RF uplink and downlink to support communications between the tag and the reader in an RFID system. End-users need not worry about these issues as long as they comply with the manufacturer's recommendations for coaxial cable, connectors, antenna, and installation practices.

RETURN-LOSS

Match and power transfer are vital to the performance of
RF circuits. Return-loss augments the concept of VSWR
(RL), which is measured in decibels and has widespread
use in the specification of signal cabling. Because it is
a measure of the reflected energy of the signal, there is a
direct correlation from VSWR to return-loss. Table 39.3
shows a few key conversion points.

TABLE 39.3
VSWR

VSWR	Return-Loss (dB)
1.0:1	Infinite
1.01: 1	46.1
1.4:1	15.6
2.0:1	9.5
10:1	1.7
Infinite	0

Consider a simple cable assembly: there will be a
mismatch when the connector is mated with the cable.
There may also be an impedance mismatch caused by
nicks or cuts in a cable. For RFID, the frequencies used by
electronic product code (EPC) tags are sufficiently high
to be subject to additional problems, including material
properties and the dimensions of the cable or connector, which plays an important
role in determining the impedance match or mismatch. A high value of return-loss
denotes better quality of the system under test (or device under test). For example, a
cable with a return-loss of 21 db is better than a similar cable with a return-loss of 14
db, and so on. If 50 percent of the signal is absorbed by the antenna and 50 percent is
reflected back, we say that the return-loss is −3 dB. A very good antenna might have
a value of −10 dB (90 percent absorbed and 10 percent reflected). Return-loss can be
calculated using the following equation, where Z_i is internal impedance:

$$RL = 20 \log \left| \left(Z_i - 100\Omega \right) / \left(Z_i + 100\Omega \right) \right|$$

COUPLING

Inductive and *capacitive coupling* are important terms for RFID due to the fact that
different tags use one of the two methods for transferring electromagnetic energy.
Inductive coupling is the transfer of the electromagnetic energy from one circuit to
another as a result of mutual inductance between the circuits. Inductive coupling is
created by matching the impedance of a transmitter or a receiver to an antenna to
guarantee maximum power transfer. The tendency of a change in the current of one
coil to affect the current and voltage in a second coil is called *mutual inductance.*

Capacitive coupling is the transfer of electromagnetic energy from one circuit
to another through capacitance, which is the ability of a surface to store electrical
energy. Capacitance is the measure of the electrical storage capacity between circuits. Capacitive coupling favors the transfer of higher-frequency signal components,
whereas inductive coupling favors lower frequency elements.

POLARIZATION

Polarization is a process or state in which electromagnetic waves exhibit different
properties in different directions. Electromagnetic waves are composed of two plane
waves. In most cases the amplitude and phase of the plane waves define the character
of the polarization of the product wave.

A plane electromagnetic wave is said to be linearly polarized. The transverse electric field wave is accompanied by a magnetic field wave.

If the radio wave is composed of two plane waves of equal amplitude but differing in phase by 90°, then the light is said to be circularly polarized. If you could see the tip of the electric field vector, it would appear to be moving in a circle as it approached you. If, while looking at the source, the electric vector of the radiation coming toward you appears to be rotating clockwise, the light is said to be right-circularly polarized. The electric field vector makes one complete revolution as the radiation advances one wavelength toward you. Elliptically polarized waves consist of two perpendicular waves of unequal amplitude that differ in phase by 90°.

ANTENNAS

Electromagnetic waves are sent airborne or received through an antenna. The antenna is a critical component designed to radiate energy out into free space and/or collect radio energy from space. It is important to recognize that in doing this job the antenna is the most important part of the radio system — without it, the system dies. In most systems, the antenna is common to both the transmitter and the receiver; therefore, any change in the antenna affects both transmission and reception.

The antenna changes radio energy from the transmission line into radiated energy and vice versa. The antenna's operation can be broken down into two fundamental modes of wireless communications:

- Near-field communications, aka close proximity electromagnetic, aka inductive coupling
- Far-field communications, aka propagating electromagnetic waves

Far-field radiation is distinguished by the fact that the intensity is inversely proportional to the square of the distance. In reality, obstructions, absorption, and interference make the loss more severe. On the other hand, near-field radiation intensity is inversely proportional to the cube of the distance in the region that is less then one sixth of the wavelength from a simple loop antenna. (For additional reference, see Lee, 1993).

In either mode, antennas have optimal sizes that relate to the frequency of the signal. Basically, the higher frequencies require smaller antennas because of shorter wavelengths. This becomes an even greater factor with RFID, as tags are typically designed so their geometric lengths are a fraction of the operational frequency's wavelength; for example, quarter wavelengths. Deviating from the optimum geometry "detunes" the antenna. It likely will still function, but at a non-optimized range. As an analogy, consider a portable radio. With its antenna mast fully extended, it likely will have optimum reception. With the mast retracted, the radio still will have reception, but not at the level previously achieved unless it is close enough to the broadcast tower.

Because the sizes of wavelengths vary, radio signals propagate differently through free space. Some are well suited to short ranges, while others are good for transmitting over long distances. Typically, the higher the frequency, the shorter the distance the signal will travel. The strength of the radio signal diminishes rapidly as it moves away from the transmitter antenna.

STANDARD ANTENNA IMPEDANCE

What is the meaning of 50 ohms? It is the standard RF transmission line impedance. To understand this concept, we will think of the conductor and the devices as part of a garden hose wherein the RF signal is represented by the water inside. If an RF signal is to move through a conductor and then enter a device efficiently, there will be minimal leakage of signal. The size of the garden hose must be specified to allow the optimum amount of water to flow through the system. If interconnection is to work and for water to flow in the garden hose system, the diameter and connection type must be standardized. Like the garden hose, some of the water leaks out, depending on the quality of the connection and how well the male and female couplings are matched. To standardize for RF, engineers have specified the size of the hose to carry the RF energy. When talking about an RF resistance, we use impedance. Remember, this is the measurement of resistance for the signal to move through a conductor (aka garden hose size). The standard for RF is 50 ohms of resistance. Impedance is dictated by the size of the conductor, the material, and the temperature.

IMPEDANCE MATCHING

Impedance matching is the lifeblood of RF circuit design. From the end-user's point of view, all the work for impedance matching is necessary to create an interoperable RFID system. It can be shown mathematically that any source of power — for instance, an RFID reader — will deliver its maximum possible power output when the impedance of the load is equal to the internal impedance of that source. The ideal condition provides only 50 percent efficiency because half the power is consumed in the source. This can be explained through the following example.

Choose a value for ESource = 100 volts and RSource = 50 ohms. These will be held constant.

Use the formulas:

$$I = E_S / (R_S + R_L)$$

$$W_S = I^2 * R_S$$

$$W_L = I^2 * R_L$$

Recalculate I, W_S, and W_L for each occurrence of R_L to generate the graph below. The intersection of the source and load lines proves the power to the load given by W_L is maximum when $R_L = R_S$.

From the graph we can infer that:

- Maximum power to load occurs when the source impedance = load impedance. At this condition the source expels the same amount of power in heat as it delivers to the load.
- As load impedance increases the power converted to heat from the source decreases.

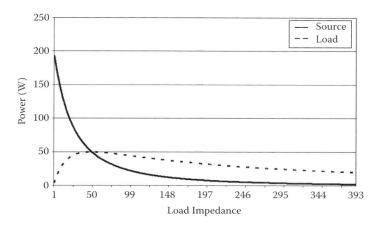

FIGURE 39.3   Effects of impedance matching.

TUNING

For each particular radio transmission there will be a certain number of cycles completed each second. As defined earlier, the frequency of the transmission is the most basic property of radio waves. Tuning of a transmitter or receiver is achieved by changing frequency. Frequency is the property that controls the pitch of a sound wave, the color of a light wave, and the band and channel of a radio signal.

It is because of differences in frequencies that many radio signals can coexist in the airborne atmosphere and be sorted out by the radio's receiver circuitry. Differences of propagation are also largely related to the frequency and governed by the equation:

$$\lambda = c/f$$

Where:

      λ = the wavelength
      c = the speed of light
      f = the frequency (cycles per second).

The wavelength for RFID in the United States is typically 13½ inches or .33 meters.

In a vacuum, c is equal to the speed of light (299 793 077 m/s), but radio waves are slower when passing through other materials; hence, the wavelengths are shorter. This is of great importance when designing antennas.

Isolation of frequencies is based on the fact that there are electrical components and circuits that respond differently to signals of different frequencies. In some cases, the selective response to a small range of frequencies can increase the signal rejected outside the pass band by a factor of up to one hundred times compared to the desired signal. A series of these circuits may be arranged to work on the signal one after the other as the signal flows through the transmitter or receiver and can be used to provide the desired rejection of the unwanted signal to effectively make the desired signal clearly recognized.

Tuning may be performed by using a variable capacitor or inductor to change the resonant frequency of the circuit. This has the effect of electronically changing the center frequency of bandwidth for desired signals.

RANGE AND PATH LOSS

Another key consideration is the issue of read range. It is important to realize that read range is a nonlinear relationship and is governed by the concept of path loss. As radio waves propagate in free space, power falls off as the square of range for the radio waves (E field) and the fourth power for the magnetic field (which is used in the 13.56-MHz RFID applications). For a doubling of range, power reaching a receiver antenna is reduced by a factor of four. Path loss reduces signal strength. In free space, this effect is caused by the spreading of the radio waves as they propagate. It can be calculated thusly:

$$L = 20 \log_{10} \left(4\pi D/\lambda \right) \tag{1}$$

Where:
> D = the distance between receiver and transmitter
> c = speed of light (3×108 m/s)
> f = frequency (Hz)
> L = path loss

The equation above describes line-of-sight or free space propagation path loss. This is the best case for a radio wave as free space reduces the signal the least amount as it travels. On the other hand, earthbound radio wave travel faces such obstructions as buildings, trees, and mountains, among other things. Propagation losses indoors can be significantly higher because of building walls, glass, steel, and concrete. RFID may be even higher due to the combination of attenuation by walls and ceilings, conveyors, pallets, and blockage caused by forklift trucks, equipment, furniture, and even people. For example, a 2 by 4 wood stud wall with sheetrock on both sides results in about 6 dB loss per wall. Experience has shown that line-of-sight propagation holds only for about the first twenty feet. Beyond twenty feet, indoor propagation losses increase at up to 40 dB per one hundred feet in dense warehouses, office environments, or factories. This is a rule of thumb and will have to be measured for each use case. Actual propagation losses will vary significantly depending on building construction and layout.

MODULATION

Signal Propagation

Once an RF signal is airborne, it is attenuated by something called *free space loss*. The further away a receiver is from the transmitter, the smaller the signal is because of free space loss. Power density is a measure of an airborne signal's strength and always is used in the RF world. Imagine a square that is one meter on each side. The amount of RF energy passing through the square is watts per square meter or power density. This tells us how powerful the RF energy is at this location.

Just about everything an RF signal encounters while airborne changes it in some way. These changes tend to do one of three things to the signal: they make it smaller, change its direction, or create heat. Many of the attenuators the RF signal encounters are such common items as the air we breathe, rain, glass, steel, brick, wood, and even foliage. We may model these things as passive devices with some insertion loss. Insertion loss exhibited by nature is called *absorption*, because it absorbs the RF signal. Absorption explains how your microwave oven works. An RF signal is radiated inside the oven at a frequency that water likes to absorb. As the RF signal encounters water, it gets smaller, translating its energy into heat. This is the basis for microwave cooking.

Not everything encountered by the RF wave absorbs its energy. Some things have the ability to change the signal's direction, called *reflection*. The amount of reflection depends on the frequency of the signal and the material of the object. As a rule, RF waves tend to reflect off the objects at the same angle at which they encountered them.

Modulation

The purpose of radio signaling is to carry some intelligent information. If a steady RF carrier is transmitted such that the frequency and amplitude do not change, then no information is transmitted beyond the fact that a radio wave is present in the environment. To encode intelligence onto the radio wave, some property needs to change. A method of varying some property to encode intelligence is called *modulation*. It is the lifeblood of carrying information within radio waves.

Radio waves make this easy to do because there are only two primary properties that may be changed.

- Adjusting the power of the signal over time: Known as *amplitude modulation*, you witness this by listening to an AM station.
- Adjusting the frequency of the signal over time: Known as *frequency modulation*, you witness this by listening to an FM station.

Of course, there also exist a number of permutations and combinations of these two basic properties to increase the amount of information carried within the radio wave. A modulated signal does not exist as a separate entity from the radio wave. The signal must be processed through a detector or demodulator circuit to reverse the process and extract the information that was encoded. Some basic forms of modulation techniques are

- Amplitude modulation
- Frequency modulation
- Phase modulation
- Pulse modulation

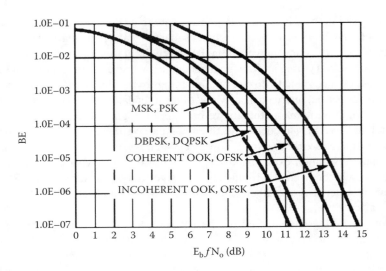

FIGURE 39.4   Eb/No vs. BER.

Selection of modulation method determines system bandwidth, power efficiency, sensitivity, and complexity. For the purposes of link budget analysis, the most important aspect of a given modulation technique is the signal-to-noise ratio (SNR) necessary for a receiver to achieve a specified level of reliability in terms of BER (bit error rate).

A graph of Eb/No versus BER is shown in Figure 39.4. Eb/No is a measure of the required energy per bit relative to the noise power. Note that Eb/No is independent of the system data rate. To convert from Eb/No to SNR, the data rate and system bandwidth must be taken into account as shown below:

$$SNR = \left(E_b / N_o \right) + \left(R / B_T \right)$$

Where:

E_b = Energy required per bit of information
N_o = thermal noise in 1Hz of bandwidth
R = system data rate
B_T = system bandwidth

Frequency Modulation

In frequency modulation (FM), the frequency of the carrier wave is time varied based on the original signal to be modulated. Specifically, the change in frequency at any instant is proportional to the modulating signal that varies with time. Its principal benefit over AM is increased noise immunity and decreased distortion; however, this is achieved at the expense of requiring more bandwidth. The FM band has become the choice of music listeners' desire for quality and faithful reproduction of a musician's talents.

In analog applications, the carrier frequency is varied in direct proportion to changes in the amplitude of an input signal. In digital applications, the carrier frequency is varied in accordance with a set of discrete values — to encode a zero or one. This technique is known as frequency shift keying.

The main advantages of FM over AM are

- Improved signal to noise ratio (about 25 dB) w.r.t. to manmade interference
- Smaller geographical interference between neighboring stations
- Less radiated power
- Well-defined service areas for given transmitter power

The disadvantages of FM are

- Much more bandwidth (as much as twenty times)
- More complicated receiver and transmitter

Amplitude Modulation

Amplitude modulation (AM) is the modulation used in the AM radio broadcast band. In this system, the intensity, or amplitude, of the carrier wave varies over time based on the signal to be modulated; for example, speech or music. This varying signal embeds the information in accordance with the modulating signal onto a carrier radio signal of higher frequency. When the RF carrier is AM modulated, the amplitude of the carrier radio wave varies in symmetry to the input signal. A fraction of the power is converted to sidebands extending above and below the carrier frequency by an amount equal to the highest modulating frequency. If the modulated carrier is rectified and the carrier frequency filtered out, the modulating signal can be recovered.

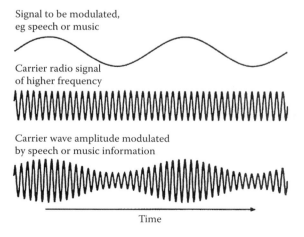

FIGURE 39.5   Amplitude modulation.

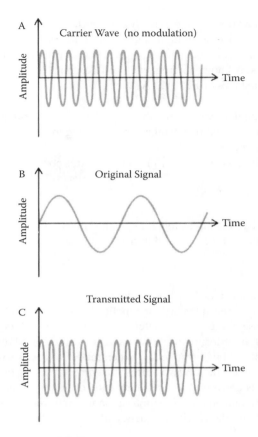

A   Carrier Wave (no modulation)

B   Original Signal

Transmitted Signal

C

FIGURE 39.6   Frequency modulation.

AM modulation is not an efficient way to send information, mainly because the power required is relatively large because the carrier, which contains no information, is sent along with the information.

In a variant of amplitude modulation, called *single sideband modulation* (SSB), the modulated signal contains only one sideband and no carrier. The information can be demodulated only if the carrier is used as a reference. This is normally accomplished by generating a wave in the receiver at the carrier frequency. SSB modulation is used for long-distance telephony (as in amateur radio bands) and telegraphy over land and submarine cables.

Phase Modulation

Phase modulation, like frequency modulation, is a form of angle modulation (so called because the phase is shifted to the radio wave carrier is changed by the modulating wave).

The detector discerns the intelligence in the carrier wave by measuring the phase shift from the original carrier. This information may then encode digital data to represent a specific combination of ones and zeros.

The two methods are similar in the sense that any attempt to shift the frequency or phase is accomplished by a change in the other. An RFID tag and reader use pulse modulation; the data is contained in changes in the phase of the carrier wave sent out by the reader.

Pulse Modulation

Pulse modulation involves modulating a carrier that is a train of regularly recurrent pulses. The modulation may vary the amplitude (PAM or pulse amplitude modulation), the width (PWM or pulse width modulation), or the presence of the pulses (PCM or pulse code modulation). Pulse code modulation is the most important form of pulse modulation because it can be used to transmit information over long distances with little interference or distortion. Although PCM transmits digital instead of analog signals, the modulating wave is continuous.

Amplitude Shift Keying (ASK)

Amplitude shift keying, or ASK, is useful in transmitting RFID tag data because it is simple and effective for digital communications.

One of the disadvantages of ASK is that it has a varying envelope, making power amplification more difficult. However, this makes it easy to demodulate with an envelope detector. ASK, in the context of digital communications, is a modulation process that provides two or more discrete amplitude levels to a sinusoidal signal. For a binary message sequence there are two levels, typically one and zero. The modulated waveform looks like bursts of a sinusoid. There are sharp discontinuities

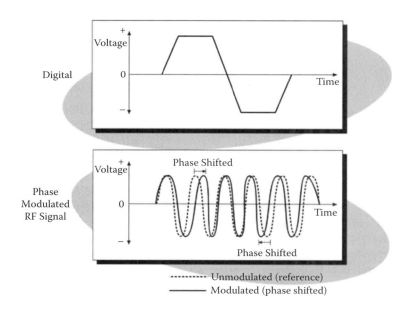

FIGURE 39.7   Pulse modulation.

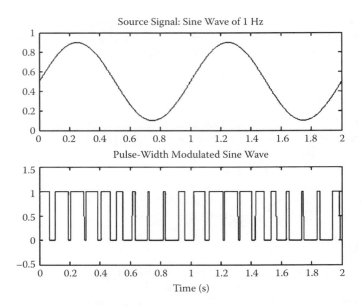

FIGURE 39.8 Pulse width modulation.

shown at the transition points. Using a submultiple of the carrier frequency is typical for the data rate.

HANDSHAKING

Once the radio engineering link is operational, you may consider how it transports information from one location to another. To explore a high-level description of the typical transmitting sequence for a generic tag-antenna-reader system, you start with the greeting. When you meet someone, you usually shake hands. An analogous situation occurs in electronics with a system handshake. The typical handshake for a passive tag is as follows.

First, a reader looks for modulation of its radio frequency sine wave to indicate the presence of a tag. When a tag's antenna captures the EMF generated by the reader's antenna, it initiates a process to respond with a data stream, which is encoded in the carrier frequency.

With a successful handshake, the system begins transmitting information as follows: the tag typically starts clocking its data messages against an output transistor, which is connected across coil inputs. In this case, the RF link behaves like a transformer, wherein the tag is the primary coil and the reader the secondary coil.

As the tag's output transistor shunts the coil, it effectively modulates the carrier to experience a momentary voltage drop. The pattern of voltage drops corresponds to the information to be uploaded from the tag to the reader.

The reader must detect these small voltage drops, which represent the modulation. This requires a sensitivity that can pick up 1/1000 of a change from the original carrier wave's amplitude as sent by the reader. By constantly monitoring these voltage drops, the reader detects and decodes a bit stream according to the modulation being used. To further complicate things, the modulation scheme also incorporates algorithms to affect error recovery, bandwidth, synchronization and other system needs.

In addition to these basic tasks, the system needs to handle collision avoidance during the simultaneous reading of several tags in the same radio frequency field. In this case, the tag and reader must be intelligent enough to detect that more than one tag is present. Failure to recognize this condition leads to all the tags modulating the carrier frequency at the same time; these multiple waveforms arrive at the reader only to create a garbled signal. This is referred to as a *collision*. No data would be transferred to the reader when this happens.

Consider the problem of having a telephone conversation with three people. If everyone talks at once, it is impossible to understand the conversation. Some order will allow everyone to be understood. The RFID radio interface requires arbitration so only one tag transmits data at one instance in time.

While it is possible to transmit all the data from the tag to the reader through amplitude modulation, the practical electronic circuit's modulation of data bits is enhanced by using other methods:

- FSK — frequency shift keying: two different frequencies are used for data transfer. A 0 is transmitted as amplitude-modulated clock signal with a different frequency, while a 1 is sent on a different amplitude-modulated frequency.
- PSK — phase shift keying: similar to FSK, except only one frequency is used and the shift between 1 s and 0 s is accomplished by shifting the peak and trough of the wave forms.

Data is also sent using NRZ (non-return-to-zero), differential biphase, and Manchester coding schemes. They are used to improve noise immunity, interference, and efficiency.

These factors make the air interface the most complicated component of system design. In other words, the radio channel is the weakest link in the system and requires sophisticated engineering for peak performance; however, once that task is complete, the radio link operates with the greatest efficiency and highest reliability.

For RFID, the interrogator sends information to one or more tags by modulating an RF carrier using double-sideband amplitude shift keying (DSB-ASK), single-sideband amplitude shift keying (SSB-ASK), or phase-reversal amplitude shift keying (PR-ASK), using a pulse interval encoding (PIE) format.

Tags receive their operating energy from this same modulated RF carrier. An interrogator receives information from a tag by transmitting an unmodulated RF carrier and listening for a backscattered reply. Tags communicate information by backscatter-modulating the amplitude and/or phase of the RF carrier. The encoding format, selected in response to interrogator commands, is either FM0 or Miller-modulated subcarrier. The communications link between interrogators and tags is half-duplex, meaning that tags will not be required to demodulate interrogator commands while backscattering. A tag will not respond using full-duplex communications to a mandatory or optional command.

FREQUENCY HOPPING

The term *spread spectrum* simply means that the energy radiated by the transmitter is spread out over a wider amount of the RF spectrum than would otherwise be used. By spreading out the energy, it is far less likely that two readers sharing the same spectrum will interfere with each other. This is an important consideration in an unlicensed band and explains why the FCC imposed spread spectrum requirements on part 15 radios that transmit over −1 dBm (about 0.75 mW). It also explains why a dense reader environment for RFID is defined as fifty readers operating within one thousand feet of each other.

In the United States, these bands are collectively designated as industry, science, and medicine (ISM) bands. Operation in these bands with approved devices does not require an FCC license. By waiving licensing requirements, these bands have been made generally accessible to virtually anyone. This is why the ISM bands are so important for commercial and consumer applications. It is critical for end-users to realize that RFID does operate in a dedicated band and may catch interference from other devices operating within the band. As mentioned above, radios employing spread spectrum methods are allowed to radiate up to 1.0 W (30 dBm) of RF energy, as compared to less than 1 mW for nonspread radios.

There are two common types of spread spectrum systems. The easiest to understand is frequency-hopped spread spectrum (FHSS), used in RFID. In this method, the carrier frequency hops from channel to channel in some prearranged sequence. The receiver is programmed to hop in sequence with the transmitter. If one channel is jammed, the data are retransmitted when the transmitter hops to a clear channel. The major drawback to FHSS is limited data rate. In the 2.4-GHz band, FCC regulations require that the maximum occupied bandwidth for any single channel is 1 MHz. This effectively limits the data rate through this type of system to about 1 Mbps.

VALUE PROPOSITION: THE WAVE OF THE FUTURE

Since MIT commercialized RFID with the formation of EPC Global, there has been a great deal of interest in the application of RFID technology in the supply chain, pharmaceuticals, and health care, to name prominent vertical markets. Several vendors, including Alien, Symbol, TI, Intermec, Samsys, and Impinj, offer products that comply with the United States' FCC regulations for unlicensed operation in the 902- to 928-MHz spectrum. These regulations permit radiated RF power of up to 4 W when spread spectrum modulation techniques are used.

STUDY QUESTIONS

1. What units measure radio frequency?
   (a) Hertz
   (b) Amps
   (c) Volts
   (d) None of the above

2. How do you create radio waves?
   (a) When ohms flow through an antenna
   (b) When alternating currents flow through an antenna
   (c) When direct current flows through an antenna
   (d) None of the above
3. What word(s) refer to the signal direction for an antenna?
   (a) Horizontal pattern
   (b) Vertical pattern
   (c) Read range
   (d) None of the above
4. What units measure the antenna signal strength?
   (a) Voltage
   (b) Current
   (c) Watts
   (d) None of the above
5. What determines an RFID system's write range?
   (a) Antenna pattern
   (b) Transmitter output power
   (c) Link budget
   (d) All of the above
6. What does polarization mean?
   (a) The direction of the antenna relative to the ground
   (b) The direction of the radio energy relative to the ground
   (c) Both a and b
7. What frequencies does passive RFID use?
   (a) 125 khz
   (b) 13.56 Mhz
   (c) 902–928 Mhz
   (d) 2.45 Ghz
   (e) Both b and c
8. What does frequency hopping mean?
   (a) Changing frequencies from one location to another to avoid interference
   (b) Changing frequencies from one channel to another
   (c) Both a and b
9. Which of the following is true about multipath signals?
   (a) Multiple versions of the signal reach the receiver at different times due to the varying lengths of their paths
   (b) Multiple versions of the signal arrive at different times they create more work for the receiver because it has to decode the information more then once
   (c) Multiple versions of the same signal may arrive out of time synchronization and recombine at the antenna to cancel each other out and significantly reduce the signal

   (d) Multiple versions of the same signal may arrive out of time synchronization and recombine at the antenna to amplify each other and significantly increase the signal

   (e) None of the above

10. Why is the write operation to a tag more resource intensive then a read operation in consuming resources?

   (a) To write a tag requires the following operations: read/write/verify. As a result of the additional steps, the write operation will take longer

   (b) Write operation requires a different wavelength for the radio channel and the tuning to that channel takes additional time

   (c) To latch the memory requires more energy then a read and therefore the signal strength requirements are higher to give the tag access to more power to perform the necessary write operations to the on-board memory

   (d) A read operation does not need to perform the binary exclusive or computation and as a result it is faster

   (e) None of the above

11. What does a 3-dB gain do to a signal?

   (a) It changes the phase of the signal and this increases the power significantly

   (b) Double the original power

   (c) Triples the original power

   (d) Cuts the original power in half

   (e) None of the above

12. What is the tag attenuation factor?

   (a) A method of noting how much gain a tag has relative to its peers

   (b) A method of noting how much attenuation a tag has relative to its peers

   (c) A method of measuring when a tag ceases to respond when optimally presented

   (d) The amount of path loss before a tag fails to respond

   (e) None of the above

13. What important information does SWR tell you?

   (a) Measures antenna output power

   (b) Measures the voltage to the antenna

   (c) Measures the gain of the antenna

   (d) Confirms the characteristic impedance is 50 ohms and the system is providing maximum output power to point of measurement

   (e) None of the above

14. What is modulation?

   (a) The to-and-from pattern of a wave cycle

   (b) The length of a wave

   (c) The additional information added to a wave

   (d) The height of a wave

   (e) The distance from one wave to another

   (f) None of the above

REFERENCES

Clampitt, H. G. (2006). *RFID certification textbook*. Edited by Erick C. Jones. Houston, Tex.: PWD Group.

Lee, S. W. and Y. T. Lo. (1993). *Antenna Handbook: Antenna Theory* 1st ed. NJ: Springer.

Stallings, W. (2007). *Data and computer communications*. 8th ed. Upper Saddle River, N.J.: Pearson Prentice Hall.

ADDITIONAL REFERENCE

Clampitt, H. G., D. Galarde, M. Hendricks, M. Johnson, A. De La Serna, and S. Smith. (2006). *The RFID certification textbook*. 2d ed. Edited by Erick. C. Jones. Houston, Tex.: PWD Group.

End of Book Questions

1. Which of the following is *not* a passive RFID application?
   (a) Ignition immobilizer
   (b) Item tagging
   (c) Pallet tagging
   (d) Case tagging
   (e) None of the above
2. What does RFID stand for?
   (a) Radio frequency identification
   (b) Real-time factory identification
   (c) Rapid frequency identification domain
   (d) Radar frequency identification
   (e) None of the above
3. Which of the following benefits does RFID present over the bar code (BC)?
   (a) BC has unlimited lifespan, whereas RFID times out when radio waves are not present
   (b) RFID protects against counterfeiting
   (c) RFID is smaller and holds less information than a BC
   (d) RFID is less complex
   (e) All of the above
4. From what development do historians claim RFID was derived?
   (a) Radar in the 1920s
   (b) Morse code
   (c) Bell Labs research
   (d) None of the above
5. Which of the following are challenges preventing adoption of RFID technologies?
   (a) Hardware and software cost for items such as tags, readers, antennas, and middleware
   (b) Standards
   (c) Volume of data to be processed
   (d) Consumer's resistance due to privacy concerns
   (e) All of the above
6. What future event will cause a profound change in RFID usage?
   (a) Data overload causing reduced data speed of the Ethernet networks
   (b) Embedded readers in devices using speed pass–type payment systems
   (c) Serialization requiring reevaluating on how businesses use individual product serial numbers
   (d) The tipping point
   (e) All of the above

7. Which of the following is a measure of radio frequency?
   (a) Hertz
   (b) Amps
   (c) Signal bars
   (d) None of the above

8. Which best describes how radio waves are created?
   (a) When current flows through an antenna
   (b) When alternating currents flow through an antenna
   (c) When direct current flows through an antenna
   (d) None of the above

9. What selections best describes the signal directions for an antenna?
   (a) Horizontal/vertical patterns
   (b) Up/down patterns
   (c) Top/bottom patterns
   (d) a and b only
   (e) a, b, and c
   (f) None of the above

10. What units measure the antenna signal strength?
    (a) Voltage
    (b) Current
    (c) Watts
    (d) None of the above

11. Which of the following does *not* determine an RFID system's write range?
    (a) Antenna pattern
    (b) Transmitter output power
    (c) Path loss
    (d) Radar patterns
    (e) Both b and d
    (f) None of the above

12. What does polarization mean?
    (a) The orientation of the tag and the antenna relative to each other
    (b) The direction of the electromagnetic field (EMF) relative to the ground
    (c) Both a and b
    (d) None of the above

13. What frequencies does an RFID animal tag for livestock utilize?
    (a) 125 Hz
    (b) 13.56 Mhz
    (c) 902–928 Mhz
    (d) 2.45 Ghz
    (e) Both a and b
    (f) All of the above
    (g) None of the above

14. What is the difference between a tag and transponder?
    (a) Tag has no battery while a transponder incorporates an on-board battery
    (b) Tag incorporates an on-board battery while a transponder has no battery

    (c) Both a and b

    (d) None of the above

15. What is the difference between an interrogator and reader?

    (a) Readers are unable to write to a tag, whereas interrogators are able to read/write to tags

    (b) Interrogators may read only, whereas readers are able to read and write to a tag

    (c) Both a and b

    (d) None of the above

16. What is modulated backscatter most similar to?

    (a) Light refracted through water

    (b) Sunlight focused through a mirror

    (c) Flashlight reflected back from a mirror

    (d) None of the above

17. Which type of tag can transmit its own signal

    (a) Active tag

    (b) Passive tag

    (c) Transmission tags

    (d) SAW (surface acoustic wave) tag

    (e) All of the above

18. Which type of tag(s) can use radiated energy and transmit a signal back to the original transmitter?

    (a) Active tag

    (b) Passive tag

    (c) Battery tag

    (d) Semi-passive tag

    (e) Both c and d

    (f) Both b and d

19. Which tag uses on-board energy to transmit back to the original transmitter?

    (a) Active tag

    (b) Passive tag

    (c) Battery tag

    (d) Semi-passive tag

    (e) Both c and d

    (f) Both b and d

20. What are the most common means of powering RFID tags?

    (a) Backscatter power

    (b) Battery power

    (c) Both a and b

    (d) None of the above

21. Which of the following characteristics are associated to a passive tag?

    (a) It uses beam power

    (b) It uses modulated backscatter

    (c) It has no on-board battery

    (d) All of the above

22. Which of the following characteristics are associated to an active tag?
    (a) It has an on-board battery to power the CPU
    (b) It has an on-board battery to power the radio circuitry
    (c) It uses beam power
    (d) It has a transmitter
    (e) Both b and d
    (f) Both b and c
    (g) Both a and c
23. Which task takes more energy and CPU cycles?
    (a) Read operation with verify
    (b) Write operation
    (c) Read operation without verify
    (d) None of the above
24. Which tag offers maximum read distance?
    (a) Battery-powered tag
    (b) Beam-powered tag
    (c) Modulated backscatter tag
    (d) None of the above
25. Which component has the largest impact on the RFID system performance?
    (a) Antenna
    (b) Tag
    (c) Reader
    (d) Substrate
26. What is the primary role of the antenna?
    (a) Radiate energy
    (b) Capture energy
    (c) Both a and b
    (d) None of the above
27. What are the differences between a passive tag and an active tag?
    (a) Active tags can use cheaper readers; passive tags' readers are more expensive
    (b) Passive tags' frequencies can be tuned easier; active tags do not have a frequency range
    (c) Active tags are mostly used for item-level tacking of inventory items
    (d) Passive tags do not have the ability to have sensors and active tag can have sensors
    (e) Passive tags are EPC compliant and active tags are not EPC compliant
    (f) None of the above
28. Which statements are true about Gen 2 tags?
    (a) The tags are larger
    (b) The tags have more transistors
    (c) The tags are cheaper
    (d) The tags transmit farther than active tags
    (e) None of the above

29. How does the tag antenna size affect performance?
    (a) Tag antenna geometries are critical to performance
    (b) Frequency is more important than the tag's antenna size
    (c) The tag attenuation factor is more important to performance
    (d) None of the above
30. What are the characteristics of a linear polarized antenna?
    (a) RF energy radiates from antenna in a linear pattern
    (b) The wave has a single E-field component
    (c) Generally longer range than a circularly polarized antenna
    (d) Best for applications with known tag orientation
    (e) All of the above
31. What are the characteristics of a circular polarized reader antenna?
    (a) RF energy radiates from antenna in a circular pattern
    (b) The two E-field components are equal in magnitude, 90 degrees out of phase and spatially oriented at 90 degrees from one another
    (c) Offers more signal strength in presence of multipath and high scattering
    (d) All of the above
32. Where is the best location to tag a large bottle of a liquid detergent?
    (a) On the bottom of the jug
    (b) On the side
    (c) In the top, clear measuring cup
    (d) All of the above
33. Where is the best location to tag a package of Q-tips?
    (a) Package bottom
    (b) Package top
    (c) Package side
    (d) All of the above
34. Describe the radiation pattern of a patch antenna?
    (a) Emits RF energy in a donut shape
    (b) Emits RF energy in a fixed concentrated direction
    (c) Directs RF propagation in a fixed omni direction
    (d) Emits RF energy in a concentrated antenna aperture
    (e) None of the above
35. What does the acronym EPC stand for?
    (a) Electronic process control
    (b) Electronic product code
    (c) Electromagnetic product code
    (d) None of the above

Lecture Notes

INTRODUCTION TO RFID

- What is all the hype about RFID?
- What is RFID?
- Why is it an emerging technology?
- What is Supply Chain Logistics?
- Focus: Why do companies care?
- Scope: Will RFID really work?
- Purpose: How can I integrate RFID into the Supply Chain?

RFID HISTORY

- RFID history
- Introduction
- The evolution of Logistics and Supply Chain Management in America
- The use of data acquisition devices in distribution and logistics
- Barcodes
- Overlaying the history of RFID development into the Supply Chain
- Prior to IFF
- Research on RFID
- In the 20th century
- The first RFID patents
- Toll road and animal tracking
- Development of cost effective protocol

BASIC RFID SYSTEM COMPONENTS

- General component overview
- Tags
- Reader
- Antennas
- Host
- Tags
  - Power sources
  - Passive Tags
  - Active Tags
  - Semi-Active Tags
  - SAW RFID tags
  - Tag Frequencies

- Writing capabilities
  - Read only
  - Write once read many
  - Read/write
- Tag components
  - Tag Integrated Circuitry
  - Tag Antennas
  - Tag substrate or tag housing
  - Tag generations
- Scanners and readers
  - Scanners
  - Readers
  - Reader frequencies
  - Reader interrogation modes
- Antennas
- Hosts
- Communication protocols
- RS-232
- RS-485
- Ethernet
- Summary
- Chapter questions

PASSIVE RFID SYSTEM COMPONENTS

- Introduction
- Major advantages to passive RFID systems
  - Lower expense
  - Smaller sizes
  - Greater operational life
  - Environmental robustness
- Major disadvantages to passive RFID systems
  - Less range
  - Less identification capability
- Chapter organization
- Trovan Electronic Identification Systems
  - Trovan Passive Tags
  - ID 100 Series
  - ID 200 and 300 Series
  - ID 400 Series
  - ID 600 Series
  - ID 700 Series
  - ID 800 Series
  - ID 1000 Series
  - Trovan Portable Readers

- LID WAPR Workabout Pro Reader
- GR-250 High Performance Reader
- LID Pocket Series Readers
- SmartCode
  - SmartCode Inlays
  - SmartCode Passive Tags
- Symbol Technologies
  - RFX3000 Series Inlays
  - RFX3000 1 x 1 Read/Write Tag
  - RFX3000 1 x 6 Read/Write Tag
  - RFX3000 2 x 2 Read/Write Tag
  - RFX3000 4 x 4 Read/Write Tag
  - Gen 2 RFX6000 Series Read/Write Inlay
  - RFX6000 1 x 1 Series Read/Write Inlay
  - RFX6000 2 x 4 Series Read/Write Inlay
  - Cargo Tag
- Symbol Antennas
  - AN200 General Purpose Antenna
  - AN400 High Performance Area Antenna
- Symbol readers
  - RD5000
  - XR400 Series
- Intermec
  - Intellitag windshield tag
  - Intellitag container tag
  - Intellitag ID Card
  - Intermec readers
  - IF Series of fixed readers
  - IP4 hand held Reader Handle with Intermec 700 series computer
  - IV7 vehicle mount reader
- Summary

ACTIVE RFID SYSTEM COMPONENTS

- Introduction
- Major advantages to active RFID systems
  - Greater range
  - Greater identification capability
- Major disadvantages to active RFID systems
  - More expensive
  - Less operational life
  - Larger physical size
- Savi Corporation
  - Savi Active Tags
  - SaviTag ST-602
  - SaviTag ST-604

  - SaviTag ST-656
  - Savi Fixed Readers
  - SR-650 Fixed Reader
  - Savi Signpost
  - Savi Mobile Readers
- Mark IV Industries
  - Mark IV Transponders
  - Mark IV Internal Flat Pack Transponder
  - License Plate Transponder
  - Roof Mount Transponder
  - Fusion Transponder
  - Ubiquity Transponder
  - Mark IV Readers
  - Badger Reader
  - MGate Reader
  - Mark IV Antennas
- Summary

SYSTEM DESIGN AND TESTING

- System Design Approach
- Step 1: Gain ideas through understanding
  - On-site analysis
  - Equipment evaluation
  - Environmental evaluation
  - Human factor evaluation
- Step 2: Create preliminary designs
- Step 3: Prototype Development
- Step 4: Choose an alternative
- Step 5: Test and re-test chosen
- Step 6: Implement the solution

STANDARDS ORGANIZATIONS AND RFID STANDARDS

- Introduction
- International Standards Organization (ISO) Standards
- ISO Standards and RFID
- 18000-1 Part 1 – Generic Parameters for the Air Interface for Globally Accepted Frequencies
- 18000-2 Part 2 – Parameters for Air Interface Communications below 135 kHz
- 18000-3 Part 3 – Parameters for Air Interface Communications at 13.56 MHz
- Intellectual Property

- 18000-4 Part 4 – Parameters for Air Interface Communications at 2.45 GHz
  - Frequency
  - Interface Definitions
- 18000-5 Part 5 – Parameters for Air Interface Communications at 5.8 GHz
  - Intellectual Property
- 18000-7 Part 7 – Parameters for Air Interface Communications at 433 MHz
- Work Group on RFID for Item Management (WG 4)
- ISO Standards Summary
- EPC Global Standards
- GS1 and GS1 US
- EPC/GTIN Integration
- EPC Generation 2
- Other standards
- The Electronic Product Code details
- The Department of Defense (DOD) UID
- EPCglobal Tag Data Construct Option
- FCC Part 15 radiation regulation

IMPORTANT RFID MANDATES

- Introduction
- Department of Defense (DOD) Mandate
- Requirements commencing January 1st, 2005
- Requirements commencing January 1st, 2006
- Requirements commencing January 1st, 2007
- Guidelines and requirements
- Wal-Mart Mandate
- Other organizations

RFID IN LOGISTICS

- Introduction
- RFID supports information use in the Supply Chain
- Data analysis and information gathering
- Push and Pull Operational Strategies
- Supply chain coordination
- Forecasting and Aggregate Planning
- RFID and other enabling technologies
- EDI Business Transmissions
- Web based application systems
- Business operations systems
- Overall Trade-Off: responsiveness versus efficiency
- eCommerce and technology
- RFID as part of the Information Supply Chain

- RFID as an Intelligent Agent System
- Summary of RFID and Information Enablers
- RFID provides timely visibility in Logistics
- Inventory in the Supply Chain
- Business responsiveness
- Cycle inventory
- Safety inventory
- Seasonal inventory
- Level of product availability
- Inventory-related metrics
- The Bullwhip Effect
- Summary

INVENTORY CONTROL BASICS

- Introduction
- Inventory carrying costs
- Stock-out costs
- Safety Stocks
- Economic Order Quantity
- Inventory flows
- Fixed-Order-Interval System
- Just-in-Time inventory systems
- RFID and inventory control
- Automatic replenishment
- Safety-Stock reduction
- Picking and routing
- Order batching of waves
- Summary

RFID SUPPLY CHAIN PLANNING LEVELS

- Introduction
- RFID supports Supply Chain Planning and operational optimization
- Tactical-Level
- Intermediate-Level Problems
- Transportation Strategy
- Common transportation decisions
- Transportation mode
- Intermediate level summary
- Strategic level
- Facilities strategy
- Facilities decisions
- RFID Best Practices for Success

RFID PROJECT MANAGEMENT

- Introduction
- RFID project selection
- Project selection models and factors
- Non-numeric Project Selection Models
- The Sacred Cow
- Operating necessity
- Competitive necessity
- Comparative models
- Numeric Project Selection Models
- Payback time
- Average rate of return
- Unweighted 0–1
- Unweighted scoring
- Weighted scoring
- Constrained weighted scoring
- RFID Project Parameters
- RFID Implementation Lifecycle
- Conceptual phase
- Planning phase
- Installation phase
- Startup phase
- RFID Project Manager
- RFID Project Manager authority
- RFID Project Manager functions
- Planning
- Organizing
- Motivating
- Maslow's Theory
- Herzberg's Theory
- Directing
- Situational Leadership Theory
- Controlling
- Developing the project plan
- Work break down structure
- Linear Responsibility Chart
- Gantt Chart
- Finish to start relationship
- Start to start relationship
- Finish to finish relationship
- Lags
- Compressing and crashing projects
- Compressing the acquisition of hardware and software
- Compressing the testing of RFID tags
- Compressing the installation of hardware and software

- RFID project tasks which cannot or should not be compressed
- Hardware and software selection
- Avoid compressing pilot testing

IMPLEMENTING RFID SYSTEMS

- Introduction
- Make the ROI case for RFID
- Choose the right RFID technology
- RFID system details
- Six Sigma Methodology
  - 3P's theoretical model
    - Plan
    - Define
    - Measure
    - Predict
    - Analyze
    - Design
    - Perform
    - Optimize
    - Verify
- Conclusion

THE ENGINEERING ECONOMICS OF RFID

- Introduction
- Problem statement
- Background
- Cost justification
- Audit costs
- Rework costs
- Scrap costs
- Management costs
- Customer Service costs
- Total annual cost
- Tag costs
- Reader costs
- Software costs
- Implementation costs
- Net Present Value Comparison
- Comparison
- Sensitivity analysis
- Limitations
- Conclusions

ANIMAL TRACKING RFID APPLICATIONS

- Introduction
- Tag placement methods
- Size of the animal
- The presence of a previously existing external tag
- Natural and aesthetic considerations
- External versus Internal tag placement
- Internal placement methods.
- External tag placement
- Internal tag placement
- Animal RFID technology
- Existing systems for domestic food related animals.
- Existing systems for domestic pet related animals
- Animal antenna readers and portals
- Nature of the application
- Position of the tag on the animal
- Frequency of required reads
- Livestock tracking standards
- Related human applications
- Summary

CREDIT DEVICE RFID APPLICATIONS

- Introduction
- Form factors
- General transaction process
- Standards
- Credit card RFID readers
- Summary
- Questions

SECURE DOCUMENT RFID APPLICATIONS

- Introduction
- Basic passport background
- E-Passport RFID chip
- International Civil Aviation Organization (ICAO) Protocol
- Other developments
- Deployment
- Summary

DEPARTMENT OF DEFENSE RFID INITIATIVES

- Introduction
- The past

- The present
- The future
- Conclusions

ENTERTAINMENT RFID APPLICATIONS

- Introduction
- Conventional approaches
- Wrist bands
- Access cards
- RFID wrist bands and tags
- General advantages to RFID wristbands to entertainment facilities
- Resource distribution
- Marketing behavior
- Patron locating
- Patron restriction
- Medical records
- Locker access
- Disadvantages to RFID wristbands
- Specific benefits to entertainment application areas
- Amusement parks
- Waterparks
- Ski-resorts
- Special events
- Summary

EVALUATING RFID SOLUTIONS FOR HEALTHCARE IMPROVEMENT

- Introduction
- RFID: the emerging technology
- Comprehensive RFID Application System in Healthcare
- Drug supply chain network
- Point-of-care passive system/patient management.
- Active system/ hospital RTLS system/asset tracking
- Combined RFID system/surgical operation
- Cost and performance analysis of the comprehensive network
- Conclusions

RFID APPLICATIONS IN LIBRARIES

- Introduction
- Existing applications
- Background
- Advantages of RFID library systems
- Disadvantages of RFID systems

- RFID Supply Chains and Libraries
  - Application of RFID in libraries
  - The basic components of a typical RFID-based library system
  - Sensor gates
  - Self check station
  - Staff service center
  - Other options
  - Discussion about anti-theft and privacy issues
  - Cost and benefits of integrating RFID into existing library system
  - Experiments and Results
  - Experiment design
  - Patron self check-out experiment
  - Handheld reader for shelf inventory and maintenance
  - Experiment discussion

MARINE RFID SECURITY APPLICATIONS

- Introduction
- Special RFID hardware considerations
- Water resistance and water resistance ratings
- Circuit board hardening
- Shock resistance
- UV protection
- RFID tag positioning
- Infrastructure considerations
- Marine portals
- Antenna mounting
- Other considerations
- Marine RFID security applications
- Vessel registration tag applications
- Scanning recreational vessel RFID tags
- Stolen vessel identification
- Hostile vessel identification
- RFID chaff
- Summary

INVENTORY TRACKING ON INTERNATIONAL SPACE STATION USING RFID TECHNOLOGY

- Introduction
- Plan
- Define problem statement
- Measure
- Predict
- Analyze

- Design
- Perform
- Optimize
- Verify
- Conclusion

INDIVIDUAL SPORT COMPETITION RFID APPLICATIONS

- Introduction
- Application considerations
- Tags
- Mounting considerations
- Antenna systems
- Reader systems
- Performance issues
- Extensions to other sports competitions
- Special cycling RFID considerations
- Special skating RFID considerations
- Summary

SURGICAL RFID TECHNOLOGY APPLICATIONS

- Introduction
- Materials and methods
- Results
- Discussion

TOLLWAY RFID APPLICATIONS

- Introduction
- Tollway applications
  - Tollway RFID technology
  - Active Tollway Tags
  - Passive Tollway Tags
  - Tollway Antenna Reader Systems
  - Problems with reads
  - Multiple vehicle registrations
  - Tollway consortiums
  - New developments in Tollway RFID technology
- Associated applications
- Summary

RFID TRANSPORTATION SYSTEMS APPLICATIONS

- Introduction
- Transportation in SCM

- Information technology and SCM
- Real-time technologies
- Conclusions

MARINE TERMINAL RFID APPLICATIONS

- Introduction
- Tracking containers
- Container tags
- Tag operation
- Tag mounting

RFID USES IN WAREHOUSING

- Introduction
- Warehouse applications
- Receiving
- Storage
- Pick / pack
- Shipping
- Reliability
- IT infrastructure issues
- RFID warehouse implementation Examples
- Gillette
- International Paper
- Proctor & Gamble

OPTIMIZING RFID PORTAL LOCATIONS IN DISTRIBUTION USING SYSTEMATIC LAYOUT PLANNING (SLP)

- Introduction
- Modeling procedure
- Layout improvement alternatives and numerical results
- Computer-aided program algorithm approach (BLOCPLAN)
- Relationship data
- Discussion and conclusion

OBSOLETE INVENTORY REDUCTION WITH MODIFIED CARRYING COST RATIO

- Introduction
- The two-echelon model
- The one-echelon model
- The Modified Carrying Cost Ratio model
- Results: case study
- Facilities costs

- Purchasing costs
- The Modified Carrying Cost Ratio
- Inventory turn analysis
- The decision
- Conclusion

A CASE STUDY OF A SUPPLY CHAIN MANAGEMENT NETWORK MODEL IN GOVERNMENT PUBLIC WORKS DEPARTMENT

- Introduction
- Background
- Case description
- Lessons learned
- Implications for the engineering manager
- Conclusions

THE FUTURE OF RFID IN ARMY LOGISTICS

- Introduction
- Background
- Discussion of RFID and its alternatives
- Current RFID system
- Third Generation RFID (3G RFID)
- Next Generation Wireless Communication (NGWC)
- Economic analysis
- Annual tag cost
- Maintenance cost
- Infrastructure cost
- Savings in lost container material
- Savings in detention charges
- Engineering analysis
- Information capability
- Implementation cost
- Maintenance cost
- Asset visibility
- Ease of expansion
- Operations cost
- Real time data capability
- Conclusion/Recommendations

RFID IN GOLF — APPLICATIONS AND PARALLELS

- Introduction
- Testing and experimentation
- Results
- Conclusion and recommendations

RAILROAD CAR TRACKING BY AN RFID SYSTEM TO ORGANIZE TRAFFIC FLOW

- Introduction
- Current problem
- Reason for improvement
- Strategy
- Methodology
- Testing the active tags
- Test results
- Finding a practical way to send data to the control center
- Determining the appropriate layout to set the devices
- Simulation results
- Cost analysis
- Recommendations

RFID MIDDLEWARE AND WEB SERVICE

- Introduction
- EDI vs. Web service
- Applications of Web services in RFID
- Web services Return on Investment
- Direct and indirect measures
- Discount rate or Weighted Average Cost of Capital (WACC)
- Net Present Value (NPV)
- Internal Rate of Return (IRR)
- Discounted Cash Flow Analysis
- Payback Period Analysis
- ROI analysis becoming a Necessity
- ROI and Web services
- Calculating ROI of Web services
- Factors to be included in ROI calculation
- Applying the ROI formula
- Not the only model
- XML and PML language

RADIO FREQUENCY THEORY

- Introduction
- Common terms
- Units and prefixes
- Wave theory
- Electromagnetic waves
- Radio waves
- Frequency spectrum
- Measuring power loss

- Smith Chart
- Return-loss
- Coupling
- Polarization
- Antennas
- Standard Antenna Impedance
- Impedance matching
- Tuning
- Range and path loss
- Modulation
- Signal propagation
- Modulation
- Frequency modulation
- Amplitude modulation
- Phase modulation
- Pulse modulation
- ASK Amplitude Shift Keying
- Handshaking
- Frequency hopping
- Value Proposition: the wave of the future
- Study questions

References

Capone, G., D. Costlow, W. L. Grenoble, and R. A. Novack. (2004). *The RFID-enabled warehouse*. Center for Supply-Chain Research, Penn State.

Clampitt, H. G., E. C. Jones, eds. (2006). *RFID certificate handbook*. 1st ed. Houston, Tex.: PWD Group.

DoD suppliers' passive RFID information guide, Ver. 1.0 [Online]. Available at http://www.acq.osd.mil/log/rfid/implementation_plan.htm [Accessed]

Kinsella, B. (2003). The Wal-Mart factor. *Industrial Engineer* 35(11):32-36.

Rogers, A., E. Jones, and D. Oleynikov. (2007). RFID technology can assist in laparoscopic procedure and prevention of gossypiboma. Working paper.

Suprina, D. Security risks with RFID. *RFID Journal* [Online]. Available at http://www.rfidjournal.com/article/articleview/1564/1/82/ [Accessed August 30, 2007].

Wyld, D. C. (2005). *RFID: The right frequency for government*. IBM Center for the Business of Government. http://www.businessofgovernment.org/pdfs/WyldReport4.pdf. [Accessed August 30, 2007].

Index